Archetypal Explorations

Archetypal Explorations is a ground-breaking study, which examines one of Jung's most important theories and the link it forms between analytical psychology and the social sciences. Richard M. Gray uses the concept of archetypes as a basis for understanding the reciprocal interaction of individuals and cultures as coevolving systems. In a systematized approach to the subject he reveals the implicitly cross-cultural and interdisciplinary nature of Jung's work.

Despite the depth of the Jungian contribution to understanding social phenomena, little has been done to apply it to sociology. Beginning with a re-examination of the literature of archetypes, the author makes enlightening comparisons between Jung's words and the formulations of the century's prominent sociologists. Elements of modern biology and systems theory are introduced to achieve a clearer and non-reductionist definition of archetypes. Basic terms are defined and particular attention is paid to patterns of archetypal activity, the role of instinct and libido and the significance of mandala images. The author establishes the fundamental issues that a reformulated sociology must address and in the final part develops the sociological themes which emerge from detailed analysis of the *Collected Works*.

Archetypal Explorations is a full assessment of Jung's statements on social theory. A significant addition to the literature of archetypes, it will appeal to psychologists, sociologists and all those interested in an integrative outlook on human behavior.

Richard M. Gray is a Senior United States Probation Officer, specializing in drug treatment in Brooklyn, New York, and a Lecturer in Sociology at Brookdale Community College, Lincroft, New Jersey.

Archetypal Explorations

An integrative approach to human behavior

Richard M. Gray

 London and New York

First published 1996
by Routledge
11 New Fetter Lane, London EC4P 4EE

Simultaneously published in the USA and Canada
by Routledge
29 West 35th Street, New York, NY 10001

Routledge is an International Thomson Publishing company

© 1996 Richard M. Gray

Typeset in Times by
Keystroke, Jacaranda Lodge, Wolverhampton

Printed and bound in Great Britain by
Mackays of Chatham PLC, Chatham, Kent

British Library Cataloguing in Publication Data
A catalogue record for this book is available from the
British Library

Library of Congress Cataloguing in Publication Data
Gray, Richard M.
    Archetypal explorations : towards an archetypal sociology /
Richard M. Gray.
        p.   cm.
    Revision of the author's thesis (doctoral)—Union Institute,
Cincinnati, Ohio, 1993.
    Includes bibliographical references and index.
    1. Archetype (Psychology) 2. Archetype (Psychology)—Social
aspects. 3. Jung, C. G. (Carl Gustav), 1875–1961. 4. Social
sciences and psychoanalysis. I. Title.
BF175.5.A72G73 1996   95-37516
    155.2′64—dc20

ISBN 0–415–12116–7
    0–415–12117–5 (pbk)

Contents

List of illustrations   vii
Acknowledgments   viii
Introduction   1

Part I Archetypal explorations

1 The nature of the archetype   11
2 The archetypal dimensions   32
3 The emergence of new properties   43
4 Archetypes and images   50

Part II The archetypal sequence

5 The archetypal set   69
6 The archetypes and their images   88

Part III Sociological considerations

7 The sociological prospect   125
8 The paradigms   132

Part IV The elements of an archetypal sociology

 9 The roots of intersubjectivity   161
10 The nature of groups   176
11 Families, nations and thought   181
12 The structure of large groups   199
13 Archetypal patterns in large groups   230
14 The problem of deviance   250

Part V Retrospect: analysis, conclusions

15 Review   257
16 Retrospect: Jung and sociology   272
17 Prospects: further research   280

Notes   287
References   293
Index   301

Illustrations

FIGURES

Figure 1.1	The spectrum of psychic activity	14
Figure 1.2	The poles of biological activity	30
Figure 2.1	The spatial octahedron	37
Figure 2.2	The ouroboros	38
Figure 5.1	Four levels of archetypal complexity	73
Figure 5.2	Primary elements of the Jungian psyche	73
Figure 6.1	The trefoil and the triple ring	117
Figure 12.1	The fundamental roles of society and their corresponding traditions	207
Figure 17.1	The fractal octahedron	282

TABLES

Table 5.1	Archetypal affects	79
Table 6.1	Some Greek gods and their attributes	108
Table 6.2	Attributes of the Greek Pantheon according to Bolen	112
Table 6.3	The Greek gods as rulers of the zodiac and the primitive elements	120
Table 12.1	Archetypal figures from Mitroff and Moxnes	205
Table 12.2	The fundamental roles of society translated into four disciplines	208

Acknowledgments

Like most books, this work reflects contributions and inspirations from many people. My first and most important debt is to God, whose mercy and long-suffering have placed me in a position to undertake such a task. In the final analysis the inspiration and energy for the undertaking come from Him.

Much of the style of the book is a reflection of study habits learned from my parents who inspired my brothers and me with their great love of learning. I recall especially my father's pride over his preceptor's instruction to "exhaust the law" as he prepared a case. To him, that meant seeking out the source of every principle of law down to their roots in the Common Law. It was an example that I learned early and that has served me well.

The text as it now stands is a revision of my doctoral dissertation, originally presented at the Union Institute, Cincinnati, Ohio in 1993. The subject matter has been of particular interest to me for many years. At Union, it was Doug Davidson who convinced me to pursue it. I owe him a debt of gratitude for helping me along the way. My faculty advisor and friend, Bob McAndrews was a great help and a constant inspiration. It was he who introduced me to general systems theory and shared my excitement over the progress of the work as he guided me through the maze of regulations at the school. My friends and peers, Jim and Cathy Elliot and Sarah Tyler MacPherson, were great sources of encouragement and strong allies through the process. Their words of inspiration and early edits of the text were invaluable. More profoundly, however, my special thanks go to Ira Progoff and Betsy Landau for their careful guidance and deep care, not only for the work, but for me as an individual.

When I originally approached Ira Progoff for his assistance, I knew little, except that he was one of the few Jung scholars who had looked at the social implications of analytical psychology. In fact, his doctoral dissertation, published as *Jung's Psychology and its Social Meaning*, was a major influence in choosing the topic of this book. Expecting a scholar, I found a deeply caring and personally involved friend. It is with some pride that I see the current work as a continuation in the spirit of his work.

Betsy Landau, a psychologist in private practice, was my constant confidant and worked to keep me on focus. Her balanced analyses kept me mindful of the wider audiences to whom the material might be of interest and helped in the crucial task of setting and keeping limits as the work proceeded. Her continuing friendship is a special treasure.

Among those who labored with me in editing the text, my good friend Florence Tomasulo has been an exceptional help with the final version. Her care for detail and her sensitivity to nuances of meaning and grammar have been irreplaceable.

There are others who stood by me and assisted me in one way or another. My thanks to Steve Rackmill who provided space when I really needed it. Thanks to Ed Willis at Central, and Dan Gilmore, Dave Wilson and Peter Sissons, wherever they are, for the foundations they laid and the continuing inspiration that they have provided. Thanks to Ken Aldritch and the family at Trinity, and to Sister Wood and my other church family at Union Beach for their encouragement and prayers.

Last but not least, I give special thanks to and for my wife, Kim, and our three children, Rick, Mike, and Rachel. Together, they endured my continuing sojourn in the basement with humor, grace and love. Their love and sacrifice of time and energy, their good spirit and encouragement, has made me appreciative of just how fortunate I am to have them in my life.

My thanks also to the following publishers who have granted permission to quote from the works indicated.

Princeton University Press and Routledge & Kegan Paul Ltd, for the use of material from the *Collected Works of C. G. Jung*, edited by G. Adler, M. Fordham and H. Read, and translated by R. F. C. Hull, as follows: Vol. VI, *Psychological Types*, copyright © 1971 by Princeton University Press; Vol. VII, *Two Essays on Analytical Psychology*, copyright © 1953 and 1966 by Princeton University Press; Vol. V, *Symbols of Transformation*, copyright © 1956 and 1967 by Princeton University Press; Vol. IX (i), *The Archetypes of the Collective Unconscious*, copyright © 1959 and 1968 by Princeton University Press; Vol. IX (ii), *Aion: Researches into the Phenomenology of the Self*, copyright © 1959 and 1968 by Princeton University Press; Vol. X, *Civilization in Transition*, copyright © 1964 and 1970 by Princeton University Press.

Princeton University Press is again acknowledged for permission to quote from Neumann, Erich, *Art and the Creative Unconscious*, translated by Ralph Mannheim, copyright © 1959 and 1974 by Princeton University Press.

Thanks to the University of California Press for permission to quote from Weber, Max, *Economy and Society*, 2 vols, edited by Guenther Roth and Klaus Wittich, copyright © 1968 and 1978 by the Regents of the University of California.

Quotes from *The Protestant Ethic and the Spirit of Capitalism* by Max

Weber are reprinted with the permission of Simon & Schuster Inc., from the Macmillan College text *The Protestant Ethic and the Spirit of Capitalism* by Max Weber, translated by Talcott Parsons, copyright © 1958 by Charles Scribner's Sons.

Quotes from *The Rules of the Sociological Method* by Emile Durkheim are reprinted with the permission of The Free Press, a division of Simon & Schuster Inc., from *The Rules of the Sociological Method* by Emile Durkheim, translated by Sarah A. Solovay and John H. Mueller, and edited by George E. G. Catlin, copyright © 1938 by George E. G. Catlin; copyright renewed 1964 by S. A. Solovay, J. G. Mueller, and G. E. G. Catlin.

Quotations from *Depth Psychology and a New Ethic*, by Erich Neumann, copyright © 1990, reprinted by arrangement with Shambhala Publications Inc., 300 Massachusetts Avenue, Boston, MA. 02115.

Quotes from *Hamlet's Mill* by Georgio de Santillana and Hertha von Dechend are reprinted by permission of David R. Godine, Publisher, Inc., copyright © 1969 by Georgio de Santillana and H. von Dechend.

Quotes from George Ritzer, *Sociology: A Multiple Paradigm Science*, copyright © 1980 by Allyn and Bacon, are reprinted by permission.

Quotes from *The Structure of Scientific Revolutions* by Thomas Kuhn, copyright © 1969 by the University of Chicago, are reprinted by permission.

Introduction

Jung observed that whenever humankind looks into the void, he/she projects there the structure of their own psyche. The more formless the void, the more fearful or abstract the image. In this observation was an implicit warning. There is a level at which we cannot with definite assurance differentiate between projected patterns and the reality about us, but must always be ready to withdraw the projected image in order to replace it with a better one.

James Hillman notes:

> Fantasy especially intervenes where exact knowledge is lacking; and when fantasy does intervene, it becomes especially difficult to gain exact knowledge. Thus, a vicious circle forms, and the mythical usurps theory-forming; furthermore, the mythic is given fantastic witness in observation. Seeing is believing, but believing is seeing. We see what we believe and prove our beliefs with what we see.
>
> (Hillman, 1972, p. 220)

Lawrence Blair (1991) recounts the story of how the indigenous people of Tierra del Fuego were unable to see Magellan's ships when he first visited their land. The natives' visual repertoire apparently had no tools with which to apprehend the explorer's fleet.

Modern physics has underscored the problem by acknowledging the observer variable in his/her efforts to measure location and velocity in the behavior of subatomic phenomena. As soon as we measure one dimension, the other becomes inaccessible. Indeed, from some experiments it would almost seem that the decision to measure one determines the impossibility of measuring the other. Is it a wave, or is it a particle? Is it here, or does it possess this amplitude?

The same problem applies in psychology. The minute we seem to have identified some basic facet of human nature, we are made aware of a new dimension of ourselves, and the reality is then revealed as only a new projection against which we must question our finding. Should we then analyze that projection, understand its root in the deepest levels of the psyche and eliminate it from our observations, we may then again face the external reality we originally sought to map, measure and understand. With every new discovery, however, we awaken one day to discover the same pattern in our own depths. The ouroboros, the snake that swallows its own tail, is a fitting symbol for our inquiry.[1]

It would be very nice to be able to say that what follows is the truth. Unfortunately, it is not. It is only a version of the truth based upon the state of the observer and the nature of the instrument. It is one of many possible maps of many possible territories.

It would appear that the contingencies that have placed humankind and every other creature on the planet have so arranged things as to fit the observer and the observable into a reciprocal relationship so that the things perceived are exactly those needed to ensure the survival of the individuals involved. Whether by a Benevolent Creator or blind evolution, the effect is the same. Humans stand in respect of their environment so that, for the most part, their probable projections will match the probable configurations of the external world. That is to say, the projection mechanism whereby we understand the world is, in some manner (whether by evolution or creation we cannot tell), matched to the world in which we live so that the world shapes our perceptions just as our perceptions shape the world.

This suggests that archetypal patterns exist in relation to a real world. They are matched to the world as the roots of perception and action, and are in some manner inherited to ensure that they retain a certain level of consistency from generation to generation. Jung understood them to be the images of instinct in consciousness. What is inherited, and the specific means of inheritance is, of course, debatable and will be part of the discussion that follows (Samuels, 1985).

The discussion of archetypes inevitably embroils the participants in an argument as to the relative weights of nature and nurture in the development of the individual. For the purposes of this discussion, a radical epigenetic perspective is assumed so that the two perspectives are viewed as equal poles of a single reality. There is no heredity that operates purely outside the shaping influence of environmental factors, there is no environmental influence on development without a specific genetic predisposition that it may affect. This perspective is limited to the normal experience of the individual organism or population of organisms. It does not include being crushed by a rock although there is even there a specific environmental impact on a specific genetic propensity.

All in all, this is not an easy topic. On the one hand, I am led to the reductionist pole in order to more fully understand the archetype *an sich*. On the other, I am fully aware that the Jungian position not only held the abstract archetype to be inaccessible, but developed a strong aversion to reductionistic arguments and analyses. In response, I can only observe, first, that progress in biology, physics and systems theory in the years since

Jung's death have made a classical reduction of psychic phenomena to this or that class of inanimate interactions nearly impossible. Except for the few truly blind men among us, there is none that can point to either a biological or physical first cause and claim thereby to have understood a phenomenon in any absolute sense. Second, it is my belief and my argument that the patterns that form what we recognize as archetypal are either so fundamental to our perception, or to the nature of things, or both, that their illustration at one level will be followed by their illustration at others. That is to say that what is fundamental to the archetypal is equally fundamental to the animate, inanimate, psychic and spiritual worlds. If this is so, then a proper reduction will result in a general principle of perception.

In so saying, I return to my original warning. Whether what follows describes some portion of the principles of reality or only our perception of that reality, we cannot tell. It is only a piece of a map of part of the truth.

Despite the depth of material that Jung provides for the understanding of social phenomena, little has been done to apply it at the sociological level. To my knowledge, there exist only six works that make any such attempt. These are: H. G. Baynes's (1941) *Germany Possessed*; Ira Progoff's (1953) *Jung's Psychology and its Social Meaning*; Walter Odjanyk's (1976) *Jung and Politics: The Political and Social Ideas of C. G. Jung*; Joseph Henderson's (1984) *Cultural Attitudes in Psychological Perspective*; Erich Neumann's (1990) *Depth Psychology and a New Ethic*; and, more recently, Andrew Samuel's (1993) *The Political Psyche*. That leaves us on fairly untraveled terrain. I think, however, though difficult at points, the journey will be worthwhile.

WHY A JUNGIAN SOCIOLOGY?

One of the first questions that many people will ask as they pick up this book is: why a Jungian sociology? For most people Jung's theories lie in the dark hinterlands of science. Many have relegated Jung to the mystics and visionaries. For others, the century-long competition between psychology and sociology for some kind of scientific pre-eminence will have made them seem more like opposite perspectives than complements. Still others emphasize only the spiritual dimension of Jung's work with little or no appreciation for the wealth of its implications on the path into biology and matter. Most have entirely missed the potential of Jung's psychology to serve as an integrative framework for the behavioral sciences.

On the outside, a claim for the Jungian model as an integrative frame seems extravagant. Jung was a theorist whose ramblings are notoriously hard to follow and whose appeals to phenomenological, clinical and empirical levels of explanation defy any possibility of clean categorization. But it is Jung's breadth, his refusal to be tied down into one or another pet domain, that recommends him to the task. From every perspective we find Jung bridging conceptual territories that lesser lights often find difficult to follow. If we lapse into the popular jargon of Kuhnian analysis we might easily call Jung a paradigm bridger (Kuhn, 1969; Ritzer, 1980; Brooke, 1991).

In the process of weaving what becomes a rich tapestry of concepts, Jung maddeningly, repeatedly and without warning, jumps logical levels. As a result, his definitions suffer so that archetype, self and other constructs so closely identified with his writings are subject to understanding on many more levels than Jung may have intended. These are easy targets. When they enter the line of sight of more systematic thinkers, it is often easy to forget that Jung's central task was to make the world of meanings that he had discovered in the unconscious available to the therapeutic process (Fordham, 1957).

When we move from the spiritual themes and non-systematic elements of Jung's thought, we discover the elements of theoretical structure that effectively tie meaning simultaneously to biology and spirit without violating the integrity of either. Moreover, we discover there the broad brushstrokes of a theory of humankind lying dormant, just below the surface. In harmony with most modern thinking, Jung saw that mind and spirit were essentially inseparable from, though not reducible to, the physical world. Indeed, in his psychoid realm he found matter and spirit meeting at the far end of his spectrum of the psyche, indissolubly linked outside the then regnant paradigm of Cartesian dualism. In sketching some of the broad implications of Jung's explorations, we find ample foundation for the articulation of the Jungian view into the world of sociology.

Beginning at the most basic level, we find Jung aligning himself with biology and ethology without becoming either reductionistic or vitalistic. He understands that the archetypes are connected to something more basic than the brain and sees their close relationship to instinct. He is nevertheless careful to avoid leaving us with only ethological response systems, or the less respectable instincts. Like Piaget and Mead, he understands that the workings of human consciousness arise out of the space that has developed between stimulus and response, in the loosening of absolutely dependent responses (Furth, 1969; Miller, 1973).

Redeeming Jung's formulations from the archaic language of instinct, meaning becomes linked closely to innate and emergent response systems but again not reducible to them. At every turn, a careful reading of Jung finds meaning and growth appearing at emergent levels of integration that are not predictable from the simple assembly of their constituent elements.

Expanding on this link, it will be apparent later on that the structure of archetypal systems, especially as reflected in symbols of the self, reflect some of the most basic patterns of living systems. This is implicit in Jung's material and helps to provide a core of meaning that unites all levels of existence. Whether possessed of a human mind, or functioning on the level of the Protista, certain of Jung's formulations provide meaningful links between all living creatures.

Anticipating Damasio and other modern neurophysiologists, Jung understood that thought processes were dependent upon a feeling tone that was the *sine qua non* of meaning. Without delving into the mysteries of the papez circuit and cortical–limbic interactions, Jung formulated his feeling-rooted, complex theory based upon the unconscious responses of his human subjects (Damasio, 1994; Redfearn, 1973; von Franz, 1970).

In harmony with Piaget and Pavlov, Jung saw that learned responses were systemic responses, not isolated behaviors. Their assimilation into the complex structure of the psyche was ultimately determinative of whether a response perseverated or was extinguished. No behavior stands alone but is part of a dynamic feeling with its root in the deeper systems of complex and archetype (Piaget and Inhelder, 1969; von Franz, 1970).

Modern neurophysiology seems to vindicate not only the link between affect and memory, but also between affect and image and the level to which meaning is rooted in imagistic terms strongly reminiscent of Jung's early formulations. The ambiguity that surrounds his use of the words *archetype*, *archetypal image* and *primordial image* becomes understandable when, in harmony with modern theory, memory moves beyond the brain and involves the whole of the organism in somatic states. Anticipating Maturana and Varela, the Jungian organism and psyche are autopoetic (Maturana and Varela, 1987; Samuels, 1989; Damasio, 1994; Hochman, 1994).

Linking the multiple levels that differentiate the simplest of life-forms from consciousness as experienced by humans is a definition of meaning derived from Piaget that remains wholly compatible with Jung. When meaning is defined as the organism's capacity to assimilate new experience to pre-existing structures, it has the effect of extending the range of conscious activity so that living things at every level are understood to participate in a progressive spiral of growing awareness. In the Jungian system, it is the archetype that expresses the root values and into which new patterns are assimilated through the complexes. Linking new contents back to root complexes, libido charges each level of experience with the numen of living energy so that each experience integrated into the complex becomes a structural foundation for further levels of meaning and understanding (Piaget, 1970a; Hillman, 1983/1988).

It is these archetypal potentials – these potentials for perception and action and their seemingly unlimited capacity for articulation with the inner and outer worlds – that provide the power of the Jungian perspective to integrate the social with the psychological and the biological. Because they represent universal perceptions, situations and needs, the archetypes provide for the possibility of a shared world of meanings. Because in the world of the infant they presume the presence of a responsive other and build a world of distinctive meanings and potentialities based upon interaction with that other, the archetypal dynamic represents the root of social interaction. They present the possibility for understanding the interplay between individual and society, nature and nurture, the world of inborn potential and its socially mediated fulfillment. With this rich foundation, Jung provides an implicit theoretical structure into which the sociological perspective merges in almost seamless fashion.

Significantly for the study of sociology, Jung provides a basis for understanding the reciprocal interaction of individuals and culture as coevolving systems. Out of the archetypal core of human consciousness there arise the great symbolic patterns that provide its organization. These mythic themes arise out of the collective and are clothed in the dress customary to the time and place of their arising. On one level they fulfill the functions identified by Lévi-Strauss by providing the answers to the questions which life always presents to individuals and to groups: Whom should I marry? What does it mean to become an adult? Where are the boundaries of my tribe or group? How can I know that I belong? On another level they reach down to primal roots of lived experience and contact the spiritual realities that reflect the world to come, the age gone by and the hope of contact with the eternal (Lévi-Strauss, 1966; 1963).

The anthropological question as to the primacy of myth and ritual is mooted by the revelation that both arise from universal patterns that share the dual function of ordering life in terms of locally mandated forms and of providing access to the numinous root of those forms. From the perspective of a Jungian sociology we find myth and ritual serving a deeper reality than most conventional anthropologies imagine.

For as many typical situations as humankind endures, there is an archetypal pattern. But because the archetypes are clothed in symbolic forms that arise in interaction with a real-world experience (including an experience of culture), the mythic systems give varying expression to the underlying archetypal cores. So, there arises out of the uniformity of the collective unconscious the rich cultural diversity that we know as humankind in its many cultural manifestations.

In the dynamic between individual and culture, culture and the collective unconscious, we find reflected in Jung's psychology the great themes of sociology. Weber's routinization of charisma and his view towards the centrality of religious thought is readily harmonized with Jung's pattern of the regression of libido. Durkheim's conception of the collective consciousness can easily be made compatible with Jung's ideas of group identification and the participation mystique. Labeling and role theory are compatible with the idea of the shadow and the projection of its contents on outsiders (Weber, 1958; Durkheim, 1938/1964; Neumann, 1990).

Jungian theory presents a particularly fine groundwork for an approach to sociology for several reasons. First, his work is implicitly systems theoretical.[2] This has the happy consequence that the theory is, by its nature, not limited to its present form but may be extended to the biological, spiritual and sociological poles. Second, his theory is explicitly cross cultural. It is based upon the comparison of patterns as they occur across many times and many cultures. Third, Jungian theory carries at its heart basic assumptions that allow for a smooth transition from the realm of individual experience to the realm of group action. These include, on a certain level, the social determination of the expression of symbolic images and a substratum of potential that is necessarily other-seeking, including the cross-gender archetypal figures of anima and animus. He includes a mechanism that accounts for role-related behavior in the animus/a and persona/ae, and a biological-level commonalty of experience as the basis for symbolic interaction in the psychoid collective unconscious. He has uncovered, moreover, among the several layers of consciousness, explicitly sociological levels including the cultural and regional unconscious. Despite his general intolerance for group action and his championing of the individual, the theoretical structure left by Jung is more than adequate to the task of providing, with little modification, a bridge to sociology.

ORGANIZATION OF THE TEXT

The following exposition is partly exegetical and partly integrative. At heart, it is an attempt to bring into clear definition and systematic form the idea of the archetype as Jung saw it. On the other hand, it is an attempt to understand that definition in light of data from biology and systems theory. It is further an attempt to integrate insights from various perspectives on the Jungian corpus into a reasonably coherent picture of what the archetypal *can* mean. If there is any one thing it is not, it is not a claim for the ascendency of one perspective over any other. From here, we seek to extend the theory of archetypes to the realm of sociology.

In Part I I have made an attempt to clarify the nature of the archetype and to define the archetype and archetypal action in terms of the principles of modern biology and systems theory. The need for this section is rooted in the classical Jungian reticence to examine the biological pole of the collective unconscious and in the ambiguity that often attaches to the archetype and the mode of archetypal action. This section is also necessary in order to provide a firm foundation for our later inquiry into archetypal mechanisms at the level of sociology.

Part II examines typical patterns of archetypal activity. It provides a basic vocabulary for the identification of the kinds of archetypal patterns already seen at the individual and familial levels and that may be expected to reappear at the sociological level.

Part III tackles the problem of how to approach a sociology from the design level and asks the question: what are the essential issues that a sociology must address? It examines sociology from the perspective of Kuhn's (1969) paradigm and leans heavily upon Ritzer's (1980) application of the idea to sociology. It finally derives an outline for later use in the examination of sociology from an archetypal perspective.

Part IV develops basic sociological themes as they emerge from an exhaustive analysis of the *Collected Works*. Part V is a review of the entire enterprise and suggests practical applications and directions for future research.

Part I

Archetypal explorations

Chapter 1

The nature of the archetype

It has been previously noted that Jung's most important contribution to the world of psychology was the concept of the collective unconscious and the archetypes of which it is comprised. Having never formalized his work with archetypes as a systematic theory, the Jungian account reads more like the continuing narrative of discovery than a clear exposition of the nature of the archetype *an sich*.

Archetypes are commonly enumerated in terms of specific motifs that appear in the myths of all cultures. These include the mother, father, senex, puer and trickster among others. These, with the anima/us, may be seen to represent the psychic templates for the biologically inevitable interactions within a normal person's life experience. They simultaneously reflect stages in the development of the psyche.

To this group, Jung added the shadow, the anima/us, the self and the personae as archetypal structural elements that were regularly personified in dreams, myths and fairy tales.[1] Beyond these classes, Jung also mentioned a class of transitional archetypes, archetypes which give rise to symbols of transformation or change (1959/1968a).

Jung indicated that while these were common classes of archetypal expression, they were not in themselves the archetypes, but symbolic representations of the abstract dynamisms which actually characterize the archetypal realm. The archetypes were far more abstract than these lists suggest and, for Jung, were most closely approximated by the number series understood in its qualitative aspect.

Jung warned that the archetype was not accessible as a thing, but was only perceptible insofar as its ordering influence was reflected in the contents of consciousness. He insisted that the archetypes were a set of formal invariants which, like the stereometric systems of crystals, give form to the molecules attracted to them, but are in themselves undiscoverable (1959/1968a).

Jung also indicated that the archetype *an sich* was undiscoverable, because all of the archetypes were said to be contaminated one with another.[2] That is to say that one cannot tease out one archetype without dragging with it significant elements of others. This is amply demonstrated by von Franz (1970) and Edinger (1972) as they illustrate how all of the elements of a net of associations centered in any one archetype can be related to every other archetype, and it is only through a specific feeling tone[3] that the limits of each are to be distinguished.

Again, from the perspective of Fordham, where the archetype is a "deintegrate"[4] of the self, we come upon another reason for the inability to differentiate clearly between one archetype and another. Here, the self is the primary actor in psychic activity. The archetypes themselves are aspects of the self that express the focus of libidinal[5] activity. They approximate the activation of an instinct but are in practice much more diffuse. In the process of their expression, certain behavioral and affective elements are marshaled together to form an active archetypal center. Because the center partakes of the whole, one may never say that the archetype exists *per se*, but only that it exists as one of many centers of libidinal activity within the organism. Every archetype, according to Fordham (1957), is a reflection of the self. For similar reasons Jacobi (1974) points out that the functions of the gods in primitive mythology always overlap, each a partial function of an integrated whole, only deriving its reality from its participation in the whole.

It is also useful to recall Jung's (1956/1967, para. 294) statement to the effect that there are as many archetypes as there are typical situations in human life. This suggests the existence of a not incalculable number of archetypes, but it simultaneously suggests that because of the possibility for overlap and imprecision in definition, the task of specifically defining the archetypes would be nearly impossible. Moreover, as Jacobi (1974) points out, if the number of archetypes is great, then the number of symbols associated with them is incalculably greater.

It is, in part, for these reasons that I have decided to refer in general, not to the archetypes, but to the archetypal as a realm, a field of inquiry, a class of experience. Grammarians may shrug at the bastardization of the adjectival form; however, because the archetypes are known through their adjectival influence on the contents of consciousness the form itself becomes especially significant. This is in line with the observation by James Hall that it may be more correct to speak of an archetypal field rather than archetypes as individual entities. Individual archetypes in this perspective represent nodal points where the field is most dense (1977/1991).

THE ARCHETYPAL SPECTRUM

There are points in his discussion of archetypes where Jung seems to contradict himself. One of the most significant of these appears in his discussion of the archetype in relation to instinct. Early on, Jung goes to great pains to correlate archetypal activity with instinct. He notes that for each archetype there is, or must be, an instinctual companion. Further, he declares the archetypes to be the psychic correlates of instinct and their reflection in consciousness. In a later passage, Jung now declares, to the confusion of many readers, that the instincts and the archetypes are the most polar opposites imaginable (1960/1969).

Although confusing at first, the statements point to the self-consistency of the archetypal phenomena. As a whole, the group is said to be Janus-faced, that is, looking both up and down, forward and back. Janus was the Roman god of portals. He had one face that looked out and one that looked in. Morally, he symbolizes confusion and ambiguity. One might suggest that calling someone two-faced is a reference to the moral ambiguity of the god (Jung, 1959/1968a; Matthews, 1986).

This two-facedness is plainly seen in the bipolar origin of the archetype. As the psychoid[6] manifestation of instinct, it mediates the biological drive on the level of intellect and emotion. As the reflection of the order of the universe and the root of abstract thought, it separates humankind from the biological and moves him to the spiritual. So, the archetype is two-faced. In its thrall one might as easily be drawn down into the world of sensuality as drawn upward into the rarefied realm of spirit (Jung, 1960/1969).

The whole issue of archetypal polarity is in part clarified by Jung's map of consciousness as a spectrum ranging from the material and biological at one pole to the spiritual and transcendent at the other. In the middle, balanced and often sliding between the two, is the realm of consciousness (see Figure 1.1). All psychic processes exhibit the bipolarity of the archetype, the extent to which they partake of either pole is dependent upon the position of the listener (von Franz, 1974; Jung 1960/1969).

THE CIRCLE OF MEANING

An essential part of the archetypal definition was included in Jung's insistence that archetypal patterns were not reflections of the observed patterns of nature as they are presented to each individual on a daily basis, neither were they the result of the cross-cultural migration of symbols. He was adamant in his insistence that the archetypes and the patterns to which they gave rise were psychic in origin and would appear autochthonously[7] without exposure either to nature or to other cultures from which they might be learned.

Hidden in this declaration was the understanding that the self mediated a superordinate reality to which it and the whole of the material universe were equally bound and from which both emerged. This reality was called by Jung, after the manner of the alchemists, the *Unus Mundus*, the singular reality. Because of its contact with and determination of the archetypal nodes of the collective unconscious, he came to call the latter the objective psyche. It was Jung's belief that both matter and psyche met in this unity

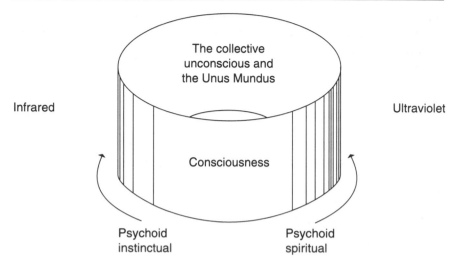

Figure 1.1 The spectrum of psychic activity

and that, there, all of the elements of reality were unified in terms of a singular reality and a single law. This being so, there existed a necessary correspondence between the inner world and the outer world. The archetypes necessarily corresponded with the outward reality as they sprang from the same underlying inner reality.

In the Jungian Universe, not only are the physical and psychic aspects of reality mutually conditioned by an underlying transcendental level, but both are mutually codetermined on the physical level. While Jung explicitly denies that archetypal motifs are determined by the direct, historical interaction between the mind and the external world, his perspective holds that on an evolutionary level, the environment has left its mark in the patterns of the instincts and archetypes which we see today (1960/1969, para. 328).

A mechanism for just such an inheritance of culturally determined patterns has been identified by Lumsden and Wilson in *Genes, Mind, and Culture: the Coevolutionary Process* (1981). Lumsden and Wilson have hypothesized that it takes something on the order of 1,000 years for a cultural element, or a propensity to express some culturally defined trait, to become established in the gene pool as an inherited trait. That is, during 1,000 years of selection for a specific tendency towards culture or the manipulation of cultural artifacts, a group will result that exhibits an increased propensity for displaying that trait or being able to use that artifact. This is strongly suggestive of Jung's observations that the archetypes represent the accretion of endless repetitions of typical patterns of behavior (Jung, 1959/1968a, para. 99; Lumsden and Wilson, 1981).

From this it may be understood that the human organism is born ready to respond to diurnal cycles, the patterns of seasons and the patterning of the world, not because he/she sees them and adjusts his/her behavior accordingly (although there is a secondary level of attunement mediated by the pineal body), but because they correspond to ancient rhythms that are part of his/her biological heritage. Millions of years of evolution have implanted the rhythms of life upon the fabric of human existence in the form of instinct and archetype so that the natural projections emerging from the human psyche fit perfectly the planet for which they were formed. One might say that the archetypes are environmentally determined in phylogenesis, but are genetically determined in ontogenesis.

> From this standpoint [the primordial image] ... is a psychic expression of the physiological and anatomical disposition. If one holds the view that a particular anatomical structure is a product of environmental conditions working on living matter, then the primordial image, in its constant and universal distribution, would be the product of equally constant and universal influences from without, which must, therefore, act like a natural law. ... We are forced to assume that the given structure of the brain does not owe its peculiar nature merely to the influence of the surrounding conditions, but also and just as much to the peculiar and autonomous quality of living matter, i.e., to a law inherent in life itself. The given constitution of the organism, therefore, is on the one hand a product of external conditions, while on the other it is determined by the intrinsic nature of living matter.
>
> (Jung, 1971, para. 748)

Because both the world of matter and the world of mind and spirit arise out of the same ground, Jung, again following the alchemists, expected to find a considerable level of correspondence between the physical world and symbolic/archetypal realm. His researches, and those of his followers, found repeated evidence of just such a correspondence that ranged from the easily observed regularities of the sun, moon and planets to the biological necessity of a mother and father. Among the successors of Jung, Marie Louise von Franz has had special success in tracing the existence of archetypal pattern at the level of micro-physics and abstract number theory.

In the realm of micro-physics, remarkable correspondences were found between religious views, philosophical perspectives and the hard data of science. Moreover, this correspondence could be expected to exist in the patterns of life as well as in the patterns of inanimate matter. From the Jungian perspective, the universe is united with an archetypal ordering, a logos that suffuses all and orders all (von Franz, 1974).

GETTING IT FROM THE RIGHT PERSPECTIVE

Understanding that Jung's approach to the archetypal was not theoretically oriented, but aimed at the immediate need of a psychological practice, it is clear how his terminology could afford to be less precise than one might wish. In the day-to-day realities of the therapeutic session, the image is the practical handle on the archetype. The clarity of its abstract expression is far less valuable. In such a circumstance, the motif, filled with meaning and affective value, is a far more valuable commodity than the underlying structure. Indeed, the abstract structure is, on this level, of little value. Because of his necessary focus, Jung could reasonably hold the underlying principle as unknowable. This very perspective, however, may have been itself a function of one of the central qualities of the archetypes, their numinosity.

The numinosity of the archetypal is the quality by which it draws the center of consciousness to itself. It is sometimes likened to a magnet. The numinous charge of the archetype tends to obscure all else from the field of consciousness. All things lead back to it. This charge of libido is expressed as spirituality, compulsion and goal directedness. The point is made clearly in *Symbols of Transformation* (1956/1967). There, Jung notes that the archetype "has a characteristically numinous effect, so that the subject is gripped by it as though by an instinct. What is more, instinct itself can be restrained and even overcome by this power . . . " (para. 225). Jung indicates that the archetypes fascinate, actively oppose the conscious mind and "mold the destinies of individuals by unconsciously influencing their thinking, feeling and behaviour" (para. 467).

Insofar as Jung was caught in the *fascinens* of the archetype (as we all are to some degree), it is not unreasonable to assume that the numen of meaning obscured the less accessible roots of the mechanism, thus making it not only unreachable, but unappealing as well. We perhaps see this in the conflict between scientific/empirical efforts in Jung's presentations and the experience-oriented attempt to provide the reader with a sense of the archetypal itself. According to Jung's own statements, the latter was an absolutely necessary part of psychological understanding. It provides the crucial difference in understanding between a man who has endured a severe illness and one who has only read about it (1959/1968b).

Combining the practical need of the therapist with the power of the archetype to overshadow, and both with Jung's stated desire to provide a taste of the archetypal, we might easily come to the conclusion that the abstract archetype may in fact have been unreachable to Jung. It need not, however, elude researchers with a different perspective.

In the following paragraphs, some of the very principles which Jung saw as precluding an analysis of the nature of archetypal activity will be summoned up to provide a new look at the invisible archetype.

The biological perspective

It is very possible to take another view of the archetype that builds up from the data of biology to the point where an instinctual/archetypal continuum meets with Jung's observations on the level of psyche. It is my belief that it is at the psychoid pole nearest the biological that we can best discover the roots of archetypal activity.

This is not to suggest that the archetype is any less a spiritual or psychic force than Jung imagined it. If indeed the archetype is the expression of an ordering Logos (whether personal or impersonal) that reaches into the depths of matter as well as into the heights of the spirit, then no true reduction becomes possible. From this perspective, any validation of the biological pole is only evidence for the continuing validity of the construct at the more spiritual and archetypal pole. With Jung we point to the Tabula Smagdarina, holding the same principles true on every level of analysis – "As it is above, so it is below" (1959/1968a, para. 193).

With this in mind, we note that there are several characteristics of the archetype that suggest that the nature of the archetype is to be discerned most clearly at the level of biology. Among these are the universality of archetypal patterns, their mutual contamination and interpenetration, the fact that they are discerned one from another by affective tone and their relationship to instinct.

The universality of archetypal patterns

One of the basic evidences for the existence of the archetypal was Jung's observation that certain patterns of thought appeared more or less universally. In his extensive study of myth and religion, as well as in his daily work with clients, Jung found the same mythemes and motifs appearing in myth, dream and psychotic episode over and over with great consistency. After many years of studying these correspondences, Jung was able to conclude that their universal occurrence was not dependent upon cultural transmission, nor upon similarity of experience, but arose out of the very structure of the human psyche.

Although mustered in defense of a perspective on the origins of myth that is diametrically opposed to Jung's position, de Santillana and von Dechend point to the universality of certain mythic themes as evidence that the themes themselves point to a common origin.

Take the origin of music. Orpheus and his harrowing death may be a poetic creation born in more than one instance in diverse places. But when characters who do not play the lyre, but blow pipes get themselves flayed alive for various absurd reasons, and their identical end is rehearsed on several continents, then we feel we have got hold of something, for such stories cannot be linked by internal sequence. And when the Pied Piper turns up both in the medieval German myth of Hamelin and in Mexico long before Columbus, and is linked in both places with certain attributes like the color red, it can hardly be a coincidence. Generally there is little that finds its way into music by chance.

(de Santillana and von Dechend 1969, p. 7)

After a careful examination of the theory of archetypes, Hobson provides an analysis of the criteria used by Jung to adjudge a theme or image as archetypal (Hobson, 1973; Hall, 1977/1991). He reports that there are four criteria which must be satisfied in order to classify any theme or image as archetypal. He notes, however, the criteria are extremely difficult, with the fourth almost impossible of validation. The four criteria are:

1 A theme must be isolated clearly enough to recognize it as a typical phenomenon, i.e. a particular motif must occur in the imagery of different individuals and must recur in a series of dreams or fantasies of one person.
2 The theme must be shown to occur in many parts of the world in many ages.
3 The motif must have a similar context and functional meaning whenever it occurs.
4 The fantasy image must not have been acquired through education, tradition, language, or indirectly via religious ideas, and all motifs must be excluded which have been known and forgotten.

(Hobson, 1973, p. 72)

Despite the seeming difficulty of passing such stringent criteria, there exist abundant examples of the recurrence of many such themes throughout the world. Von Franz (1980/1988) points specifically to the healer, the hero, the great mother, the treasure hard to attain, the helpful animal and the tree of life as particularly familiar examples.

One of the more striking of these common archetypal themes is the idea of the *axis mundi* as the center of the home, village and individual.[8] This theme has been treated extensively by non-Jungian and Jungian authors. Jung encountered it in mandala symbolism and the symbols of the self. In that context he counted the *axis mundi* in combination with the quaternio[9] of orientation (i.e. North, South, East, West) the most fundamental of archetypal patterns (1959/1968a, b). Other authors including Mircea Eliade have traced the phenomenon worldwide as representing the fundamental orientation towards self, home, city, world and universe (Eliade, 1954/1971, 1976; Stewart, 1989).

Further evidence for the universality of archetypal influence is mustered by von Franz (1980/1988) when she points out that even where clear evidence exists for cultural contamination, an archetypal predisposition may be evidenced by the spread of one idea or pattern in contradistinction to another. We may interpret this to say that if we are presented with two versions of a myth or fairy tale, or two alternate symbols of an archetypal reality, the one corresponding more closely to the archetypal substrate as it is locally experienced would be the more readily incorporated into the system under study. This is strikingly similar to the conclusion by Lumsden and Wilson (1981), that even small genetic predispositions to the adoption of what they call culturgens are significantly magnified by ethnographic and cultural mechanisms.

In their 1981 exploration of the coevolution of culture, Lumsden and Wilson hypothesized the existence of an hereditary mechanism which could account for the development of culturally defined behavioral tendencies. In the context of a relatively stable culture, these rules had the consequence that certain kinds of behavioral traits and abilities would become more frequent and accessible over time. While some of these traits would pass quickly in and out of the epigenetic landscape, others, more fundamental to the human condition, might appear universally. Thus, the physiological basis of Jungian archetypes (Lumsden and Wilson, 1991).

Jung's criteria and Lumsden and Wilson's epigenetic program suggest that the archetypal is to be found in the fundamental realities of human life, if not in the qualities of living systems themselves. Indeed, there is strong reason to believe, especially in light of their link to the instincts, that the archetypes are biologically more fundamental than the data that they organize. This is further emphasized by their role as the organizers of perception and action. As such, they must exist on a more fundamental level than either.

Affective tone

One of the more striking characteristics of the archetypal realm is the observation that the archetypes are distinguishable one from another only in terms of affective tone. Marie Louise von Franz makes the point that it is intellectually possible to connect everything with everything else at the level of the collective unconscious. It is, however, only through the use of the feeling function that the relevant limits of the individual archetypal nets are clearly demarcated (1972/1986).

Jung notes that the feeling tone is a description of the energic value of a psychic element. It describes the idea's "energic potential," how much the individual is affected by the idea, and what it means to him. He also indicates very clearly that a content cannot be integrated into consciousness unless it is appreciated in terms of both the feeling and the analytic function (1959/1968b).

Jung defined the personal unconscious as consisting largely of feeling-toned complexes, each built up upon their specific archetypal base. The feeling tone is the subjective pattern of feeling aroused by the activation of a complex. It may be thought of as the emotional shape of the complex and of the underlying archetype or archetypes. These were said by Jung to be founded upon a twofold core. The first part was a biologically based, innate element: the psychoid archetype. The second part, and essential to the growth of the process, is an original set of experiences which set the feeling tone that will characterize the complex from then on. The complexes are the accretions of experience about this twofold archetypal foundation. This body of past experience gives each complex a specific feeling tone (1960/1969).

The idea of a feeling tone is very like those times in an individual's life when a specific physical or emotional experience evokes memories of similar situations from the past. There is a specific physiological state, a specific emotional response and other variables which evoke the memory in a powerful and undeniable manner. In ghost stories we hear that someone senses a presence in the room. My father told the story of standing in his kitchen one night, shortly after his mother's death, and feeling her presence. Not any presence, mind you, but a feeling tone that he recognized as the presence of his mother. In the same fashion, the archetypes bind to themselves, out of their original encounter with the world, a specific and identifiable feeling tone which marks the flavor of their associative complexes from then on.

With this lead we find the fundamental nature of the archetype pointing us back to the ideas of instinct and imprint, so that the archetypal finds its root in the more primitive levels of human existence. The data from *The Structure and Dynamics of the Psyche* clearly indicate that the archetype – the biological element – is joined to an environmental element, and that these together constitute the core of the complex. From this we can surmise that the archetypal element consists in a predisposition to seek a correspondence between some internal organismic state and some possible match or complement in the external world (Jung 1960/1969; Fordham, 1957).

Mutual contamination

One of the important reasons that Jung gives for the inability to discern the individual archetype *an sich* is that all of them mutually interpenetrate and are mutually contaminated by one another. As noted on p. 12 of this text, Hall (1977/1991) takes this to be an indication that the objective unconscious is a field in which the archetypes are individually represented by higher concentrations of libidinal energy. Likewise, von Franz compares the archetypes to excited points in the field of the objective psyche which behave like "relatively isolatable nuclei" (1980/1988, p. 86).

By way of illustration von Franz (1972/1986) relates the idea to a species of "Chinese grass."

In studying any archetype deeply enough, dragging up all of its connections, you will find that you can pull out the entire collective unconscious! I am always reminded of the Chinese who speak of a certain kind of grass whose roots spread so far that you never get it all up. The Chinese say that if you pull up a root of this grass the whole lawn comes up with it! It is the same with archetypes, for if you pull at one of them long enough, the whole collective unconscious follows.

(von Franz, 1972/1986, p. 160)

When one makes the mistake of identifying the archetypal with a specific image or content, it is very easy to see how the parable of the grass can apply. The archetypal lies at a lower logical level than the elements by which it is expressed, and so uses the elements of experience interchangeably in a Lévi-Straussian bricolage in order to manifest itself in consciousness (Lévi-Strauss, 1966).[10]

We may also conclude from the suggested linkage between the archetypes that the archetypal functions more by manifesting different aspects of a unitary reality than in terms of discrete entities. There may, in fact, be only a single archetypal mechanism, more or less identical with the self, rather than many individual archetypes.

Jung notes:

It is necessary to point out once more that the archetypes are not determined as regards their content, but only as regards their form and then only to a very limited degree. A primordial image is determined as to its content only when it has become conscious and is therefore filled out with the contents of conscious experience. . . . In principle it can be named and has an invariable nucleus of meaning – but always in principle, never as regards its concrete manifestation.

(Jung, 1959/1968a, para. 155)

We must therefore conclude that the archetypal is something that exists below the level of content and is expressed through the form of the archetypal image or theme. Interpenetration and contamination suggest that, underneath the images and associative nets, there lies a more formal archetypal reality which suffuses but remains untouched by the nodal points that we observe. This is again reflected in Fordham's view of the archetype as a deintegrate of the self, and the view that the self is reflected in the structuring of each and every archetype. In reality, the archetypal represents a unifying dynamic, relating all conscious activity to the program of individuation.

In his essay, *Maturation of Ego and Self in Infancy*, Fordham notes:

The study . . . showed that, though apparently distinct forms could be separated out, to consider each archetype as a discrete substructure of the self was fallacious. Each always carried within it associative connections with other archetypes and each had a remarkable capacity to become interchangeable and to transform itself. In other words, each archetype implied the whole self and therefore could be thought of as a deintegrate of the self ... since the archetypes were unconscious structures and the conscious is formed out of the unconscious they could also be conceived as the substructures of ego formations – islets of consciousness – which develop during periods of deintegration.

(Fordham, 1973/1980, p. 88)

From the holographic perspective suggested by Zinkin (1987), we may expect that each archetype reflects the whole of the self, and comes into manifestation only as the indicator of the necessary direction of individuation. That is, whenever a specific need or compensation becomes the center of psychic attention, the archetype, or complex associated with that need, rises into salience. When it is not activated, the individual experiences which it has drawn to itself in the form of complexes give expression to other complexes while the archetypal core itself recedes into the general libido pool of the self. When, therefore, we pull at the archetype, we pull not at an individual entity, but at one of those points of the self that lie closest to the focus of the plan of self realization.

Systems organization

Samuels, Zinkin and others have suggested that the Jungian psyche is subject to systems analysis (Zinkin, 1987; Samuels, 1985; Lester, 1986, 1987). When one views the self simultaneously as the central archetype and as the whole system; when one sees the archetypal self moving the existential self towards the realization of specific systemic patterns in the unfolding of the teleological self (the process of individuation),[11] a set of directing systems principles including wholeness, hierarchical organization and systems integration are immediately brought to mind. The holistic perspective of Jung and Fordham suggests that the expression of the individual archetype is but a special case of what Bertalanffy called centration (Laszlo, 1972; Fidler, 1982; Progoff, 1959).

From the systems perspective pioneered by Bertalanffy, a complex phenomenon or organism can often be shown to be composed of a group of interacting subsystems. Systems have the special quality that the specific characteristics of the whole are unpredictable from the nature of the parts or subsystems. Wholes are instead said to be the emergent properties of the interactions between their parts or subsystems. They differ specifically from aggregates in this property: the whole possesses a quality that is irreducible to its parts.

Bertalanffy described centration as the tendency for whole systems, though differentiated into separate subsystems, to retain the capacity to center their energy upon one or another of those subunits. That is to say that the whole, at any moment in time, is capable of temporarily redefining itself in terms of the subunit. When, for example, I burn my finger on the stove, the whole of my body reacts as if the finger were the center of the whole: my muscles tense, my heart rate increases, my back arches away from the source of pain, my legs propel me across the room and my lungs fill to elicit a loud cry of pain: "Ouch!" According to Bertalanffy, centration is the only way a system changes from one state to another (1968).

This process is described in perfect parallel with Fordham's concept of the archetype as deintegrate of the Self. The primordial self breaks apart into component subsystems or archetypes and each becomes capable of becoming the more or less temporary center of the psychic system. In the adult, centration becomes the source of the compulsive nature of the archetype, its numinosity and its ability to function as a subordinate personality (Bertalanffy, 1968, pp. 69–71; Fordham, 1973/1980, pp. 84–7).

This perspective is also fully compatible with Samuels's (1989) call for a rethinking of the concepts of hierarchy and the relative importance of synchronic and diachronic perspectives on the psyche. A systems theoretical approach implies a dynamic hierarchy in which the organism is intentionally reconfigured in terms of the centrating subsystem. Moreover, the self-same approach preserves all of the structures and subsystems as contributing members and potential centers of the whole. There is an implicit balance between synchronic and diachronic modes of organization. Synchrony is maintained as a mutual arising of the property of wholeness expressed as a function of the interaction of all of the parts. Diachrony is revealed in the capacity for development and its dependence upon successive levels of emergents over time.

The appeal to systems points us again to a level below consciousness for the root of archetypal activity. Indeed, the parallel to systems theory suggests that the archetypal may find its expression in the general characteristics of living systems. It further suggests, as living systems are by nature complex systems, that archetypal patterns are expressed in some form at all levels of life and consciousness. This reflects Piaget's observation that the activities of humans and all living things were on some level analyzable into the basic characteristics of complex systems. In his perspective these included, as root qualities, systems organization and adaptation, with adaptation divided into his hallmark accommodation, assimilation and equilibration (1970b).

Fundamental considerations

Ira Progoff (1953/1981) studied with Jung and was a Bolingen fellow at the Jung Institute at Kusnacht during the 1950s. He indicates that Jung placed great emphasis upon a Bergsonian-style vitalism. Indeed, he suggests that Jung owed a great intellectual debt to Bergson that was never properly acknowledged.

A perusal of the index to the *Collected Works* finds Jung's minimal acknowledgment of Bergson's understanding of intuition as "a mere pointer" (Jung, 1971, para. 540–1). Later he acknowledges Bergson's crystalline metaphor for abstraction, but acknowledges no debt (para. 871). In paragraph 55 of that work he explicitly denies that his concept of energy is at all "vitalistic." In *Two Essays on Analytical Psychology*, Jung acknowledges that Bergson struck a powerful blow against a monistic intellectualism when he forced other scientists and philosophers to acknowledge multiple causal forces (1953/1966). Finally, in *Civilization in Transition* he points again to his idea of psychic energy and notes that it is as well explained by Bergson's *elan vital* as by any other construct (1964/ 1970, para. 55).

It is not difficult to find a Bergsonian thread in Jung's writings. The idea of the self as the source and goal immediately recalls Bergson's entelechy: "the determination of the parts by the function and purpose of the whole" (Durant, 1926, p. 500). Moreover, the Bergsonian call for a transcendence of mechanism and finalism recalls Jung's early discussions of their relation to psychology and his later transcendence of both in the principle of synchronicity (1960/1969).

That a vitalistic thread might be found in the Jungian corpus is suggested by the foregoing analysis of the archetypal phenomenon. Over and over again, the root of the archetypal points to lower and lower levels of integration. The distinction between the archetypes and the semantic nets that they form point to sub-cortical mechanisms. The association between the archetype and emotion suggests that the level of action lies beneath the limbic structures which map out the emotional shape of experience. The association between archetypal action and instinct brings the level of action to the brain stem and below. Finally, the association of the Jungian psyche with the principles of systems theory suggests that the archetypal may at root represent the most basic qualities of living organisms.

This at last arrives at what appears to be one of Jung's underlying assumptions: the psyche is rooted in the processes of life. And we find that from the beginning, the archetypal image, as well as the entire structure of the psyche, was associated with the processes of life.

> We are forced to assume that the given structure of the brain does not owe its peculiar nature merely to the influence of the surrounding conditions, but also and just as much to the peculiar and autonomous quality of living matter, i.e., to a law inherent in life itself. The given constitution of the organism, therefore, is on the one hand a product of external conditions, while on the other it is determined by the intrinsic nature of living matter.
>
> (Jung, 1921/1971, para. 748)

THE PROPERTIES OF LIFE

The Piagetian patterns of life

It was observed on p. 23 that Piaget had analyzed living systems and their behaviors into certain basic elements. These elements consisted of the rules of organization and the principles of adaptation. They were contained in his theory of biological structure (Piaget, 1970b).

According to Piaget, organization is the tendency of the living system to structure itself and its environment in accordance with the principles that characterize complex systems. These were defined by Piaget as wholeness, transformation and self regulation (ibid., p. 5).

Wholeness is defined as that quality of systems that separates them from heaps or aggregates. It means that the individual elements, while not losing their own identity, become joined in accordance with identifiable laws into a unit. The unit then reveals properties which are not predictable from the properties of the parts as individuals. The properties of the whole, however, are not to be construed as emergent, qua the almost mystical appearance of qualities as the simple consequence of the joining of the parts. No, the new qualities are the results of the interactions of the parts. It is these interactions which become the determinants of the nature of the whole (ibid., pp. 7–9).

The second characteristic of structure is that it is subject to transformation. Insofar as the nature of "structured wholes" is dependent upon the laws which order their parts, those laws are themselves the structural agents which govern the transformations of the system which they define. In short, the rules that govern the interrelations between the elements of a whole system define the amount to which that system may vary without losing its identity. Transformation occurs on the level of the individual elements while the rules remain invariant (ibid., pp. 10–13).

Self regulation, the third criterion, then appears as "self maintenance and closure" (ibid., p. 14). These require that despite constant change and self renewal, the system retains a basic identity, it does not become something else. A human being remains a human being, a dog remains a dog. Further, the idea of closure indicates that transformations within the system always give rise to new elements that are members of the system. That is, they conform to the defining properties of the system and are regulated by its laws.

> It is in this sense that a structure is "closed," a notion perfectly compatible with the structure's being a substructure of a larger one; but in being treated as a substructure, a structure does not lose its own boundaries; ... the laws of the substructure are not altered but conserved and the intervening change is an enrichment rather than an impoverishment.
>
> (Piaget, 1970b, p. 14)

The idea of structure is seen by Piaget as the expression of a continuously evolving system in which structure blends seamlessly with system construction. They are inseparable. Indeed, form and content are seen by Piaget as different levels of analysis within the same structure. He notes: "there is no 'form as such' or 'content as such,' . . . each element . . . is always simultaneously form to the content it subsumes and content for some higher form" (ibid., p. 35).

These structures then reappear on the levels of physical reality, mathematics, biology and psychology. Always and in each system the growth of the system involves the transformation of the meaning of the whole. In each case progress

> never takes the form of simply "adding on" new information – new discoveries . . . always lead to a complete recasting of preceding knowledge . . . while leaving room for some future discovery; . . . even in physics attempts to reduce the complex to the simple . . . lead to syntheses in which the more basic theory becomes enriched by the derived theory, and the resulting reciprocal assimilation reveals the existence of structures as distinct from additive complexes.
>
> (Ibid., p. 45)

Self regulation generally takes the form of homeostasis and is differentiated from inorganic models by three factors. First, organisms develop specific organs of self regulation that take over the systemic function. Second, the function of a living structure is tied to the effective function of the entire structure; structure and function are intimately tied together. Third, biological structures are dependent upon meaning (ibid., p. 44 ff.).

Deriving his definition of meaning from linguistics, Piaget describes meaning in terms of signification. Meaning is the assimilation of the signified object to familiar action schemes. Meaning is achieved, that is, when a new stimulus can be fitted into a pre-existing response category. I know what a bird is. Two-legged creatures with beaks, wings and feathers, however new their coloring, all assimilate to the pre-existent pattern of birds. Such assimilations occur on multiple levels and lie at the root of the human ability to develop categories and symbols (Ginsburg and Opper, 1969).

But from this perspective, meaning becomes accessible to any system capable of learning. It further redeems learning from the stimulus response chains of behaviorism and relates it in every organism to a holistic concept of meaning. Insofar as an organism is capable of assimilating a stimulus to some pre-existing scheme of behavior, the stimulus may be said to have meaning. This insight will prove to be important later in our discussion.

Adaptation consists of the individual's tendency to respond and adapt to his environment. Piaget classes adaptations as assimilative and accommodative. They are assimilative insofar as an external event becomes incorporated into the structure of the organism. They are accommodative insofar as the structure of the organism is adapted to suit the requirements of the environment. At the level of humans, assimilations and accommodations generally apply at the level of the sensori-motor scheme (Ginsberg and Opper, 1969, pp. 17–18).

Assimilation is defined in terms of global reorganization and redefinition. It involves, at the most primitive level, the reorganization of the organism as it incorporates the stimulus object into its own structure. In a real sense the biological model of physical assimilation is the archetypal image for this concept. It is closely reliant upon the Bertalanffian operation called centration. It is a universal pattern, associated with the simplest forms of life (Piaget and Inhelder, 1969, pp. 5–6; Bertalanffy, 1968).

Biologically considered, assimilation is the process whereby the organism in each of its interactions with the bodies or energies of its environment fits these in some manner to the requirements of its own physico-chemical structures, while at the same time accommodating itself to them (Piaget, 1970b, p. 72).

On the other hand, just as assimilation relates to the filtering of the stimulus or modification of the object to meet the need of the organism, accommodation refers to the shaping of the response schema, or the restructuring of the organism to fit the current environmental constraint. Neither represents a simple response, but is part of a global tendency brought together through equilibration.

Equilibration is the tendency for the system to seek the most economical definition, meaning or form afforded it. Equilibration proceeds as first one assimilative or accommodative pattern is applied to the situation and then another, through a process involving a succession of alternations and approximations. The process finally results in the pairing of the most appropriate response system with the environmental event, and the subsequent accommodation of that response to the situation at hand. It represents an alternation of possible solutions until a stable pattern of alternations is established. These equilibrating patterns assimilate to one another and produce the third accommodated response scheme.

If we apply these very basic definitions of living patterns to archetypes we find that even at this level the archetypal character is retained. Among the systems principles, wholeness is manifested as the self as central archetype, goal and existential reality. Fordham's definition of the archetypes as deintegrates of the self underline the unity of the system. Moreover, we find that each of the complexes centered about an archetype is in itself a whole system, a provisional ego capable of functioning at the level of consciousness when and if necessary. The principle of wholeness is also manifested in the top-down mode of analysis emphasized by the existence of a self that defines the entire system and is yet more than the sum of its parts.

The property of transformation is reflected in the ability of the psyche to change, grow and individuate while maintaining its own identity. It is further emphasized by Jung's perception of the archetypes as sets of relations, not content-filled categories.

It is necessary to point out once more that archetypes are not determined as regards their content, but only as regards their form and then only to a limited degree. A primordial image is determined as to its content only when it has become conscious and is therefore filled out with the material of conscious experience. Its form, however ... might perhaps be compared to the axial system of a crystal, which, as it were, preforms the crystalline structure in the mother liquid, although it has no material existence of its own. This first appears according to the specific way in which the ions and molecules aggregate. The archetype in itself is empty and purely formal, nothing but a ... possibility of representation which is given a priori. The representations themselves are not inherited, only the forms. ...

(Jung, 1959/1968a, para. 155)

The archetypal is identified by the feeling tones that it draws to itself, the shape of the relations that hold between its libido-charged elements. Thus, Hillman, through application of the systems principle, is justified in identifying anything having archetypal impact as an expression of the archetype. Just so, Fordham can legitimately see each archetype as an expression of the self (Hillman, 1983/1988; Fordham, 1957).

Here, we find Jung once again in agreement with modern physics which declares that the permanent qualities of atoms lie not in their possession of some indivisible substance but in their organization and shape (Augros and Stanciu, 1987).

Self regulation bespeaks the continuity of the archetypal subsystems, their reappearance in every culture and each individual. It recalls the re-emergence of the repressed and never-conscious contents of the psyche as well as the persistence of the submerged ego identity in psychosis. It foreshadows the development of the ego out of the more salient complexes in the developing individual and the assimilation of the ego to the self in the process of individuation.

At this level of adaptation archetypal principles appear in the assimilation of conscious contents to a complex and the building of such complexes about just such an archetypal core. Accommodation recalls the withdrawal of projections as truly new information reaches consciousness, while equilibration recalls nothing so strongly as the enantiodromia of the conscious poles of an unconscious content breaking through into conscious life.

Since these most basic definitions of the properties of living systems suggest archetypal mechanisms we may do well to extend our inquiry to the nature of living systems more generally.

The classical properties of life

Augros and Stanciu indicate that modern biology is hard pressed to provide a definition of life. However, after a foray into modern biological perspectives, they come up with one characteristic of living systems that differentiates them from the inanimate. This is the property of self-originated movement – "Life is the capacity for self-motion. Nutrition and growth, found in all living things, are both self-initiated, self-directed changes" (1987, p. 32). Maturana and Varela (1987) have argued that the single characteristic of life is that it is autopoietic: "continually self producing" (p. 43).[12] Classically, however, living systems have been characterized as displaying several basic properties, including metabolism, irritability, adaptation, growth and reproduction (World Book, 1987).

Metabolism and reproduction may be considered special cases of adaptation and organization. Growth similarly relates to these properties but also bears close affinity to the system properties of wholeness and self regulation. For our purposes we will concentrate on irritability and adaptation.

Adaptation, as we have seen from the Piagetian perspective, consists of two complementary processes: accommodation and assimilation. They are, moreover, both resolutions of the more diffuse response to environmental contact that Piaget has identified as equilibration. Equilibration, in its turn, is the movement of the organism from a relatively unordered and diffuse state of activity to a focused mode that I have identified with Bertalanffy's centration. Centration, on the other hand, contrasts very nicely with diffusion, which is to say that organismic processes (much like consciousness) may have a specific focus, or may be diffuse.

As noted on page 22, Bertalanffy (1968) was the originator of the term centration, and he described it as the only means whereby an organism can pass from one state to another. As such, it becomes a crucial element in the repertoire of living systems. Augros and Stanciu reflect the same process when they note that "Living things move themselves ... by producing *qualitative* changes in those parts" (1987, p. 43).

Classical biology assumes the property of irritability, or the ability of the organism to respond to the world in which it lives. The most primitive of such responses are called taxes and tropisms. In classical biology, a tropism refers to a growing process, while a taxis is a locomotor movement effected by a reorganization of cellular material. Maturana and Varela (1987) have noted, however, that there is no practical difference between growth and other kinds of movement. This makes the distinction somewhat arbitrary. Taxes come in two varieties: positive taxes that move towards the stimulus and negative taxes that move away.

We may now introduce a positive and a negative polarity to centration. In the case of a negative taxis, the centration will occur in a direction opposite to the stimulus and probably be expressed as an accommodation. In the case of a positive taxis, centration will occur in the direction of the stimulus, but the response will remain relatively diffuse until a proper reorganization of the organism through equilibration is completed.

To this point, our analysis of the elementary properties of living systems suggests that they progress from state to state following in a dialectical progression. The organism begins in a relatively diffuse state, it is quiescent. No one process dominates the system as a whole. With the occurrence of an external stimulus, the organism responds by shifting its energy resources to the nearest subsystem; centration begins. As the stimulus becomes stronger, further subdivisions of the system occur and an alternation is set up between positive and negative taxes. At a specific threshold of stimulus intensity the system centrates at either an approaching system or an avoiding system. The final equilibrations alternate between and ultimately produce the assimilation and accommodation schemes that most closely match the nature of the external phenomenon.

We have here defined three axes of function: the axis of centration/ diffusion, that of accommodation/assimilation or equilibration, and the axis of the tropisms, positive/negative. Curiously, with these three axes we may describe all of the functions of a living organism in its interactions with the environment. It may be centered in a subsystemic activity, or non-centered. It may be moving towards an object or moving away. It may be assimilating the environmental stimulus to its own structure, or accommodating its structure to the requirement of the environment.

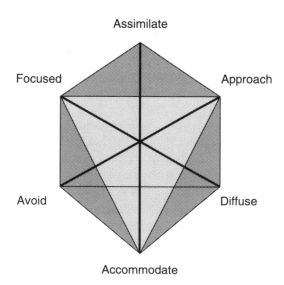

Figure 1.2 The poles of biological activity

These three bipolar elements can be used to build an octahedron that can schematically describe the state of the organism at any one time (see Figure 1.2), in just the same manner as Jung used an octahedral model to describe the process of individuation as revealed in gnosis (Jung 1959/1968b).

In the primary axis we may place central tendency. Is the organism responding to a specific stimulus out of a specific subsystem, or is its activity noncentrated, diffuse? Is its activity focused or diffuse? In the secondary axis we place movement, taxes. The organism may be approaching or avoiding a stimulus. In the third axis it may be assimilating or accommodating to the stimulus.

With this small excursion into the patterns of life, we are immediately faced with the recognizable patterns of archetypal activity: diffuse, non-directive activity at one pole is paired off against focused "purposeful" activity at the other; focus in turn is seen to differentiate into the distinct and complementary options of assimilation and accommodation. Accommodation and assimilation are then further modified by the positive or negative nature of the stimulus. Let us now turn to a further examination of these patterns as the dimensions of archetypal activity.

Chapter 2

The archetypal dimensions

If the basic processes of living systems are truly equivalent to the properties of archetypal systems, then there should be a ready match between the archetypal and biological phenomena. In fact there is just such a match. In the preceding arguments we have seen that living systems typically exhibit positive and negative polarity, centration, accommodation and assimilation. Although many of these characteristics have already been shown to be characteristic of archetypal systems, it is important now to recapitulate that relationship.

BIPOLARITY

Bipolarity is, of course, an essential property of the archetype. While not a dimension in and of itself, it describes the basic patterning of all of the other dimensions. Bipolarity is an expression of the dialectic progress evidenced in biological systems and psychic process. The one inevitably becomes two, and the two uniting at the higher level produce a new unity which will, in turn, split into poles.

Typical among the archetypes that clearly express the property of bipolarity is the trickster figure. On the one hand, he is often part of a pair of creator gods, on the other, he is a symbol of the shadow and the dark side of the spirit. He is the source of the idea of the devil, but is also revered as a god and teacher of magic. A similar figure is the Philosopher's Stone: it is itself most precious, but is created from the most vile and common substances; it is rare, but its substance is everywhere (Jung, 1959/1968a).

That this bipolarity is the rule on the level of the products of intellect was observed by Lévi-Strauss who noted that natural classification schemes proceed on a binary pattern. "[A]ll classification proceeds by pairs of contrasts: classification only ceases when it is no longer possible to establish oppositions" (1962/1966, p. 217).

In the Jungian psyche the symbolic process draws contents from the unconscious and represents them in conscious awareness as symbols. Although most contents at the archetypal and unconscious levels are bipolar, they normally present themselves to consciousness in terms of separate, polar opposites, without any conscious recognition of their complementarity. When the process of individuation requires that a deeper understanding of an unconscious element is necessary, there begins to appear an emotional and intellectual swing between the consciously opposed poles of the underlying truth. One position is presented to consciousness, then the other. Back and forth, back and forth with gradual adjustments of meaning, slow broadenings of definitions. At some point a synthesis occurs ending the pendulum swing by uniting the opposites on a new level of understanding. No sooner is this new equilibrium found, but it constellates its own opposite which in turn restarts the pendulum at this next level of understanding.

The principle of oppositions is pointed out by Jung as an essential characteristic of conscious thought: "There is no consciousness without discrimination of opposites" (1959/1968a, para. 178). The following quote, from *Aion*, reflects an oppositionally based dynamic that Jung saw at the heart of the psyche.

As opposites never unite at their own level (*tertium non datur!*), a super-ordinate "third" is always required in which the two parts can come together. And since the symbol derives as much from the conscious as from the unconscious, it is able to unite them both, reconciling their conceptual polarity through its form and their emotional polarity through its numinosity.

(Jung, 1959/1968b, para. 280)

This same bipolarity also seems to appear as a basic trait in living systems. Activity may be focused or unfocused, assimilative or accommodative, moving towards or moving away. In sexual systems there are males and females. The bipolar nature of most processes seems ubiquitous.

The archetype, as we have seen, exhibits its bipolarity on multiple levels:

- It is the most polar opposite imaginable to the instinct, yet each archetype corresponds to, and is intimately related to, an instinct.
- It is the deintegrate of the self, an autonomous content, but also an expression of the integrated self.
- It is capable of acting as the bearer of meaning but can also dominate consciousness to the exclusion of conscious direction.
- It has a specific affective tone that determines its meaning, but it can never be reduced to a single content.
- It is capable of motivating the highest spirituality and the deepest carnality.
- Although an expression of unconscious function the archetype focuses attention.

CENTRATION, DIFFUSION

The primary polarity in a living system is the distinction between focused and unfocused activity. Every system has its relatively passive state in which vegetative functions predominate. These are contrasted with active, focused states where the entire organism focuses upon some stimulus. On the level of the psyche the same polarity exists between conscious and unconscious contents, archetypally energized contents and the contents of normal consciousness.

Consciousness is characterized by focused attention. Jung noted that conscious processes were primarily linear and analytic. Subconscious processes tended, on the other hand, to be non-linear, synchronistic and atemporal. Consciousness is mediated by the ego, the organ of consciousness *par excellence*, the diffuse imaginal realm is governed by the collective unconscious and the complexes. Without focus or purpose, without an archetypally determined focus, consciousness tends to dissipate.

Jung also noted that a central characteristic of the archetype was its ability to focus the attention. He indicated that the archetype has numinous power, and that it takes hold of its subject with the power of instinct. This same power may resist or contradict instinct and redirect the normal directions of conscious activity (1956/1967). This is a far cry from a diffuse consciousness.

The same poles are again emphasized in the self–ego polarity. The self represents the goal and totality and is, in its origins, unconscious. Through the ego it develops a focus, a center of consciousness, while it continues to operate largely in terms of unconscious functions.

In humans the centration/diffusion polarity becomes associated not only with conscious and unconscious poles, but with left and right brain functionality. It describes in a very clear manner the extent to which our thoughts and actions are dominated by the linear patterns of left brained consciousness, or the more holistic, global and spatially oriented right brain functions (Leary, 1989). Further, Pribram (1984) has pointed to the discovery of energy-saving and mobilizing systems related to the hypothalamus in human subjects. These trophotropic and ergotropic systems are complementary one to another and represent on another level the opposition between centrated and diffuse systems.

APPROACH, AVOID

The organismic polarity that corresponds to the taxes appears in higher animals as approach and avoid, good and bad. These poles were immortalized on one level by Freud in his perception of the drives towards life and death – Eros and Thanatos. They more generally apply, in the Jungian perspective, as the polarities between physical and spiritual or instinctual and archetypal. They appear also in the ubiquitous tendencies toward self protection and the preservation of life. If archetypal activity is patterned on living systems, as we propose, then the tendencies towards self definition, self motivation and self preservation constitute an approach pole; while external determination, the passivity of death and self destruction constitute an avoidance pole.

For Jung, however, the polarities, even of approach and avoid, are artifacts of consciousness that are resolved in the collective unconscious where a *coincidentia oppositorum*[1] prevails. This appears at the cellular level with the need of certain cells in growing systems to die off so that others can take their place, and for populations to grow old and die so that newer versions of organisms can have their day. There remains, however, a hint from his work on alchemy that Jung may have seen even the coincidence of opposites itself resolved into a final, absolute and paradoxical "absolute opposition" in order to provide the system with psychological validity (1968b, para. 256).

ASSIMILATION, ACCOMMODATION

Assimilation and accommodation are represented in archetypal functions as constellation and projection. Insofar as an external object can be perceived, it must be assimilable to the archetypal structure of a complex. Fordham (1957), relying on the IRM[2] metaphor, has noted that in the early weeks of neonatal life, the archetypal structure of perception requires a perfect or near perfect fit between the external stimulus and the pattern embodied in the archetypal template. It is only later that the organism begins to accommodate its perceptions to the shape of the world.

This precedence is somewhat accounted for in the realization that even assimilation involves an adjustment of the entire organism as it centrates about the target stimulus. In this sense, accommodation to external phenomena may be viewed as an inevitable outgrowth of the assimilation process.

Object relations theorists posit a psychic level of assimilation and accommodation in terms of the child's projection of its own reality upon the external world during the stages of symbiotic dependency (Spitz, 1965; Fraiberg, 1965; Mahler, et al., 1975; Compton, 1987; Plaut, 1975). Moreover, assimilation is implicit in the idea of the introject. Here, the external object, the ethological releaser (IRM), is taken into the structure of the organism as a part through the agency of its correspondence to the archetypal template.

Accommodation occurs on various levels of the psychic organism. In the young child, the range of relatively unrelated reflexes are assimilated to a single accommodation which finds the mother, locates the breast and nourishes the infant. As the same process proceeds, the biological expectation, the sum of those responses that serve to locate, attach and relate to the mother – the maternal archetype – assimilate one to another, so that their total expression is an accommodation of the archetypal response system to the physical mother.

In general, much of what happens in the Jungian psyche can be understood in terms of accommodation and assimilation. The systems of complexes represent specific groupings of memory elements to which other such elements may be assimilated, and which, in themselves, are capable of accommodation in order to incorporate a new element into their own structure.

THE PRIMARY OCTAHEDRON

From the preceding paragraphs it is possible to understand that there is some relationship between the basic functions of living organisms and the Jungian psyche with special reference to the archetypes. Without stretching the issue, it is more than possible to schematize both archetypal functions and the functions of living systems into a three-dimensional figure that corresponds perfectly to the octahedral schema specified by Jung in *Aion* (1959/1968b).

The octahedron, one will recall, is a quaternio suspended by a third axis (see Figure 2.1). In general, it represents the three dimensions/degrees of freedom of normal experience: up and down, left and right, forwards and backwards. Of this time–space quaternary Jung notes:

> The space–time quaternio is the archetypal *sine qua non* for any apprehension of the physical world – indeed, the very possibility of apprehending it. It is the organizing schema par excellence among the psychic quaternities. In its structure it corresponds to the psychological schema of the functions.
>
> (Jung, 1959/1968b, para. 398)

Stewart, in *The Elements of Creation Myth*, points to the directional pattern of three axes as one of the fundamental patterns of nature. He notes its ubiquity as an underlying pattern in most myths and its capacity for complex articulation. Moreover, it was firmly integrated into the common life of the people.

> we find that the cosmic map was quite intentionally mirrored in the physical organization of ancient cultures. Cities, regions, entire lands, were appointed directions, quarters allocated to certain forces and qualities in the ancient world.
>
> (Stewart, 1989, p. 19)

From the work of Mircea Eliade, we find the same theme repeated at all levels of human existence. As the axis mundi, the vertical axis provides the sense of place-as-meaning from which the other directions receive their

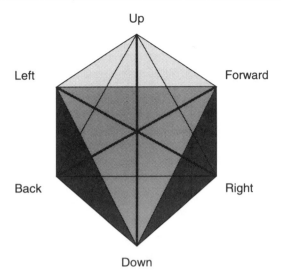

Figure 2.1 The spatial octahedron

relevance. As the pole that joins heaven and earth the axis becomes the seat of all meaning and the point from which the cardinal directions become meaningful. It is home. It is no less the urbs or the omphalos from which the four corners of the city arise and the heart of the city itself (Eliade, 1954/1971, 1976; Stewart, 1989).

Lévi-Strauss analyzes the relations of meaning in totemic classifications and finds such systems reproducing a structure similar to Jung's octahedron (1966).

The pattern applies down into the further reaches of human and sub-human experience. We have already noted Leary's identification of the three axes with man's primary response systems: forwards and backwards – approach and avoid; up and down – dominance and submission; left and right (in humans) – focused and unfocused responses. We have also seen how in animals the left and right polarity recalls Bertalanffy's centration as opposed to more diffuse behavioral organization and Herr's trophotrophic vs. ergotrophic response systems (Pribram, 1984). We are once again brought face to face with the double pyramid as representing an archetypal scheme of organization.

THE OUROBORIC CAVEAT

The ouroboros is a snake which swallows its own tail (see Figure 2.2). Like all good, archetypally determined symbols it has many meanings that depend upon the context in which it appears. Those meanings, moreover, are divided into polar opposites.

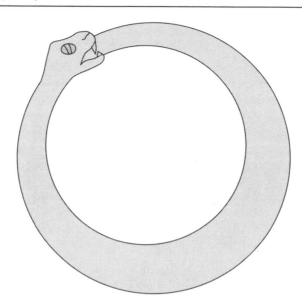

Figure 2.2 The ouroboros

In the context of our investigation, the ouroboros can represent, on the one hand, a self-similar system, which eternally and simultaneously folds in upon itself as it expands to encompass new levels of operations – an eternal pattern of self-similar principles repeating at every level of integration. It can also refer to the circular logic of the familiar. Whenever I project my understanding upon the world, the world becomes somewhat more understandable to me. If, however, I am not careful to examine the goodness of fit between my projection and the world upon which I project it, should I fail to accommodate my understanding to the stimulus, I have learned nothing. I have only swallowed my own tail. The warning of the ouroboros is this: don't swallow your tail.

While we may clearly see the presence of the octahedral model in what has gone before, and in what follows, it would be wise to remain mindful of the fact that it is the most common means at our disposal for dealing with physical existence. Left, right, up, down, forward, backward are primary data of our existence. Our bilateral symmetry naturally divides our world into left and right. Our dorso-ventral asymmetry likewise divides the world into front and back, while the pull of gravity daily defines the third axis. Is it reasonable to assume that this pattern is any more or less fundamental to life or to living systems than any other, or has our whole discussion fallen under the glamour of the archetypal numen? Are we only caught up in a projection? Are we justified in characterizing these patterns as fundamental as opposed to ubiquitous, or must we search elsewhere for acceptable explanations?

Jung was careful to note that while archetypal patterns reflect the patterns of nature, they did so independently of current experience; acting, as it were, from a phylogenetic perspective. If this is indeed true then we have come upon a paradox expressed symbolically by the ouroboros. As noted earlier, the archetypal dimension developed out of the instinctual level of action. Instincts, presumably, reflect the needs of living systems at the level of multicellular organisms. All of them, presumably, developed in the context of a three-dimensional world with similar restrictions on experience.

The problems of organismic symmetry are obviously not the source of the phenomenon, but adaptations to it. Were the interpretation at hand only a projection, we would not expect lower organisms to display the basic patterns. Strikingly, however, they do.

The amoeba, considered structurally, has neither top nor bottom, front nor back, left nor right. These are only assigned by the observer as the organism responds to its environment. Its leading surface encounters the world frontally, producing only then a functional rear. It is bound by the law of gravitation no less than other creatures and so exists in a world where up and down are realities. Paramecia clearly show differentiated anterior/posterior, dorso/ventral and lateral differentiation. Radiolaria swim free but respond to various stimuli by approach and avoidance. Their physical form is marked by a differentiated vertical patterning of organelles and flagella. Euglena and other protozoans display a clear differentiation between anterior and posterior surfaces. Ciliates show definite anterior, posterior differentiation. Sessile forms inevitably show a clear differentiation between peduncle and apex.

Likewise, the Piagetian position rests upon the insight that human intelligence is only a special instance of biological adaptation. The movements to which intelligence refers are extensions of the normal responses of living systems to their environment. As such, they include an inherited propensity towards environmental adaptation. This suggests that the patterns which are ultimately expressed as intelligence are reflected in the organization of all life and all of nature (Furth, 1969, p. 175 ff.).

These things being so, we must assume that life in general has evolved in such a way that it takes three-dimensional reality into account. If this is so, then the dimensions which we use to describe spatial existence are reflections of the adaptations that living systems have developed to deal with the world.

THE DIMENSIONS OF EXPERIENCE

Writing in the essay, *The Structure and Dynamics of the Psyche*, Jung points to symbols of wholeness arising out of the collective unconscious. He notes that in their most basic form, the symbols of the self are circular or spherical. These are often combined with symbolic quaternaries, squares and crosses to form the root forms of symbols of wholeness, symbols of the self. But the process does not stop with the simple mandala.

> From the circle and quaternity motif is derived the symbol of the geometrically formed crystal and the wonder-working stone. From here analogy formation leads on to the city, castle, church, house and vessel. Another variant is the wheel. The former motif emphasizes the ego's containment in the greater dimension of the self; the later emphasizes the rotation ... psychologically, it denotes concentration on and pre-occupation with a center, conceived as a center of a circle and thus formulated as a point.
>
> (Jung, 1959/1968b, para. 352)

Wholeness is always regular, and for Jung the quaternio always required a specific context. The context itself was graphically represented as a third dimension of development perpendicular to the other two. Thus the four psychological functions were placed into a true psychological context along the introversion/extroversion axis. Similarly, the four directions of spatial orientation take their meaning in the context of the axis mundi. This results in the octahedral system of relations that Jung used to understand the recurrence of the quaternio principle.

In Eliade's writings the center is described most often as a holy place, a place of creation. It is the place where heaven and earth meet, the birth-place of the god, the holy place where the eternal contacts the temporal. It is the provision of physical location that seems to give the center its true value. As the god dwells with me, I am in a good place. As the god has specially sanctified this place, it is identifiable. But the holy place is always carried within. As much as it is shared, it is recreated *de novo* with each birth, with each new building, with each new beginning. In a sense, he reflects the Freudian idea of a body ego, the experiential reality of the continuing existence of a single biological individual in time and space (Eliade, 1954/1971, 1976; Hall, 1977/1991). This is the primitive locus of the individual. It is the child undifferentiated from the maternal matrix. It is the primordial self. It is the simple unconscious organism.

In kabbalistic writings it appears as Kether, represented geometrically as the point. It is undifferentiated, a singularity. It is the one, indivisible, alone. Out of it flows all else. Yet, it is, in itself, identified by the interaction of the poles of being and non-being, heaven and earth. Where the *axis mundi* intersects the phenomenal world, real meaning is born (Regardie, 1973/1988; Halevi, 1987).

Here too is created the original polarity, up and down, dominance and submission, spiritual and carnal, archetypal and instinctual. And, by its interaction with the phenomenal world, the *axis mundi* creates meaning and focus. By the act of intersection, focus is differentiated from diffusion, conscious from unconscious and centrated from non-centrated.

Moving from the world of conscious experience, our example translates into the world of existence, primitive existence with no dimensionality, no consciousness as we know it, no verbal tags to differentiate one stimulus from another. Here, centration is an expression of autopoiesis. It is part of the mechanism of life itself, intrinsic to the faculty of self maintenance.

Can we then define centration, biological focus, as the most primitive level of meaning and the root of consciousness? Donovan (1989) has suggested that both life and consciousness in the human organism are indeterminate as to their beginning. Where does the individual life start? If we take the argument that the continuity of personal identity extends at least to the level of the single celled zygote, then we may find a root of consciousness there as well. The metaphor of focus as consciousness is very useful. The Jungian ego may be viewed as that complex which focuses psychic energy on the conscious dimension.

Reiser (1990) has used the metaphor of focus as a very explicit model for consciousness. He points to the perceptual field as an unintelligible confusion without the focusing and filtering action of the ego. He pictures the ego as a small beam of light illumining and bringing into high relief an otherwise confused landscape.

Central to Jung's spatial scheme was the understanding that, within each quaternio, one element bears a special duplex relation to the others and so becomes capable of generating a third axis. In the psychological functions, the inferior function has the duplex relation to conscious and unconscious worlds and it becomes the axis of movement from unconscious to conscious. This is the meaning of the words of Maria Prophetessa:

> We know that three of the four functions of consciousness can become differentiated, i.e., conscious, while the other remains connected with the matrix, the unconscious, and is known as the "inferior" function. It is the Achilles heel of even the most heroic consciousness: somewhere the strong man is weak, the clever man foolish, the good man bad, and the reverse is also true . . . the enigmatic axiom of Maria runs " . . . from the third comes the one as the fourth" – which presumably means, when the third produces the fourth it at once produces unity.
>
> (Jung, 1959/1968, para. 430)

This double function, in the context of living systems would seem to appear in the centration/diffusion pole. In comparison with the other biological elements, this is the more basic, for it applies to all interactive systems, not only those that are alive. In a living system it is closely related to the assimilative/accommodative pole and on some level, especially when viewed in terms of salience, behaves as a double attribute.

Implicit in the twin ideas of centration and focus is the idea of differentiation. The current focus is differentiated from the unfocused. What is not conscious fades back into relative unconsciousness. In biological systems, centration brings the organismic focus to various dimensions of the environment: approach/avoid, forward/backward, up/down, assimilate/accommodate. Focus itself becomes differentiated and the possibility of relative direction flows out of focus itself.

This once again raises the question of context. One of the important functions of centration and the placement of the center is the determination of context. In the context of noxious stimuli the organism moves into an avoidance state. In the presence of assimilable or otherwise attractive stimuli, the reorganization tends to move the organism towards the stimulus. Such internal changes in combination with various external stimuli provide contexts for actions as additional elements of meaning.

In the case of the archetype it is its numinous charge, its power to draw the contents of attention to itself, that reflects the same function. Each archetype is capable of becoming the center of consciousness and the center of human activity.

We again come to the octahedral structure as somehow primary. It is rooted in our genes and in our experience, and through it we and all other creatures on earth, whether explicitly, or implicitly, filter our worlds. The space–time quaternio, the dimensions of experience, left, right, up, down, forwards, backwards, are evident to every child. Their ubiquity argues for their insignificance. Yet on an archetypal level, it is just their common occurrence that gives them special significance.

Eliade notes that

> The space inhabited by man is oriented and thus anisotropic, for each dimension and direction has a specific value; for instance, along the vertical axis, "up" does not have the same value as "down"; along the horizontal axis, left and right may be differentiated in value.
>
> (Eliade, 1976, p. 30)

In the following sections we will attempt to show how the archetypal elements of everyday life are related to the tri-axial scheme of the time–space quaternio. However, before we can proceed, the process of emergence must be elucidated.

Chapter 3

The emergence of new properties

One of the concepts necessary for the prosecution of our program is the idea of an emergent property. As we noted earlier, it is the notion of emergence that separates systems from heaps and aggregates. Simply stated, the emergent property of a system is a quality of a system that *Emergent* appears as a result of the interaction of the subsystems of which it is *Property* comprised. The trick is this: the emergent property can not be predicted from the properties of the individual subsystems. It emerges out of their interactions.

We have already defined the Jungian psyche as being susceptible of systems theoretical analysis. One of the keys to such an analysis is the observation that one level is differentiated from the next by the appearance of properties that are unexplainable in terms of the individual properties of the subsystems. These are the emergent properties of the whole.

The idea of emergent properties is similar to Buckminster Fuller's (1991) idea of synergy. Fuller found that in the construction of geodesic domes and certain other kinds of structurally integrated systems, the net strength of the whole surpassed the total strength of the individual members. To this added property Fuller applied the pre-existing term synergy, which then came to mean not only the confluence of energy, but the magnification of energy in structural combination.

Emergent properties are similar but somewhat more elusive. Fishman, et al., provide the following example of emergent properties.

> Emergent properties are ubiquitous in nature. The classical example of emergent properties concerns the individual properties of hydrogen and oxygen as atoms versus the unique properties that emerge when hydrogen and oxygen unite and become the molecular system called water. The unique properties of water expressed as a liquid at room temperature cannot be predicted by studying the behavior of hydrogen and oxygen independently (i.e., un-united) as separate gases at room temperature.
>
> ... the properties that are unique to water can only be revealed

(i.e., discovered) when the *particular components are allowed to interact as a unique, integrated system.*

(Fishman et al., 1988, pp. 308–9)

Emile Durkheim, the great French sociologist, wrote:

The hardness of bronze is not in the copper, the tin or the lead, which are its ingredients and which are soft and malleable bodies; it is in their mixture. The fluidity of water and its nutritional and other properties are not to be found in the two gases of which it is composed but in the complex substance which they form by their association.

(Durkheim, 1938/1964, p. xlviii)

The emergent properties of systems are clearly described in an article on robotics in the March 1991 issue of *Discover* magazine. The issue in question covered progress in robotics at MIT and other centers of robotics research. Much of the article centered on the unorthodox approach to artificial intelligence championed by Rodney Brooks.

Most researchers in artificial intelligence (AI) had, to that time, assumed that it was possible to analyze specific behaviors, develop algorithms for their reproduction and program robots to behave, based upon the embedded algorithms. They thus assumed that a rigorous analysis of the behavior of walking (the motions of walking, the motions of balancing, the motions involved in shifting the center of gravity, and the feedback controls that link all of the motions together, along with specific rules for problem situations – if you fall to one knee . . .), would allow them to write a series of routines that would result in a robotic behavior that we could identify as walking. Most of the AI community was committed to that approach and was obtaining mediocre to poor results. The algorithms were never quite sophisticated enough, the rules usually failed to anticipate some eventuality and none of it was ever as flexible as it needed to be.

Brooks, on the contrary, thought such attempts unfruitful. Instead, he created robots capable of all of the motions necessary for walking. He built no central logic and decision engine, but connected all of the elements in a neural network. Instead of creating a sophisticated walking algorithm, he instructed the processing system to strengthen the linkages between any combination of movements that resulted in forward movement (Freedman, 1991).

Discover reported that, when actuated, the robot shuddered and began to vibrate. After a few minutes of chaotic motion, the movements became more or less rhythmic, the machine clambered on to its feet. In a few more moments it was walking away from its starting position. This is an emergent property.

The central idea here is that there was no specific encoding of the idea "Walk." The parts necessary to accomplish it were provided as well as an overall purpose which guided their assembly. However, no explicit instructions on how to walk were included. The instructions developed out of the design constraints of the system as they were acted upon by the driving program: "If it makes you move forward, do it more often."

The example of Brooks's machine illustrates something else. The design of a system has a powerful effect on how it works and on how it interacts with other systems. It is plain that Brooks's robots were designed. Each leg was specifically designed to be capable of all of the degrees of motion necessary to do its part in walking. Similarly, all six legs were so arranged that they could cooperate and provide the sequence of motions necessary for walking. In fact, we may assume that the whole was designed in such a way that coordinated walking provided the optimal means of moving forward (Freedman, 1991).

It is important, however, not to see the idea of emergent properties as a mechanistic answer to the question of behavior; for, in the same article I recognized a pattern of organization described by Piaget some years previously. In fact, in passing the article on to a friend, I noted that it was a Piagetian scheme for Artificial Intelligence.

Jean Piaget saw that an essential part of the genetic predetermination of behavior was encoded not so much in specific instructions to perform this or that action, but in the physical design of the limbs and body of the individual (Ginsburg and Opper, 1969). This is an essential part of the message of emergent properties. The interactions possible between the subsystems are constrained by their structure, and it is that very constraint that helps to determine the properties that emerge when systems interact (Piaget, 1970b).

Beyond the general structure of the body, according to Piaget, the child is born with a relatively small number of in-built reflexes, a penchant for global and rhythmic movement and the capacity to assemble these through the process of assimilation into meaningful groupings of movements called schemata. All meaning, for Piaget, reduces to combinations of movements, or their representation internally. The development of intellect is viewed as a continuous increase in complexity as spontaneous movements give rise to reflexes, reflexes to habits, and habits to intelligence (Piaget and Inhelder, 1969, p. 4 ff.).

Unlike other scientists, Piaget does not see the reflex as the most primitive element in this developmental sequence. The reflexes are consolidated from more diffuse global and rhythmic responses. Within the genetic scheme that creates needs and their satisfactions, reflexes become differentiated as the initial building blocks of action schemes. Through an unspecified genetic mechanism, reflexes become the subjects of spontaneous repetition which strengthens them as distinct activities. This strengthening of the reflex actions by spontaneous repetition has been called functional or reproductive assimilation. As, however, any individual reflex is one of many reflexes embedded in a general pattern of rhythmic movement, there is a propensity within the organism to associate reflex actions into consistent and repetitively occurring groups called schemata.

As the early complex of reflex patterns, e.g. sucking, head turning, grasping, finds a reinforcement in the infant's world, e.g. the breast and milk, and insofar as the association can be assimilated into the pattern of actions that form the primitive scheme, the scheme is consolidated as a habit pattern. The habit is not a simple stimulus–response chain, but the result of active participation by the infant as, in assimilation, it reconstructs the stimulus in terms of the motor scheme; and in accommodation, it modifies the specific character of the response chain so as to streamline the transformation of the random reflex scheme into the goal-seeking response. Such an assimilation is recognitive as it leads to a similar response in similar situations. As this results in a general strengthening of the scheme so that it may repeat outside of the original situation it gives rise to generalizing assimilation (ibid., pp. 5–7; Piaget, 1970b, pp. 72–3).

What we see in the emergence that Brooks built into his robotic systems is a recapitulation of the property of emergence just as it appears in the world of living systems. Specific in-built propensities emerge as the various subsystems combine in proper sequence. Random rhythmic motions give way to recognizable patterns of action. The patterns then coalesce about an environmental stimulus whose reinforcing power forges the assimilation of the individual elements into the whole, new behavior.

We must not be too quick to assign precedence to genetic or environmental variables, however, for, although the genotype predetermines the possible range of behavioral variation, it is the environment which actually selects the pattern of development. Jung reflected this when he said that the archetype represents the "possibility of representation" (1959/1968a, para. 155). The content is dependent upon the organism's interactions with the environment.

Just as Brooks's machine needed the external realities of friction, inertia and their measurement to give meaning to the range of movements built into the machine, so the archetypal pattern relies upon the externally present mother-figure, father-figure or other target object for its own fulfillment.

Michael Fordham (1957) sees the developmental origin of the archetypal response in the differentiation of reflex actions out of the diffuse, rhythmic activity of the neonatal nervous system. Instincts themselves grow out of combinations of these reflex actions at the next level of integration. The archetypes reflect instinctual patterns at the next higher level of the psyche, with the self representing the final integration of all levels. Implicit in the genotypic plan is the expectancy of environmental stresses which will allow the manifestation of the potential pattern.

Fordham, like Jung, goes on to show that the archetype, as expressed in individual experience, only becomes capable of expression as it is filled with the data of individual experience. Thus, the mother archetype, as it is expressed in the individual, depends less upon a single genetic predisposition to perceive the mother than it does upon the summation of many lesser predispositions – to suck and grasp and follow and look – and the total image that they create. He notes, moreover, that the development of the child is dependent upon specific responses that bind the child to the mother and, reciprocally, the mother to the child (1957, p. 32; 1981, p. 113).

So we might see in a given organism a specific tendency to close the hand upon stimulation, a random flexion response of the arm, a head turn at the brush of a cheek, and sucking in response to lip stimulation. By themselves they may or may not resolve into a coherent response like thumb sucking. However, given a specific environmental stimulus that is graspable, projected into the mouth region and that moreover provides nourishment, the probabilities are that upon interaction with that object the individual elements will combine in such a way as to produce the neonate's characteristic nursing response. It is an emergent property of the interaction of two living organisms.

Jung viewed the archetype as an experiential reflection of instinctual response systems. These systems are composed of a releaser and an action pattern. They are somehow passed on at the level of biology. The transmission of the archetypal image or releaser does not include an image, but a propensity towards perception, a form without content. He further understood that the releasing element might not be simple or singular but part of a complex circumstance that in its entirety evoked the instinctual action pattern.

Brooke (1991) clarifies Jung's understanding of the instinctual by pointing out that he typically emphasized instinctuality as a quality of behavior, not in-built patterns. They are, most simply, behaviors which are not subject to conscious regulation. Nevertheless, Jung presses the examples derived from ethology.

Turning to ethology, it would appear that we again come to instinctual response systems as emergent properties of complex systems of relatively unrelated behaviors. Hinde (1983, pp. 149–61) lists six factors which contribute to a chick's final ability to identify its mother, i.e. that constitute the imprinting scheme for the chick.

1 At the outset of the sensitive period, the chick seeks out and approaches conspicuous moving objects.
2 As the chick repeatedly encounters the mother a differentiation between the now-familiar mother and the less familiar environment begins to take place. This has the result that the mother-object becomes positively associated with what we might anthropomorphize as safety.

3 The intensification of contact with the mother, who is now identified as "the protector," leads to further differentiation of the mother from other organisms in the environment.
4 Because the mother serves the specific function as a conditioned stimulus for multiple "filial responses," and
5 because the chick tends to learn associations in terms of temporal and spatial contiguity, the mother's identity as the primary source of nurturance is steadily reinforced. She thus becomes
6 the first recognizable entity in the chick's immediate environment.

Were we to apply the logic of archetypes to the chick, we might say that the maternal archetype as it exists in the chick is constellated through the environmental expression of a specific group of reflexes specifically attuned to an expected chicken environment. In one sense we may say there exists an implicit image of the mother in that the chick has been selected to express certain patterns of behavior which in the majority of cases will result in the identification and bonding of an appropriate mother object. Further, as a result of the imprint, the chick will internalize a mother image which will begin to guide the chick's development from that point on. In another sense, however, we may say that there was no pre-existent mother-image, only the probability that a group of reflexes acting in concert would provide access to an appropriate imprint object. This is a near perfect reflection of Fordham's version of the Jungian model. And here we are presented with the archetypal image as an emergent property of a complex system (1957, p. 32; 1981, p. 113).

Fordham notes that:

The images started as part-objects, and evolved into a whole object. Just as the infant first experiences parts of his mother's body in numerous images which gradually coalesce into a single one of her whole body. . . .

(Fordham, 1957, p. 32)

Following the course of similar genetically directed learning in human children, Lumsden and Wilson (1981, p. 68) point to the progression of preferences in the neonate's visual system. As early as the first ten minutes of life, visual preferences begin with a preference for larger or more numerous elements of specific design types. Among these preferences there quickly appears a specific preference for designs that bear some similarity to human faces. Soon thereafter the child displays a marked preference for normally arranged facial objects. The preferences then narrow and grow in strength showing specific preferences for the mother's face followed by other familiar faces.

Lumsden and Wilson again note that during the sensitive period for mother/infant bonding a cascade of reciprocal interactions begins between the mother and her baby, which interlocks them and ensures the further development of attachment. A close contact between the mother and her infant during the first hours following birth appears to be crucial for the formation of subsequent strong bonding.

(Lumsden and Wilson, 1981, pp. 80–1)

Chapter 4

Archetypes and images

THE PRIMORDIAL IMAGE

Originally, the archetype was formulated as an image. In *Symbols of Transformation*, Jung used the term *primordial image* to describe patterns of meaning that seemed to reappear consistently in myths, dreams and legends, independent of cultural transmission. Jung pointed to the repeated appearance of the image of the fire-bearer along with its consistent association with the ideals of forethought and prudence as an example of the reappearance of the archetypal. These associations occurred on a worldwide basis, independent of the mechanisms of etymology and cultural transmission. He understood this to be evidence of the existence of "autochthonous primordial images" (1956/1967, para. 209).

In the definitions chapter of the same work, Jung defines the primordial image as follows:

> I call the image *primordial* when ... the image is in striking accord with familiar mythological motifs. It then expresses material primarily derived from the *collective unconscious*, and indicates at the same time that the factors influencing the conscious situation of the moment are *collective* rather than personal. ...
>
> The primordial image, elsewhere also termed *archetype*, is always collective, i.e., it is at least common to entire peoples or epochs [sic]. In all probability the most important mythological motifs are common to all times and races. ...
>
> (Jung, 1921/1971, para. 746 ff.)

Jung next makes some attempt to account for the existence of the archetype by appealing to a relationship between the archetype and environmental pressures. But he discards a simple developmental reflection of environmental influences, holding that such reflection would probably not appear in symbolic form. Instead, he points to an evolutionary mechanism. The means of inheritance, however, is related by Jung to the properties of life in general, positing no specific genetic mechanism.

We are forced to assume that the given structure of the brain does not owe its peculiar nature merely to the influence of the surrounding conditions, but also and just as much to the peculiar and autonomous quality of living matter, i.e., to a law inherent in life itself. The given constitution of the organism, therefore, is on the one hand a product of external conditions, while on the other it is determined by the intrinsic nature of living matter. Accordingly, the primordial image is related just as much to certain palpable, self-perpetuating, and continually operative natural processes, as it is to certain inner determinants of psychic life and of life in general.

(Ibid., para. 748)

This begins to suggest that the primordial image was viewed by Jung as a second-order phenomenon, an emergent property of underlying inter-actions. This perspective seems to be confirmed in the next paragraph where Jung makes the following characterization: "The primordial image is thus a condensation of the living process. It gives a co-ordinating and coherent meaning both to sensuous and to inner perceptions, which first appear without order or connection . . ." (ibid., para. 749 ff.).

We may understand that the archetypal image, the primordial image, is an emergent property of the underlying biological processes. As the emergent whole representing their interactions, it provides a coordination, a direction, an image that can be presented to consciousness that expresses the biological and psychological needs of the organism. The archetype itself, however, would seem to consist of the potentially emergent properties which give rise to the image. It is no one thing, but one of many possible biological constellations, expressible to consciousness in the form of an image. Thus, Jung's insistence on the inexpressibility of the archetype *an sich* is rooted in the fact that without an expression in consciousness, a symbolic image, the archetype remains an inchoate mass of biological impulses. It is the image or symbol that unites, expresses and brings the archetype into the realm of being.

It is necessary to point out once more that archetypes are not determined as regards their content, but only as regards their form and then only to a limited degree. A primordial image is determined as to its content only when it has become conscious and is therefore filled out with the material of conscious experience. Its form, however . . . might perhaps be compared to the axial system of a crystal, which, as it were, preforms the crystalline structure in the mother liquid, although it has no material existence of its own. This first appears according to the specific way in which the ions and molecules aggregate. The archetype in itself is empty and purely formal, nothing but a . . . possibility of representation which is given a priori. The representations themselves are not inherited, only the forms.

(Jung, 1959/1968a, para. 155)

Although we have spent considerable energy in an effort to differentiate between the image and the archetype, it is now clear on some level that the field of archetypal action is in and through the image. From the perspective of later researchers, the value of the image per se is far greater than the idea of an abstract archetype.

Naomi Goldenberg, writing from the perspective of the school of archetypal psychology, notes that the separation between the abstract archetype and its experience in the imaginal realm of the soul lies at the heart of the critique leveled at classical archetypal theory by the followers of James Hillman. For them, image and archetype need not be separated. Because each image "partakes of numinosity" it no longer needs to be differentiated from the archetype. Similarly, because the image is the point at which the archetypal energies coalesce, they should not be treated as a sub-category of archetypal activity: they are the archetypal actors (Goldenberg, 1975, p. 216).

Thus, from the archetypal perspective of Hillman and Goldenberg, the archetypal is "always phenomenal;" that is to say, it is defined by the experience that the image imparts. Hillman sees no pre-existent list of archetypes, but an imaginal realm that symbolizes all things, empowering them in experience as archetypal elements identified by the numina that they bear, and the place of their manifestation in relation to the mythic structure of the imagination (Goldenberg, 1975, p. 216; Hillman, 1983/1988, pp. 2, 3, 13).

A similar view is held forth by Brooke (1991) who sees the archetypal as expressive of the possibilities for relationship and the imaginal worlds implied by each such image. Like the Post Jungians, he sees the archetype as an affect image expressive of the whole net of relations implied by the context. The whole is held in the image and needs no reification of an unconscious archetype to make it work.

Progoff identifies the archetype with a "protoplasmic image" (1959, p. 160). The protoplasmic image is an "encompassing image" holding within itself the goal, the necessary energy to reach the goal, the outer stimuli upon which the end depends and the pattern of behavior needed to reach the end. All this, he says, occurs on a level far below consciousness. It is rooted in the biological/protoplasmic history of the individual.

These "dark images" come to consciousness in humans only in symbolic form. They can never be fully expressed consciously because their nature is preconscious, organic, protoplasmic. As such, they arise as urges, impulses and symbols.

[T]he main frame of reference of the unconscious processes of the organic psyche is composed of the goals and directions of life growth that are inherent in the protoplasmic organism. The individual is not and has never been conscious of them to more than a slight degree.

(Progoff, 1959, p. 163)

In humans, the protoplasmic image takes the form of a stream of images which may or may not be apperceived on a conscious level, but that are often available through dreams. These images represent the direction in which the individual potential is unfolding, and how that potential may be realized.

It is as though a tulip bulb, with the style and color of its flower were already contained directly within it, grew toward the unfoldment of this flower by a process in which images followed one upon another until the ultimate image contained originally in the bulb was fulfilled. What was present as potentiality at the very outset acts as the pervading and unifying principle throughout the life of the organism.

(Ibid., p. 166)

This flow of images has roots at an organic level, below consciousness. However, because the lower levels participate in the whole and can become the center of systemic attention, the needs of the lower levels are reflected in the needs of the whole. We may expect that the unconscious and organic "image" reflects an accurate image of the organism's present state. So, then, despite the fact that the basic impulses expressed in those images may reflect a much lower form of consciousness, they are adapted to human goals, strivings and conditions. At each level of development, the organismic goals of survival and self expression are extended to their current expression in life. Like nesting Russian dolls, each level of consciousness holds within itself all that preceded it and is, in some essential manner, isomorphic to those that follow.

This can be pictured in terms of the idea of resonance. If bells attuned to the same tone, one octave apart, are set next to one another, striking one will start vibrations in the others. If the bells are of a different scale, or the interval wrong, little or no resonance occurs. By the same token, because the archetypal structure links all of the levels of a system, changes in one level are reflected in all the others. Like the bells, however, there may be different levels of response depending upon the level of core similarity in their characteristic feeling tone.

It is less than obvious, however, that the image need not be a visual construct. Redfearn's affect image is as real a representation as anything visual. Even on the visual plane an image may consist less in what is seen than how it is seen. In all, Progoff's characterization of the archetypal image as a "dark image" is most apt (Redfearn, 1973; Hillman, 1983/1988; Casey, 1974; Progoff, 1959).

A further and already noted view of the image is the fundamental characterization of the archetypal in terms of a feeling-toned complex. Jung indicates that the complex takes its feeling tone from the combined interaction of the archetypal energy-charge and the early experience with which it is first associated. These produce a characteristic level and pattern of energy; as Redfearn calls it, an affect image (Jung, 1960/1969, para. 17 ff.; Redfearn, 1973, p. 128).

Fraiberg (1969) divided early memory into two varieties called recognitive and evocative memory. In recognitive memory, experience of the stimulus awakens appropriate non-verbal responses, but they are insufficient to call up the image of the stimulus in its absence: the event is only recognized. In evocative imagery, the actual mnemonic image is called to mind and can be described despite its physical absence. In conscious processing we most often make use of evocative imagery. As we delve below the level of consciousness, the images grow increasingly abstract until they fail to provide a clear conscious referent.

As process descends below the level of conscious awareness, we pass from evocative consciousness and memory – memory which can produce the image of the absent object – to the level of recognitive memory and consciousness. We no longer summon up the image, but the experience reactivates the affective tone of the earlier experience; there is a form of recognition. Image has moved from a visual formulation to a state of muscle tonus, visceral response and physical state. It is sufficiently complex to differentiate one individual or one context from another, but it is preverbal and preconscious: I feel comfortable around you ... I have a sense that we've known each other for a long time ... There's something funny about him ... She or he turns me on.

Next further down comes the non-cognitive response: I don't know in any real sense who you are or what you are, but your presence evokes a specific stereotypical response. The image consists of involuntary physical movements and physiological responses. I am frozen with abject terror, devoured by rage, eaten up by lust, consumed with jealousy. The world consists of objects that elicit specific responses. There is no meaning or purpose beyond the moment of response.

To this level the psychoid realm provides a possible handle for conscious appreciation, but there may be yet further levels of image that we can only vaguely apperceive. At the organ level there are tropisms, accommodations, and assimilations, all controlled in accordance with physical law.

THE IMAGE AS METAPHOR

We have, in the present context defined the archetypal image as an emergent property of the interaction of psychoid and biological processes occurring at lower levels of organismic integration. Indeed, we have gone so far as to identify the archetypal realm as being identical with the processes of life, with both subject to the same kinds of ordering.

At the level of human understanding, we have seen these emergent properties in their expression as archetypes and that these are presented to consciousness as images. The word "image" connotes most often a visual percept, something seen. But as we noted on p. 53, it is not our intent to make the visual element primary, as indeed we may not in light of the consistent definition of archetypal action in terms of affective tone.

Jung recognized that the archetypal represents a more abstract level of action than the image. He notes:

> An archetypal content expresses itself, first and foremost, in metaphors. If such a content should speak of the sun and identify it with the lion, the king, the hoard of gold guarded by the dragon, or the power that makes for the life and health of man, it is neither one thing nor the other, but the unknown third thing that finds more or less adequate expression in all these similes, yet – to the perpetual vexation of the intellect – remains unknown and not to be fitted into a formula.
>
> (Jung, 1959/1968a, para. 267)

James Hillman said of the archetype:

> The curious difficulty of explaining just what archetypes are suggests something specific to them. That is, they tend to be metaphors rather than things. We find ourselves less able to say what an archetype is literally and are more inclined to describe them in images. We can't seem to point to one or to touch one, and rather speak of what they are like. Archetypes throw us into an imaginative discourse. In fact, it is precisely as metaphors that Jung ... writes of them, insisting on their indefinability. ... All ways of speaking of archetypes are translations from one metaphor to another. Even sober operational definitions in the language of science or logic are no less metaphorical than an image that represents the archetypes as root ideas, psychic organs, figures of myth, typical styles of existence, or dominant fantasies that govern consciousness. There are many other metaphors for describing them: immaterial potentials of structure, like invisible crystals in solution, or form in plants that suddenly show forth under certain conditions; patterns of instinctual behavior like those in animals that direct actions along unswerving paths; the *genres* and *topoi* in literature; the recurring typicalities in history; the paradigmatic thought models in science; the world-wide figures, rituals and relationships in anthropology.
>
> (Hillman, 1975, p. xiii)

If we take Jung and Hillman at all seriously, then we must admit that the primordial image is for the most part a metaphor. It is a best fit from among the available data of experience for the experience of archetypal energy. It is only striking for the consistency with which the same images are chosen. And we apply it not only to the levels of human experience, but to levels that will never know a consciousness that even approaches human. On this level we call our metaphors anthropomorphisms.

We have previously argued that the archetypal source of meaning lies in the organization of living systems per se. If this is so, may we not assume that, although not subjectively labeled as we might label them, the experience of life is reducible to the same basic dimensions on every level? This would suggest that the archetypal categories are categories which are not only reducible to the common elements of human experience, but to the common elements of life.

We are here dealing with the matter of perception. If perception is dependent upon the existence of archetypal categories, and our claim is that perception in humans bears some relationship to a similar archetypal phenomenon that is characteristic of all living systems, then how do we deal with perception?

Jung differentiated between perception and apperception. The first was the physiological registering of a stimulus, the second was defined as follows.

> APPERCEPTION is a psychic process by which a new content is articulated with similar, already existing contents in such a way that it becomes understood, apprehended, or "clear." We distinguish active from passive apperception. The first is a process whereby the subject, of his own accord and from his own motives, consciously apprehends a new content with attention and assimilates it to other contents already constellated; the second is a process by which a new content forces itself upon consciousness either from without (through the senses) or from within (from the unconscious) and, as it were, compels attention and enforces apprehension.
>
> (Jung, 1921/1971, para. 683)

The key word here is assimilation. Can the Jungian use of the term have any relation to the idea expressed in Piagetian biology? Piaget notes:

> Biologically considered, assimilation is the process whereby the organism, in each of its interactions with the bodies or energies of its environment fits these in some manner to the requirements of its own physico-chemical structures.
>
> (Jung, 1970b, p. 72)

Similarly, Jung defines assimilation thus:

> ASSIMILATION is the approximation of a new content of consciousness to already constellated subjective material, the similarity of the new content to this material being especially accentuated in the process. ... Fundamentally, assimilation is a process of *apperception*, but is distinguished from apperception by this element of approximation to the subjective material.
>
> (Jung, 1921/1971, para. 685)

I use the term assimilation . . . as the approximation of object to subject in general. . . .

(Ibid., para. 686)

It would appear then, that Jung's idea of assimilation requires a certain similarity or matching between the external object and some, presumably archetypal, element in the structure of the subject. If that structure consists of "already constellated subjective material" we find an essential equivalence between Jung's constellations and Piaget's schema.

Boulding, in *The Image*, describes the behavior of a paramecium placed in a petri dish whose carefully controlled water supply grows ever hotter:

> If the little one-celled animal known as the Paramecium is observed in water, the temperature of which is slowly being raised, it will at first exhibit a somewhat livelier movement simply as a result of the energetics of the system. . . . At a certain critical temperature, however, the behavior of the tiny animal changes. Instead of merely speeding up its rather random movements in search of food it now develops what can only be described as "seeking" behavior. The animal swims around in ever-widening circles as if it seeks to escape the hot water in which it finds itself. There is something here like perception. Simple as it is, the paramecium has an image of the universe around it in which cooler waters may be found for the seeking.

(Boulding, 1966, p. 38)

However one may deny that the paramecium possesses an image as we know it, one cannot deny that on some level there exists a series of responses that, upon expression, interact in such a way as to provide a behavioral image that we can identify as searching. We can be sure that the paramecium cannot say to itself, "Whew, I'd better find some cooler water!" Yet, the expression is apt and recognizably appropriate to the situation. It is an archetypal situation as it is common to all living things.

We might observe once more at this point that the archetypal situations are those situations that are common to all humankind, but are also reducible to those situations that are common to all living systems. Moreover, except for the dark image of inexpressible motions and affects, the archetypal image expresses a certain isomorphism with the archetypal intent, but as Jung notes regarding symbols, the relationship is non-exhaustive.

If it is permissible to align the patterns of living systems with those patterns peculiar to *homo sapiens*, we may find that, to a large extent, meaning operates metaphorically as it moves between logical levels. Insofar as a pattern is associated with or subsumed under the driving force of a biological pattern (e.g. assimilation, accommodation, moving towards, moving away, centering, non-centering), we may say that it has meaning.

The power of any concept is related to its isomorphism to root categories of life and their basic expression in human society.

This means that living systems give rise to meaning by two parallel and often simultaneous mechanisms of metaphor. First, meaning exists as a concrete need. This is an indication of archetypal action at the instinctual pole, it is relatively pure. The same may occur at the spiritual pole where the individual interacts with the self or self image. Both touch the psychoid extremes of the archetypal range.

The second form of meaning is dependent upon metaphorical extension of those same root categories. That is, because the affective tone surrounding this person or event evokes or resonates with the tone of a root experience, it becomes clothed with the significance of the first: it is assimilated to its associative complex. Similarly, if the event itself is sufficiently similar in its merely formal aspects to evoke the affective tone of some experience assimilated to a strongly centrated complex, it too will assimilate to the complex and take on the numen of significance.

Things are important for one of three reasons. Some things are important in themselves. Other things evoke feelings which are recognizable as being like those evoked by other things which actually are important, and still others look like important things and so remind us of the feeling of importance.

The archetypes, said Jung, are the images of the instincts on the level of psyche. They are the organizers of the contents of consciousness, and the channelers of psychic energy.

THE IMAGINAL DIMENSIONS

Hillman identified the archetypes with the ancient gods and suggested that each assigns intelligibility to sensory phenomena in terms of its placement in an ordered cosmos.

> The Gods are places, and myths make place for psychic events that in an only human world become pathological. . . . All phenomena are "saved" by the act of placing them which at once gives them value. We discover what belongs where by means of likeness, the analogy of events with mythical configurations.
>
> (Hillman, 1983/1988, pp. 36–7)

De Santillana and von Dechend likewise point to the mythic world as being one of places and relationships:

> As we follow the clues – stars, numbers, colors, plants, forms, verse, music, structures – a huge framework of connections is revealed at many levels. One is inside an echoing manifold where everything responds and everything has a place and a time assigned to it.
>
> (de Santillana and von Dechend, 1969, p. 8)

It would appear that even the gods of the ancient Greeks were spatially constrained. According to Francis Cornford (1991) and de Santillana and von Dechend (1969), the Greek Kosmos was ordered by the Moirae, or fates. Both men and gods were constrained by this pre-existent and superior power. When, however, Cornford traces the root concept of the idea of fate, it equates to a province, a bailiwick, a place. The key ordering principle of the Greek Kosmos is the idea of place.

The arrangement of the archetypes in time and space, their distribution in a matrix, brings us back to the time–space quaternio and the three dimensions of spatial existence. The gods themselves represent foci of affect, centers of libidinous energy. Each represents a center from which the world may be viewed and from which other directions may be established. Each focus draws to itself certain kinds of data and repels others.

Eliade refers to just such a pattern as it exists for religious and primitive people as the non-homogeneity of space:

> [I]t is the break effected in space that allows the world to be constituted, because it reveals the fixed point, the central axis for all future orientation. When the sacred manifests itself in any hierophany, there is not only a break in the homogeneity of space; there is also a revelation of an absolute reality, opposed to the nonreality of the vast surrounding expanse. The manifestation of the sacred ontologically creates the world. In the homogeneous and infinite expanse, in which no point of reference is possible and hence no *orientation* can be established, the hierophany reveals an absolute fixed point, a *center*.
>
> (Eliade, 1976, pp. 21–2)

Psychic reality, no less than the reality of the external world, depends upon the existence of a center or reference point. Jung called them nodal points, the archetypes. They order psychic activity and direct the possible flow of energy and behavior. Jung also suggested that there existed an implicit ordering of archetypes and pointed to the works of Cornelius Agrippa and Paracelsus as providing strongly suggestive tables of correspondences (Jung, 1960/1969).

Edward S. Casey makes the significant observation that, as the ordering elements of the psyche, the archetypes must, in themselves, be subject to an ordering. He suggests, following Hillman's statement that the archetypal is characterized by places, that the archetypes occupy metaphorical positions which determine their relations one to another (Casey, 1974; Hillman, 1972).

Following Casey's suggestion, an examination of the ancient art of memory, as explicated by Frances Yates (1966), finds most such systems rooted in archetypal and/or place relations. In that work we find the efforts of the mnemotechnicians oriented about places, rooms, houses and theaters, or relations between archetypal figures, analyzable in terms of grids.

In his commentary on Yates's treatment of the memory theater of Giulio Camillo, Casey notes that the organization proposed by Camillo holds out a clear methodology for the mapping of the archetypes. He notes that there are two fundamental elements involved. They include:

> a nuclear term (e.g., a name designating a given astral-affective quality) with its own semantic depth – a "shimmering symbol", as Jung called it – together with a network of internal relations by means of which this nuclear term is given a determinable locus in imaginal space.
>
> (Casey, 1974, p. 16)

This immediately recalls Eliade's description of non-homogeneous religious space. It has a center that is endowed with meaning, and a specific relationship to other kinds of space within the same framework.

It is also important to note that the mnemonic systems studied by Yates and Casey, especially those rooted in the Renaissance occult revival, seemed to draw much of their claimed efficacy from the interaction of affective value with relative position. The mnemotechnicians in general believed in the special value of their symbols. They were not only learning how to memorize effectively, they were restoring and controlling the order of the cosmos.

In Camillo's system, each of the planetary bodies provides a central core of meaning. Each of these meanings is in turn modified by seven interpretive relations named likewise for the seven planets. Thus, in the abstract, each idea may be classified in terms of its specific position relative to forty-nine classes of phenomena (Yates, 1966).

A similar system appears in the Kabbalist's tree of life. Here the seven planets, with the moon, sun and Divine Source, interact in four worlds along twenty-two interrelated paths. Each of the ten spheres (sephiroth) is associated not only with a planet, but with a visual image, a name of God, an archangel and a demon, a specific virtue and vice, specific body parts, a series of Bible stories and innumerable other associations. The paths that join the sephiroth have been associated with the letters of the Hebrew alphabet, the signs of the zodiac, the major arcana of the tarot deck and other symbolic/affective data. Some authors have even mapped out psycho-affective states and stages of development in the areas between the paths. In general, it provides a significant mnemotechnical aid, as well as an archetypal map of associations (Halevi, 1987; Regardie, 1973/1988).

We are again confronted with Eliade's idea of non-homogeneity and it maps on to the idea of an archetypal map with little or no distortion. We may travel from any of the centers in a relative direction, and in so doing derive a specific meaning in imaginal space relative to that center. At any given point we may either continue to make our interpretations in terms of the original sphere of meaning, or acknowledge a new center, a new balance and a new meaning.

A similar structuring of experience is suggested by the semantic networks outlined by von Franz. She holds that archetypal relations are best understood topographically in terms of a net. She notes:

> The idea of a fieldlike arrangement of the archetypes, or the collective unconscious . . . derives from the fact that the archetypes exist in a state of mutual contamination; they overlap in meaning. . . .
>
> [The archetypes] are contained in a field of inner qualitative nuances. This field may be termed a manifold of psychic contents, whose relations are defined by meaning.
>
> [E]very archetype forms the *virtual center of a field like realm of representational contents* definable strictly in relative terms, a region overlapping other realms.
>
> (von Franz, 1974, pp. 144–7)

Throughout the study, certain names for the archetype have resonated more than others as revealing something of the nature of the thing itself. Among these are affect image, feeling-toned representation, and proto-plasmic image (Redfearn, 1973; Fordham, 1957; Progoff, 1959). Another significant descriptor is provided by Redfearn's definition as "the direction towards which sensory data, perceptions, images and motor patterns tend to be modified and organized by spontaneous human psychic activity" (1973, p. 128).

Direction has appeared as a significant metaphor for the development of the psyche throughout the study. Early on, Jung posits the self as the telos of the system. Each archetype, moreover, insofar as it is a reflection of that end, provides a specific goal for the period of its own dominance. The idea of a direction, a goal or image is strongly reflected in Progoff's idea of an archetypal or protoplasmic image.

The twin concepts of centering and focus reappear in the ability of the archetypal to draw the contents of consciousness to themselves and to act as "nodal points" in the collective unconscious. The numinosity of the arche-typal is partly manifested in their ability to provide meaning. Their numen, the meaning that they provide, is magnified as it transcends the immediate referent and provides meaning for successive levels of operations.

Centering and focus also call up the ideas of centrifugal and centripetal force: the center may draw and it may repel. Part of the essence of centra-tion is the possibility of differentiation. The organism centers on a response system as a means of dealing appropriately with a given stimulus. As a result, a content may be accepted or rejected, drawn in or cast out, assimilated or accommodated to.

Another dimension is added in the complementary ideas of depth and relative height. Up and down, heaven and earth, are archetypal dimen-sions. Down into the underworld, down into the abyss are common themes. Up into the heavens, ascent into glory are just as common.

Assimilation and dominance are suggestive of the same pole. Insofar as the stimulus is subsumable to my structure, it is below me, I will dominate it. Likewise accommodation suggests deference, submission. Insofar as I am subsumable to its structure, I am below it, it will dominate me.

Left and right are dexter and sinister: the one associated with right–rectitude, the other with darkness and evil, the sinister side. Accordingly, Jung sees them also as expressing conscious and unconscious, as well as male and female. The two orientations imply a specific feeling tone and a moral valuation (1959/1968b, 1953/1968). However, in the East, the association may be reversed with left associated with activity and benevolence, and right with passivity and suspicion (Matthews, 1986). Turning towards the left is associated with turning towards the unconscious, while turning towards the right symbolizes awakening and consciousness (Jung, 1959/1968a; Cirlot, 1962).

Cirlot lists the following associations with left and right:

left side with the past, the sinister, the repressed, involution, the abnormal and the illegitimate; the right side with the future, the felicitous, openness, evolution, the normal and the legitimate.

(Cirlot, 1962, p. 287)

We are here left with a three-dimensional representation of the feeling tone and a rationale for its association with the image.

The dimensions are those which we have mentioned before: centration/diffusion, assimilation/accommodation, approach/avoid. They might easily be understood as salience, interactive style and valence. Together, they form an octahedron which maps on to the Jungian system perfectly.

The image itself is provided by the interaction of the developing individual with the environment. All of the intersystemic interactions, length of bone, strength of muscle, relative activity level, hormonal concentrations and others conspire to prepare the individual for an encounter with an external stimulus. This "dark image" or affect image interacts with the world as a filter, or as a lock awaiting the peculiar key that will open it. Like the IRM of the ethologists it awaits a specific stimulus. Unlike the IRM, it is responsive over a longer period of imprinting.

Several authors have noted that the human infant does not imprint on the same level as do other mammals, but extends the critical period over several months.

Few human behaviors have learning regimens limited to periods of less than three months. Human infants and children engage in undoubted directed learning, but it is concentrated in longer, less well-defined periods.

(Lumsden and Wilson, 1981, p. 64)

During this period, we may assume that there occurs a pairing of the innate, biological element, the psychoid archetype, with the initial environmental encounters with parents and the world at large. These interact with one another to produce the core of the unconscious complex. This imago feeds back into the biological system and becomes the affective and visual foundation for the archetypal image. Insofar as the interacting external figure is isomorphic to, or meets the "expectation" of, the archetype, there is constellated a well-balanced archetypal imago. Insofar as it fails to meet those "expectations" the imago is perverted and the future growth patterns distorted (Jung, 1960/1969; Bowlby, cited in Stevens, 1982/1983, p. 100).

SUMMARY

Up to this point, we have analyzed the idea of the archetype as it appears in Jungian literature and have seen that it possesses certain specific characteristics. Broadly, these have included the following traits:

- It is an inherited predisposition to action and/or perception that has resulted from the "Crystallization of experience over time" (Samuels, 1985, p. 27; Jung 1953/1966, para. 151).
- It possesses a strong charge of libidinal energy and resultantly impels the organism to find corresponding data in the environment. It possesses a numinosity (Jung, 1971, para. 748).
- The archetype is never expressed except in terms of the accretions of life experience that it gathers to itself. It is then expressed in images, themes and motifs that reappear independent of cultural transmission or other non-heritable mechanism (Jung, 1959/1968a, para. 155).
- The archetypal image is related to the instincts as it represents them to consciousness, evokes them as stimulus, and represents their fulfillment as a goal or telos (Samuels, 1985, p. 29).
- The archetype is bipolar, Janus faced. That is, it always presents two faces, upward and downward, inward and outward, good and bad, male and female, etc. (Jung, 1959/1968a, para. 413).
- Although individually distinct, the archetypes are contaminated with one another in their expression. Their contamination is rooted in their common or singular source, the *unus mundus* of the collective unconscious (Jung, 1956/1967, para. 660).
- The archetype represents the organ of meaning as it mediates the instinctual and spiritual poles of reality to the level of conscious experience through the symbolic function. It is simultaneously the voice of nature and the voice of spirit (Jung, 1971, para. 446).

Beyond these defining characteristics, other properties of the archetype have suggested to many that the nature of the archetype *an sich* is undiscoverable. We have, however, suggested that it is just those properties which obscure the individual archetype that provide the clues to the biological roots of archetypal activity.

The major clues to the relationship between the archetypes and the patterns of living systems appear in the following characteristics of the archetypes and archetypal activity.

- All of the archetypes intermingle and are mutually contaminated by each other.
- The operations of the Jungian psyche and the archetypes in particular are subject to systems theoretical analysis.
- Jung described the archetypes as psychoid elements, originating in the living patterns of the organism and associated with instinct.
- Jung saw that the archetypes could only be differentiated one from another by affective tone, not by intellectual analysis.
- The archetypal patterns were seen to reappear autochthonously throughout the world.

These items strongly suggested a link between the archetypes and patterns observable in living systems. For this reason, we examined the properties of life and there discovered that the properties of living systems from both classical and Piagetian perspectives compared well with the characteristics of the archetypes.

- Both living systems and archetypes seem to divide the universe into a binary response system. As Jung noted, the archetypes are Janus-faced.
- Both the Jungian psyche and living systems differentiate between states by focusing on one or another subsystem.
- The result of the centration process, focusing, is often expressible in terms of the Piagetian concepts of assimilation and accommodation.
- Both the archetypes and living systems may be positively or negatively motivating. That is, they may move towards or away from various stimuli.

Having determined that there existed a fair degree of correspondence between archetypal systems and living systems, we then saw how the commonalties between living systems fit into the octahedral scheme developed by Jung from gnostic materials as a symbol of the psyche. Moreover, we saw that the patterns already enumerated were on some level isomorphic to the six basic orientations in space: up, down, left, right, forwards and backwards.

Although these patterns were seemingly basic elements of archetypal action on all levels of interaction, they failed to capture the specific form of the archetypes known to us in any satisfactory manner. That is to say, up to this point we have been able to account for the general formal attributes of the archetype, but have been able to provide no explanation of content.

In order to solve this problem, we turned to the idea of emergence and suggested that from the evidence provided by biology, artificial intelligence, ethology and developmental psychology, the archetype is no thing, but the emergent property of systems, selected or designed to emit specific behaviors in "expectation" of specific environmental consequences. The archetype, we saw, was more akin to a direction that received its meaning from the response it received. This observation led us to reconsider the archetypal image, Jung's original formulation, and to acknowledge that Progoff's idea of a "dark image" rooted in the processes of life provides a clear indication of the nature of the archetype *an sich*.

After an exploration of the archetypal image as metaphor and the root of metaphor, we returned to an examination of the spatial metaphor as somehow basic to the archetypal realm. Touching on the works of Yates, Casey and Hillman we found that much of archetypal activity can be interpreted in terms of a three-dimensional affective grid. Every instinctual urge that emerges as an archetypal element will become a central element or lack focus, it will draw certain contents towards itself and repel others, it will appear to be desirable or repulsive, good or bad, worthy of approach or worth avoiding. Depending upon its relative salience or libidinal charge, it will either assimilate other patterns to itself, or accommodate to another pattern.

In summary, we have seen that:

- Archetypal responses are isomorphic with the basic response characteristics of living systems.
- The idea of image is crucial to the idea of the archetype.
- The archetype *an sich* may not exist until it emerges from systemic interactions as an image of the instant state of the system, thus vindicating Hillman's statement that the archetype is always phenomenal.
- The abstract archetype exists only as a developmental pole, a set of possibilities of expression whose fullness of expression is characterized by the archetypal image.
- The affective tone of an archetype may be described in terms of a three-dimensional scheme based upon salience or libidinal activity (Is it the center of activity, or does it function in the background? Does it draw into focus or consciousness, or does it move from consciousness out of focus?); interactive style, its primary mode of interaction (Does it draw to itself or assimilate other psychic contents, or does it accommodate to them?); and valence (Is it "good" or "bad," does it attract or repel?).

Having provided a basis for understanding the archetypal mechanism in its relation to living systems and, further, having outlined a means for analyzing the dimensions of archetypal activity, we will now turn in Part II to an exploration of the patterns of archetypal activity at the psychic level.

Part II

The archetypal sequence

Chapter 5

The archetypal set

We have already determined that the archetype represents the emergent property of the biological system as it crosses from unconscious, determined activity to consciousness. Until the archetype is symbolized by an archetypal image, its existence consists of a body of kinesthetic and affective states that characterize a certain inchoate organismic "expectancy." This expectancy is closely related to a developmental direction or chreode[1] that has been shaped by selective pressure. It is closely related to instinct. It is aimed at an encounter with a tacitly specified object with which it will bond for the often mutual fulfillment of specific organismic functions: nurturance, food, protection, reproduction, etc. In the course of its interaction with the environment the organism internalizes a representation of its early experiences with the object as the object imago. These early experiences, in combination with the psychoid archetype, give rise to the archetypal image which tends to dominate the development of that facet of the individual's life from that point forward.

From the archetypal images common to all of humankind, Jung developed a characteristic psychic topology, and a population of archetypal characters susceptible to organization into several possible hierarchies. Some of the hierarchies seem to be structurally organized in terms of depth and sequence as they are encountered in the therapeutic domain, viz. persona/ae, ego, shadow, animus/a, self. Others are ordered in terms of a developmental scheme: mother, puer, father, mana figure, etc. It is also possible to produce a structural analysis in terms of the psychic function of each element beginning with the primordial self[2] at the root and passing on through the mother, "the first of the archetypes," to the development of the ego, the father and other interpersonal relations. One more organizational scheme suggested by Samuels consists of a synchronic ordering that is rooted in present experience (Jung, 1956/1957, 1959/1968a; Samuels, 1985, 1989).

In rejecting any single classificatory scheme, I see archetypal phenomena as representing an unconscious infrastructure upon which psychic life depends. Archetypal systems may be understood as giving rise to levels of learning and experience corresponding to reflexive and instinctive patterns of behavior at the biological root. At the interface between human and non-human systems they give rise to broadly human patterns. As the individual proceeds through maturation and individuation they also appear as topographically structured elements and as personified characterizations of the current state of the psyche.[3]

Jung's understanding of the phylogenetic development of libido provides a possible underlying schema for the organization of the psyche. Libido is defined by Jung as:

> a desire or impulse which is unchecked by any kind of authority, moral or otherwise. Libido is appetite in its natural state. From the genetic point of view it is bodily needs like hunger, thirst, sleep and sex, and emotional states or affects, which constitute the essence of libido.
>
> (Jung, 1956/1967, para. 194)

Libido has its root in an undifferentiated life urge, "a will to live which seeks to ensure the continuance of the whole species through the preservation of the individual" (ibid., para. 195). This simple urge is later differentiated or channeled into specific functional categories which we interpret in terms of reproduction, nourishment, self maintenance, etc. These innate centers of libido – the natural appetites – are also the nodal points that define the organization of the collective unconscious, they are the archetypal roots of the complexes.

The undifferentiated life urge, as we have seen, expresses itself in terms of the essential patterns of living systems. It becomes differentiated as it moves to different levels of complexity and as it is channeled into specific definable needs. If the earliest differentiations appear as oral, anal and reproductive urges, their later differentiation gives rise to impulses that are clearly independent of those primitives (ibid.).

Each such differentiated function expresses the primal life-energy, and each can become the root of further differentiations of libidinal process in more complex forms. From the perspective of the sexual urge alone, Jung sees

> many complex functions, which today must be denied all trace of sexuality, were originally derived from the reproductive instinct. . . . Thus, we find the first stirrings of the artistic impulse in animals, but subservient to the reproductive instinct and limited to the breeding season. The original sexual character of these biological phenomena gradually disappears as they become organically fixed and achieve functional independence. Although there can be no doubt that music originally belonged to the reproductive sphere, it would be an unjustified and fantastic generalization to put music in the same category as sex.
>
> (Ibid., para. 194)

Thus, we may observe a certain hierarchical organization of the collective unconscious that suggests the phylogenetic differentiation of libido into separate functions. This further suggests that the archetypal field is capable of continuous refinement so that an almost infinite set of archetypally defined urges may be differentiated from the underlying matrix.

In articulating his theory of libido, Jung showed that the expression of the urge to live may occur at multiple levels simultaneously. That is to say, although it has been differentiated into higher functions, hindrances, whether from fear or frustration, may have the effect of channeling the libido or life-energy into more primitive (and, hence, more potent) modes of release. At such times, the symbology associated with these more archaic levels mixes with and is expressed in terms of the current level of experience. Jung noted that just such a conflation of psychic level was responsible for the ongoing incest fantasy in Freudian theory.

All things considered, it would appear that there are several levels of archetypal action and several distinct varieties of what may be classed as archetypes. All of these intermingle and cross-fertilize with one another across logical levels as part of an integrated, complex system. At the lowest level of this organization, which is clearly identifiable with the immediate underpinnings of the psyche, is a relatively undifferentiated set of tendencies strongly linked to the biological level of organismic existence. These relate most closely to the abstract, psychoid archetypes as Jung described them. They exist only as dominants, nodal points, tendencies about which behavior accumulates. They are the preconditions of perception and action. They are the roots of meaning. They have no individual existence beyond the biological *per se* until they coalesce and deintegrate from the background of self as a response to the need of the organism.

At this level, the archetypal is rooted in rhythmic movements and the genetically determined physical characteristics of the organism. They are here identical with the physical range of movements and perceptions possible to the organism, as well as the innate drives. Jung referred to the archetypal at this level as holding forth " a . . . possibility of representation which is given a priori" (1959/1968a, para. 155). Out of the interaction of these elements with each other and the environment, there emerge the instinctual and reflex actions, the foundation of experience and action.

On the next level of organization come those well-defined and internalized archetypes which define humankind at the biological level. These are the uniformities of human existence. At this level, each archetype seems to have a correspondent in some instinct: "There are as many archetypes as there are typical situations in life" (ibid., para. 99). These include the great events and significant persons in life, family, friends, birth, death, marriage and sexuality. Included in this group are transitional archetypes, archetypes which give rise to symbols of transformation or change (ibid.). In their root forms they correspond to general instinctual patterns. In their expression, however, they are subject to modifications that reflect selection within ethnic groups and the peculiar circumstances in which they arise.

Next, we find a level consisting of structural elements derived from the interactions of the previous elements and further interactions with the environment. Their organization is predetermined and corresponds to the typical Jungian topological model of persona/ae, ego, shadow, anima/us and self. While their structural relations are not in general dependent upon environmental variables, significant elements of their interrelations, content and means of expression are susceptible to cultural and social influences. The personae especially take the form of socially determined roles, while anima/us manifestations may be significantly impacted by the character of the parental imagos, the general attitude of the ego towards the unconscious, and the relative salience of those symbols most important to the individual within the current social matrix.

At last we come to the level of the archetypal images, and the archetypes as more generally understood in popular literature. These are actually symbols that represent the specific relations of the individual to the unconscious, of the ego to the shadow, the anima/animus, and the self. They characterize the direction of wholeness, the means to wholeness and the goal itself. In general, they present the psyche's self regulatory system to consciousness in symbolic form. Although already functional at the previous level, here, as symbolic images, they meet with the common conception of the archetype as a conscious image or symbol (see Figure 5.1).

This scheme immediately recalls the diagrams of the Jungian psyche presented by Jung in the Tavistock Lectures and recreated by von Franz in *Projection and Recollection* (Jung, 1968b; von Franz, 1980/1988), and not surprisingly so, for, the closer to consciousness the archetypal influence is led, the more easily its external form is determined by environmental factors. So, the personae and the ego, as well as the shadow and the anima representation, are strongly influenced by personal history (see Figure 5.2). Moreover, the symbolic vocabulary that communicates both type and direction for the movement of individuation is also determined by conscious and environmental variables which combine in an artful bricolage[4] to communicate the unknowable (Hillman, 1975/1977).

THE PSYCHOID ELEMENTS

One of the difficulties associated with the theory of archetypes and its analysis in a reasonably rigorous manner is the insistence by Jung and his colleagues that the archetypes are pre-existing and do not develop. Faced with such a statement, most non-Jungians are driven to the assumption that Jung relied upon a mystical, Platonic ideal.

We propose that the archetypes do not develop, but that the human organism develops in such a way that non-manifest archetypes are

Topological/Structural archetypes (persona, ego, shadow, anima, self)	Psychic archetypes
Archetypal elements (archetypes as psychic entities, and as universal patterns of human thought and action)	
Instinctual psychoid elements (IRMs, instincts)	Psychoid archetypes
Psychoid structural elements (the possibility of perception and action)	

Figure 5.1 Four levels of archetypal complexity

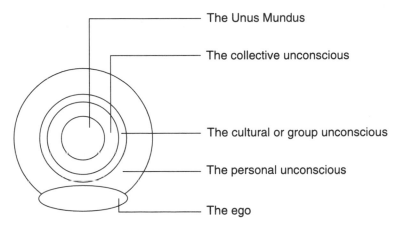

The Unus Mundus

The collective unconscious

The cultural or group unconscious

The personal unconscious

The ego

Figure 5.2 Primary elements of the Jungian psyche

pre-nascent, though predetermined both as to their form and the time of their emergence.[5] They appear in a developmentally ordered sequence that is determined by the interacting elements of the physical and psychological organism. As such, the archetypes give expression to emergent behavioral properties characteristic of the next logical level in the development of the organism. They are new, however, only in the sense that they were to this point maturationally inaccessible to the organism. Insofar as they represent consistently appearing dominants of human experience, they are part of the archetypal armamentarium of the organism.

That is, archetypes are predetermined insofar as a human organism must have certain physical parts, and behave in certain ways in order to qualify as being human. These behavioral and structural elements are broadly predetermined, but depend upon previous developmental factors and environmental interactions to determine just how and when they will be expressed. Because all humans share a common biology, there are certain unavoidable, biologically predetermined developmental sequences that give rise to specific foci of biological investment – libido. These are the psychoid archetypes.[6]

As noted earlier, the archetypes exist as part of the survival repertoire of humankind. They are developmentally structured expectancies aimed at corresponding stimuli in the environment. They function first to coordinate the linkage between the organism and the environment through perception, and then to ensure the bonding of mother and child, child and family, individual and society.[7] While they do not develop *per se*, they are activated in accordance with a specific and predictable developmental sequence that some have wrongly interpreted as development of the archetypes themselves (Neumann, 1954/1973; Fordham, 1981; Geigerich, 1975).

In the interaction between the ethological expectancy and its environmental fulfillment there forms a base set of behaviors for dealing with the class of stimuli and behaviors peculiar to that developmental stage. As the most primitive levels interact with each other and the environment, they in turn give rise to the next level of predetermined emergents. With each level, the absolute specificity varies from the common mold more and more so that each individual quickly begins to display the marks that distinguish one person from every other.

Jung and Fordham point to the early development of the oral, anal and genital areas as centers of libidinal activity. At an early age archetypal materials regarding eating, excreting and sexuality are differentiated as specific and basic ways of relating to the world. These archetypally defined functions combine with life experiences and other archetypal formations to provide the developmental and experiential circumstances under which more complex archetypal systems may find expression (Jung 1956/1967; Fordham, 1957).

Simultaneously, archetypally defined perception systems are interacting with physical response systems to locate and bond to the mother. The emergent property of their interaction will be expressed in terms of the mother archetype and its developing imago. Around them will develop the mother-complex and with it the root of the child's later interactions with women, other people and the world.

In the early years and months, life is characterized by a pulsing rhythmic character. First it is physically rhythmic and out of those rhythms develop reflexes, movements and perceptual skills. In the background there is a psychic rhythm as one and another of the archetypes moves into salience and moves again into the background as the predetermined forms of actions and perceptions are filled with the material of experience. With the accretion of experiences about the archetypal core, individual patterns begin to manifest themselves as typical modes of interaction with the mother, the father, siblings and life in general (Fordham, 1957; Jung, 1956/1967).

THE STRUCTURAL ELEMENTS

As noted, the Jungian psyche is often analyzed in terms of the archetypal structures encountered as one progresses from the most external structures inward towards the self, the inner man. In speaking, however, of structural elements, we should be careful to understand throughout that Jung perceived these more as dynamic systems than as specific loci.

What characterizes the structural elements are typical modes of action and typical kinds of relations. It is essentially a functional description. The ego is typically the center of consciousness. It may to a lesser or greater degree incorporate previously unconscious materials, it may fragment, dissolve and reappear, yet there remains, except in the deepest psychosis, some focus identifiable as the center of consciousness, the ego. The shadow lies immediately behind the ego. At its most superficial level, the shadow contains forgotten and repressed materials. At lower levels it represents collective ideas that cannot become conscious and merges with the anima. As with the ego, the momentary borders and particular outlines are variable, but the relations remain constant (Jung, 1956/1967, 1960/1969; Williams, 1963).

Although often not classed with the archetypes, Jung's typology of consciousness is held as a sigil of the self, the quaternio, as well as an archetypal structuring element. He identifies this fourfold structure as one of the unconscious dominants, the archetypes:

> [I]nvestigation of the products of the unconscious yields recognizable traces of archetypal structures which coincide with the myth-motifs, among them certain types which deserve the name of dominants. These are archetypes like the anima, animus, wise old man, witch, shadow, earth-mother, etc., and the organizing dominants, the self, the circle and the quaternity, i.e., the four functions or aspects of the self or of consciousness.
>
> (Jung, 1956/1967, para. 611)

So, then, within the self, and reflected in the structure of the ego, there exists a tendency to a fourfold division of energy corresponding to the four functions of consciousness: thinking, feeling, sensing and intuiting. Of these, one generally becomes the dominant mode of function through differentiation, while the least used and therefore the least differentiated tends to remain submerged in the unconscious. Of the four, two are seen as rational, thinking and feeling, and two are seen as non-rational, sensing and intuition.

Jung originally held that the inferior function was always opposed to the dominant function as a polar opposite of the same broad type. Thus, feeling was opposed to thinking and sensing to intuiting. This suggested that if the dominant function were a rational function, then the inferior function must necessarily be the other rational function. Only the most primitive individual could be expected to function equally in all modalities (1971).

More recent research suggests, however, that the functions do not relate in an altogether polar fashion, but that the dominant/inferior limitation applies only to specific contexts in which one or another of the functions becomes dominant. In other contexts, not only may another function become dominant, but functions may alternate. Bolen has suggested that different dominants may, at different times, express completely different if not contradictory patterns. Metzner, et al., and others have pointed out that the very goal of individuation requires conscious differentiation of the inferior function. From this perspective it is not only possible, but desirable, that all of the functions should develop as fully as possible (Bolen, 1990; Metzner, et al., 1981; Larsen, 1990).

Closely allied to the four functions is Jung's concept that individuals are broadly differentiable into two types: introverts and extroverts. Introverts tend to turn inward for validation, while extroverts look outwards.

After reviewing the available data, Metzner, Burney and Mahlberg found that empirical data validated the introversion/extroversion dichotomy, but failed to support the idea that cognitive functions of the same type necessarily exclude the complementary type. They note:

> Jung and others have argued that the functions are opposites because one cannot use them simultaneously – i.e., one cannot think and feel simultaneously, or intuit and sense simultaneously. Although this is an assumption that could be questioned, even if true it would not negate the possibility that the two functions, as personality functions, could be equally strongly developed in an individual. Indeed, the theory of the individuation process calls for this kind of balanced development of all the functions.
>
> (Metzner et al., 1981, p. 34)

Following our lead from Part I, we are again brought to the archetypal dimensioning of experience in terms of a quaternio, a bipolar relationship between activities. We find, moreover, that this quaternio takes its meaning in part from another axis along which Jung described an individual as either externally oriented/extroverted, or inwardly oriented/introverted.

Jung defined the introversion–extroversion pole in terms of the individual's orientation towards information. The extrovert determines all things by external data. He is good or bad depending upon the response of those around him. An action is right or wrong depending upon the accepted custom. Things can be weighed, measured, evaluated and decided upon by their external qualities. Von Franz says that the extrovert's libido "habitually flows toward the object," which is to say he desires to incorporate the external by accommodating to it. On the contrary, the introvert feels himself in danger of being overwhelmed by externals and seeks refuge in the internal. He validates all things against an internal standard. For the introvert all things must assimilate to an internal reality before they can make sense (Jung, 1971; von Franz and Hillman, 1971). Jung says:

I propose to use the terms extroversion and introversion to describe these two opposite movements of libido. . . . We speak of extroversion when he gives his whole interest to the outer world, to the object, and attributes an extraordinary importance and value to it. When, on the contrary, the objective world sinks into the shadow, as it were, or undergoes a devaluation, while the individual occupies the centre of his own interest and becomes in his own eyes the only person worthy of consideration, it is a case of introversion.

(Jung, 1971, para. 860)

Jung believed that the tendency to introversion and extroversion was rooted in biological reproductive strategies. One depends upon fending off the outside world through few offspring possessed of powerful protective mechanisms and the other seeks security by multiplying its influence in the environment through multiple, relatively unprotected, offspring. The first corresponds to an introverted strategy, the second to an extroverted one. In conformity to our own model, it may be convenient to label introversion as assimilative and extroversion as accommodative (Jung, 1971; von Franz and Hillman, 1971).

That such a label is acceptable is suggested by Larsen's paraphrase of the Piagetian position:

In cognitive assimilation as described by Piaget, a person has an unchanging model or schema about reality that bends incoming data from the world to its own form. Its complementary and necessary counter principle is accommodation, which allows for modification of one's internal schema to "accommodate" new information.

(Jung, 1990, p. 62)

Returning to the four functions of consciousness, we find that the rational functions relate to information on an evaluative basis. A thing is good or bad, true or untrue, based upon a standard of some sort. In the case of thinking, the standard is abstract and hierarchical. In the case of feeling, it is relatively concrete. Both are relatively focused upon some specific aspect of the situation or the individual's feeling about the situation. Here again, the archetypal directions, the root patterns of living systems – towards and away, focused and non-focused – reappear.

Similarly, for the non-evaluative functions, the same archetypal pattern reappears. These, however, are generally less differentiating, tending towards response patterns more than evaluations. Jung noted that the non-evaluative functions were more archaic. Sensation "is given a priori and unlike thinking and feeling is not subject to rational laws." Intuition is defined partially as unconscious perception, while the two together assemble to create a context in which the rational functions may become operative. By comparison with the rational functions they are more diffuse, less focused, less conscious (1971, paras 795–6).

Challenging the doctrine of opposites as it applies to the four functions, Metzner, et al., suggest that the four functions are independent of one another and that they can combine in any of twelve possible configurations of personality type. Their research suggests that each of the four functions is capable of its own characteristic means of interacting with the universe and is also provided with its own evaluative processes.

According to this view, thinking involves the perception and evaluation of "prerational" descriptions, thoughts and hypotheses. Each may be judged in terms of its truth or falsity, clarity or obscurity and whether it possesses meaning. Feeling involves feelings, e.g. love, joy, peace, fear, rage, anguish, terror, grief, depression. These may be good or bad, pleasant or unpleasant, acceptable or unacceptable. Likewise, sensation, working on the raw data of experience, can be adjudged as recognized, unrecognized, pleasant or unpleasant, real or unreal. Intuition, the perception of possibilities, can be interesting or boring, relevant or irrelevant, practical or impractical (Metzner, et al., 1981, pp. 36–7).

Joseph Henderson (1964, 1968, 1984) has suggested that there exists an archetype of culture which expresses itself in terms of four specific perspectives on the world of social interactions. These are the Philosophical, rooted in thought and, more specifically, thought about origins and meanings; the Social, which views the world in terms of people and relationships; the Aesthetic, which experiences the world artistically and sensually; and the Religious view.

The archetypal nature of the fourfold division of the psyche is further underlined by Stewart's 1987 analysis of the archetypal dimensions of affect. Stewart indicates that beyond the orienting response (startle) and the basic experience of libido (joy/interest), there are four primal affective categories: fear/terror, sadness/anguish, anger/rage and contempt/shame or disgust/humiliation. These are related, in turn, to the four functions of consciousness, four archetypal situations and Henderson's four cultural attitudes. For the sake of brevity the four elements are presented in tabular form (see Table 5.1), with an added column analyzing each in accordance with our previously detailed pattern of living systems.

The persona/ae

According to Jung, the most external facet of the personality is the persona. This is the context-dependent mask that an individual assumes on

Table 5.1 Archetypal affects[1]

Stimulus	Image	Affect	Adaptive response	Cultural attitude	Ego function	System analysis
The unknown	The abyss	Terror	Ritual	Religious	Intuitive	Away Accommodate Focused
Loss	The void	Anguish	Rhythm Harmony	Aesthetic	Sensation	Towards Assimilate Non-focused
Restriction	Chaos	Rage	Reason	Philosophic	Thinking	Away Assimilate Focused
Rejection	Alienation	Disgust Humiliation	Relationship	Social	Feeling	Towards Accommodate Non-focused

[1]Adapted from Stewart, 1987, p. 142.

a day-to-day and context-to-context basis. It is this mask that allows him or her to provide appropriate and consistent responses in accordance with socially defined roles in various contexts. These roles develop in response to the day-to-day needs of the individual and coalesce out of the habitual responses that characterize specific situations. The personae explain the differences in personality that people often show between separate contexts.

Jung makes the following definition: "The persona is ... a functional complex that comes into existence for reason of adaptation or personal convenience, but is by no means identical with the individuality. The personal is exclusively concerned with the relation to objects" (1971, para. 801).

Jung was careful to differentiate between the person who identified with his or her persona and those who understood themselves to exist on a deeper level. The former were said to be personal, the latter, individual. While he might function effectively, the personal human offers little depth and often suffers from neurotic disorders. The individual human, however, has begun to plumb the depths of his own reality through introspection, religious practice, analysis or some other method. Through these he has discovered a depth of personal reality that transcends any socially determined role.

Relative to the process of individuation, Jung also observed that the persona exists in a complementary relation to the anima/us. Just as the persona reflects the habitual manner of our relations with the external world, so the anima/us reflects our manner of relating to the collective unconscious.

> As to its common human qualities, the character of the anima can be deduced from the persona. Everything that should normally be in the outer attitude, but is conspicuously absent, will invariably be found in the inner ... when a man is identical with his persona, his individual qualities will be associated with his anima. ... For in the same way as the persona, the instrument of adaptation to the environment, is strongly influenced by environmental conditions, the anima is shaped by the unconscious and its qualities.
>
> (Jung, 1921/1971, para. 806)

There is also a complementary relationship between the persona and the shadow. Both Progoff (1953/1981) and Neumann (1990) emphasize that just as the persona reflects the socially acceptable mask, so the shadow contains, among other things, those contents which society rejects, abhors or ignores. In terms of susceptibility to social demands, the persona represents the most malleable facet of the Jungian psyche.

The ego

The word ego refers to that part of the psyche that is conscious. It is the conscious "I" that serves as the mediator between the self and the world about it. It is the realm of rational choice and the gate of consciousness.

> We understand the ego as the complex factor to which all conscious contents are related. It forms, as it were, the centre of the field of consciousness; and, insofar as this comprises the empirical personality, the ego is the subject of all personal acts of consciousness.
>
> (Jung, 1959/1968b, para. 1)

Within the Jungian economy, the ego is seen not as the center of the psyche, but only the center of consciousness. The difference is crucial. Jung reserves to the self the center (as well as the periphery) of the psyche, the ego is only its conscious expression. Jung notes:

> By ego I understand a complex of ideas which constitutes the center of my field of conscious-ness and appears to have a high degree of continuity and identity. Hence I also speak of an *ego-complex*. The ego-complex is as much a content as a condition of consciousness, for a psychic element is conscious to me only insofar as it is related to my ego-complex. But inasmuch as the ego is only the center of my field of consciousness, it is not identical with the totality of my psyche, being merely one complex among other complexes. I therefore distinguish between the ego and the self, since the ego is only the subject of my conscious-ness, while the self is the subject of my total psyche, which also includes the unconscious.
>
> (Jung, 1971, p. 706)

In another context he refers to it as a "relatively constant personification of the unconscious" (1963/1970, para. 129).

The Jungian ego develops over time from "islands of consciousness" arising out of the interaction of the archetypes with the environment and the overlap of archetypal claims upon environmental events. Fordham indicates that the ego develops out of an original self, present at birth, which deintegrates to produce a field of consciousness. Among the early archetypal elements that contribute to ego formation are the three erogenous zones whose mutual competition and complementary interaction reinforce a continuing sense of "I" or me-ness in the developing child. Fordham points to these erogenous zones as the original loci of consciousness and suggests that they are of primary importance in the development of the mature ego. Developmentally we may view the ego *in part* as the abstracted "I" in the area of psychic activity where the most salient complexes interact. It is rooted in a bodily ego that provides a locus and a sense of continuity in time and otherwise integrates the scintillae[8] closest to its realm of dominance (Fordham, 1957; Jung 1959/1968b).

These processes result in a continuing experience of identity and continuity in time. A consistent "I" develops that recalls past events and can choose to respond or not to respond. Fordham produces the following list of ego functions: perception, memory, organization of mental functioning, control of mobility, reality testing, speech, defenses and the ability to relinquish dominance (Fordham, 1973/1980; Samuels, 1985, p. 74 ff.).

The shadow

The shadow is the personified form of the personal unconscious. It exists as a negative component of the personality; a compensatory and complementary opposite to the ego (Jung 1963/1970). It is a "sort of second personality, of a puerile and inferior character" (Jung 1959/1968a, para. 469). It is metaphorically a shadow by virtue of its unconsciousness in comparison to the sphere of ego-consciousness, in much the same way as a natural shadow exists only by virtue of the presence of a light source: "The [shadow] . . . usually presents itself as the inferior or negative personality. It comprises that part of the collective unconscious which intrudes into the personal sphere, there forming the so-called personal unconscious" (1963/1970, para. 129n).

It is the repository of things repressed, forgotten and other elements which can never become conscious. Jung says: "The Shadow personifies everything that the subject fails to acknowledge about himself and yet is always thrusting itself upon him directly or indirectly – for instance, inferior traits of character and other incompatible tendencies" (1959/1968a, para. 513).

The shadow brings to mind the Fool in the tarot deck. Like the Fool, the shadow is: "A minatory and ridiculous figure, he stands at the very beginning of the way of individuation, posing the deceptively easy riddle of the sphinx . . . " (ibid., para. 486).

The position of shadow as guard over the repressed, forgotten and unknowable has led at least one author to point out the essential continuity between the personal unconscious and the collective unconscious. Mary Williams, in what Samuels has characterized as a seminal paper, raises the easily overlooked issue of whether, if the contents of the personal unconscious did not threaten to overwhelm consciousness by virtue of their numinosity, they would need to be repressed. She suggests that it is precisely *because* of the continuity between the personal and collective unconscious that repression becomes an issue (Williams, 1963; Samuels, 1985).

The shadow, however, is also the repository of instinctual impulses and drives that can be necessary for survival. They can even be beneficial (Jung 1959/1968b; Neumann, 1990). Through the trickster archetype, the shadow is associated with wisdom and the beginnings of spiritual endeavor (Jung 1959/1968a). It also represents the first obstacle to true self knowledge.

The shadow is the source of projections. A projection is

> an unconscious, automatic process whereby a content that is un-
> conscious to the subject transfers itself to an object, so that it seems
> to belong to that object. The projection ceases the moment it becomes
> conscious, that is to say when it is seen as belonging to the subject.
>
> (Jung, 1959/1968a, para. 121)

In the case of a projection of the contents of the shadow, the object
(victim) is almost always of the same sex as the subject (projector). Jung
indicates that the first stage of personal growth is the recognition of
projections and their subsequent withdrawal.

> During the process of treatment the dialectical discussion leads logically
> to a meeting between the patient and his shadow, that dark half of the
> psyche which we invariably get rid of by means of projection: either by
> burdening our neighbors – in a wider or narrower sense – with all the
> faults which we obviously have ourselves, or by casting our sins upon a
> divine mediator with the aid of *contritio* or the milder *attritio*.
>
> (Jung, 1953/1968, para. 36)

Having recognized the reality of the shadow, the way opens for the
confrontation of the anima/us.

The anima

Directly behind the shadow and often intimately connected to it, lies the
anima or animus, the contrasexual archetype. Once the shadow has
been encountered, and its contents integrated, the contrasexual archetype
first presents itself as an autonomous complex, then as the bridge to
the collective unconscious. She may be the controlling force behind the
shadow, or shadow possessed.

> [The animus and anima] ... evidently live and function in the deeper
> layers of the unconscious, especially in that phylogenetic substratum
> which I have called the collective unconscious. This localization explains
> a good deal of their strangeness: they bring into our ephemeral conscious
> an unknown psychic life belonging to a remote past. It is the mind of our
> unknown ancestors, their way of thinking, their way of experiencing life
> and the world, gods and men.
>
> (Jung, 1959/1968a, para. 518)

In the unawakened, or relatively unconscious psyche, the anima is an
unknown quantity showing itself in dreams and the projection of unrealistic
idealizations and fears upon members of the opposite sex. It is, in most
people, completely unconscious and is not confronted by consciousness
until the shadow has been confronted and acknowledged. Like the shadow,

the anima or animus is the source of projections, but its projections are usually not on members of the same sex, and are much harder to recognize as projections than are the projections of the shadow.

> The anima is a factor of utmost importance in the psychology of a man wherever emotions and affects are at work. She intensifies, exaggerates, falsifies, and mythologizes all emotional relations with his work and with other people of both sexes. The resultant fantasies and entanglements are all her doing. When the anima is strongly constellated, she softens the man's character and makes him touchy, irritable, moody, jealous, vain, and unadjusted. He is then in a state of "discontent" and spreads discontent all around him.
>
> (Ibid., para. 144)

Von Franz calls her the "fate-spinning core of the unconscious psyche" and relates her to the Indian goddess Maya, who dances and spins the world of illusion – *samsara* – into existence (1980/1988, p. 123). Encountered as an autonomous complex, the anima/us is often a frightening, devouring, overpowering element of psychic life. It represents that beyond oneself which may provide perfect nurturance or absolute oblivion.

> The East calls it the "spinning woman" – Maya, who creates illusion by her dancing ... the enveloping, embracing and devouring element points unmistakably to the mother, that is to the son's relation to the real mother, to her imago, and to the woman who is to become a mother for him. His Eros is passive like a child's, he hopes to be caught, sucked in, enveloped, and devoured. He seeks, as it were, the protecting, nourishing, charmed circle of the mother, the condition of the infant released from every care, in which the outside world bends over him and even forces happiness upon him.
>
> (Jung, 1959/1968b, para. 20)

For a man, the anima is rooted in the mother archetype, which is to say the organizing factor of all things feminine from the devouring mother to the Virgin Mary. All of his understandings of things feminine are rooted here; out of the unconscious womb is woven the web of illusion that for him becomes the world. From her, his world derives a connectivity and emotionality that is expressed in her erotic capacities (ibid., para. 20 ff.).

Similarly, the animus in the female is rooted in the father archetype which is again the organizing principle of all things masculine. From him flows the logos, the faculty of separation and discrimination, the need to discuss and argue. Also from him comes her ability to seek new artistic and spiritual goals (ibid., para. 20 ff.).

> Turned towards the world, the anima is fickle, capricious, moody, uncontrolled and emotional, sometimes gifted with daemonic intuitions,

ruthless, malicious, untruthful, bitchy, double-faced, and mystical. The animus is obstinate, harping on principles, laying down the law, dogmatic, world-reforming, theoretic, word-mongering, argumentative, and domineering. Both alike have bad taste: the anima surrounds herself with inferior people, and the animus lets himself be taken in by second rate thinking.

(Ibid., para. 124)

All of a man's associations and preferences for women, beginning with his mother and continuing onward, are determined for men by the anima. Similar relations are determined for women, from the father onward, by the constellation of the animus. They are archetypal male and archetypal female within the psyche of their contrasexual host.

Von Franz notes that

the animus is a rejuvenated form of the father-image. As "father" he represents a traditional spirit which expresses itself in "sacred convictions" that the woman herself has never really thought through. The animus as divine *puer aeternus*, on the other hand appears as a creative spirit who can inspire a woman to undertake her own spiritual achievements. This spirit is a spirit of love, that is, love of her own living inner mystery, which comes into realization in the Eros between man and woman.

(von Franz, 1980/1988, p. 145)

As one learns to cooperate with the movements of the unconscious and begins to recollect the projections of anima/us, real growth towards personness begins.

This, of course, never means full integration of the anima/us, since they are archetypes and can never become fully conscious. Further, as personifications of the unconscious, they represent the limitless expanse of the unconscious realm as Jung understood it. As the anima/us is brought into a cooperative relationship with the ego, in bringing unconscious contents to consciousness, the process of individuation continues and accelerates.

Through [the transformation of the anima from an autonomous complex to a bridge between the ego and the collective unconscious:] ... the anima forfeits the daemonic power of an autonomous complex; she can no longer exercise the power of possession, since she is depotentiated. She is no longer the guardian of treasures unknown; no longer Kundry, daemonic Messenger of the Grail, half divine and half animal; no longer is the soul to be called "Mistress," but a psychological function of an intuitive nature, akin to what the primitives mean when they say "He has gone into the forest to talk with the spirits" or "My snake spoke with me" or in the mythological language of infancy, "A little bird told me."

(Jung, 1953/1966, para. 374)

The self

From his observations of the recurring patterns of myth, religion and personal symbols, Jung came to identify certain patterns as referring to a central image or dominating archetype from which all others within the psyche took their meaning. The evidence of this consistent tendency was the mandala.

> [M]andala means "circle." There are innumerable variants on this motif ... but they are all based on the squaring of the circle. Their basic motif is the premonition of a center of the personality, a kind of central point within the psyche, to which everything is related, by which everything is arranged, and which is itself a source of energy. The energy of this central point is manifested in the almost uncontrollable urge and compulsion to become what one is, just as every organism is driven to assume the form that is characteristic of its nature, no matter what the circumstances.
>
> (Jung, 1959/1968a, para. 634)

Jung characterized the archetype of the self as a God image; deep in the center of every psyche, there is an image of perfect balance, perfect wholeness towards which psychic life naturally strives. This image, the self, is what is most often reflected when people refer to a God (1958/1969, para. 231).

> The content of all such symbolic products is the idea of an overpowering, all-embracing, complete or perfect being, represented by either a man of heroic proportions, or by an animal with magical attributes, or by a magical vessel or some other "treasure hard to attain," such as a jewel, ring, crown, or, geometrically, by a mandala. This archetypal idea is a reflection of the individual's wholeness, i.e. of the self, which is present within him as an unconscious image.
>
> (Jung, 1959/1968a, para. 417)

Again, Jung notes that the unconscious may have no limits that can be known and suggests that part of the sense of the numinous associated with the contents of the unconscious comes precisely from their seemingly limitless expanse: "[W]e should not be in the least surprised if the empirical manifestations of unconscious contents bear the marks of something illimitable, something not determined by space and time. This quality is ... alarming" (1953/1968, p. 247).

In his long experience with the human condition, Jung found that this archetype was not "only" a psychic construct, but represented both a reflection of something greater and a link to that realm of objective psyche that corresponded to it.

> An archetype – so far as we can establish it empirically – is an image. An image, as the very term denotes, is a picture of something. ... We

find numberless images of God, but we cannot produce the original. There is no doubt in my mind that there is an original behind our images, but it is inaccessible.

(Jung, 1958/1969, para. 1,589)

This image provides a central tendency that draws mankind into seeking something more than a biological existence. It presents, as an inwardly perceived and real need, the urge to spirituality: the sense that life must have some meaning beyond mere survival. Out of this primal direction arise all of the religions of the earth as an expression of an in-built need to fulfill the perfection reflected at the heart of his being.

Jung's definition makes the self first, the source of psychic activity. It also represents the totality of mental activity. Out of it, but continuing to participate in it, come the archetypes. During the first half of life, the self as center provides direction to the process of ego development. During the second half of life, the self orchestrates the absorption of the ego into its own sphere in self realization. The whole process moves from the self as an unconscious and helpless unity, through a dissociation in which the ego provides a field of conscious action, to a conscious reintegration of the archetypal elements of the original dissolution.

The idea of the self as archetype, the archetype of order, has been severely criticized by Fordham who indicates that much of Jung's logic in regard to its relation to the self as the whole psyche is contradictory. He resolves the problem by redefining the archetypes as deintegrates of the self and the self archetype as a deintegrate related to the archetype constellated as the central ego (1973/1980).

In these elements we find a series of subsystems and levels of integration capable of interrelation one with another and whose contents are modifiable one by another. It is in the context of the systemic interrelations of these parts that the archetypes as images and motifs are found.

Chapter 6

The archetypes and their images

Archetypal imagery, as already noted, finds its external referents in the common themes of myth, dream and folklore. Over and over, the same themes and images with minor variations appear in each individual, culture and race.

Jung indicates that as we observe the patterning of archetypal images in various media, we are watching the transformation of libido as it flows from one container to the next. Because libido interacts with the world and psyche in a characteristic manner, the patterns that give it expression are likewise universal.

> The various meanings of the tree – sun, tree of paradise, mother, phallus – are explained by the fact that it is a libido symbol and not an allegory of this or that concrete object. Thus, a phallic object does not denote a sexual organ, but the libido, and however clearly it appears as such, it does not mean itself but is always a symbol of the libido. . . . The sole reality is the libido, whose nature we can only experience through its effect on us. Thus, it is not the real mother who is symbolized, but the libido of the son, whose object was once the mother . . . we always forget that it is the unconscious creative force which wraps itself in images. When, therefore, we read: "His mother was a wicked witch," we must translate it as: the son is unable to detach his libido from the mother-imago, he suffers from resistances because he is tied to his mother.
>
> (Jung, 1956/1967, p. 329)

However expressed, archetypal themes represent the typical patterns of the flow of energy as it moves from one level of the psyche to another. Whether the object is ego, anima/us, shadow or self, the theme is a representation of the flow of energy in the drama of individuation. Archetypal themes most clearly appear in fairy tales, myths, dreams and in the waking dreams of psychotics.

According to von Franz, fairy tales focus on *that part of the archetype of the Self which is the model of the ego complex and its general structure*

(1980b, p. 16). They have to do with the patterns of growth and compensation in the development of healthy relations between the ego and other complexes; they are tales of the experience of individuation. While it is tempting to identify the main characters with Jungian structural archetypes, von Franz warns that the relations change from tale to tale and that each must be allowed to interpret itself without formulaic preconceptions:

> Different fairy tales give different average pictures of different phases of this experience. They sometimes dwell more on the beginning stages, which deal with the experience of the shadow and give only a short sketch of what comes later. Other tales emphasize the experience of animus and anima and of the father and mother images behind them and gloss over the preceding shadow problem and what follows. Others emphasize the motif of the inaccessible or unobtainable treasure and the central experiences. There is no difference of value between these tales, because in the archetypal world there are no gradations of value for the reason that every archetype is in its essence only one aspect of the collective unconscious as well as always representing also the whole collective unconscious.
>
> (von Franz, 1970, p. 2)

One of the most popular sources of archetypal material is mythology, with special reference to Greek mythology. Here the archetypes are set forth as the gods, each with its peculiar tradition, realm and characteristics. But unlike the fairy tales, whose psychological elements appear in bare-bones form, the myths characterize the archetypes in the forms appropriate to a specific group, they carry a national character. Among other things, myths carry poetic and ritualistic accretions imposed upon them by the keepers of the tradition under examination (ibid., p. 17).

Myth is always deeply intertwined with the cultural expressions of specific peoples. For this reason it tends to express the generalities of human existence from the perspective of specific cultural contexts. Von Franz gives the example of the story of Ulysses. On the one hand he represents the "essence of the Hermetic–Mercurial" figure in Greek culture and so can be compared with other, similar trickster figures. On the other hand, he is very Greek and thus limited in many ways to the specific manifestation of the archetype in that culture (ibid., p. 18).

In general, one may view myths and fairy tales as the average representation of the patterns of psychic life common to humankind. Both reflect the patterns of energy flow in the psyche.

When, in common parlance, people discuss archetypes, they typically have in mind a particular set of symbols that gives expression to the more fundamental archetype. The archetype, of course, is by definition irrepresentable. As one of the dominants of the collective unconscious it cannot become conscious. It may, however, be reflected in consciousness by a symbol (Jung, 1959/1968a). Because of this common error, we must look at the difference between archetypes, complexes and symbols in somewhat more detail.

ARCHETYPE, COMPLEX AND SYMBOL

From the biological pole, as we have already noted in Part I, the archetype consists of a combination of innate elements related to the possibility of perception in a specific context, which may be compared to the perceptual half of the ethologists' Innate Releasing Mechanism (IRM). In the process of animal imprinting the organism bonds to the specific image determined by the IRM, just as the human infant bonds to its mother, father and other objects to create the parental imagos and root experiences – the primordial images. The images are the roots of the psychological complex combining multisensory perceptions into a feeling-toned image that will affect the individual's perception of himself, his parents and all others throughout life. This archetypal combination provides the active root for the development of the complexes.

As these core complexes are exposed to the data of ongoing existence, they collect about themselves the personal experiences which most appropriately correspond to the root image. On some levels, different complexes interact by attracting similar contents to produce multileveled complexes of complexes. On other levels, the archetypal core remains relatively pure. In all, the underlying affective tone provided by the archetypal core and its early experience with fulfillment or frustration defines the character of the complex as it contributes to the balance of the psyche on the road to individuation (Fordham, 1957; Gordon, 1987; Jung 1960/1969, 1959/1968a; Jacobi, 1974). The archetypes themselves are expressed only through the complexes. The complexes in turn communicate their archetypal burden to the world of consciousness through symbols.

A symbol, according to Jung, is much more than a token or sign. In standard usage, a symbol may stand as a simple mark or token that tells one something about its referent. It is often man-made, or consciously chosen. Where the word symbol is used in its traditional sense, the referent is wholly known or knowable, but not necessarily through the sign or symbol. In Jungian parlance, however, a symbol is the best possible representation of a wholly unknown or unknowable referent. It more often than not provides a new perspective from which opposing perceptions can be integrated and is not a product of the conscious mind.

The most frequent source of symbols is the emergence of unconscious contents into the level of consciousness. Contents emerging from the unconscious usually have a specific role in the balance of the psyche. More often than not, they serve the purpose of bringing the psyche into equilibrium or leading the individual to a new level of functioning.

Jung explained that because the contents of the collective unconscious were *concidentia oppositorum*, or unions of opposites, they could not enter consciousness unmodified. These contents were blocked from consciousness because one of the defining properties of consciousness is the discrimination of opposites. Any time an unconscious content presents itself to consciousness, the conscious function can only perceive one side of the issue while repressing the other.

This principle is readily seen in the classic field-ground illusion. In one common manifestation a figure alternates between a beautiful young woman and an old hag. In another, the figure shifts between a glass and two faces. The simultaneous perception of both images is said to be impossible.

Since the arising content bears fresh energy from the unconscious, it drives the ego first to acknowledge one of its poles, then, through the principle of complementarity, the system is driven to recognize the opposite pole. This enantiodromia[1] results in the ego's final stagnation in its inability to define the content. In stagnation the ego weakens and recedes to the point where a symbol expressing the synthesis of the two opposites can arise in consciousness. If the ego is resilient enough it will gradually integrate the symbol on a new level and be drawn to the next higher level of function. If it is weak, it will reduce the symbol to one or another pole and lose the opportunity to grow towards individuation (Jung, 1971).

The character of the symbol depends upon the relationship between the complex that gives it birth and the conscious economy. If the complex is active at or near the level of the personal unconscious, there is a great deal of probability that the symbol will be clothed in the guise of a familiar person. A father-complex might appear as the actual father, the school principal, a local policeman, or another known authority figure who closely fits the average feeling tone of the complex. If, however, the complex has been repressed, or has never yet come near conscious realization, it is likely to appear as a god, an animal or a monster. This is in accordance with the rule that the further from consciousness a content derives its meaning, the less human and the more numinous it becomes (Jung, 1956/1967, 1959/1968a, 1971).

Jung's perspective on the nature of symbols holds them protean, and of limitless depth.

They are genuine symbols precisely because they are ambiguous, full of half glimpsed meanings, and in the last resort inexhaustible. The ground principles, the αρχαι, of the unconscious are indescribable because of their wealth of reference, although in themselves recognizable . . . what we can above all establish as the one thing consistent with their nature is their manifold meaning, their almost limitless wealth of reference, which makes any unilateral formulation impossible.

(Jung, 1959/1968a, para. 80)

THE ARCHETYPES AND THEIR RELATIONS

The list of archetypes is extensive, but also deceptive. What often passes for a list of archetypes is really a list of the typical symbols by which the archetypes, in their most familiar forms, enter consciousness. Often, as in the case of the phallic images, they are symbols of the libido. Others, especially those following maternal and watery themes, are symbols of the collective unconscious. But all of these rules can only be applied within an affective context giving them this or that specific meaning.

Jung, in the *Collected Works*, lists many such archetypal themes including: bird/spirit, boy, butterfly/resurrection, cave, child, city, conjunctio, crowds, crucifixion, daughter, demiurge, devil, dioscuri, divine child, divine harlot, divine son, dragon, family, father, fire, flowers, foot, giant, god and goddess, goddess, gods, guard, hand, healing serpent, jesters, king and queen, kore, lingam, lover in remote land, magic demon, mana personality, marriage, marrying the city, marrying the land, mistletoe, mouth, others, phallus, powerful animals, puer, quaternity, sacrifice, separation, shadow, speech, sphere, square, sun, tree, tree of death, tree of life, tree and snake, trickster/ mercurius, twins, vulva, water, women, wood, worm, yoni, syzygy. In turn, these are represented by further multiplying and overlapping symbols (1956/1967, 1959/1968a, 1959/1968b).

We note once again, that with the exception of the self as it appears in mandala form, archetypal symbols tend not to appear as isolated forms, but in multi-layered contexts. There is an immediate emotional context, the feeling tone and affect image, a general psychic context that describes the unconscious situation and a conscious context that provides the material for projection and dream imagery. We should also recall that the links between specific images are only determined by their shared affective tone.

The gods as psychic dominants and response systems

Progoff divides the archetypes into dynatypes, or "enacting images," that pattern motivational structures and personalities, and cognitypes, or "formative images," that structure perception and intellect in a more general manner. Of the dynatypes he says:

> The quest for life is the starting point and the original source of energy in the organism. . . . It is life moving ever towards its own continuation, altering its forms, but ever extending itself. The patterns that provide the forms and directions for this movement of life are derived from the organic psyche, for the organic psyche acts as the organ of meaning and of protoplasmic guidance toward survival in the human species. It draws the life process forward with imagery of many kinds, but the most fundamental of these images are the dynatypes. . . .
>
> (Progoff, 1959, p. 238)

Here the protoplasmic image, or dynatype, is an "encompassing image" holding within itself the goal, the necessary energy to reach the goal, the outer stimuli upon which the end depends and the pattern of behavior needed to reach the end. In man, the protoplasmic image as revealed in the dynatype takes the form of a stream of images which may or may not be appreciated on a conscious level, but that are often available through dreams. These images represent both the direction in which the individual potential is unfolding and how that potential may be realized (ibid., p. 160).

The dynatypes provide "patterns of behavior for specific types of individual development." They reflect the nature of the whole, the quality of character towards which the individual is moving. They enfold the specific weighting of dynamic principles that define each individual as to style and potential. Each person embodies a characteristic dynatype which fulfills some variant of a limited number of basic types like the adventurer, the prophet, the leader, the seer, the teacher and the seeker after truth (ibid., pp. 184–6).

The cognitypes are the more familiar archetypal categories that allow us to apprehend reality. They are the "basic forms of thought, the images within the structure of the organic psyche which set both the limits and the possibilities for man's knowledge" (ibid., pp. 186–8).

In order to rightly understand the archetypes, it is necessary to see that they do not exist as separate entities. They are part of a continuum, embedded in a matrix, part of the fabric of the protoplasmic image, nodes in the collective unconscious. As such, each archetype bears a special relation to the others around it. It might be useful to envision this relation in terms of each archetype occupying or having its own place (Jacobi, 1974; Progoff, 1959; Hillman, 1975).

Von Franz observes that the archetypes are interconnected in a continuous field:

> The idea of a fieldlike arrangement of the archetypes, or the collective unconscious . . . derives from the fact that the archetypes exist in a state of mutual contamination; they overlap in meaning. . . .
>
> [The archetypes] . . . are contained in a field of inner qualitative nuances. This field may be termed a manifold of psychic contents, whose relations are defined by meaning.
>
> . . . every archetype forms the *virtual center of a field like realm of representational contents* definable strictly in relative terms, a region overlapping other realms.
>
> (von Franz, 1974, pp. 144–7)

In accordance with this view, she notes repeatedly that the field of influence of a specific archetype must be differentiated, not simply by logical analysis, but by its own characteristic feeling tone (1972/1986, 1974).

For Jung, the archetypes appear as part of the unfolding of the plan of individuation for each individual, in the patterns of canalization of libido; for Progoff, they appear as an expression of the unfolding protoplasmic image; and for both Jung and von Franz there exist definable relations between the archetypes.

Abstracting from the primary view that the archetypes represent the patterns of energy exchange within the psyche, we may see different archetypes as representing different perspectives on the journey itself. One such perspective, embodied in Progoff's dynatype, may reflect the individual goal – the full expression of the potential held within the psyche. This would be equivalent to the archetype of the self in its teleological aspect.[2] Another may represent the current condition of the individual as a typical stage in the journey, expressing either the ego state or the current condition of the self.[3]

Pattern 1: The archetypal journey

The basic pattern of individuation[4] is provided in the Hero's Journey. Leo Frobenius first described it as the journey of the Solar Hero. Later, Jung, Campbell, Kerenyi and others saw the same pattern as it reappeared in dreams, myth and fairy tales as the Hero's Journey, the nekiya,[5] the monomyth and the path of individuation. Jung identified the journey with the introversion and reemergence of libido and saw the pattern as recurring many times through the life of an individual (Jung, 1956/1967, 1959/1968a; Campbell, 1949/1972, 1972/1988; Jung and Kerenyi, 1949/1973; Pearson, 1986/1989; Larsen, 1990).

Jung presents Frobenius's pattern as follows:

A hero is devoured by a water monster in the west (devouring). The animal travels with him to the east (sea journey). Meanwhile, the hero lights a fire in the belly of the monster (fire-lighting), and feeling hungry, cuts himself a piece of the heart (cutting off of heart). Soon afterwards he notices that the fish has glided on to dry land (landing); he immediately begins to cut open the animal from within (opening); then he slips out (slipping out). It was so hot in the fish's belly that all his hair has fallen out (heat and hair). The hero may at the same time free all those who were previously devoured by the monster, and who now slip out too.

(Jung, 1956/1967, para. 310)

The pattern itself can be used to represent the entire path of individuation or a current portion of it. In general, when it represents the life as a whole, the end result is the realization of the teleological self through fulfillment of the growth tasks encountered on the journey. When it represents a segment of the path, the goal is usually the realization in consciousness of a previously unknown content of the unconscious, or a reorganization of the psyche in accordance with the course of the greater journey.

Regression carried to its logical conclusion means a linking back with the world of natural instincts, which in its formal or ideal aspect is a kind of *prima materia*. If this prima materia can be assimilated by the conscious mind it will bring about a reactivation and reorganization of its contents. But if the conscious mind proves incapable of assimilating the new contents pouring in from the unconscious, then a dangerous situation arises in which they keep their original, chaotic and archaic form and consequently disrupt the unity of consciousness.

(Ibid., para. 631)

The Hero's Journey follows point for point Jung's understanding of the cycle of libido. Over time, the symbols that vivify consciousness stagnate or otherwise become depotentiated. In other circumstances, the ego function is weakened, or intentionally brought to a level of lowered intensity. It must then turn inward and descend to its sources in the depths of the psyche for renewal and re-creation.

When the libido leaves the bright upper world, whether from choice, or from inertia, or from fate, it sinks back into its own depths, into the source from which it originally flowed, and returns to the point of cleavage, the navel, where it first entered the body. The point of cleavage is called the mother, because from her the current of life reached us. Whenever some great work is to be accomplished, before which a man recoils, doubtful of his strength, his libido streams back to the fountainhead – and this is the dangerous moment when the issue hangs between annihilation and new life. For if the libido gets stuck in the wonderland of this inner world, then for the upper world man is nothing but a shadow, he is already moribund or at least seriously ill. But if the libido manages to tear itself loose and force its way up again, something like a miracle happens: the journey to the underworld was a plunge into the fountain of youth, and the libido, apparently dead, wakes to renewed fruitfulness.

(Ibid., para. 449)

This cycle of energic transformation follows a predictable sequence within which the renewed libido is often symbolized as a treasure, or a maiden who must be redeemed and whose redemption gives the hero the right to inherit the kingdom. Trials and tests assault the hero throughout the adventure.

Jung notes that the return to the womb calls upon the most primitive forms of libidinal energy. It is essentially a nutritive and reconstitutive regression. Because, however, the adult is a sexual being, the descent becomes colored by his sexual nature. The sexual coloration then arouses the paternal prohibitions against incest and the fear that they evoke in the child. These fears are represented in the heroic sequence as the Dragon or guardian giant who must be overcome.

[T]hese introversions and regressions only occur at moments when a new orientation and a new adaptation are necessary, the constellated archetype is always the primordial image of the need of the moment. ... If the libido connects with the unconscious, it is as though it were connecting with the mother, and this raises the incest taboo. But as the unconscious is infinitely greater than the mother and is only symbolized by her, the fear of incest must be conquered if one is to gain possession of those "saving" contents – the treasure hard to attain. Since the son is not conscious of his incest tendency, it is projected on the mother or her symbol. But the symbol of the mother is not the mother herself, so in reality there is not the slightest possibility of incest, and the taboo can be ruled out as a reason for resistance.

(Ibid., para. 450)

Jung's version of the myth differs only slightly from Frobenius's:

This is the almost worldwide myth of the typical deed of the hero. He journeys by ship, fights the sea monster, is swallowed, struggles against being bitten and crushed to death (kicking or stamping motif), and having arrived inside the "whale-dragon," seeks the vital organ, which he proceeds to cut off or otherwise destroy. Often the monster is killed by the hero lighting a fire inside him – that is to say, in the very womb of death he secretly creates life, the rising sun. Thus the fish dies and drifts to land, where with the help of a bird, the hero once more sees the light of day.

(Ibid., para. 538)

One version of the myth appears in alchemy as the *conjunctio*, or royal wedding. In typical Jungian fashion, the *conjunctio* consists of four basic steps. In the first, the old King, enfeebled with age, is found dying. In the second he is approached and devoured by the body of his mother, or he drowns in a mystical bath with the Queen. In the third stage the Queen/mother becomes pregnant or lies in a sick bed. In the final stage the Queen/mother gives birth to the *Filius regius*, the King reborn as his own son. These symbolic images corresponded to a well-defined process of introversion of libido, Jung's process of psychic renewal (1963/1970).[6]

Whenever the conscious system becomes ego-bound with a feeble and inflexible dominant (the old King), the self begins a compensatory operation. This operation may start with either an ascent of unconscious contents that overwhelm the ego, or a relatively voluntary descent of the ego into the unconscious (the bath and swallowing). In the course of this descent, the ego is first dissolved (pregnancy and sickness), and then re-formed on a higher level. Finally, the new conscious dominant emerges as the reborn or transformed ego, now somewhat better equipped to express the needs of the self (the emergence of the *filius regius*) (ibid.).

Campbell briefly describes the journey as having three distinct stages: separation, initiation and return. His classic formulation of the journey is as follows:

> A hero ventures forth from the world of common day into a region of supernatural wonder: fabulous forces are there encountered and a decisive victory is won: the hero comes back from his mysterious adventure with the power to bestow boons on his fellow men.
>
> (Campbell, 1949/1972, p. 30)

Like Jung, he provided a psychological context for its interpretation:

> [T]he usual pattern is, first a break away or a departure from the local social order and context; next, a long, deep retreat inward and backward, as it were in time, and inward, deep into the psyche; a chaotic series of encounters there, darkly terrifying experiences, and presently (if the victim is fortunate) encounters of a centering kind, fulfilling, harmonizing, giving new courage; and then finally, in such fortunate cases, a return journey of rebirth to life.
>
> (Campbell, 1972/1988, p. 208)

Barbara Stevens Sullivan (1987) reports that the Hero's Journey is the archetypal root of the therapeutic experience. She indicates that the pattern reappears in every culture and presents a significant variant of it in her review of Sylvia Brinton Perera's *Descent to the Goddess* (1981).

Standing out from the typical versions of the solar myth, Perera presents the mythic Journey from the perspective of the ancient Sumerian myth of Inanna, and holds that it requires not only a descent to the preverbal depths of the unconscious but a total surrender to the Terrible Mother.[7] Denying the intrinsic value of the images of the treasure and the redemption of the heroine that appear in other formulations, she interprets the journey in terms of a surrender to the inchoate depths of the Terrible Mother for restructuring in terms of the world of the dark mother (1981).

Jung cites the myths of Moses and Khidr, Jonah and the whale, Oedipus, Siegfried, Heracles, Osiris, Christ and Mithras as typical of the genre. In each case he points to the essential unity of the phenomenon.

> The Journey of Moses with his servant Joshua is a life-journey (it lasted eighty years). They grow old together and lose the life-force, i.e., the fish, which "in wondrous wise took its way to the sea" (setting of the sun). When the two notice their loss, they discover at the place where the source of life is found (where the dead fish revived and sprang into the sea) Khidr wrapped in his mantle, sitting on the ground. In another version, he was sitting on an island in the midst of the sea, "in the wettest place on earth," which means that he had just been born from the maternal depths. Where the fish vanished, Khidr, the verdant one,

was born as a "son of the watery deep," his head veiled, proclaiming divine wisdom. . . .

. . . we may compare Khidr and Elias (or Moses and his servant Joshua) with Gilgamesh and his brother Eabani (Enkidu). Gilgamesh wanders through the world, driven by fear and longing, to find immortality. His journey takes him across the sea to the wise Utnapishtim (Noah), who knows how to cross the waters of death. There Gilgamesh has to dive down to the bottom of the sea for the magical herb that is to lead him back to the land of men. On the return journey he is accompanied by an immortal mariner, who, banished by the curse of Utnapishtim, has been forbidden to return to the land of the blessed. But when Gilgamesh arrives home, a serpent steals the magic herb from him (i.e., the fish slips back into the sea). Because of the loss of the magic herb, Gilgamesh's journey has been in vain; instead he comes back in the company of an immortal.

(Jung, 1956/1967, paras. 291–3)

One of Jung's important conclusions concerning the surface structure of the myth was the realization that it was subject to various modifications and transformations.[8] Thus, the exact number of parts was far less important than their relation one to another and the fact that certain specific archetypal configurations consistently appear.

[N]o part of the hero myth is single in meaning, . . . all the figures are interchangeable. The only certain and reliable thing is that the myth exists and shows unmistakable analogies with other myths . . . investigation of the products of the unconscious yields recognizable traces of archetypal structures which coincide with the myth-motifs, among them certain types which deserve the name of dominants. These are archetypes like the anima, animus, wise old man, witch, shadow, earth-mother, etc., and the organizing dominants, the self, the circle and the quaternity, i.e., the four functions or aspects of the self or of consciousness.

(Ibid., para. 611)

Following this logic, Carol Pearson has reinterpreted the monomyth in terms of a sequence of archetypes through which all of us pass as we live out the Hero's Journey:

It begins with the complete trust of the Innocent, moves on to the longing for safety of the Orphan, the self-sacrifice of the Martyr, the exploring of the Wanderer, the competition and triumph of the Warrior and then the authenticity and wholeness of the Magician.

(Pearson, 1986/1989, p. xxvi)

Pearson characterizes the archetypes noted in the following terms:

The Innocent lives in the prefallen state of grace; the Orphan confronts the reality of the Fall. . . . The Wanderer begins the task of finding one's self apart from others; the Warrior learns to fight to defend oneself and to change the world in one's own image; and the Martyr learns to give, to commit, and to sacrifice for others.

... After learning to change one's environment by great discipline, will, and struggle, the Magician learns to move with the energy of the universe. ... Having learned to trust the self, the Magician comes full circle and like the innocent, finds that it is safe to trust.

(Ibid., pp. 4–5)

Pearson characterizes her sequence as expressing the archetypes that dominate consciousness through the quest. Each is simultaneously a stage in the journey and a perspective from which the journey may be experienced. She also points out that although the stages are the same, women tend to take more time with those roles that emphasize relatedness – Martyr and Magician, while men take longer with those emphasizing isolation – Wanderer and Warrior. Thus, she emphasizes the difference between the genders as they are reflected in subjective preferences within an essentially similar structure.

The typical male journey tends to follow the sequence, Orphan, Warrior, Wanderer, Martyr, Magician; and the typical female pattern, Orphan, Martyr, Wanderer, Warrior, Magician. Finding that it is not uncommon for the warrior and martyr motifs to coincide, Pearson (ibid., p. 8) describes the general pattern of the journey:

	Martyr		
Orphan		Wanderer	Magician
	Warrior		

This conceptualization matches Jung's analysis of the transformation of libido in the archetype of the divine child. He indicates that both the archetypal "child" and the young hero share the characteristics of extraordinary birth, abandonment and persecution. Both also look forward to a future fulfillment of the promise of self realization. In fact, says Jung, identification with the child archetype implies that the individual will likewise identify sooner or later with the Hero. So, Pearson's Orphan is none other than the Child archetype and the Young Hero, holding out the promise of growth towards completion (Jung, 1959/1968a).

As the individual continues to mature into adulthood, the blossoming hero must early on encounter the anima/us, and claim its power for his or her own use. Once the anima has been encountered and assimilated, it ceases to be an unconscious compulsion, but begins to appear as an unconscious advisor, the "bridge to the collective unconscious" (Jung, 1953/1966).

Jung argues that with this transformation of the anima her libido now becomes the property of the ego. He supports the contention with the age-old belief that when a mana-person is killed, the power turns to the killer's benefit. Now, the ego, having absorbed the creative power of the anima, becomes itself the mana-personality. The ego may now manifest in the character of the "hero, chief, magician, medicine-man, saint, the ruler of men and spirits, the friend of God." In general, however, it will tend to appear as the Magician, the figure beyond opposites, before it recedes again into the collective, reappearing as the reborn ego (1953/1966, para. 377).

This sequence would seem to support Pearson's basic outline, as would the general pattern of the path itself. Paraphrasing Jung, we see it beginning in a normal condition. With the onset of stagnation, or crisis, the theme of the Orphan appears. This signals, by its weakness and vulnerability, the miraculous birth of the Child – the earnest of individuation. Inevitably, the birth of the Child is followed by the emergence of the Hero. The Hero may choose the Martyr's way of self sacrifice, like Jonah who threw himself into the sea and was swallowed by the fish, or he may take the Warrior's path and, like Siegfried, seek out and slay the Dragon in its den. In either case, having faced the fear of incest and dissolution, the Hero spends some time in wandering but finally returns home transformed and empowered (1956/1967).

Pearson also notes that her conception of the movement of the process of individuation is a three-dimensional spiral. Each cycle through the mythic journey leads the individual to a new journey begun on the next logical level. This recalls the ever-cycling progress of the alchemical quaternio expressed in the revolution of the mandala through analysis, abstraction and synthesis until the unconscious is made conscious and becomes a new content ready for analysis at the next level of operation (Jung, 1956/1967, 1959/1968b).

Jung also points to the path of the hero as a spiral way:

> The way to the goal seems chaotic and interminable at first, and only gradually do the signs increase that it is leading anywhere. The way is not straight but appears to go round in circles. More accurate knowledge has proved it to go in spirals: the dream-motifs always return after certain intervals to definite forms, whose characteristic it is to define a centre. And as a matter of fact the whole process revolves about a central point or some arrangement around a centre. . . .
>
> (Jung, 1953/1968, para. 34)

And, citing Plotinus, Jung quotes:

> Self-knowledge reveals the fact that the soul's natural movement is not in a straight line, unless indeed it have undergone some deviation. On the contrary, it circles around something interior, around a centre. Now the centre is that from which proceeds the circle, that is, the soul.
>
> (Jung, 1959/1968b, para. 342)

As Pearson's roles also appear as stages in the work, their formulation bears an archetypal similarity to Western occult systems like astrology and tarot cards, as well as Eastern symbol systems like the chakras of Kundalini Yoga. In each of these, the individual elements simultaneously represent stages in the evolution of the psyche, individual types of psychic function available to all humans, and also specific styles of mentation characteristic of specific individuals (Jung, 1959/1968a).

This first examination of archetypal patterning is rooted in the process of psychic rejuvenation. Its source is the descent of libido into the depths of the unconscious for revivification and reformulation. It is expressed universally as the Hero's Journey.

The Journey itself follows predictable stages. Beginning with a lowering of the threshold of consciousness there is a descent into childhood memories, dreams and archetypal material. The ego in this state reverts to earlier patterns or totally fragments. In the case of a positive journey, the ego finds renewal and redefinition in the archetypal contents of the collective unconscious, returning renewed and reshaped into the conscious realm. In less fortunate cases the ego fails to reformulate in an adequate fashion and psychosis results.

Externally, in myth, dream and fairy tale, the journey takes the form of descent, battle, obtaining the treasure and returning. In a variant suggested by Pearson, the journey involves the assumption of a sequence of characters: the orphan, the martyr, the warrior, the wanderer and the magician. The path is traveled through the living out of the character traits of each.

Although the classical application of the pattern of the descent of libido is to individual psyches, there may be reason to believe that a similar pattern applies in larger groups. In such cases, a group or national identity, suffering irremediable loss, might regress to an historically and socially earlier pattern in order to recreate its identity.

Pattern 2: The gods and personality

Mythic systems show a great deal of the overlap that is characteristic of the archetype. Just as the path can be broken into characteristic styles, so the styles can be personalized in terms of the gods. Wandering gods immediately bring to mind Dionysius and Hermes. The warriors in the Greek pantheon are surely Ares and Artemis, but Zeus and Poseidon also figure in here. Martyred gods include Dionysius and Demeter–Persephone. Orphaned gods include Hephaistos and Dionysius. Yet, a hard and fast one-to-one correspondence is almost impossible.

The gods, however, appear at a different logical level than the path; they are more primary elements of experience and must be treated as more fundamental. This is in part suggested by Julian Jaynes (1976). Jaynes found that the ancient Greeks immortalized by Homer almost never thought as we experience it. Thought was an external event; it came from without. If a thought came, it came as the voice of a god or goddess. If an emotion overcame one, he or she was literally *enthused*, possessed by the god. It is only in the very last stages of the epic that individuals began to be portrayed as thinking, responsible individuals.

> The characters in the *Iliad* do not sit down and think out what to do. They have no conscious minds such as we say we have, and certainly no introspection. . . . It is one god who makes Achilles promise not to go into battle, another who urges him to go, and another who then clothes him in a golden fire reaching up to heaven and screams through his throat across the bloodied trench at the Trojans. . . . In fact, the gods take the place of consciousness.
>
> (Jaynes, 1976, p. 72)

Long before Jaynes, Jung indicated that the primitive does not think, rather, thought happens to him. In a passage strongly reminiscent of Jaynes's thesis, but preceding it by nearly forty years, Jung notes that all thinking is rooted in archetypal predispositions dating from a time when

> consciousness did not think, but only perceived. "Thoughts" were the objects of inner perceptions, not thoughts at all, but sensed as external phenomena – seen or heard, so to speak. Thought was essentially revelation, not invented but forced upon us or bringing conviction through its immediacy and actuality.
>
> (Jung, 1959/1968a, para. 69)

Jung, of course, identifies the gods with the archetypes. The archetypes were understood also to be expressible as partial personalities, the dominants of the collective unconscious. Of the archetypes Jung says: "They are the ruling powers, the gods, the images of the dominant laws and principles and of typical, regularly occurring events in the soul's cycle of experience" (1953/1966, para. 151). As gods they were projected upon the outer world and spoke from tree and bush, idol and icon (1956/1967, para. 388).

We should also note that the path of individuation that Jung outlines is the path of self discovery which, among the ancients and many peoples today, is only held out to the extraordinarily gifted. Note how the path is clearly reflected in the esoteric systems of initiation. Tarot, astrology, Kundalini yoga and alchemy are all systems of initiation with an ultimate goal of what we now call individuation (1959/1968a).

In our time, however, what was once the special gift of the few enlightened ones has become the provenance of the many. In the West, thought is for the most part internalized. While the vast majority of individuals have little interest in individuation, its relative democratization is a striking part of the Western heritage.

That this represents a qualitative change in the Western psyche is suggested by Jung's visit to a temple while in India.

When we left the temple and were walking down a lingam lane, he suddenly said, "Do you see these stones? Do you know what they mean? I will tell you a great secret." I was astonished, for I thought that the phallic nature of these monuments was known to every child. But he whispered in my ear with the greatest seriousness, "These stones are a man's private parts." I had expected him to tell me that they signified the great god Shiva. I looked at him dumbfounded, but he only nodded self-importantly as if to say, "Yes, that is how it is. No doubt you in your European ignorance would never have thought so!"

(Jung, 1965, p. 278)

The esoteric wisdom of yesterday has become almost commonplace. The gods precede the path.

Von Franz details the evolution of the gods and of human consciousness in terms of the withdrawal of projected consciousness. In the ancient world the gods suffused all.

In the Greek world of antiquity, before the period of relatively reliable records, the original, mythical, psychic condition of archaic identity prevailed, as it did everywhere, a condition in which inner psychic facts were not differentiated from outer natural facts. The whole world was alive with demons and spirits, or, in other words, single components of the human psyche were for the most part unreflected and were seen out there in nature where the human being was confronted with them as parts of an objective "world."

(von Franz, 1980/1988, p. 36)

In the next stage the gods are no longer identical with the elements over which they rule. Zeus rules over the heavens, Poseidon rules over the seas, Demeter rules over the earth and Pluto over Hades and the souls of the dead. They are nonetheless projected images of psychic dominants. Individuals do not yet experience consciousness as we do, but thought comes upon them as the revelation of a god, emotions drive them as possession by the god. This is the stage of classical Greek mythology.

As time goes by, the people draw to themselves more and more of the perquisites of the gods, growing more and more conscious, more and more responsible. In the next phase the morality of the gods becomes questionable, are they good gods, or are they bad gods? Do they intend me good or evil? Light has begun to dawn. The possibility of contrasting values has arisen and with it the possibility of conscious choice. It is to people at this stage of psychic development that St. Paul directs his observation in I Corinthians 12: 1–3.

You know how, in the days when you were still pagan, you would be seized by some power which drove you to those dumb heathen gods. For this reason I must impress upon you that no one who says "A curse on Jesus!" can be speaking under the influence of the Spirit of God. And no one can say "Jesus is Lord!" except under the influence of the Holy Spirit.

(New English Bible, 1961/1970)

At last there comes a denial of the reality of the spirits, followed by the realization of their origin in the individual psyche (von Franz, 1980/1988; Jung, 1968).

Although we have been speaking of the gods up to this point as archetypes, we must again remember that the archetypes never reach consciousness until they have passed through a dual filter. First, they are enclothed with the data of experience as the root values of a complex. Then, they are presented to consciousness as a symbol which is the emergent property of the interaction of personal experience, cultural history and archetypal formalism.

When the gods do appear, they appear in culturally appropriate forms. These are determined by the manner in which the local culture has responded to the unfolding of archetypal intent in the individual and by the manner in which these dictates have been culturally expressed in the myths, rituals and customs that provide symbolic vehicles for their manifestation. So, the gods are universal in their presence, and the mythologems – the repeated story elements that accompany them – are repeated from culture to culture. The individual character of the gods, and the stories appropriate to them, vary from place to place. We also find that individual places are dedicated to specific gods around whose cult the local culture rotates. Individuals are likewise drawn to a specific god or goddess in accordance with the structure of their personality. Just as the archetypes overlap in meaning, so the gods, as their symbolic representatives, overlap in their attributes, powers and personalities. The gods are ubiquitous, their stories are universal, but their boundaries are fluid.

We again recall de Santilla and von Dechend:

Take the origin of music. Orpheus and his harrowing death may be a poetic creation born in more than one instance in diverse places. But when characters who do not play the lyre, but blow pipes get themselves flayed alive for various absurd reasons, and their identical end is rehearsed on several continents, then we feel we have got hold of something, for such stories cannot be linked by internal sequence. And when the Pied Piper turns up both in the medieval German myth of Hamelin and in Mexico long before Columbus, and is linked in both places with certain attributes like the color red, it can hardly be a coincidence.

(de Santillana and von Dechend, 1969, p. 7)

When we begin to look to the gods as expressions of archetypal dynamics, it is important to recognize that, as archetypal expressions, we can relate to them on several levels. The most common of these is metaphor.

An archetypal content expresses itself, first and foremost, in metaphors. If such a content should speak of the sun and identify it with the lion, the king, the hoard of gold guarded by the dragon, or the power that makes for the life and health of man, it is neither the one thing nor the other, but the unknown third thing that finds more or less adequate expression in all these similes, yet – to the perpetual vexation of the intellect – remains unknown and not to be fitted into a formula.

(Jung 1959/1968a, para. 267)

By using metaphor and simile we miss the errors of hubris that lead to possession and inflation. The archetypes, represented by the gods, can provide a sense of place and context for the vagaries of human existence and a rationale for the outworking of pathology where needed. These benefits, however, are more usually gleaned from metaphorical processes than from identification. In any event, the use of myth must steer between the Scylla of over-identification, on the one hand, and, on the other, the Charybdis of substituting an avowedly mythical diagnostic for one based in the myth of nineteenth-century empiricism (Jung 1959, 1968a; Hillman, 1975/1977; Miller, 1980).

Hillman suggests the following approach to the gods:

Mythical metaphors are not etiologies, causal explanations, or name tags. They are perspectives toward events which shift the experience of events; but they are not themselves events. They are likenesses to happenings, making them intelligible, but they do not themselves happen.

(Hillman, 1975, p. 101)

We have so far seen that, in general, the gods represent constellations of specific archetypal contents. In a very real sense we may characterize the gods as representing the kinds of selves that our cultural and physiological environment make available to us. They are for the most part fragmentary and partial personalities in need of other aspects before they can qualify as fully human. We have already cited Jung as indicating that the gods represent personified complexes.

The major exponents of the view that the gods have something to tell analytical psychologists have been James Hillman (1975/1977, 1980/1988) and the archetypal psychologists, and Jean Shinoda Bolen (1984, 1989/ 1990). Hillman has led the way in pointing out the value of the examination of the gods as representing a truly humanizing and ensouling perspective for psychotherapy and living.

In archetypal psychology Gods are imagined. They are approached through psychological methods of personifying, pathologizing, and psychologizing. They are formulated ambiguously, as metaphors for modes of experience and as numinous borderline persons. They are cosmic perspectives in which the soul participates. They are the lords of its realms of being, the patterns for its mimesis. The soul cannot be, except in one of their patterns. All psychic reality is governed by one or another archetypal fantasy, given sanction by a god, I cannot but be in them.

(Hillman, 1975/1977, pp. 169–70)

Hillman sees the archetypes as defining, ruling and organizing psychic experience. The gods are imagined, not as an exercise in idle fantasy, but in the recognition of the existence of archetypal dominants that preceded us and that make us human. The gods are not seen as another means of categorizing personality, but they are its source as well as the background against which life obtains meaning.

Gods are imagined as the formal intelligibility of the phenomenal world, allowing each thing to be discerned for its inherent intelligibility and for its specific place of belonging to this or that *kosmos* (ordered pattern or arrangement). The Gods are places, and myths make place for psychic events that in an only human world become pathological.

(Hillman, 1983/1988, p. 36)

In pathologizing, archetypal psychology sees the gods as providing a context for suffering in which every event is infused with the meaning shared by all of its archetypal variants.

The link between Gods and diseases is double: on the one hand, giving the dignity of archetypal significance and divine reflection to every symptom whatsoever, and on the other hand, suggesting that myth and its figures may be examined for patterns of pathology. Hillman has called this pathology in mythical figures the infirmitas of the archetype, by which is meant both the essential "infirmity" of all archetypal forms – that they are not perfect, not transcendent, not idealizations – and that they therefore provide "nursing" to human conditions; they are the embracing backgrounds within which our personal sufferings can find support and be cared for.

(Ibid., p. 38)

The archetypes may then provide a means of understanding the dynamics that motivate a person, a group or a culture. Each god has his or her pattern of behavior, emotion and pathology. The curse of the god and the god's blind spot are as important in understanding the pattern as the virtues he or she bestows.

Outside the realm of archetypal psychology, the gods are sometimes represented in terms of just that classificatory grid that Hillman eschews.

Dan McAdams at Loyola University in Chicago analyzed biographical narratives for evidence of archetypal or mythic influence. His data, derived from two-hour interviews in which subjects provided narratives of significant life-events, found that without any special awareness of mythology or the character of the gods, mythic themes tended to dominate the lives of the individuals interviewed.

The themes that emerged in any one subject were found to be consistent with the attributes of a given god or goddess as assessed by the researchers. In the narratives, the significant events were matched not so much to the pattern of the mythic events in the lives of the individual gods, but to specific traits which identified the gods on the level of theme and role (Goleman, 1981). According to McAdams's study, which treated the Greek gods as the archetypal exemplars for specific styles of life and work, the Greek gods were related subjectively to specific activities (see Table 6.1).

It is significant that Hades and Poseidon are missing, as are Artemis, Persephone and Hephaestus. These are missed all the more as the relative late-comers Dionysius and Prometheus are included. Nevertheless, the data is interesting, as even a cursory examination of the attributes leads one to easily characterize each row with a short summary:

Apollo: Messiah, the Son
Athena: Mediatrix, the Logos
Zeus: Source, the Father
Prometheus: the Advocate
Hermes: Opportunist, Freedom
Ares: Warrior, the Protector
Demeter: Giver, the Mother
Hera: Relation, the Spouse
Aphrodite: Sensualist, Attraction
Hestia: Doer, the Home
Dionysius: the Child

While it cannot be claimed that the above exercise was completed without some preparation, even the unprepared will see some validity in the attributions. The importance of the study is the empirical validation of the gods as representing affective categories. Within these archetypally based categories affinities appear between occupations and avocations which may not be otherwise related.

In the above example it is not difficult to identify the relations between the stated roles and their synthesis. The surprising thing is that these are the very associations that one would expect from an occult table of correspondences such as Crowley's 777 (Regardie, 1973/1988). This underlines Jung's perception of a tendency towards a hierarchical organization in the psyche that led many of the great occultists to attempt to create universal tables of correspondences. It also helps to explain the attempts by Lully,

Table 6.1 Some Greek Gods and their attributes[1]

Apollo	healer	prophet	artist	protector	organizer	legislator		
Athena	counselor	arbiter	therapist	teacher	guide	peacemaker	sage	celebrity
Prometheus	humanist	defender	revolutionary	evangelist				
Zeus	ruler	judge	conqueror	seducer	creator			
Hermes	swift traveler	explorer	adventurer	trickster	rabble-rouser		persuader	entrepreneur
Ares	warrior	fighter	soldier	policeman				
Demeter	caregiver	altruist	martyr					
Hera	loyal friend	spouse	helpmate	chum	confidante	sibling	assistant	
Aphrodite	lover	charmer	seducer					
Hestia	homemaker	domestic	ritualist					
Dionysius	escapist	pleasure-seeker	hedonist	player	epicure	child		

[1] After Goleman, 1988

Bruno and others to create memory systems based upon the affective patterns identified with the gods and planets. A mind immersed in the already familiar attributes of the gods would find such a powerful symbol set intuitively self-validating and filled with magical power (Jung, 1964/1970; Yates, 1966; Casey, 1974).

One of the very important recurring patterns in archetypal studies is, as we have noted, the spatial regularities of three-dimensional existence. We have seen that they may be correlated with the most basic properties of living systems, affective relations and the physical world.

Cornford (1991) has traced the central ideas of destiny and law as they appear in Greek religion and philosophy to spatial concepts relating to one's rightful place and the right to apportion that space. Associated with the directions are elements and with the elements Gods who originally personify and then rule over the elements. Built into the structure of myth, religion and thought, there seems to be an implicit spatial ordering whose presence is revealed in the octahedron, the quaternio and the square (Jung, 1959/1968b).

Hillman (1983/1988), Casey (1974), Brooke (1991) and Samuels (1989) all refer to an imaginal space: the *Mundus Imaginalis*. Here, the nodal points of the collective unconscious are ordered spatially in terms of the images that give them life. It exists no less as an interpersonal space as a subjective space. It is imagined as the net of meaning that allows interpersonal relations and structures personal experience. It is the ground of meaning and metaphor. It is this space which is reflected in the memory theaters of Renaissance thinkers.

A further evidence of the ubiquity of the spatial metaphor is the recurrence of the superior and inferior or inside/outside elements in social, psychological and even linguistic materials. Jung and Freud, of course, have conscious and unconscious, Chomsky has surface structure and deep structure, Marx has infrastructure and superstructure. It is ubiquitous.

One of the principal exponents of the archetypal patterning of personality has been Jean Shinoda Bolen. Her popular volumes on the relevance of mythic images to the structure and expression of personality have been widely received. Bolen, besides holding out the archetypes as reflected in the mythological gods as the determinants of personality, recasts Jungian theory to allow for several pure feminine types. These derive no benefit from the psychic balance allegedly afforded the female ego by the animus, despite the fact that a vital female element is provided to the male psyche by the presence of the anima. Interestingly, no such accommodation is made for the male psyche (1984/1985, 1989/1990).

One of the clues leading her to the determination of the existence of the pure female types was the existence of three virginal goddesses who never submit to sexual contact with males. These are Artemis, Athena and Hestia.

The virgin goddesses represent the independent self sufficient quality in women. Unlike the other Olympians, these three were not susceptible to falling in love. Emotional attachments did not divert them from what they considered important. They were not victimized and did not suffer. As archetypes they express the need in women for autonomy, and the capacity women have to focus their consciousness on what is personally meaningful. Artemis and Athena represent goal-directedness and logical thinking, which make them achievement oriented archetypes. Hestia is the archetype that focuses attention inward, to the spiritual center of a woman's personality. These three goddesses are feminine archetypes that actively seek their own goals. They expand our notion of feminine attributes to include competency and self sufficiency.

(Bolen, 1984/1985, p. 16)

It is especially when either Artemis or Athena is activated that a woman needs to be conscious of the possibility that traits of intelligence, goal-centeredness and competence are not the fruit of an internal male element upon which the woman must lean, but rather that they are expressions of the power of the feminine archetypes. Activation of the goddesses is often characterized by a sense of comfort in what might be perceived as the otherwise male world of ideas and action. On the contrary, she has observed that animus-related strivings in the world of men are characterized by a sense of strangeness and unfamiliarity.

One of Bolen's important contributions is an analysis of the patterns of response exhibited by each of the major gods and goddesses that she observes. This includes typical response patterns for each archetypal figure in childhood, adolescence, adulthood and old age as well as predictions of response styles in various basic life-situations and contexts. She also makes the important step of relating the gods to Jung's personality types (1984/1985, 1989/1990).

Bolen points out the important effect that family and culture have on the development of the individual. Children in every culture are born into a "Procrustean bed," but Bolen emphasizes that the patriarchal culture of the West has crippled many men and women psychologically.

Some men fit the Procrustean bed exactly, just as there are men for whom the stereotype (or the expectations from outside) and the archetype (or the innate patterns) match well. They find ease and pleasure at succeeding. However, conformity to the stereotype is often an agonizing process for a man whose archetypal patterns differ from "what he should be." He may appear to fit, but in truth he has managed at great cost to look the part, by cutting off important parts of himself. Or, he may have stretched one dimension of his personality to fit expectations but lacks depth and complexity, which often make his outer success inwardly meaningful.

(Bolen, 1989/1990, p. 4)

In the drama of life, Procrustes is played by the patriarchy which systematically favors certain personality types while inhibiting others. Moreover, according to Bolen's thesis, the patriarchy has also systematically victimized women and minorities as a function of the same pathology. The remedy to such culturally imposed "dis-membering" is the active cultivation of the virtues inherent in those gods or goddesses most lacking or repressed in our individual make-up. Initially, growth comes through resonance with the conscious style of one or another of the gods. This occurs as an "Aha!" experience, a moment of revelation when the archetypal core is constellated by the familiar pattern to which we can now provide a name. Afterwards it can come through the acknowledgment of particular deficits in our conscious make-up, and taking action to invoke the character of the necessary god or goddess.

Most of the basic characteristics of the gods are presented in tabular form at the end of Bolen's books. Table 6.2 reproduces some of her data.

After reviewing the catalog proposed by Bolen, several questions arise. How is it that the gods chosen are not those typically identified with the Greek pantheon as they appear either on Olympus or as reflected in the classical attributions of the zodiac? Although it may be true that the gods chosen are the specific forms that most closely represent the archetypal structure of the current American psyche, she nowhere explains her choice. Further, since she has gone so far towards systematizing the archetypes in terms of their relations to the typology of attitudes and functions it is surprising to find that she has paid no attention to their classical attributes with regard to the four alchemical elements and their relations to typology.

These are relatively minor points. The first may be the result of the fact that the entire scheme is rooted in the population of patients and their real problems rather than in the relatively more abstract realm of classical mythology. In this case the myths represent an ordering tool and need not be exhaustively classified in accordance with ancient formulae. This explanation would bring Bolen's work closer to the archetypal perspective of James Hillman than might otherwise be expected.

The second issue may also be explained by the same therapeutic emphasis. It also implies that Dr Bolen's sources were more classical and less occult or alchemical than is often the case in Jungian literature.

This second pattern of archetypal influence is the pattern of personality reflected in the gods as archetypes. These mold the character and general attitudes of individuals. Insofar, however, as they represent the ideal of a group, whether conscious or unconscious, they will also shape the values of that group. This pattern molds perspective and Weltanschauung.[9] It was at this level of archetypal activity that Jung observed the coming blood bath in Europe as the spirit of Wotan possessed the German populace (1964/ 1970). It is also at this level that groups are most powerfully influenced and directed (as will be seen in Part IV).

Table 6.2 Attributes of the Greek pantheon according to Bolen

God/ Goddess	Domain	Disposition	Functions	Deficit	Virtue
Zeus	Will and power	Extrovert	Superior: thinking Inferior: intuiting and sensing	Ruthlessness Immaturity Inflation	Generativity power Decision
Hera	Marriage	Extrovert	Superior: feeling Inferior: sensing	Jealousy Vindictive rage, Monogamy	Commitment Fidelity
Ares	War	Extrovert	Superior: feeling Inferior: sensing	Reactive Abuser Low self esteem	Integrates emotions Expressive
Aphrodite	Love and beauty	Extrovert	Superior: sensing	Promiscuity Lack of foresight	Enjoyment of pleasure and beauty, Sensual Creative
Hephaestus	Forge	Introvert	Superior: feeling Inferior: sensing	Inappropriate Low self esteem	Creativity Handy
Athena	Wisdom Crafts	Extrovert	Superior: thinking Inferior: sensing	Distance Lack empathy Crafty	Pragmatic Strategist Friend to men
Hermes	Messenger	Extrovert	Superior: intuiting Inferior: thinking	Impulsive Sociopath	Understanding communication Friendship
Hestia	Hearth and temple	Introvert	Superior: feeling Inferior: intuiting	Distance No persona	Solitude Deep meaning
Apollo	Sun	Extrovert	Superior: thinking Inferior: intuiting	Distance Arrogance Venom	Set and reach goals Appreciate clarity, form
Artemis	Moon and hunt	Extrovert	Superior: intuiting Inferior: feeling	Distance Ruthlessness Rage	Independence Autonomy Sisterhood
Poseidon	Emotion and instinct	Extrovert/ introvert	Superior: feeling	Emotional instability Low self esteem	Loyalty Access to feelings
Demeter	Grain	Extrovert	Superior: feeling	Depression Burnout Over-mother	Nurturant Generous
Hades	Soul and the unconscious	Introvert	Superior: sensing	Depression Low self esteem Destructive	Inner riches Detachment
Persephone	Kore Queen of Hades	Introvert	Superior: sensing	Depression Manipulation Withdrawal	Receptive Imaginative Psychic
Dionysius	Ecstasy and wine	Extrovert/ introvert	Superior: sensing	Distorted self perception Poor self esteem	Sensual Natural Passionate

To a large extent, when seen as personality factors, the archetypes determine the nature of the individuation process. They determine the specific goals during each segment of the journey and the character of the individual at the end of the process. They strongly impact upon which of Pearson's archetypal roles will begin the path and how they will progress through the sequence of tasks. Further, the exact means of fulfilling the task – attitude, spirit, demeanor, etc. – will likewise be determined by the particular archetypes constellated.

Pattern 3: Heavenly relations

Beyond the personality traits identified with individual gods, there are specific regions of overlap and relationship within the archetypal field. These give rise to special affinities between the gods that are sometimes expressed as common characteristics, sometimes in terms of special relationships and other times in terms of real confusion between the players. These commonalties are partly the expression of the mutual contamination that holds between the archetypes. On another level, however, they suggest a means of predicting and contextualizing the probable and actual directions of attitude shift in a given person or group.

Kerenyi noted that the narratives of the gods often include a childhood narrative as well as a set of stories appertaining to the mature god. In general, he found that, for the male gods especially, there were specific themes that seemed to appear in most of the childhood narratives. These themes included abandonment, emergence from water or near water, a cave, association with dolphins, and the performance of one or more mighty deeds. On the basis of this identity, he regarded the gods Zeus, Apollo, Hermes, Dionysius and others to have evolved out of a single "mythological primordial child, who originally comprised both begetter and begotten" (Jung and Kerenyi, 1949/1973, p. 105).

Recognizing here the same attributes that Jung identified as characteristic of the archetype of the divine child, we see in the archetypal narratives the general pattern of the beginning of self realization. Most importantly we have what Jung called the futurity of this aspect of the self emphasized in the undifferentiated individuality arising out of the womb of the unconscious (Jung and Kerenyi, 1949/1973; Jung, 1959/1968a).

This undifferentiated aspect of the child god suggests not only the primordial self, but also the root of identity between the mature gods in the self, which as archetypes must overlap and interpenetrate.

We know now that the prime element whose symbol – and nothing more than a symbol – is the sea has the peculiarity that floating in it and rising out of it mean the same thing. Both imply a state of being not yet separated from non-being, yet still being. The dolphin-riding boy of the coins – the first representation of the Primordial Child-god – is sometimes shown winged, sometimes holding a lyre, sometimes holding the club of Heracles. Accordingly he is to be viewed now as Eros, now as an Apollonian, now as a Hermetic or Herculean figure; we must take him, in fact as these divinities while they were in the womb of the universe, floating in their embryonic state, on the primal waters.

(Jung and Kerenyi, 1949/1973, p. 67)

Here we also see the unity of the collective unconscious as well as its vitality. Jung points to Proteus, the old man of the sea, as an image of the collective unconscious (1959/1968b). Proteus always tells the truth, but he must be held fast or else he will change shape and slip away.

Proteus . . . saw into the future and he spoke the truth. But, since he never spoke oracularly unless forced to do so, it was first necessary to catch hold of him – no simple matter, for Proteus could change shape at will and in order to escape from whoever held him would in succession turn himself into a lion, a dragon, a panther, into water, fire, a tree. . . . The important thing was not to be intimidated by these metamorphoses, for then Proteus would admit himself vanquished and talk.

(Hamlyn, 1959/1981, p. 147)

So it is with the archetypes and the collective unconscious. They readily shift form and slip away unless they are held to with great tenacity.

We have noted that the gods are related to processes, the process of individuation and its fundamental unit, the regression of libido. It is, therefore, possible to find patternings that depend more upon the character of the traveler than on the stage of the journey. In this case we would look for clues to the order in which the archetypes succeed one another in the outworking of personal existence. James Hillman calls this the processional characteristics of the archetypes.

Their tales and their figures move through phases like dramas and interweave one with another, dissolve into one another. Whether expressed as instincts or as gods, archetypes are definitely not distinct. One instinct modifies another; one god implicates another. Their process is their complication and amplification, and each individual's psychic process involves attempting to follow, discriminate, and refine their complications.

(Hillman, 1975/1977, pp. 147–8)

The procession of the archetypes is suggested by the overlaps in oversight, background and attributes, as well as the friends, relatives and associates: the relationships to which the god is drawn. Some of these possibilities are suggested by issues of identity between Demeter, Persephone and Hecate in the Kore as well as between Hades and Dionysius. Other clues to probable processional paths are provided by classical and modern groupings of the gods in terms of their relations one with another and their similarities in function, form or habit.

At the points of closest contact with other archetypes a different archetypal configuration may be constellated and a new subjective context required. For example, Hades and Dionysius were both associated with the souls of the dead. Both can be associated with intoxication: Hades through the intoxicating flowers that rendered Persephone vulnerable, Dionysius as the god of wine. Both also bear titles that associate them with the dead: Dionysius is the Lord of Souls and a psychopomp,[10] Hades is the Lord of the Underworld, the realm of the souls of the dead. Some ancient authors have explicitly identified the two (Bolen, 1989/1990; Jung and Kerenyi, 1949/1973; Hillman, 1980/1988a).

With so many elements in common it is suggested that an archetypal constellation around one or another of the elements symbolized by these gods could easily shift from one to the other. This would partially depend upon the emotional and structural context in which the symbol is placed. In Hillman's terms, it depends upon the place afforded the god (1975/1977).

With the possibility of a fluid movement between archetypal dominants, the danger of identification with any one archetype becomes especially great. Both Jung and Hillman warn against such identification and suggest rather that the archetype be used to inform the conscious attitude by simile and metaphor and by providing a context for pathologizing (Jung, 1959/1968a; Hillman, 1975/1977; Stein, 1980/1988; Miller, 1980/1988).

If my current mental health has become overly dependent upon an identification with Dionysius and I suddenly find myself instead enacting Hades, it may take some serious adjustments before I can recover a level of balance. If, however, I am aware of their affinities beforehand, aware that a Dionysian revel may imply a visit to the underworld, and have maintained a relation to the archetype that is relatively external and imaginal, then the change becomes understandable and acceptable.

It is not only possible that the procession of archetypes may involve an identifiable sequence, but it is not unlikely that it may involve enantiodromic shifts as the opposites are constellated through common contents. As a musician I may begin as a classicist believing in the Apollonian virtue of my art, but music is tied also to the realm of Dionysius, and one must never forget that the temple of Apollo at Delphi became the shrine of Dionysius during the winter months. This juxtaposition makes it no great surprise that someone beginning as a classicist might turn to jazz, or someone over-attached to the world of rationality might take great joy in altered states (Bolen, 1989/1990; Jung and Kerenyi, 1949/1973).

Jung identifies significant similarities between Rhea, Cybele and the Ephesian Diana. All are mother goddesses and all wear the mural crown[11] as a representation of their maternal care for cities. However, the association with cities links them again to Hestia, the virgin worshipped at the heart of every city, and with Athena, the patroness not only of Athens but of all civilized places as Athena Polias. Moreover, although a virgin, Athena is addressed as Mother especially in the context of institutionalized thought and ritual (Jung, 1956/1967; Hillman, 1980/1988b; Hamlyn, 1959/ 1981).

The depth of some of these associations is suggested by Hestia. Externally, she is the virginal keeper of the hearth; but by virtue of her vow to abstain from sexual relations and marriage she also obtained the right to be the first and the last remembered of the gods at every feast: she is religious focus. Her shrine marks the center of the home, the temple and the world. She is memorialized as the *focus*, the hearth, and can be said to be constellated in attention and in centering.

Focus again points us to the biological dimensions, and the patterns of living systems. Focus is one of the primal responses and is contrasted with diffusion. From the smallest of organisms to the greatest society, focus – centration – defines the center of consciousness and of activity. In this mythical vocabulary it is contrasted with a hermetic diffusion. Hermes, he who dwells at the edge, the god of commerce and speed, the swift traveler, presents the opposite extreme to the goddess who stays at home. His statues marked the periphery and the outer bounds (Kirksey, 1980/1988). We may again recall that the focus or center of the home, according to Eliade (1976), is its rooting in sacramental space. Accordingly, Hestia, the guardian of the hearth and the center of ritual, defines the center of the home in cosmogonic/sacramental space.

That such a situation allows for considerable variability in the procession of archetypes goes without saying, but it suggests two things. First, in accordance with von Franz's dictum, the pattern is to be found in terms of the affective tone of the situation, not in a simple intellectual enterprise. Second, there are no simple concepts. All are intertwined and capable of leading almost anywhere (1972/1986).

Common patterns that express the archetypal possibilities of a situation, like the mother/city situation just described, are the trefoil and triple ring (see Figure 6.1). Both are represented by the intersection of three circles of equal size. In the trefoil, the center is removed so as to emphasize the tri-unity. In the triple ring the center remains. If we imagine a central concept like the mother of cities occupying a central circle, and the overlaps of the other circles as the token of their common theme, then any train of thought within the central circle is a legitimate and probable link between them all, independent of which circle is its source. Moreover, in proportion to the level to which the archetypes are constellated by this central issue, any function of the individual circuits becomes accessible as an expression of the central idea.

Figure 6.1 The trefoil and the triple ring

Superficial associations with gods or goddesses are often given the lie when deep relations are revealed through amplification of mythical themes. Kerenyi has shown the essential identity between Demeter, Persephone and Hecate and holds that this was the mystery of the "nameless Kore" at the heart of the Eleusinian mysteries.

Hecate is shown by Kerenyi to act as a double of the bereaved Demeter. She hears the daughter's cries, repeats the mother's words regarding the seduction as she meets her for the search and joins her to find the witness. In different versions of the myth one or the other descends to the underworld, and at the restoration of Persephone becomes her companion forever. Kerenyi notes that by the end of the drama, "Hecate and Persephone are as inseparable as Persephone and Demeter" (Jung and Kerenyi, 1949/1973, p. 110).

Further parallels between the three are the symbol of the torch, associations with the moon, associations with the spirits of the departed, and grain. In fact, all three easily substitute one for the other.

That Kore might exist independently of Demeter is to Kerenyi unthinkable. He finds them bound into a single unit whose specific and archetypal message is the message of rebirth. The daughter enfolds the mother and the mother the daughter. "It is always the grain that sinks to earth and returns, always the grain that is mown down in golden fullness and yet, as fat and healthy seed, remains whole, mother and daughter in one" (ibid., p. 117). Kerenyi synthesizes the singularity of the mother/daughter pair as follows.

[Demeter] ... is wroth because of the rape of her daughter and *at the same time* because of the marriage by rape which she herself had to undergo. In the legend that has come down to us, it is said that she was overpowered by Poseidon while she was looking for her ravished daughter. This mythological elaboration *doubles* the rape, for the goddess experienced the rape in *herself*, as Kore, and not in a separate girl. A daughter with the name of "mistress" or "she who is not to be named" was born of this rape. The goddess becomes a mother, rages and grieves over the Kore who was ravished *in her own being*, the Kore whom she immediately recovers, and in whom she gives birth to *herself* again. The idea of the original Mother-Daughter goddess, at root a single entity, is at the same time the idea of *rebirth*.

(Jung and Kerenyi, 1949/1973, p. 123)

The unity of the Kore/Persephone dyad and their further union in Hecate strongly suggest the underlying dialectic that drives the symbolic process. A further triad is identified by Kerenyi as representing the polarities in the concept of Kore independent of the Demeter/Persephone myth. Two maiden goddesses, Artemis and Athena, were present at the abduction of Persephone. Both bear the title "Kore." Neither made any attempt to assist her. Artemis expresses her virginity in terms of a natural state that, though capable of sexuality, was never subdued. Athena is a virgin whose sexuality could never have been offered to a man. Persephone is a maiden in the twofold aspect of her relation to her mother – the eternal daughter, and to her husband – the eternal bride (Jung and Kerenyi, 1949/1973).

Just as there is significant overlap between the goddesses just discussed, as we have already seen, there is a significant identity between Hades, Lord of the Underworld and Dionysius, Lord of Souls. Another strong relation that may extend to the level of identity is the unity of function between Hermes, Aphrodite and Eros.

Kerenyi reports again that anciently, among the Etruscans, Hermes and Aphrodite were worshipped together and their unity celebrated in Hermaphroditos. In Hermes, Kerenyi finds the male correspondent to Aphrodite. The Hermaphroditos is linked to Eros as a primal form of the bisexual god. Aphrodite and Eros are both imagined as emerging from the waters, while both Eros and Hermes have special affinity for the image of the eternal child (ibid.).

In a striking passage Jung points out the principle of identification that united Christ with Wotan for much of post-Weimar Germany.

As a supra-individual factor the numen of the hunter is a dominant of the collective unconscious, and its characteristic features – hunter, magician, raven, miraculous horse, crucifixion or suspension high up in the boughs of the world-tree – touch the Germanic psyche very closely. Hence the Christian Weltanschauung, when reflected in the ocean of the (Germanic) unconscious, logically takes on the features of Wotan. In the figure of the hunter we meet an imago dei, a God-image, for Wotan is also a god of winds and spirits, on which account the Romans fittingly interpreted him as Mercury.

(Jung, 1959/1968a, para. 442)

Other associations become apparent when we turn to a table of the classic Olympians in their association with the signs of the zodiac. The normal ordering of the zodiacal archetypes, beginning with Aries and continuing through Pisces, reveals little in terms of the relations between the gods. A reordering, however, based upon their associations with the Greek elements, is very interesting. It is interesting also in that a significant arrangement does not appear until the classification is ordered by functional element, as opposed to the constructive element.

Jung, of course, spent a great deal of time investigating the significance of the number four in relation to the self and the functions of personality. One of the sources of this emphasis was the idea of the four elements, earth, air, fire and water. These may not only represent the four functions of consciousness and the four stages of the alchemical work, but by combination with one another are capable of producing twelve or sixteen individual expressions. Given that Bolen's (1989/1990) distribution of the functions among the gods is unbalanced, this scheme may suggest an archetypal arrangement.

In Table 6.3 the Greek gods, not the planets, are associated with the signs of the zodiac over which they rule.[12] The signs themselves are classed first by their functional element – the element that most closely expresses their function and mode of action – and then by their constitutive element or realm. The opposite configuration failed to provide any significant associations.

Following this arrangement, the gods appear in natural pairs either as lovers, complements, opposites or rapist and victim. Hera and Zeus are married. Ares is the despised son of Zeus. The association between Ares and Aphrodite is so strong that most people assume that they were married, even though they were not. Their union is described as the perfect union of opposites. Hephaestus was the husband of Aphrodite and the brother of Ares. Hephaestus was also the midwife of Athena and sought to make love to her when she came to collect a suit of armor he was making for her. Athena and Hermes represent opposite styles of life and thought. There is virtually no mythological record of significant contact between them. Hermes and Hestia are paired as the center and the periphery. Hestia was the subject of a proposal by Apollo, and presumably, the subject also of his affection. Apollo and Artemis are brother and sister, the sun and the moon. Artemis and Poseidon have almost no contact except for Artemis' defeat of his two monstrous sons. Artemis is the regularity of the lunar cycle, Poseidon is the unpredictable sea. Poseidon raped Demeter (Graves, 1955/1957; Jung and Kerenyi, 1949/1973; Bolen, 1984/1985, 1990; Hillman (ed.), 1980/1988; Hamlyn, 1959/1981).

If the gods suggest archetypal character formations we may then expect that individuals, whose personalities are constructed in a similar fashion to these archetypal figures, might reflect personal styles similar to those

Table 6.3 The Greek gods as rulers of the zodiac and the primitive elements

Element	Sign	Deity
air of air	Aquarius	Hera
air of fire	Leo	Zeus
air of water	Scorpio	Ares
air of earth	Taurus	Aphrodite
fire of air	Libra	Hephaestus
fire of fire	Aries	Athena
fire of water	Cancer	Hermes
fire of earth	Capricorn	Hestia
water of air	Gemini	Apollo
water of fire	Sagittarius	Artemis
water of water	Pisces	Poseidon
water of earth	Virgo	Demeter

The elemental attributions of the signs are derived from Crowley's attributions in *777* while the gods that appertain to them are derived from Paul Christian's data in *The History and Practice of Magic*. The latter source was chosen for its reliable use of the twelve traditional Olympians and its general correspondence to Crowley's data

exhibited by the gods. In light of von Franz's observation that the gods represent culturally specific versions of more general archetypal patterns, we can expect those patterns to change from country to country. Further, if the gods are personality types, then the mythical relations between the gods should be reflected in the relations between the relatively pure personality types that correspond to them. There is also a strong temptation to identify the twelve gods arranged in accordance with their functional element with the twelve modified psychological types suggested by Metzner, et. al. (1981).

Metzner, Burney and Mahlberg have suggested a reclassification of the psychological types based on the general inability of empirical research to validate Jung's assertion that the dominant function absolutely determines the inferior function due to their mutual incompatibility. Their research found that there is both empirical and archetypal evidence for the existence of twelve, not eight personality types.

That the patterns of personality reflected in the gods may also reflect the personalities and affinities of groups or nations has already been suggested. Jung himself identified the structure of the Young National Socialist Party in Germany during 1936 with the spirits of Wotan and Dionysius. He later pointed out that it was the constellation of the ancient German archetype of Wotan that fired the Holocaust not long after (1964/1970; 1959/1968a).

In this third level of patterning, we have seen that the archetypal styles can shift from one to another. These styles may also be predictable on the basis of affinities revealed in amplificatory material. Typical elements in such material indicate hidden identities between gods – or phases in the personality types that they reveal, affinities that fog the borders between one type and the other, and the strong possibility that interpersonal styles like personality traits may follow relationship patterns similar to those displayed by the gods who reflect their archetypal constitution.

SUMMARY

In Part II we saw that archetypes are organized in several general patterns. The most subtle of these is their capacity to operate at many logical levels simultaneously. Although the pattern was discussed as an essential property of the archetype, it should be remembered as crucial to archetypal functioning. This is the key to the pattern of the descent of the libido. The same primal patterns that energize the single-celled amoeba are capable of energizing the adult human. The same part-objects that serve to link the newborn to its mother still operate in the ancient. Every level remains accessible to every other level and can reappear in the clothing of maturity at almost any time. This is the central reason for the effectiveness of Hillman's (1983/1988) definition of the archetypal: any level of experience can be charged with archetypal energy and function as a symbol.

The archetypal patterns are next seen as susceptible to patterning in terms of functional entities, whether as distinct elements of a psychic topology or as the personalized inhabitants of an inner stage. The archetypes tend to take on patterns of action expressible as more or less specialized *topoi*, or as personalized expressions of the internal relations of the psyche. These, in turn, may be identified with the gods as the culturally averaged manifestations of the personality types generally expressed within that group. The gods, as dominant patterns, overpower and dominate the psychic landscape. They can, however, provide a metaphorical background against which specific patterns of behavior are emphasized and given a meaningful context.

The gods are protean. Like all archetypal contents they have a tendency to overlap and merge one with another. Some quickly merge into more archaic forms, while others retain some level of individual identity throughout the process. In any event, the progress of the archetypes through a life or situation provides specific clues for contextualizing current activities and predicting future directions.

The gods also reflect the attitudes that a person might take with regard to the path of individuation. As expressions of stages of evolution along the path of individuation, the gods provide specific challenges and benefits as they become recognized along the way.

The most crucial pattern of archetypal activity appears to be the pattern of the introversion of libido, the Hero's Journey. In it is expressed the basic theme of libidinal activity for the renewal and/or the destruction of an individual or nation. It is in the return to the depths of the archetypal realm that self definitions are recreated to the good or ill of an individual or society. If there is to be a Jungian sociological perspective it must be rooted in the reality of this pattern.

Jung and others, before and since, have outlined the pattern clearly: there is a lowering of the level of conscious energy – the ego fails, the identity is lost, meaning fades, life grows stale. Under such conditions, unconscious contents may draw the individual down into their own depths or unconscious contents may rise up to flood the conscious landscape. Willingly or unwillingly, as Odysseus or Persephone, the ego is drawn down into a more archaic and less differentiated level. There it obtains contact with the patterns of childhood, the patterns of early life or perhaps the primitives of life themselves. In contact with these archetypal primitives, it must restructure itself, regain meaning and return to the world of light. In returning, it discovers whether it has found the treasure hard to attain, the princess, the elixir of life or the poison of poisons.

On a personal level we see this happen in every major transition of life to a greater or lesser degree. On the larger scale of the whole life it is the path of individuation. In the life of nations it can be a revivifying of national identity or the emergence of unspeakable monstrosities.

Part III

Sociological considerations

Chapter 7

The sociological prospect

Up to this point we have carefully examined the archetype on multiple levels. We have explored its relation to systems theory and the properties of living systems. We have looked at it as the organ of meaning and as providing the root elements of human experience. All of this has related to the biological and psychological levels of human experience.[1] Insofar as our purpose is to outline an approach to sociology based upon Jung's insights into the archetypal dynamic, we now turn to an overview of sociology.

Sociology is a complex field. In order to explore the possibility of an archetypal sociology we must develop an acceptable definition of sociology. Like the archetype, the nature of sociology is protean. Every effort to define it will raise some objection from one or another of the competing perspectives that seek to define it and give it form; and as soon as a satisfactory approach appears, it soon becomes unsatisfactory.

On the surface, we might be content to broadly define sociology as the study of groups, their nature and their relations to individuals and to other groups. Although this very general definition has satisfied many, for other theorists such a definition is highly inadequate. An alternate definition, provided by Timasheff and Theodorson, makes sociology the study of human interdependencies. Ultimately, the specific questions that define sociology are determined by the specific perspective taken by the author of the definition (Chinoy and Hewit, 1975; Broom and Selznick, 1963; Timasheff and Theodorson, 1976).

The problem of definitions in sociology has been taken up by several authors who agree that there is no one metatheoretical definition that comprehends the field. Indeed, there is no unanimity as to the paradigmatic status of sociology generally. As a result, the field suffers from the tendency for each metatheoretical stance to spend its time either justifying its own perspective or attacking the perspectives of others in the field (Ritzer, 1980; Abrams, Reitman and Sylvester, 1980). In order to make our task of defining the implications of the theory of archetypes for sociology, we will examine the paradigmatic status of sociology in accordance with the works of Thomas Kuhn (1969) and George Ritzer (1980) and outline the perspectives of the major paradigms. Having done that we will then outline a set of questions that should be addressed by an archetypally based sociology.[2]

As sociologies are complex theoretical models, we cannot hope within the breadth of Part III to present an entire articulation of an archetypal sociology. Instead, we will enumerate a series of root questions that, on the whole, bridge the differences in fundamental perspectives between the paradigms, and which will be examined from an archetypal, or Jungian, perspective in Part IV.

This effort is at best an exploration. In propounding a synthetic overview of sociology, we seek to provide a meaningful context in which to frame Jung's insights; no ultimate paradigm or theoretically perfect sociology is anticipated or attempted. Thus, at the outset, the author recognizes that there will be certain inadequacies in the outlined sociology. This problem is further underlined by the lack of unanimity in the field. Were it a perfect outline, someone would nevertheless complain. Just as the analysis of sociology is suggestive, so the analysis of Jung's work and its application to the level of sociology will be exploratory, not exhaustive.

The idea of a paradigm as a scientific perspective has gained much popularity among New Age enthusiasts, especially in light of the currency of the rumor of a coming paradigm shift in the natural sciences. While this has brought the concept of the paradigm into question for certain audiences, it should not allow the fundamentally sound insights of Thomas Kuhn to be set aside with other popular ideas coinciding with the end of the twentieth century.

THE KUHNIAN PERSPECTIVE

Until the emergence of Kuhn's work, *The Structure of Scientific Revolutions* (1969), it was generally assumed that sciences were unified fields of knowledge that grew incrementally through the slow build-up of knowledge. Part of this assumption was the idea that every line of thought is, in some manner, the direct heir of its predecessors in a long line of unbroken ascent. Science was a gradually evolving organism in which every pattern emerged as the natural result of its logical precursors.

Kuhn discovered, to the contrary, that the development of scientific thought was discontinuous. Each historical stage of scientific growth was characterized by an outlook or paradigm that specified every facet of the enterprise. And each stage was in a significant manner discontinuous with the last. An important part of his discovery was that the historical progress of science was essentially a political and a sociological process with little to do with science as we normally conceive it. In fact, science as normally conceived was seen to be the invention of school teachers (Kuhn, 1969; Ritzer, 1980).

Besides the fact that many teachers are often not engaged in science itself and have little appreciation for its workings, Kuhn noted that most textbooks are written from a perspective that is dominated by the very outlook that they seek to describe. Because the paradigm orders the perspectives of both the author and the student, its discovery is seen to be self-evident; the natural conclusion to be drawn from the evidence that preceded it.

According to Kuhn, the progress of science is discontinuous, and characterized by changes in scientific perspectives, or paradigms, that are, at heart, radical socio-political shifts in perspective. They are more akin to religious conversions than to gradualist Darwinian evolution; much more like revolution than evolution.

> The transition from a paradigm in crisis to a new one out of which a new tradition of normal science can emerge is far from a cumulative process, one achieved by articulation or extension of the old paradigm. Rather, it is a reconstruction of the field from new fundamentals, a reconstruction that changes some of the field's most elementary theoretical generalizations as well as many of its paradigm methods and applications. . . . When the transition is complete, the profession will have changed its view of the field, its methods, and its goals.
>
> (Kuhn, 1969, pp. 84–5)

Every period of productive science is governed by a paradigm. Mature sciences have one ruling paradigm, immature sciences may be governed by several competing paradigms. Ill-defined sciences, or pre-sciences, may be characterized as possessing no paradigm at all (Banville and Landry, 1989).

The paradigm supplies a relatively complete set of investigative tools including theory, methods and standards for evaluation in a coherent scientific Weltanschauung. This perspective then guides all of the scientist's researches within the field. It also provides a convenient "map" of the field in which one can discern the fundamental underpinnings of any theoretical stance (Kuhn, 1969; Ritzer, 1980; Burell and Morgan, 1979)

> by telling the scientist about the entities that nature does and does not contain and about the ways in which those entities behave. That information provides a map whose details are elucidated by mature scientific research. And since nature is too complex and varied to be explored at random, that map is as essential as observation and experiment to science's continuing development. Through the theories they embody, paradigms prove to be constitutive of the research activity. . . . paradigms provide scientists not only with the map but also with some of the directions for map making.
>
> (Kuhn, 1969, p. 108)

According to Burell and Morgan, paradigms are defined

> by very basic meta-theoretical assumptions which underwrite the frame of reference, mode of theorizing and *modus operandi* of the social theorists who operate within them. It is a term which is intended to emphasize the commonality of perspective which binds the work of a group of theorists together in such a way that they can usefully be regarded as approaching social theory within the bounds of the same problematic.
>
> (Burrell and Morgan, 1979, p. 23)

Similarly, George Ritzer offers his definition of a paradigm, based upon Kuhn's. It is often quoted and may have become a more-or-less *de facto* standard.

> A paradigm is a fundamental image of the subject matter within a science. It serves to define what should be studied, what questions should be asked, how they should be asked, and what rules should be followed in interpreting the answers obtained. The paradigm is the broadest unit of consensus within a science and serves to differentiate one scientific community (or *sub-community*) from another. It subsumes, defines, and interrelates the exemplars, theories, and methods and instruments that exist within it.
>
> (Ritzer, 1980, p. 7)

Each successful paradigm is, in some respect, a response to previous failed paradigms which have passed through several stages. In the first stage, the newly adopted paradigm is fully accepted by the community at large. During this period of "normative science" little innovation takes place, as all of the energy of the scientific community is given over to puzzle-solving within the new world and extending the grasp of the new perspective into previously uncharted waters. Insofar as the paradigm works, it tends to limit the focus of the community on what it defines as real. Thus, for the long period of behaviorism's paradigmatic regnancy in psychology, an archetypal approach was, for the most part, deemed to be non-existent or unworthy of study. During the same period there are other conceptions of the science, but they tend to be relegated to the fringes of the community and discounted. The bulk of the enterprise, as well as the bulk of its rewards, are channeled to the major players within the dominant paradigm.

As normative science proceeds, the puzzles that occupy standard science begin to be replaced by more trying issues. Problems from the edge of the field begin to stretch the imagination of the scientists and the articulation of the paradigm begins to grow unwieldy. Kuhn gave the example of the Ptolemaic universe. By the time of Copernicus's discovery of the heliocentric solar system, the Ptolemaic system was stretched, literally, to the breaking point in its efforts to satisfactorily explain the motion of the planets. The calculations and explanatory impedimenta had become so cumbersome, and efforts to resolve them had endured for so long, that a new perspective could only mean relief.

During the transitional period that precedes the period of crisis, several things happen. First there is a growing dissatisfaction with the inelegance of the regnant paradigm: less and less is accomplished at the cost of more and more complex justifications. Often, one anomaly comes so much to the front of the scientific endeavor that it becomes the subjective center of the science.

When ... an anomaly comes to seem more than just another puzzle of normative science, the transition to crisis and extraordinary science has begun. The anomaly itself now comes to be more generally recognized as such by the profession. More and more attention is devoted to it by more and more of the field's most eminent men. If it still continues to resist, as it usually does not, many of them may come to view its resolution as the subject matter of their discipline. For them the field will no longer look quite the same as it had earlier. Part of its different appearance results simply from the new fixation point of scientific scrutiny.

(Kuhn, 1969, pp. 82–3)

At other times, a growing number of anomalies appear with which the paradigmatic scientist is unable to deal. These encourage the growth of alternate approaches to the problems at hand. This is the crisis phase of the old science. Should the original paradigm prove unable to restructure, or change sufficiently to incorporate the new material, a new paradigm will emerge and threaten its continued existence. Kuhn has noted that alternate perspectives exist throughout the period of normative science. Alternate perspectives serve the function of pointing out that the puzzles on which the establishment spends its time are actually incommensurables that point towards the ultimate failure of the paradigm.

All crises begin with the blurring of a paradigm and the consequent loosening of the rules for normal research. In this respect research during crisis very much resembles research during the pre-paradigm period, except that in the former the locus of difference is both smaller and more clearly defined. And all crises close with the emergence of a new candidate for paradigm and with the subsequent battle over its acceptance.

(Ibid., p. 84)

When, at last, a competing theory proves to be a potentially viable competitor for the status of paradigm, it must accomplish two things. First, it must provide a more elegant, effective and far-reaching set of tools than those that it seeks to supplant. Second, it must address an issue that lies at the heart of scientific frustrations. The discovery of oxygen revolutionized chemistry because phlogiston and the mystery of combustion lay close to the heart of chemistry. The heliocentric theory of Copernicus changed the world because so much intellectual energy had been invested in the need to accurately predict the motion of the planets. In all such cases a certain level of pre-paradigmatic research had laid the groundwork for the final change. In the case of Copernicus, the paradigm was fully articulated at the time of the shift. In other cases, competing paradigms vie one with another for acceptance until one or the other gains hegemony. Final victory is often not declared until the old generation of scientists has died off and the champions of the new paradigm take over as the new establishment.

PARADIGMS IN SOCIOLOGY

Although the concepts of paradigms and paradigm shifts have revolutionized the history and sociology of the sciences, Kuhn was often less than precise in his definition of the paradigm. Masterman cited no less than twenty-one separate uses of the word "paradigm" in the 1962 edition of *The Structure of Scientific Revolutions*. Banville and Landry report that one author found five kinds of usage that developed through differing phases of the book. In later editions of the text, Kuhn makes a significant change on the revolutionary aspects of paradigmatic change. Kuhn's shift between editions of the book is characterized by several authors as a move from revolution to evolution (Masterman, 1970, cited by Ritzer; Banville and Landry, 1989; Ritzer, 1980).

Ritzer (1980) spends some time examining the possible definitions of the paradigm and finally settles upon the image of the subject matter as the most useful and the farthest reaching. In justifying his peculiar slant on Kuhn's definition, Ritzer indicates that without further refinement, the concept is too nebulous to serve as a reliable tool and tends to disintegrate into an equivalent of theory. Indeed, in reviewing the work of Effrat (1972) and Fredrichs (1970), he shows how their imprecision in definition leads them to multiply paradigms to the point where the concept loses all utility.

Although Kuhn imagined each scientific enterprise as being dominated by a single paradigm, Ritzer found that, especially in the social sciences, a science might legitimately be characterized by multiple paradigms. The multiplication of paradigms in the social sciences was seen to flow from the inherent difficulty of precise agreement as to the nature of the subject matter. A decision to treat sociology as a multiple paradigm science was also made by Burell and Morgan (1979).

For our purposes, the definition championed by Ritzer will guide us in the following endeavor.

A paradigm is a fundamental image of the subject matter within a science. It serves to define what should be studied, what questions should be asked, how they should be asked, and what rules should be followed in interpreting the answers obtained. The paradigm is the broadest unit of consensus within a science and serves to differentiate one scientific community (or *sub-community*) from another. It subsumes, defines and interrelates the exemplars, theories, and methods and instruments that exist within it.

(Ritzer, 1980, p. 7)

Using this definition, Ritzer comes up with three paradigms: the Social Facts Paradigm, the Social Definitions Paradigm and the Social Behavior Paradigm. In a similar effort, Burell and Morgan (1979) specify four such paradigms, to wit: the Functionalist, Interpretive, Radical Humanist and Radical Structuralist paradigms.

The differences between the two approaches lie in the grounding of the idea of the paradigm: the logical level at which it is applied. Ritzer, it would seem, aims his evaluation at the level of sociology. On a relatively simple level he asks, what commonalties of perspective link these theorists? What assumptions do they make about their field and what is their historical lineage? How are they methodologically oriented? For Burell and Morgan, however, the paradigm is rooted in more fundamental philosophical considerations as to the specific ontology and epistemology employed and the perspectives on human nature and methodology espoused by the theorist. These are arrayed against a background dimension of subjective or objective orientation to present a framework for paradigmatic assessment.

While there may be several reasons for reevaluating Ritzer's definitions, our purpose in following his plan, i.e. development of a general integrative perspective on sociology, would not seem to require going any further than Ritzer. Moreover, insofar as Ritzer's definition has obtained a *de facto* legitimacy in the discussion of paradigms in the social sciences, and because it is specifically aimed at the field of sociology, it has special utility for our purposes.

In the following discussion of the paradigms an attempt will be made to provide an outline of a theoretical approach within each of the specific perspectives examined. Our aim is the production of a short set of questions from the perspective of each paradigm to serve the broadly integrative purpose of informing an archetypal view of sociology.

Chapter 8

The paradigms

THE SOCIAL FACTS PARADIGM

The Social Facts Paradigm is strongly rooted in the works of Emile Durkheim, with special reference to his *The Rules of the Sociological Method* (1938/1964). Its primary focus is on social facts (Ritzer, 1980).

Emile Durkheim

Durkheim was an early pioneer whose efforts to define the field as distinct from both psychology and philosophy helped to provide sociology with its distinctive character. Borrowing from mechanical and biological models current in his day, he sought to bring a certain scientific rigor to the field of sociology which till then had been lacking (Aron, 1970; Ritzer, 1980; Catlin 1938/1964).

Central to his sociology is the idea that social phenomena are real. They are facts whose reality has an impact on human life and experience. According to Durkheim, human behavior is constrained by two kinds of facts: psychological facts and social facts. Psychological facts have to do with inherited predispositions, they are primarily biological and psychophysical in nature. Social facts are the forces of social life that impinge upon the individual from the outside. They are experienced as external to and coercive upon the individual (Ritzer, 1980; Durkheim, 1938/1964; Aron, 1970).

> Here, then, is a category of facts with very distinctive characteristics: it consists of ways of acting, thinking and feeling, external to the individual, and endowed with a power of coercion, by reason of which they control him. These ways of thinking could not be confused with biological phenomena, since they consist of representations and of actions; nor with psychological phenomena, which exist only in the individual consciousness and through it. They constitute, thus, a new variety of phenomena; and it is to them exclusively that the term social ought to be applied.
> (Durkheim, 1938/1964, p. 5)

Social facts occur in two forms – those possessing a physical reality and those possessing an existential, although non-physical, reality. In the first group we find architecture, law and the elements of physical culture. In the second, we find currents of opinion, the Zeitgeist, the mood of a nation and general attitudes. The one type of fact is physically real; the second is to be *treated* as real (Catlin, 1938/1964; Ritzer, 1980).[1]

Moreover, social facts have social causes, and Durkheim demanded that they be analyzed in terms of their social causation. It was his opinion that although groups were composed of individual people, the whole was more than the sum of its parts, and produced, through synergy, an entity of a different logical level than that of the individual.

The hardness of bronze is not in the copper, the tin or the lead, which are its ingredients and which are soft and malleable bodies; it is in their mixture. The fluidity of water and its nutritional and other properties are not to be found in the two gases of which it is composed but in the complex substance which they form by their association.

Let us apply this principle to sociology. If . . . this synthesis constituting every society yields new phenomena, differing from those which take place in individual consciousness, we must indeed admit that these facts reside exclusively in the very society itself which produces them, and not in its parts, i.e., its members. They are . . . in this sense, external to individual consciousnesses . . . just as the distinctive characteristics of life are external to the mineral substances composing the living being.

(Ibid., p. xlviii)

The effective agent at the level above the personal was a personalized entity that he called the collective consciousness.

[S]ociety is not a mere sum of individuals. Rather, the system formed by their association represents a specific reality which has its own characteristics. . . . Individual minds, forming groups by mingling and fusing, give birth to a being, psychological if you will, but constituting a psychic individuality of a new sort. It is, then, in the nature of this collective individuality, not in that of the associated units, that we must seek the immediate and determining causes of the facts appearing therein.

(Ibid., pp. 103–4)

Durkheim, besides laying down the essential foundations of sociology, made several important observations. First, he saw that society was evolving from a relatively unconscious and mechanical unity to a more conscious and contractually based unity. These phases of social evolution were identified as mechanical and organic solidarity. Mechanical solidarity is defined by Aron as a solidarity of resemblance. The major characteristic of a society in which mechanical solidarity prevails is that the individuals differ from one another as little as possible. The individuals, the members of the same collectivity, resemble each other because they hold the same things sacred. The society is coherent because the individuals are not yet differentiated.

(Aron, 1970, p. 11)

Organic solidarity is characterized by consensus emerging from a diverse and differentiated society. According to Aron, the terms are derived from the manifest dissimilarity of specialized organs in the human body and the interchangeability of parts on the mechanical assembly line. Because there are no individuals in the primitive society, anyone can be replaced by any other. In the differentiated society, the specific skills of each individual, or each type of individual, have a specific – organic – value (ibid.).

Among the social facts analyzed by Durkheim was the development of anomie, the sense of rootless and directionless detachment which so plagues modern man. Anomie is rooted in the boundless opportunities of modern society unbalanced by the necessary moral restraint (1951/1966).

Every society . . . where organic solidarity prevails runs the risk of dis-aggregation, of *anomie*. In fact, the more that modern society encourages individuals to claim the right to fulfill their own personalities and gratify their own desires, the more danger there is that the individual may forget the requirements of discipline and end by being perpetually dissatisfied. For no matter how great the allowance made for individualism in modern society, there is no society without discipline, without limitation of desires, without disproportion between each man's aspirations and the satisfactions available.

(Aron, 1970, p. 84)

Part of Durkheim's position assumed that any social fact performed a specific function for the society in which it was found. Good or bad, the existence of a social fact implies its utility in some larger part of the system. If this were not so, the fact in question would not be allowed to exist. "To ask what the function of the division of labor is, is to seek for the need which it supplies" (Durkheim, 1933/1964, p. 49).

It is through the functionalist perspective that the work of Durkheim lives on in its most recognizable form. According to Ritzer, the functionalists and the structuralists within sociology have retained Durkheim's orientation towards social facts and there provide the paradigm's essential image of sociology.

The image of the subject matter

As noted, the primary object of the social factist's investigation is the social fact. Social facts may be seen as institutions – the common values or norms that exist in any cultural group – and social structures – the organized nexus of relations between individuals and the medium of the division of labor. Social institutions have tended to become the central focus of the paradigm. Although they are generally viewed as accumulations of values and norms, others see them as structural entities.

> In modern sociology, institutions tend to be viewed as interrelated sets of norms and values that surround a particular human activity or bothersome problem. There are clearly numerous institutions, but some of the more important are the family, the polity, the economy, education, religion and science. Institutions can also take more specific forms such as the nuclear family, parenthood, and childhood. All institutions clearly have a structural existence. The polity has laws, offices and organizations; the same is true of all other institutions.
>
> (Ritzer, 1980, p. 47)

On the other hand, social structures are the "roles, positions, organizations, groups, collectivities, social systems and societies." They are generally less tangible than the institutions but are nonetheless real (ibid., p. 47).

Social factists concern themselves primarily with the interrelationships between structures: How do different groups interact with the society at large? What is their relationship? How or to what degree are they mutually determining?; between institutions: How does single parenthood affect the nuclear family? What is the nature of the relations between science, religion and education? How are they mutually formative?; and between individuals and structures and/or institutions: How does society mold individual consciousness? How does national policy on housing impact the self-image of inner city children? In general, their approach is macrosociological, looking at the larger elements of human experience (ibid.).

The basic perspective of the social facts paradigm is included in the structural–functionalist school which subsumes systems theory as well as conflict theory.

> To the functionalist, society is a social system. This means that society is composed of a series of interrelated parts and these interrelated parts are in a state of equilibrium. Each part of the social system contributes to the maintenance of other parts. They are in a state of equilibrium because changes in one part will, because of these systemic linkages, lead to changes in other parts of the system. Society is believed to be in kind of a balance with a change in one part necessitating changes in

other parts. The equilibrium of the social system is therefore not static, but a moving equilibrium. Parts of society are always changing, and these changes lead to sympathetic changes in other parts of the social system. Thus change is basically orderly, rather than cataclysmic, as it often is to conflict theorists.

(Ibid., p. 48)

The relatively mechanical systems orientation of the early structuralists has been critiqued by systems advocates, no less than by conflict theorists. Walter Buckley observes:

The equilibrium theorist, to support his appeal to that concept, typically points out that there are, in any society, sets of more or less common norms, values, expectations, and definitions of the situation supported by sanctions of one kind or another. However, he equally typically fails to mention that every society of any complexity also has quite stable sets of alternative, diverse, deviant, or counter norms, values, etc., as well as a vast area of ambiguities and uninstitutionalized "collective" behavior of all shades and degrees.

(Buckley, 1979, pp. 10–11)

Although modern functionalism has grown beyond this perspective,[2] it still tends to represent the sociology of the status quo and is predominantly the chosen tool of the establishment (Gouldner, 1970).

Merton, the leading structural–functionalist of the twentieth century, reports the orientation of earlier strains of functionalism (1967). To the pioneers in the field, the approach of functional analysis was based upon three primary postulates.

1 Societies are functional unities, albeit not total unities. The function of any one part is the contribution that it makes to that unity.
2 All standardized social or cultural forms have positive functions. Those that cease to function positively, that is by contributing to the unity of society, are abandoned.
3 Social functions and the implements of their expression are all vital to the society in which they appear; none is superfluous.

In response to these rather primitive and naive postulates, Merton (1967) holds out an 11-point paradigm for structural–functional sociology, paraphrased as follows:

1 The subject matter of functional analysis is limited to " . . . standardized (i.e., patterned and repetitive) item[s], such as social roles, institutional patterns, social processes, cultural pattern, culturally patterned emotions, social norms, group organization, social structure, devices for social control, etc." (p. 50).
2 The subjective motivations and purposes of the individuals who comprise society, insofar as they are deduced from the structure of social facts, must

be differentiated from the consequences of actual subjective attitudes. Intentions are not the same as their results and assumptions are not always accurate. It is often crucial to differentiate between those circumstances where motivations are related to outcomes, and those where they are not.

3 The observation of the objective consequences of a social fact requires that both functional and dysfunctional properties be observed and evaluated, and that the subjective category of motivation be differentiated from objective category of social function. "*Functions* are those observed consequences which make for the adaptation or adjustment of a given system; *dysfunctions*, those observed consequences which lessen the adaptation or adjustment of a given system" (p. 51).

The differentiation between motivations and systemic function is codified by Merton in terms of whether or not the intent of the action matches the outcome. Thus, the objective consequences of an action that contributes to the unity of the system *as planned* is a "manifest function." Latent functions are those whose consequences were neither planned nor anticipated.

4 The idea of a function must be applied to a systemic context and at a logical level appropriate to it. Functions are applicable to units at differing levels of social structure. What might be good for my group may not be good for yours. What may be functional for my group may be dysfunctional to the national polity.

5 The needs and requirements of a social system should be embodied as an explicit assumption of the functional analysis and not imposed in an *ex post facto* manner. Every theory and each approach assumes that there are such needs, proper analysis requires that they be clearly identified.

6 Functional analysis calls for the "concrete and detailed" enumeration of the specifically social factors and mechanisms which fulfill the given function. Examples include "role-segmentation, insulation of institutional demands, hierarchic ordering of values, social division of labor, ritual and ceremonial enactments, etc." (p. 52).

7 Functional analysis requires the analysis of alternative, equivalent or substitute means of fulfillment within the structure. That is, in contradistinction to the earlier formulation, no single means of function delivery is to be conceived of in and of itself to be either unique or absolutely necessary. Every function within a system implies a range of variation in the method of its delivery or expression.

8 Because social facts occur in the context of specific interrelated structures, the range of alternatives available for the fulfillment of any given function is limited by the nature of the structure itself. This further implies that the specific functions remain necessary, it is only their means of delivery that varies depending upon the context.

9 Functional analysis need not be limited to the static relations within social structures, but must also consider the sources of change in society. To this end, "The concept of dysfunction, which implies the concept of strain, stress and tension on the structural level, provides an analytical approach to the study of dynamics and change" (p. 53).

10 Functional analysis is not amenable to experimental validation. As a result, its practitioners must assure that their analysis of the data approximates the logic of an experimental evaluation. This requires a " . . . systematic review of the possibilities and limitations of *comparative* (cross-cultural and cross-group) *analysis*" (p. 54).

11 Even though functional analysis has no intrinsic ideological agenda, it must always be concerned that its results are not compromised by the application of limited findings or particular theoretical aspects for specifically ideological goals.

THE SOCIAL DEFINITIONS PARADIGM

The Social Definitions Paradigm focuses upon the works of Max Weber, especially in regard to his work on social action. Its specific interest is in how the world of social action is experienced by the individual. Unlike the Social Facts Paradigm, its formative author, Max Weber, did not fully articulate the paradigm and is often viewed as having defected from it (Ritzer, 1980).

Max Weber

Max Weber is especially well known for his massive historical analyses that properly belong to the Social Facts Paradigm. However, his central constraint, that sociology must study the subjective meaning of social phenomena, places him at the center and the root of the Social Definitions Paradigm.

> The term "sociology" is open to many different interpretations. In the context used here it shall mean that science which aims at the interpretative understanding of social behavior in order to gain an explanation of its causes, its course, and its effects. It will be called human "behavior" only insofar as the person or persons involved engage in some subjectively meaningful action. Such behavior may be mental or external; it may consist in action or the omission to act. The term "social behavior" will be reserved for activities whose intent is related by the individuals involved to the conduct of others and is oriented accordingly.
>
> (Weber, 1962/1980, p. 29)

The tool marshaled by Weber for the examination of social behavior, and which lies at the root of the Social Definitions Paradigm, he called *Verstehen*.

A correct causal interpretation of a concrete course of behavior is achieved when such overt behavior and its motive have both been correctly ascertained and if, at the same time, their relationship has become intelligible in a meaningful way. A correct causal interpretation of a typical course of behavior then can be taken to mean that the process which is claimed to be typical is shown to lend itself to both meaningful and causally adequate interpretation. If no meaning attaches itself to such typical behavior, then regardless of the degree of uniformity or the statistical preciseness of probability, it still remains an incomprehensible statistical probability, whether it deals with overt or subjective process. On the other hand, even the most perfectly adequate meaning is causally significant from a sociological point of view only if we have proof that in all likelihood the conduct in question normally unfolds in a meaningful way.

(Ibid., p. 40)

The great contribution of Weber was the movement of the locus of sociological inquiry from the externals of the world of social facts to the subjective world of meaning. From the Weberian perspective, sociology was the study of the meaning of social behavior as perceived by people. The specific focus was the meaning of social actions. Sociological understanding, *Verstehen*, was the ability to provide a meaningfully adequate understanding of how the society impacts him as an individual. It was also an effort to understand how the social world was created and maintained by the relationships between individual actors (Ritzer, 1980; Freund, 1969).

The centrality of subjective experience was the keynote of Weber's approach. It was, however, closely allied with another tool that provided the prospectus from which a clear understanding could be found. This was the ideal type (1968/1978).

A full understanding of Weber's method requires an appreciation of his view that only fully intentional acts could be completely understood by others. The more emotionally colored the act, the less predictable and less understandable it was. In this light, he delineated four kinds of action. Two were irrational and were based either upon traditional or habitual activities, or else they were dominated by feelings and affects. These two were the least subject to rational analysis and understanding. A third action-type fails to differentiate between means and ends, but reflects rational choice in the decision. In such a case, the whole may not be fully comprehensible to the external observer, but it remains accessible at some level of understanding. The most predictable and the most comprehensible behavior is fully rational action (Ritzer, 1980; Weber, 1968/1978).

[W]e also understand what a person is doing when he tries to attain certain ends by choosing appropriate means on the basis of the facts of the situation, as experience has accustomed us to interpret them. The interpretation of such rationally purposeful action possesses, for the understanding of the choice of means, the highest degree of verifiable certainty.

(Weber, 1968/1978, p. 5)

Wedded to this concept of rational action was the idea of the ideal type. Since it was possible to understand logically conceived action and to reliably predict its outcome, a properly designed model of a situation based upon the rational balance of means and ends should provide a vantage point from which the complexities of real-life situations could be evaluated.

For the purposes of a typological scientific analysis it is convenient to treat all irrational, affectually determined elements of behavior as factors of deviation from a conceptually pure type of rational action. . . . Only in this way is it possible to assess the causal significance of irrational factors as accounting for deviations from this type. The construction of a purely rational course of action in such cases serves the sociologist as a type (ideal type) which has the merit of clear under-standing and lack of ambiguity. By comparison with this it is possible to understand the ways in which actual action is influenced by irrational factors of all sorts. . . .

(Ibid., p. 6)

A further perspective that set Weber apart from the social factists was his determination that humankind was capable of free choice. Gerth and Mills note:

Weber's liberal heritage and urge prevented him from taking a determinist position. He felt that freedom consists not in realizing alleged historical necessities but rather in making deliberate choices between open alternatives. The future is a field for strategy rather than a mere repetition or unfolding of the past. . . .
. . . The decision making, morally responsible individual is, of course, a specifically modern and Occidental type of personality. This man can be more than a mere cog in his occupational groove. If he is responsible, he will have to make informed choices.

(Gerth and Mills, 1946/1980, p. 70)

Despite these beginnings, the bulk of Weber's contributions fall firmly within the Social Facts Paradigm. While it would appear to many that this apparent change in emphasis constituted a defection from his own principles, one might justify his action in terms of the need to articulate the nature of the social phenomena that mankind creates, and to which it responds, as an essential part of developing a meaningfully adequate understanding of the phenomena.

The image of the subject matter

Out of these basic insights three sociological perspectives emerge: action theory, phenomenological sociology and ethnomethodology. All three place human experience at the center of sociological inquiry. Within them there is a range of opinion as to the nature of social systems. On the one hand, the ethnomethodologists deny the existence of any ongoing social structure apart from the persons who create it in immediate experience. This view is associated with Harold Garfinkle. On the other hand, social action theorists like Parsons, and symbolic interactionists like Blumer, see social structure as a product of human activity and the enduring context of human experience (Ritzer, 1980).

Action theory was the direct heir of the Weberian conception of man. Its most formidable exponent was Talcott Parsons, who was identified by Ritzer with Durkheim, Marx and Weber as a paradigm bridger. Action theory, dating to the period before the First World War, focused upon the actions of individuals and their subjective meanings, but was seen to be rather discontinuous with post-war developments. With the exception of Charles Cooley, its exponents tended to see the social structure as coercive and external. Cooley, by contrast, rejected any mechanistic conception of human nature (Ritzer, 1980).

One of the theories closely related to, but not derived from, action theory was George Herbert Mead's school of symbolic interactionism. Mead defined himself as a social behaviorist. Unlike radical behaviorists of the Watsonian cast, he did not deny the existence of mind. He believed, rather, that mind was an expression of behavior and could only be understood through the evaluation of overt behavior. He was non-dualistic and saw that all subjective activity ultimately arose from physical actions, hence his relationship to action theory (Ritzer, 1980; Miller, 1973/1980).

Humankind was viewed by Mead as inherently social creatures. Neither mind, nor thought, nor language, could exist outside a social context. The self developed out of interactions with others and depended upon the internalization of social patterns for its existence. Language was always a social act. It involved the emission of "symbolic gestures" in socially determined contexts which would ensure a consistent response from other organisms (Miller, 1973/1980; Ritzer, 1980).

Mead believed that thought developed out of a temporal separation between stimulus and response in the simple behavioral model. Whereas an animal makes no distinction between stimulus and response, humankind has developed the capacity to intervene symbolically in the period between stimulus onset and the consummatory response. This manipulatory period is crucial to Mead's conception of mental process. He observed that animals could respond to stimuli, but that their responses were always consummatory.[3]

Killing and devouring the prey are one and the same act. Upon reaching its food the dog continues immediately to consume it. Even before they reached the meat indicated by the buzzer, the saliva in the pavlovian dogs began to flow.

(Miller, 1973/1980, p. 60)

Human beings, on the other hand, experience (or often experience) a separation between the act and its consummation; between the stimulus and the response. This was Mead's idea of a manipulatory phase, the phase of symbolic manipulation.

According to Mead, the development of the hand, the development of language, mind and society were inseparably united. The hand allowed for the manipulation of objects, this manipulation allowed for perception of the abstract physicality of the object – they could be experienced apart from the consummation of a stimulus-response loop – and the new qualities of distance, shape and permanence in time allowed for the symbolic representation of such objects in a consenting group. By practicing the manipulation of objects symbolically, through language, the range of human experience was extended significantly. Moreover, by practicing several responses to a situation on a symbolic level, humankind developed the ability to make choices and decisions about outcomes and the means to achieve them (Miller, 1973/1980).[4]

Mead was fascinated by the work of Einstein and adapted relativity to his theoretical world view. In the course of interpreting the world, the individual respondent radically recreates his past and establishes a new future of possibilities in which previously impossible options can arise as emergents. Every event influences every other, and every definition redefines the entire world. Creativity, chance and the unexpected are woven into the Meadean system in terms of the radical creativity ascribed to the thinking person and the world constructing power of the consensual group structure into which he is born (Miller, 1973/1980).

The central issues for the symbolic interactionist are the questions of how worlds of shared typifications develop, how they are passed on, and how the individual actor perceives and understands them. From the point of view of symbolic interactionism, the crucial issue of subjective experience is to be examined through the Weberian practice of *Verstehen*.

The acting units and the way they orient themselves to each other are central to symbolic interactionists. Actors fit their actions to those of others through a process of interpretation. When, through this process, actors form groups, the action of the group is the collective action of the individuals involved. Individuals, interaction, and interpretation are key terms here. . . .

(Ritzer, 1980, p. 100)

Another important heir to the Weberian heritage is phenomenological sociology, most closely associated with the work of Alfred Schutz. Schutz, like all social definitionists, focused upon internal states. In his case it was shared states:

> Schutz focuses particularly on one form of subjectivity, that is inter-subjectivity. This refers literally to shared subjective states, or simply the dimension of consciousness common to a particular social group or group of interactants. It is intersubjectivity that makes social intercourse possible, for the patterning of interaction depends on the knowledge of *rules* that are shared, yet experienced subjectively. The concept of intersubjectivity refers to the fact that groups of men come to interpret and even experience the world similarly. Such mutual understanding is necessary for cooperative tasks on which most social organization is predicated. Schutz is concerned with the conscious structures necessary for mutual activity and understanding.
>
> (Ritzer, 1980, pp. 112–13)

Although strongly influenced by Husserl, Shutz departs significantly from the classical phenomenological program by making use of intro-spection as the source of empirical data. Introspection, in his sense, was essentially identical with Weber's motivational and interpretive understandings (*Verstehen*). These, however, were very different from the everyday observational interpretations which imputed standard meanings to overt acts:

> "interpretive understanding" which is definitive of interpretive sociology cannot be observational understanding. Rather, the scientific method of establishing subjective meaning is motivational understanding [as Weber used the terms], whereas the kind of understanding proper to everyday life is observational in its character.
>
> (Schutz, 1967, p. 31)

The methodology espoused by Schutz was thoroughly Weberian. It even extended to the use of ideal types to facilitate interpretive understandings. In all of this he significantly departed from Husserl, noting that:

> The purpose of this work, which is to analyze that phenomenon of meaning in ordinary social life, does not require the achievement of a transcendental knowledge that goes beyond that sphere or a further sojourn within the area of the transcendental-phenomenological reduc-tion. In ordinary social life we are not concerned with the constitution of phenomena as these are studied within the sphere of the phenomeno-logical reduction. We are concerned only with the phenomena corre-sponding to them within the natural attitude.
>
> (Ibid., p. 44)

A final perspective, falling under the Social Definitions Paradigm, represents the school of ethnomethodology and is associated with Howard Garfinkle. Ethnomethodology is a phenomenological school with roots in Schutzian phenomenology. Its interest is, similarly, the roots of inter-subjectivity. The particular contributions of ethnomethodology lie in their radical subjectivist stance and their methodology, which includes the specific forms of observer participation now common in sociological inquiry.

Among the paradigm bridgers cited by Ritzer (1980), Berger and Luckmann in *The Social Construction of Reality* (1967) are noted for providing a particularly coherent picture of the microsociological and subjectivist pole towards which the Social Definitions Paradigm tends. Although they reach out to the great theorists in each paradigm, their perspective will be used to fill out a paradigmatic overview of the social definitionist perspective.

According to Berger and Luckmann, the central question for sociological theory is this:

How is it possible that subjective meanings *become* objective facticities? Or . . . how is it possible that human activity should produce a world of things? In other words, an adequate understanding of the "reality *sui generis*" of society requires an inquiry into the manner in which society is constructed.

(Berger and Luckmann, 1967, p. 18)

From this vantage point, the analysis of social reality must first be carried out on a phenomenological basis. Social reality consists, at heart, in the common sense facticities of the world that confront every person in their closest, most personal experience. This common sense world is socially defined, but also constraining. Sociology must determine the level to which it is socially defined, and the part each person plays in its definition and maintenance.

Social structures also represent an important part of human experience. They, like all of the data of experience, are ordered in terms of personal proximity and personal relevance through a "continuum of typifications." These common or universal definitions–typifications grow more and more abstract as they move out of the immediate realm of human experience. Part of the task of sociology is to determine the nature of the objectification and reification of social processes (ibid., p. 33).

Social structures are embodied in institutions, and these are the products of human interaction. When people agree reciprocally on the typifications that characterize their habitual interactions, those inter-actions may be said to be institutionalized. Institutions, "by the very fact of their existence, control human behavior by setting up predefined patterns of conduct, which channel it in one direction as against the many other directions that would theoretically be possible" (ibid., p. 55).

Institutionalization provides a benefit in terms of predictability. When such predictable patterns are passed on to other generations, the constructions of human interaction are perceived as givens, facticities that are external to the individual and coercive upon him.

> The objectivity of the institutional world "thickens" and "hardens," ... The "there we go again" now becomes "This is how these things are done." A world so regarded attains a firmness in consciousness; it becomes real in an ever more massive way and it can no longer be changed so readily. For the children, especially in the early phases of their socialization into it, it becomes *the* world.
>
> (Ibid., p. 59)

Although incorporating a strong dose of Marxist dialectic, the perspective of Berger and Luckmann also incorporates the major perceptions of the social definitionists. It has, in fact, been criticized as being too subjectively and microscopically oriented to provide a more general paradigmatic perspective. Their perspective is paraphrased in the following remark: "*Society is a human product. Society is an objective reality. Man is a social product*" (ibid., p. 61). From this, the following questions frame the central interests of the social definitionist paradigm:

I Society as a product of human beings

    A How do social structures arise out of individual experience?

    B What is the basis of intersubjectivity?

    C What is the nature of the group?

II Society as objective reality

    A How are intersubjective typifications transformed into facticities?

    B How do social facts gain their external and coercive properties?

    C What mechanisms exist that foster the continued existence of social systems and social institutions?

        1 What is the nature of authority?

        2 What is the nature of legitimation: why is it necessary?

        3 What is the nature and root of rationalization: why is it necessary?

III Man as a product of society

    A If society is a human product, how can man be a social product?

        1 What is the nature of socialization?

        2 How is the world of social relations perceived in the generations that have not helped to produce it?

        3 What is the role of language in shaping behavior?

        4 What is the role of religion in shaping behavior?

    B   What is the dialectic between man as producer and man as product of society?

      1 What are the parameters of the human/social cybernetic loop?

      2 To what level does man the product retain autonomy and the option to change the system?

THE SOCIAL BEHAVIOR PARADIGM

Social behavior is associated with the psychological work of B. F. Skinner. Within the world of sociology, Homans and Blau have adapted his work as exchange theory. The main focus of behaviorism is the individual and his manipulation through the contingencies of reinforcement.

B. F. Skinner

B. F. Skinner became the great exponent and popularizer of the operant conditioning paradigm that caught the attention of academic psychology through most of the 1960s and 1970s. It should be noted that in his early work Skinner did not deny the possibility of subjective states. The position of radical behaviorism originally stated that because intervening variables such as thoughts, feelings and ideas were unmeasurable and, for the most part, empirically inaccessible, science would do well to ignore such things and concentrate on the observable dimensions of behavior. These observables were limited to observed behavior and the reinforcement history that includes the schedule of deprivation and the presence or absence of reinforcement. Given the opportunity to manipulate these variables, behavior was thought to be infinitely variable (Skinner, 1965).

The centerpiece of behaviorism is the idea of reinforcement. Contrary to popular belief, the concept of reinforcement is tied to behavior and not to drives or needs, pleasure or pain. While these elements may be reflected in the properties of the reinforcing stimulus, they do not enter into its proper definition. A reinforcer is any stimulus that increases the probability of the recurrence of the behavior that immediately precedes it (ibid.).

At the outset, operant conditioning in the Skinnerian mode should be differentiated from classical conditioning in the Pavlovian mode. Classical conditioning functions at the level of the autonomic nervous system and involves involuntary behavior. Classical conditioning involves the establishment of a connection between a naturally occurring, involuntary physiological response (the unconditioned response) and a separate, neutral stimulus (the unconditioned stimulus). The neutral stimulus is paired with the unconditioned stimulus so that the originally neutral stimulus comes to evoke the response associated with the unconditioned stimulus. Thus, in his famous experiment with dogs, Pavlov paired an unconditioned stimulus (meat) with a neutral stimulus (a bell). Meat naturally caused his subjects to salivate (the unconditioned response). After a number of pairings in which the ringing of the bell preceded the appearance of the meat, the meat was no longer necessary to produce salivation. Even when the meat was removed, the bell alone was enough to produce salivation and other involuntary responses associated with eating.

Operant, or instrumental, conditioning involves the use of a neutral stimulus (the discriminative stimulus) and a reinforcing stimulus (any stimulus that increases the probability of the action preceding it) in the shaping of a random action so that the presence of the originally neutral stimulus will predictably evoke the desired activity. In operant conditioning, an essentially random behavior is gradually shaped by rewards until it becomes instrumental in obtaining the reward. Operant conditioning is associated with more complex "voluntary" actions than is classical conditioning.

In the classic Skinnerian scenario, a rat is placed into a specially equipped cage (a Skinner box). On one end is a bar which, when pushed, operates a food magazine that delivers pellets of food. Another switch is used by the experimenter to deliver pellets into the same magazine. A rat, who has been deprived of food for a measurable amount of time, is placed into the cage. Whenever the rat moves towards the bar or magazine, the researcher presses a switch and delivers a pellet to the (presumably) hungry animal.

The experimenter's first aim is to elicit behavior that indicates that the rat has associated the magazine with food. This is done by delivering pellets into the magazine after every motion that the rat makes that might orient him in the direction of the magazine. These are reinforcements for the specified behavior if the rat can be seen to frequent the magazine area. Once the rat is oriented towards the magazine, reinforcements are delivered for each behavior that brings the animal closer to bar-pressing. Once the animal learns to press the bar, the machine becomes self-operating and self-recording, and may be set to vary the number of presses necessary to obtain further reinforcement (ibid.).

Under the conditions of operant learning, the strength of a behavior, or the probability of its continued reoccurrence, is related to the way in which it was learned. If a response fails to obtain reinforcement it may be extinguished, or cease to appear. Response patterns developed under differing schedules of reinforcement reveal differing susceptibility to extinction. If a behavior is reinforced on every trial, it is vulnerable to extinction. If reinforcements are cut off, it will quickly disappear. More resilient are those behaviors which are learned under an intermittent schedule of reinforcement.

According to Skinner, all human behavior is explainable in terms of the contingencies of reinforcement and their relations to innate biological structures. Various behaviors can be chained together to produce complex series of actions that have the appearance of rational action. The strength of various behaviors – that is, the probability that they will continue to appear – can be altered by varying the scheduling of reinforcements within the learning situation. Even thought can be reduced to internalized verbal behavior (Skinner, 1969, 1965, 1957).

The image of the subject matter

For the behaviorally oriented sociologist the subject matter of sociology is profoundly microscopic. All of the patterns that control the individual in his or her behavior ultimately also control the individual as a group member and in their interactions with others.

The central theoretical application of behavioral principles at the level of social theory is exchange theory. This views social behavior as an exchange of activity between two people. In every case of social behavior, actions or behaviors on one side of the exchange are reinforced by actions or behaviors on the other (Ritzer, 1980).

George Homans, the leading exponent of exchange theory, criticized Durkheim's approach and the approach of functionalism on several levels. Most importantly, he indicated that although Durkheim had identified social causes with social problems, he had failed to specify the manner in which cause and effect were related. He acknowledged the existence of social facts, but noted that the categorization of phenomena was insufficient as a basis for a scientific discipline. It was his opinion that psychological causes, more specifically contingencies of reinforcement, provided the link between the social cause and the individual and group responses. Groups, for Homans, were only aggregates of people, and people are shaped by psychological causes (ibid.).

There are five basic propositions of exchange theory (ibid.), all of them, except the last, reducible to the basic principles of operant conditioning:

1 If situations of a certain type have been linked with behavior that was rewarded, situations similar to them will tend to evoke similar responses.
2 The frequency of occurrence of a given action is related to the frequency with which that action (or actions) is reinforced by another person's responses.
3 The more valuable the response to an action, the more likely the original action becomes. This is expressed in terms of a rate of exchange – the numerical proportion of the instances of one activity to the comparable rate of the expression of the other per unit time.
4 The more recently a certain action has been used as a reinforcement, the lower the continuing reinforcement value of the behavior becomes in subsequent trials.

5 Anger results when a person fails to realize at least his just proportion of good in accordance with principles of distributive justice.

Homan's theory never satisfactorily dealt with complex social systems and was only articulated to the level of simple interactions. Blau, continuing beyond Homans's preliminary formulations, extended exchange theory to include complex social facts. In doing so, he differentiated between two different kinds of social facts. One type of social fact emerges from exchanges between individuals. It is the emergent property of interpersonal actions. According to Blau:

> Exchange processes utilize, as it were, the self-interests of individuals to produce a differentiated social structure within which norms tend to develop that require individuals to set aside some of their personal interests for the sake of the collectivity.
>
> (Blau, 1964, p. 224)

The second type of social fact is constructed by group members for an explicit purpose. There is a qualitative difference between the two. Whereas in the smaller groups the process of exchange itself creates and maintains group structure, the larger and more complex groups are created and maintained by commonly held norms and values (Ritzer, 1980).

Blau describes four kinds of value. Each value category performs a specific function within the group. Particularistic values are those values which unite specific individuals to a given group. They also identify core from peripheral members. Universalistic values are community standards of exchange for specific actions. Legitimative values accord power and authority to certain roles within the community. Opposing values are held by the institutionalized opposition and produce the possibility of change within the society (ibid.).

Blau again differs from Homans in his humanization of the exchange process. It is real people to whom he appeals. The driving force in this version of exchange theory is the sense of trust and the experience of social exchange as encountered by human beings. "Rat psychology" is relegated to the background. Blau's later work, however, is generally placed in the functionalist camp (Blau, 1964; Ritzer, 1980; Timasheff and Theodorson, 1976).

Social behaviorism, as here defined, develops on the basis of conditioning principles and the idea of emergent properties in complex systems. Homans's principles may be extended by addition to provide a fair approximation of general exchange theory.

- If situations of a certain type have been linked with behavior that was rewarded, situations similar to them will tend to evoke similar responses.
- The frequency of occurrence of a given action is related to the frequency

with which that action (or actions) is reinforced by another person's responses.

- The more valuable the response to an action, the more likely the original action becomes. This is expressed in terms of a rate of exchange – the numerical proportion of the instances of one activity to the comparable rate of the expression of the other per unit time.
- The more recently a certain action has been used as a reinforcement, the lower the continuing reinforcement value of the behavior becomes in subsequent trials.
- Anger results when a person fails to realize at least his just proportion of good in accordance with principles of distributive justice.
- Small groups appear as emergent properties of individual interactions.
- Large groups are created for specific purposes.
- Whereas small groups are ordered by the individuals that compose them, large groups are ordered by independently existing norms and values.

THE INTEGRATIVE PARADIGM

Preliminary considerations

In our brief overview of the styles of sociological theorizing we find, on the one hand, the social factists emphasizing the externality and structural reality of social phenomena; and on the other, social behaviorists and social definitionists upholding the primacy of individual response to the social world on whatever level of reality it appears. Ritzer has identified these perspectives with the macrosociological–objective and microsociological–subjective poles that mark the extremes of a two-dimensional field of sociology.

The whole field may be classified in terms of whether the primary emphasis of the theorist deals with macrosociological issues like cultures, mass media, large groups and bureaucracies, or with microsociological issues like interpersonal relations, patterns that characterize meetings in public places, family structure and small group dynamics. On the other axis the field is divided into subjective versus objective emphasis. Shutz, Mead, Goffman and Garfinkle emphasize the subjective elements of social life, while Durkheim, Parsons, Buckley and Comte emphasize its externality and objectivity (Ritzer, 1980). A truly integrative paradigm must include a broad spectrum of elements encompassing both the microsociological/macrosociological and the subjective/objective dimensions.

Berger and Luckmann declare that any comprehensive sociology must include the sociologies of religion and language as foundational elements in the determination of human activities. These, moreover, must also be rooted in an historical context outside which they can have no real meaning.

The Frankfurt School, identified with the writings of Max Horkheimer and Theodor Adorno, makes the following important set of observations as to the nature of sociology.

[S]ocial processes are always the products of history and in the form of their immanent tensions contain historical tendencies. If one seeks to oppose a pure doctrine of the forms of human relations to the dynamics of history, one only obtains an empty mold of the social. From such entirely inessential stipulations, as the modes of behavior of diverse groups in diverse situations, one has to construct artificially what in truth can only be extracted from concrete, historically determined social structures. For this, historical analysis and construction are always required. Further, the modes of social behavior of human beings cannot be separated from psychological mechanisms, as long as it is not merely objective conditions and institutions which are being investigated. Whatever social associations of whatever kind they may enter into, human beings are individuals, and even where they throw off their usual individual traits and behave after a fashion allegedly characteristic of masses, they still act, insofar as their action is psychologically determined, according to the psychological causations of their specific individuality. This involvement has been demonstrated so strikingly by modern depth psychology that, at the very least, the special justification of sociology as the doctrine of subjective group behavior in contrast to individual psychology has been deprived of any real basis.
(Frankfurt Institute for Social Research, 1972, pp. 9–10)

The Marxist perspective, out of which the Frankfurt Institute grew, provides other important elements which a coherent science of man must consider. Marx has not been considered up to this point because, more than any other, he is a paradigm bridger. When certain facets of his earlier sociological theories are separated from their later development in the political arena, he becomes a major contributor to social thought independent of communism.

The Marxist view is essentially holistic. The average human integrates every facet of his life into the whole. He is at once biological, political, social and historical without division. He is simultaneously the product of culture and its source, living in dialectic tension between the past and the present. In the face of that dialectic he creates the future (Giddens, 1982).

Citing Marx's early writings, Giddens notes:

Each individual is ... the recipient of the accumulated culture of the generations which have preceded him and in his own interaction with the natural and social world in which he lives is a contributor to the further modification of that world as experienced by others. ... Marx asserts " ... Though a man is a unique individual ... he is equally the whole, the ideal whole, the subjective existence of society as thought and experienced."

(Giddens, 1982, p. 13)

Culture is shaped by the mode of production, the material conditions of human life as it moves through history. Engels, in *Socialism, Utopian and Scientific*, notes:

Production and, with production, the exchange of its products, is the basis of every social order; ... in every society which has appeared in history, the distribution of the products and with it the division of society into classes or estates, is determined by what is produced, and how it is produced, and how the product is exchanged.

(Cited by Laski, 1967, p. 89)

Historically, every culture has born within itself, through the nature of its economic basis, contradictions which constitute "the seeds of its own destruction." These contradictions may take the form of holdovers from the old economic system or contradictions that flow out of the current means of production and distribution. Within capitalism the central contradiction is the expansion of the modes of production without a correlated advance in the relations of production: a violation of the ideal of distributive justice. When industry prospers and the laborer upon whom it depends fails to see his fair due, the inherent contradiction inevitably becomes the seed of future transformations (Giddens, 1982; Aron, 1970).

Consciousness and the cultural superstructure is absolutely tied to the means of production and distribution, the underlying infrastructure. In fact, any conscious activity not acknowledged as being so related is by definition false consciousness. The culture in general is dominated by the values of the superordinate class (Giddens, 1982; Aron, 1970; Mannheim, 1936).

Does it require deep intuition to comprehend that man's ideas, views, and conceptions, in one word man's consciousness changes with every change in the conditions of his material existence, in his social relations and in his social life? ... The ruling ideas of each age have ever been the ideas of its ruling class.

(Marx and Engels, 1967b, p. 156)

While it is unnecessary for us to take the entire Marxist program at face value, there are certain important insights that derive from his work that an integrated sociology must include. These include holism, the view of man as a unitary being without neat compartments; and the reciprocal and dialectic relationship between humankind and culture. People are shaped by culture – which is itself a human product – over which mankind, in turn, exercises a certain level of control. The division or analysis into superstructure and infrastructure provides a strong correlate (on an abstract level) for conscious and unconscious levels of action. In Marx's determination of consciousness by the relations of production and class situation we find the root realization that thought is related to role, and that roles are determined by the division of labor.

The basic outline

In an integrative sociology we must be concerned not only with the *what* of social facts, but their meaning on an individual level. Functionalism may be seen as providing a context for meaning on a systems level, but human beings function on a level of personal experience. Meaning as such takes on two possible values (that is, in the context of the current discussion) depending upon the perspective of the assessor. To a depth psychologist, meaning may connote the personal associations evoked by the experience. It may involve transference functions and the constellation of various archetypally defined complexes. To a behaviorist, on the other hand, meaning is defined in a series of response chains rooted in the contingencies of reinforcement.

However, before a mode of action becomes ensconced as a social fact, it must first appear as an interpersonal response. These must, in turn, be derived from roots in the response systems of individuals. Therefore, in order to derive a meaningfully adequate (to use Weber's phrase) sociology we first locate its roots in individual psychology. Upon its move to a different logical level as a social fact, it then becomes susceptible of functional analysis. Yet, here too the need exists for a consistent association with personal response systems so as to provide meaning contexts for individual actors.

The following outline attempts to provide some of the basic questions that a sociology should seek to answer. At its heart lie the questions: what is the nature of the group and what is the relationship between individual meaning and group structure? No references are provided here. Most of the questions are easily traced to their forerunners in the previous sections of this chapter. While this outline asks some suggestive questions, it is only meant to be just that: suggestive. It is by no means complete or exhaustive.

At the level of the genesis of social institutions we must ask, what is the nature of intersubjectivity? More specifically we must ask:

I   What prepares an individual to communicate with other individuals?

   A   What evidence exists for a propensity for humans to form groups or group identities?

   B   Is it learned or innate?

   C   To what other behaviors is it linked?

   D   Is it a self-reinforcing behavior or does it require external reinforcement?

II What is the nature of group formation?

    A Are there primordial group structures?

        1 The mother–infant bond
        2 Families

           a Nuclear
           b Extended

        3 Tribes
        4 Communities

    B How do the experiences of the individuals in these groups influence their experiences in other groups?

        1 Are they preparatory or predictive of other roles?
        2 Are they preparatory or predictive of the roles of others?

    C Are there role definitions in these groups?

        1 What are the specific roles identified in the group?
        2 How are these roles determined or assigned?

           a If they are learned, how are they learned? And in response to what environmental demands are they shaped?
           b If they are innate, to what extent are they innate and what do we mean by innate?
           c What is the epigenetic mix?

        3 What is the impact of any specific role on the individual?

           a To what extent are roles assigned or distributed in accordance with abilities and propensities?
           b To what extent are roles assigned or distributed arbitrarily?
           c How, and under what conditions, do individuals develop role identities?

Since some theorists (Blau, 1964; Ritzer, 1980) differentiate the naturally occurring groups, like families and other small groups, from the larger, voluntary institutions, we must come to understand how large groups and institutions come into being, and the nature of the transition between small, informal institutions and large formal institutions.

I Society is a product of human consciousness: how do individuals unite to form large groups?

    A How has this happened historically?
    B How is it happening now?

II Modern society is, on some level, a product of the historical development that preceded it:

A   How do the social changes of yesterday impact upon the design of institutions today?

B   How are past decisions understood today?

III   What is the rule of legitimacy in the current context?

A   How is it defined?

B   Where did it come from?

C   How did it develop?

D   How is it currently conceived?

Once large groups come into existence they become reified as social facts. An integrated sociology must determine the nature and function of social facts not only in their own self maintenance, but as they interact with the subjective realities of smaller groups and individuals.

I   Social institutions present themselves to every individual as "facticities." How does a social construct attain to the level of fact?

A   How do the fruits of human action become determinative of that action?

B   On what level do the external facts impact on the individual?

1   How are role definitions socially determined?

2   How are individuals motivated or controlled by social institutions and social structures?

a   Are they transmitted as cultural definitions or norms?

1) What are the mechanisms of transmission?

2) How do these mechanisms function?

b   Are they contingent upon external reinforcement?

c   Are they self reinforcing? If so: what is the mechanism; i.e. what is their reinforcing property?

II   At the level of the social fact, specific functions may be defined for each subsystem in a large organization. What are the major groups represented by the system?

A   What is the group whose values are most closely identified with the social structure?

B   What are the excluded groups?

1   What function do they perform for the maintenance of the dominant perspective?

2   How specifically are they subordinated to the dominant group?

C   What contradiction does this bifurcation embody?

1   What are the manifest functions that define the institution?

    a How do they explicitly discriminate between classes or differentiate members from non-members?

    b How do they embody modes of thought and action inappropriate to the current social situation or economic era?

    c How are they maintained?

      1) Religious legitimations.
      2) Political legitimations.
      3) Negative sanctions.

  2 What latent functions define the roles of subordinate and inferior classes?

    a How do they reinforce the status quo?

    b How do they reinforce inappropriate behavior, behavioral contradictions, within the current socio-economic framework?

    c How are they maintained?

      1) Religious legitimations.
      2) Political legitimations.
      3) Negative sanctions.

D What are the historic and economic roots of the bifurcation?

  1 How are the dominant and non-dominant positions related to patterns of charisma and its routinization?

  2 Are there different social facts which spring from the same historical roots?

The foregoing represents an overview of some of the basic questions that an integrated paradigm must answer. However, our purpose is less ambitious than taking the whole project in hand. In the following chapters, we will apply the insights of Jung's psychology to the core of these issues. In order to frame our research in a manageable manner, the following questions, derived in large part from the work of Berger and Luckmann, will form a tacit background for our inquiry.

I Society as a product of human beings.

  A What is the basis of intersubjectivity?
  B What is the nature of the group?
  C How do social structures arise out of individual experience?
  D What is the relationship between the structure of the psyche and the structure of the group?

II Society as objective reality.

  A How are intersubjective typifications transformed into facticities?

B   How do social facts gain their external and coercive properties?

C   What mechanisms exist that foster the continued existence of social systems and social institutions?

1   What is the nature of authority?
2   What is the nature of legitimation and why is it necessary?
3   What is the nature and root of rationalization and why is it necessary?

D   What mechanisms exist that account for the failure of groups and societies?

1   What is the source of contradiction, the seed of destruction?
2   How do we account for deviance?

III   Humankind as a product of society.

A   If society is a human product, how can humans be a social product?

1   What is the nature of socialization?
2   How is the world of social relations perceived in the generations that have not helped to produce it?
3   What is the role of language in shaping behavior?
4   What is the role of religion in shaping behavior?

B   What is the dialectic between humankind as producer and humankind as product of society?

1   What are the parameters of the human/social cybernetic loop?
2   To what level does man the product retain autonomy and the option to change the system?

Part IV

The elements of an archetypal sociology

Chapter 9

The roots of intersubjectivity

Jung understood that humankind was inherently social. He observed that sociality was one of the necessary conditions for human existence and that without it humanity would cease to be. Progoff reflects Jung's position: "Man is by his very nature social. . . . The human psyche cannot function without a culture, and no individual is possible without society" (1953/1981, p. 161).

Jung was, however, not convinced that sociality was the purpose for which individuals existed. In fact, he was profoundly pessimistic about the power of the group and its potential for destruction. This pessimism suffused his work. Most of his reflections on group process follow a distinctly negative trend. He saw the group as precursor to the mob and the destroyer of individuality. The group was a destroyer of morality and antithetical to personal development (1954/1966, 1953/1966, 1964/1970).

> The larger a community is, and the more the sum total of collective factors peculiar to every large community rests on conservative prejudices detrimental to individuality, the more will the individual be morally and spiritually crushed, and as a result, the one course of moral and spiritual progress for society is choked up. . . . It is a notorious fact that the morality of society as a whole is in inverse ratio to its size; for the greater the aggregation of individuals, the more the individual factors are blotted out, and with them, morality, which rests entirely on the moral sense of the individual and the freedom necessary for this. Hence every man is, in a certain sense, unconsciously a worse man when he is in society than when acting alone; for he is carried by society and to that extent relieved of his individual responsibility. Any large company composed of wholly admirable people has the morality and the intelligence of an unwieldy, stupid, and violent animal. The bigger the organization, the more unavoidable is its immorality and blind stupidity (*Senatus bestia, senatores boni viri*). Society, by automatically stressing all the collective qualities in its individual representatives, puts a premium on mediocrity, on everything that settles down to vegetate in an easy, irresponsible way.
> (Jung, 1953/1966, para. 240)

In general, the group held no identity of its own, but was identical to the individuals that comprised it. Nevertheless, much like Durkheim, Jung saw that the individuals functioning as a group tended to act as a "collective entity." Jung and Durkheim, however, stood as extreme opposites in regard to their perspective on society. For Durkheim the group was the ultimate arbiter of morality. The noblest of actions and thoughts were group inspired. For Jung, on the contrary, the group pulled down the moral standing of the individual and threatened his most precious of gifts, his individuality. Because groups provide an external security from responsibility, sensuous feelings of belonging and instant power, they readily seduce the individual to surrender to their spell (Jung, 1964/1970; 1953/1966; Durkheim, 1933/ 1964, 1938/1964).

> Like the individual, a group is influenced by numerous typical factors, such as the family milieu, society, politics, outlook on life, religion. The bigger the group, the more the individuals composing it function as a collective entity, which is so powerful that it can reduce the individual consciousness to the point of extinction, and it does this the more easily if the individual lacks spiritual possessions of his own with an individual stamp. The group and what belongs to it cover up the lack of genuine individuality, just as parents act as substitutes for everything lacking in their children. In this respect the group exerts a seductive influence, for nothing is easier than a perseveration of infantile ways or a return to them.
>
> (Jung, 1964/1970, para. 891)

Jung observed that the danger of the group to individual integrity and personal growth varied with its size. The larger the group, the more thorough-going its domination and destructive potential.

> [I]nsofar as society is itself composed of de-individualized human beings, it is completely at the mercy of ruthless individualists. Let it band together into groups and organizations as much as it likes – it is just this banding together and the resultant extinction of the individual personality that makes it succumb so readily to a dictator. A million zeros joined together do not, unfortunately, add up to one. Ultimately everything depends on the quality of the individual, but our fatally shortsighted age thinks only in terms of large numbers and mass organizations, though one would think that the world had seen more than enough of what a well disciplined mob can do in the hands of a single madman. . . . People go on blithely organizing and believing in the sovereign remedy of mass action, without the least consciousness of the fact that the most powerful organizations in the world can be maintained only by the greatest ruthlessness of their leaders and the cheapest of slogans.
>
> (Ibid., para. 535)

Hope for mankind came not from mass movements or political action, but through the redemption of the individual human being. When self conscious individuals move together as a group they are both responsible and compassionate. Their consensus is freely and consciously given. As a result, their action can avoid the unconscious pitfalls of the mass mind. Humankind was destined to grow and develop as self fulfilling, self realizing individuals. Only the fully formed human could hope to provide his fellow with any meaningful help, for only he could fully appreciate what it means to be human in the broadest sense.

[T]he natural process of individuation brings to birth a consciousness of human community precisely because it makes us aware of the unconscious, which unites and is common to all mankind. Individuation is an at-one-ment with oneself and at the same time with humanity, since oneself is a part of humanity. Once the individual is thus secured in himself, there is some guarantee that the organized accumulation of individuals in the State ... will result in the formation no longer of an anonymous mass, but of a conscious community. The indispensable condition for this is conscious freedom of choice and individual decision. ...

(Jung, 1954/1966, para. 227)

Despite his general pessimism, Jung provided a significant basis for understanding group process and the nature of human societies. On the level of social behavior in the tradition of Weber, Schutz, Mead, and Berger and Luckmann, he provides a strong psychological basis for understanding the roots of intersubjectivity, and a similarly strong foundation for understanding the nature of groups. The theory of archetypes provides a significant basis for understanding how individuals can share their subjective experience, and the motivations that draw them into the group experience.

On the level of structural–functional sociology, Jung provides the basis for understanding how it is that the products of human consciousness become reified[1] as external facticities, and explains the nature of their coercive power. Using his model of the human psyche, manifest and latent functions and dysfunctions of groups are articulated in terms of the mechanisms of projection and identification.

Finally, in the application of his theory of libido, we find a mechanism that carries Weber's already fundamental idea of the routinization of charisma one step closer to full understanding. Through it, the emergence of new groups, the horror of the Nazis and the development of the United States Constitution gain a special clarity of psycho-social mechanism.

ARCHETYPAL PRECURSORS

The Jungian psyche presupposes a multileveled unconscious. It begins at the deepest levels with the biologically structured or psychoid archetypes which order the collective unconscious. These elements can never become conscious. Their influence can only be inferred by their effect as behavioral organizers as they give rise to living patterns that transcend national and cultural groupings (Jung, 1959/1968a).

The archetypes represent the mode by which the sensible world is made accessible to the psychic world. They are closely related to the instinctual releasers which form the basis for perception (Jung, 1959/1968a; Fordham, 1957; Stevens, 1982/1983). The archetypes represent at the most basic level what it means to be human. In their relation to instinct and the Innate Release Mechanisms (IRMs), they represent the psychic expression of the possibility of perceiving certain classes of objects and affective states. Moving on the analogy of the IRM, many authors have suggested that archetypal activity provides a physiological basis for understanding Kant's *a priori* categories.

> Jung equated this "*a priori* structure" with the archetypal determinants of the phylogenetic psyche (what he often referred to as the *objective psyche* as well as the "collective unconscious"): he considered that it was these archetypal structures which controlled the perceptual mechanism, determining the relative salience of differing stimuli arising from both outside and inside the individual's personal boundaries.
>
> (Stevens, 1982/1983, p. 58)

Because the archetypes were shaped over eons of human development as responses to the real world, they represent not only *a priori* categories, but common categories that link all of humankind as perceptual and response sets. Despite differences in language, culture or family structure, all of humankind responds out of the same basic organs of perception and action. What they see and hear and feel and taste and smell differs little from group to group. The way their limbs articulate, the way they walk and grasp are all basically the same. These similarities mark out what it means to be human. Their relevance is made clear by developmental psychology and sociobiology where we see archetypal and instinctual pressures orienting the neonate towards certain commonly experienced root behaviors such as locating and bonding to a suitable mother-object (Jung, 1971; Hinde, 1983; Eibl-Eibesfeldt, 1990). On the most primitive level, archetypal activity is experienced as a lack of differentiation between the subject and the object of attention. The archetypal, however, is not limited to the realm of the individual and biological.

> The processes of the collective unconscious are concerned not only with the more or less personal relations of an individual to his family or to a

wider social group, but with his relations to society and to the human community in general.

(Jung, 1953/1966, para. 278)

Such innate response mechanisms unconsciously meld with their releasers in an undifferentiated union of subject and object, stimulus and response. We recall the words of David Miller with regard to the union of stimulus and consummatory act.

Killing and devouring the prey are one and the same act. Upon reaching its food the dog continues immediately to consume it. Even before they reached the meat indicated by the buzzer, the saliva in the pavlovian dogs began to flow.

(Miller, 1973/1980, p. 60)

These phenomena – the merging of subject and object, stimulus and response – are rooted in the Piagetian concept of assimilation which is, in itself, one of the fundamental dimensions of archetypal action.[2] Assimilation reflects the extent to which an external stimulus can be included within pre-existent systems. It is Piaget's term for the special, interactive relation that holds between a stimulus and the responding organism. It expresses "an inner correspondence or sameness between an environmental phenomenon and the structure within the organism." Knowing, from this perspective, is defined as "assimilable to the organism's structure." It implies that the relationship between the organism and the environment must be based upon a prior or an *a priori* scheme of recognition (Furth, 1969, pp. 13–14).

Thus, archetypal activity, and before it, the action of ethological mechanisms, determines a primitive identity between the perceiver and the percept. To the animal or the neonate, there is no stimulus response differentiation, there is no subject/object distinction, the world is perceived as a unity without time, without dimension. Primitive understanding is, in this sense, assimilation of the stimulus object to pre-existent structures within the perceiving organism. Assimilation is complemented by the process of accommodation/compensation which balances the structure of the organism with its unmet needs against the environmental input.

In the human infant, the mechanism of compensation allows the growing child (as well as the adult) to emphasize those areas of nurture or development where the biological and psychic expectancies were unmet by the parental object. In this manner, despite wide divergence in care delivery, humans arise in a reasonably consistent manner. The roots of individual personality traits and general preference patterns are also founded in this interplay between the archetypal expectancy and the response of the real world.

The psyche is a self-regulating system that maintains its equilibrium just as the body does. Every process that goes too far immediately and inevitably calls forth compensations, and without these there would be neither a normal metabolism nor a normal psyche. In this sense we can take the theory of compensation as a basic law of psychic behaviour. Too little on one side results in too much on the other.

(Jung, 1954/1966, para. 330)

A significant example of compensation is the normal level of function attained by most children almost in spite of the level of maternal care. Imbalances in parental care are compensated by characterological dispositions which balance out the deficit.

Whatever archetypal potential we as parents fail to activate in our child still persists there as a potential and, by definition, must continue to seek actualization in reality. The extent of this unactualized potential is inversely proportional to our effectiveness as parents, the more incompetent we are, the greater the archetypal energy seeking to be discharged, and the greater the parental hunger manifested by the child.

(Stevens, 1982/1983, pp. 113–14)

Stevens notes further that:

When actualization has been deficient, an individual finds himself, despite his conscious will in the matter, "sucked into" personal involvements and situations which promise to possess characteristics adequate to constellate, or bring into birth, the unlived archetypal elements.

(Ibid., p. 115)

The most primitive levels of the collective unconscious are almost indistinguishable from instinct, but these are uniquely human responses that not only link humankind to the animal world but also distinguish it from it. The archetypes define at the most primitive level what it means to be human. On the next higher level, the unconscious is characterized by patterns that are typical of specific racial or national groups. Just as on the lower levels of the psyche there exist patterns that are characteristic of humankind as a whole, here the biologically determined characteristics of each group are registered as specific, identifiable patterns; this is the racial or regional unconscious (Jung 1959/1968a, Jung, 1960/1969).

As we move more towards the conscious psyche, the next layers become more specific to national and linguistic groups and tend to be mediated less through the biological mechanisms that order the collective unconscious as by linguistic and cultural processes. These give rise to more specific differentiations of personality and action patterns until we are eventually faced with the personal unconscious which is developed by each individual in his or her own experience of history (Jung, 1968b; von Franz, 1980/ 1988).

The individual is not only an individual but a social and collective being. There are collective needs that conflict with personal needs and personal needs that conflict with collective. The psychic functions are divided into two groups. The inferior group is the collective, unconscious and automatic part known to us as the collective unconscious. The superior part of the unconscious consists of the personal unconscious and our consciousness itself. This includes those parts of collective experience that limit the expression of the deeper archetypes in terms of racial, cultural and familial elements.

(Jung, 1953/1966)

Neumann relates that:

the individual adapts himself to the cultural canon by way of the links between the complexes and the archetypes. As consciousness develops, the childlike psyche's bond with the archetypes is continuously replaced by personal relations with the environment, and the tie with the great archetypes of childhood is transferred to the archetypal canon of the prevailing culture.

(Neumann, 1959/1974, pp. 178–9)

EARLY UNION OF THE MOTHER AND THE INFANT

Jung (1956/1967) reports that the earliest phase of human existence is characterized by an absolute identification between the neonate and the mother. Fordham continues the thought by observing that the infant's early experience is characterized by fantasies in which the acts of sucking and excreting are merged with the perception of the activity. No differentiation is made between the act and the actor, the act and its fulfillment or the act and its object. All are fused in the fantasy. This is an indication of the operation of the archetypal sphere without the intervention of consciousness (1957, p. 111).

Whitmont says of the early stages of psychic development:

The psyche of the child seems to operate like a relatively undifferentiated wholeness, a pattern of integrated, instinctual responses in an encompassing field, where subject–object separation in the adult's sense has as yet no validity. . . . Ego development gradually splits this instinctual "unitary reality" into an inner subjectivity and an outer objectivity.

(Whitmont, 1969, p. 267)

In *The Great Mother* (1955), Neumann indicated that the mother archetype begins rooted in the undifferentiated uroboric[3] consciousness. Here, all of the opposites intermingle: good and bad, male and female, low and high. There is a nearly seamless bond between mother and child that only later gives rise to the perception of a differentiated mother-object.

From the perspective of object relations theory, neonatal experience is enmeshed from the beginning with the maternal substrate. It is variously called a symbiotic relationship, an objectless stage, a stage of normal autism or a stage of biological unity with the mother. This early stage is characterized by the inability of the infant to differentiate between himself and the environment. His drives and their fulfillment or frustration are one experience. There is an essential, perceived unity between the child and its mother (Spitz, 1965; Fraiberg, 1965; Mahler, et al., 1975; Compton, 1987; Plaut, 1975, p. 207).

All of these formulations lead back to the Jungian concept of identity which is the dominant process in the formation of the mother–infant bond, and is the unconscious root of all group behavior.

> I use the term *identity* to denote a psychological conformity. It is always an unconscious phenomenon. . . . It is a characteristic of the primitive mentality and the real foundation of *participation mystique*, which is nothing but a relic of the original non-differentiation of subject and object, and hence of the primordial unconscious state. It is also a characteristic of the mental state of early infancy, and, finally, of the unconscious of the civilized adult, which, insofar as it has not become a content of consciousness, remains in a permanent state of identification with objects. . . .
>
> (Jung, 1971, para. 741)

The union between the neonate and the mother is originally rooted in the non-differentiation of subject and object. Jung, however, posits an archetypal principle which mediates the individual's future interface with other individuals. This is the anima/us. It is originally related to the ethological releasers which cause the child to bond with the mother-object but comes into full fruition as the archetypal imprint of the goodness of fit between the archetypal expectancy and actual parental behavior. Although most often identified with the unconscious and relations with the opposite sex, it is also, according to Jung, the root of the individual's relations to others of both sexes.

The anima, identified with the maternal archetype, becomes the first point of contact with the world. Assimilation of external reality takes place in the context of a pre-established maternal archetype to which the external world gradually assimilates. Jung describes the process in terms of a

> gradual drawing in of external nature into the world of the subject, and the contamination of the primary object, the mother, . . . with the secondary object, nature, which imperceptibly usurps the mother's place and takes over the sounds first heard from her, together with all those feelings we later rediscover in ourselves in our warm love for mother nature. . . . She was our first experience of an outside and at the same

time of an inside: from that interior world there emerged an image, apparently a reflection of the external mother-image, yet older, more original and more imperishable than this – a mother who changed back into a Kore, into an eternally youthful figure. This is the anima, the personification of the collective unconscious.

(Jung, 1956/1967, para. 500)

A variant of this position is presented by Tiger and Fox in *The Imperial Animal* as part of their hypothesized "biogrammar" that determines certain facets of human development.

Simply on the basis of what we know about the social mammals in general, we can predict that if the mother–child bond does not go right, the unfortunate youngster may never get any of his other bonds right. . . . Ultimately the "nonbreeding" bond with the mother has to be transformed into a "breeding" bond with a member of the opposite sex. If the initial instructions are not properly followed, the rest of the program may be jeopardized and emerge in an attenuated or skewed form. At worst the wrongly programmed animal may not be able to breed at all and thus be lost to the gene pool; at best it may breed but put the programming of its own offspring in danger.

(Tiger and Fox, 1971/1989, p. 62)

As this process continues, the individual develops bonds with the father and other family members. They, like his early responses to the physical world, are built upon the early development of the mother complex.[4] The interactions of family life form imprints which later will provide projective apparatti to which the social world will assimilate in the process of projection.

The Jungian psyche does not remain undifferentiated, neither does it remain in the state of ouroboric union with the mother. Likewise, on the level of social reality, the individual begins at some point to arise out of the group. This differentiation is rooted in his emergence from the family grouping.

All the libido that was tied up in family bonds must be withdrawn from the narrower circle into the larger one, because the psychic health of the adult individual, who in childhood was a mere particle revolving in a rotary system, demands that he himself should become the centre of a new system . . . unless this is done the unemployed libido will inevitably remained fixed in the conscious endogamous relationship to the parents and will seriously hamper the individual's freedom. . . . For if he allows his libido to get stuck in a childish milieu, and does not free it for higher purposes, he falls under the spell of unconscious compulsion. Wherever he may be, the unconscious will then recreate the infantile milieu by projecting his complexes all over again, and in defiance of his vital interests, the same dependence and lack of freedom which formerly characterized his relations with his parents. . . . When the libido thus remains fixed in its most primitive form it keeps men on a correspondingly low level where they have no control over themselves and are at the mercy of their affects.

(Jung, 1956/1967, para. 644)

THE PARTICIPATION MYSTIQUE

Jung took the position that primitive man lived in a world of shared meanings, shared consciousness and shared reality. Individuals did not exist, but man was joined to man in an undifferentiated bond of unconscious identification.

> The further we go back in history, the more we see personality disappearing beneath the wrappings of collectivity. And if we go right back to primitive psychology, we find no trace of the concept of an individual. Instead of individuality we find only collective relationship or what Levy-Bruhl calls participation mystique. The collective attitude hinders the recognition and evaluation of a psychology different from the subject's because the mind that is collectively oriented is quite incapable of thinking and feeling in any other way than by projection. What we understand by the concept individual is a relatively recent acquisition in the history of the human mind and human culture.
>
> (Jung, 1971, para. 12)

In accordance with this formulation, primitive thought encounters the world through projection of its own mental structures. The world is assimilated to a pre-existent reality. More often than not, this reality takes the form of traditional, familiar and tribal patterns similarly learned and incorporated by all members of the group. Individuality is the mark of the outcast, the witch or some otherwise powerful or dangerous being. One must not distinguish oneself, for the unity of the group is the overriding value.[5]

The shared values of a group comprise, in part, their collective representations. These are the common definitions arising out of the common structure of mind imposed simultaneously by a traditional structure of consciousness and the re-projection of those values upon the world at large. The collective contents of conscious life are bound up with emotional charges which provide a specific sensual feeling tone that stands in the place of denotative specificity (Jung, 1971, 1960/1969; Mannheim, 1936).

> COLLECTIVE: I term *collective* all psychic contents that belong not to one individual but to many, i.e., to a society, a people, or to mankind in general. Such contents are what Levy-Bruhl calls the *representations collectives* of primitives, as well as the general concepts of justice, the

state, religion, science, etc., current among civilized man. It is not only concepts and ways of looking at things, however, that must be termed collective, but also feelings. Among primitives, the *representations collectives* are at the same time collective feelings, as Levy-Bruhl has shown. Because of this collective feeling-value he calls the *represen- tations collectives* "mystical," since they are not merely intellectual but emotional. Among civilized people too, certain collective ideas – God, justice, fatherland, etc. – are bound up with collective feelings. This collective quality adheres not only to particular psychic elements or contents but to whole *functions*. Thus the thinking function as a whole can have a collective quality, when it possesses general validity and accords with the laws of logic. Similarly, the feeling function as a whole can be collective when it is identified with the general feeling and accords with the general expectations, the general moral consciousness, etc. In the same way sensation and intuition are collective when they are at the same time characteristic of a large group of men.

(Jung, 1971, para. 692)

Primitive thought is rooted in a collective participation in a singular culture that allows for little or no deviation. While individual freedom may be great, the possible thought forms and activity options are limited by the cultural milieu. Individuality generally does not arise as either an option or a goal. Such a state was also envisioned by Durkheim, who characterized primitive societies as bound together by a mechanical solidarity which was

a solidarity of resemblance. The major characteristic of a society in which mechanical solidarity prevails is that the individuals differ from one another as little as possible. The individuals, the members of the same collectivity, resemble each other because they hold the same things sacred. The society is coherent because the individuals are not yet differentiated.

(Aron, 1970, p. 11)[6]

We might also refer to Marxist sociology in which the means of production structure the available modes of thought. Where the division of labor has not appeared, thought forms must remain consistent with one another; a single infrastructure with no stratification yields no differen- tiation of thought form. Finally, we recall Jaynes's assertion, based upon patterns of linguistic change in the *Iliad*, that human consciousness slowly emerged from a collective unity some time about 5,000 years ago in the West (1976).[7]

If we take Jung's perspective to heart, we then find that Western logic possesses a mystical or emotional validity by virtue of its collective sanction that is every bit as mystical as the *representations collectives* of the non- industrialized peoples. This is the reciprocal of Lévi-Strauss's perspective on native thought. Both Western and non-Western thought may be seen to be collectively driven and, in the same sense, mystical, as they are both accompanied by an emotional charge that makes them, in Lévi-Strauss's terms, "good to think." In the hands of Alvin Gouldner, those same thought patterns are said to be rooted in the background assumptions of a culture or social stratum; thought that is consistent with those patterns is felt to be resonant with them (Jung, 1971; Lévi-Strauss, 1962/1966; Gouldner, 1970).

Progoff makes the important point that the *participation mystique* exists wherever the individual fuses with the group experience. Whenever the individual cannot clearly differentiate between his own thoughts and the thoughts of the group, the *participation mystique* prevails.

> When an individual lives completely within the spell of the collective representations, fusing himself with the group and identifying himself with the collectivity, the images of the group dominate his unconscious. Such an individual lives constantly in a relation of "participation mystique" with the collective representations. He does not distinguish the ideas of his own thinking processes from the collective images – or if so, only barely – and in this condition he can hardly be said to be individualized.
>
> (Progoff, 1953/1981, p. 171)

The participation mystique is also characteristic of the relationship between the child and his parents and, presumably, between the child and his peers. Wherever an archetypal constellation binds individuals into a common reality, the unconscious link recreates the sense of primal unity that marked the neonatal stages.

The development of the ego is firmly rooted in the child's relation to group pressures. Its structure is grounded in the values of the collective. Neumann reports that:

> The consciousness of the individual originally develops with the aid of the collective and its institutions, and receives the "current values" from it. The ego, therefore, as the centre of this consciousness, normally becomes the bearer and representative of the collective values current at any given time. The ego is in fact the authority which, in more or less complete identification with these values, represents the demands of the collective in the individual sphere and rejects any counter-tendencies that may be present.
>
> (Neumann, 1990, p. 36)

At adolescence, the child begins to seek a sense of its own power. One of the important means of acquiring this power is through identity with a group of similarly minded peers. "The prestige of the group brings prestige to each one personally, while the individual ego-needs seem to find their satisfaction in the prestige of the leader. . . . this is the moment when the developing child is susceptible to group culture" (Harding, 1948/1973, p. 222).

PATTERNS OF LIBIDO

In the course of its development the Jungian psyche differentiates distinct levels of libidinal[8] function. At the most primitive level is the undifferentiated life force, essentially identifiable with the primordial self. With it is identified the urge to life. In the early months of life this breaks up into archetypal fragments, each representing a specific instinctual urge. Peculiar to early stages of development is the threefold zonal differentiation as suggested by Anna Freud: oral, anal and sexual. These, in turn, differentiate into archetypal roots for every type of human activity (Jung, 1960/1969; Fordham, 1957; Freud, 1966).

As differentiation proceeds, the expression of libido becomes more and more susceptible to diversion, blockage or frustration. Thus, archetypal forms less efficiently reflect libidinal energies than do simple instincts. Complexes, as more differentiated expressions of the archetypal matrix, have somewhat less power to direct activity than do the archetypes *an sich*. The symbols which mediate archetypal content into consciousness are again proportionally weaker expressions of the libido. To the extent that any task is not rooted in instinctual activity, to that same extent we find it incapable of marshaling the energies of the organism (Jung, 1960/1969).

Libido, when redirected or blocked, tends to resort to more primitive and, hence, more potent means of expression. The entire range of hero stories, Campbell's monomyth, can be interpreted as a regression of blocked libido and its re-emergence in the reformulated ego (Jung, 1956/1967; Campbell, 1949/1972).

In this process Jung noted two possible outcomes. In one, the descending ego could take refuge in the maternal security offered by the more primitive mode of function and fail to restructure and re-emerge. In the other, it could resist the sensuous draw of primitive comforts and re-emerge, strengthened by its contact with the unconscious potencies.

> Regression carried to its logical conclusion means a linking back with the world of natural instincts, which in its formal or ideal aspect is a kind of *prima materia*. If this *prima materia* can be assimilated by the conscious mind it will bring about a reactivation and reorganization of its contents. But if the conscious mind proves incapable of assimilating the new contents pouring in from the unconscious, then a dangerous situation arises in which they keep their original, chaotic and archaic form and consequently disrupt the unity of consciousness.
>
> (Jung, 1956/1967, para. 631)

Therefore, in normal human experience, it is not surprising that the blocked paths of growth in the relatively differentiated individual should revert to less precarious modes of existence. In human experience, this regressive pattern often takes the form of group behavior.

Where the many are, there is security; what the many believe must of course be true; what the many want must be worth striving for, and necessary, and therefore good. In the clamor of the many resides the power to snatch wish fulfillments by force; sweetest of all, however, is that gentle and painless slipping back into the kingdom of childhood, into the paradise of parental care, into happy-go-luckiness and irresponsibility. All the thinking and looking after are done from the top; to all questions there is an answer, and for all needs the necessary provision is made.

(Jung, 1964/1970, para. 538)

The nature of groups in general depends upon this kind of regression. At heart it is characterized by two kinds of reinforcement:[9] actual enhancement of power and status, or the sensual security that mimics the earlier state of identification with the family.

The mass is swayed by *participation mystique*, which is nothing other than an unconscious identity. Supposing, for example, you go to the theatre: glance meets glance, everybody observes everybody else, so that all those who are present are caught up in an invisible web of mutual unconscious relationship. If this condition increases, one literally feels borne along by the universal wave of identity with others. It may be a pleasant feeling – one sheep among ten thousand. . . . Since this is such an easy and convenient way of raising one's personality to a more exalted rank, mankind has always formed groups which made collective experiences of transformation – often of an ecstatic nature – possible. The regressive identification with lower and more primitive states of consciousness is invariably accompanied by a heightened sense of life; hence the quickening effect of regressive identifications with half animal ancestors in the Stone Age.

(Jung, 1959/1968a, para. 226)

SUMMARY

According to Jungian thought, intersubjectivity is rooted historically in several elements of the psyche and its ontogenetic development. The central concept underlined by these elements is that social interaction is prior to individuals both ontologically and historically. Bowlby and others have made it abundantly clear that impoverished social circumstances result in irreparable damage to the growing psyche.[10]

The basic points leading to this conclusion are summarized as follows:

1 The neonate responds to, and is joined to, the mother by projective identification before it becomes an individual; indeed, the symbiotic identity is among the first response sets established by the neonate and it is essentially social.

2 The child is submerged in, and imprinted with, family patterns before it can emerge as an individual. All this occurs while in a state of unconscious identity, the root form of social interaction.
3 Early preferences and personality characteristics are determined by the interplay of archetypal expectancies and environmental fulfillments.
4 The early familial and non-familial experiences of the individual are rooted in *participation mystique*, which is to say they involve an unconscious identification between the subject and object.
5 Both language and culture exercise a determinative influence upon the development of the individual.

Intersubjectivity precedes individuality in every sense except the plain physical sense of discrete physical presences.[11] People turn to groups for many reasons; one of the reasons Jung outlined was that groups re-establish to a certain extent the neonatal omnipotence and the sense of security originally provided by the symbiotic union with the mother. These are, moreover, real places of refuge which can provide strength and direction for those unable to sustain the work of individuation.

Chapter 10

The nature of groups

THE ARCHETYPAL FOUNDATIONS OF GROUP MEMBERSHIP

Imitation

Imitation is one of the most fundamental properties of the human psyche. Meltzoff and Moore have shown that unconscious imitation is one of the basic elements of the neonatal behavioral repertoire. Later, as imitation becomes part of the child's intentional repertoire, it forms the basis of re-establishing and reinforcing the sense of unity – identification – with the mother. It is also recognized as being a root means of learning new skills (Meltzoff and Moore, 1985; Mahler, et al., 1975; Breger, 1974).

For Jung, imitation was a fundamental key to social processes.

> The mass is swayed by *participation mystique*, which is nothing other than an unconscious identity. Supposing, for example, you go to the theatre: glance meets glance, everybody observes everybody else, so that all those who are present are caught up in an invisible web of mutual unconscious relationship. If this condition increases, one literally feels borne along by the universal wave of identity with others. It may be a pleasant feeling – one sheep among ten thousand.
>
> (Jung, 1959/1968a, para. 226)

It was his view that imitation was a self-reinforcing behavior, rooted in instinct. The end of imitation was a sensuous feeling of relationship, an identity which imitated, in fact, a regression to a primitive undifferentiated state.

Outside Jungian circles, practitioners of Neurolinguistic Programming (NLP) have developed a science of rapport that emphasizes the imitation of a subject's posture, breathing rate and speech patterns as a means of establishing an unconscious identity. They suggest that such practices have the effect of opening up a subject to various treatments and practices that would otherwise be inaccessible on a conscious level (Bandler and Grinder, 1975, 1979).

Identification and projection

The projection which lies at the root of group formation follows a more or less standard path of development. In every individual the collective unconscious has provided archetypal dominants, "expectancies" which point the organism towards specific possibilities of perception. *Inter alia*, these are the commonalties of human experience: mother, father, family, children, life, death, eating, sleeping, sex, etc.

These archetypes organize experience about their objects or activities and, at first, dominate the perceptual field. Thus, the newborn infant emerges ready to respond to the perfect mother for whom it has been genetically programmed. The goodness of fit between the archetypal mother and the real experience of mothering provides an emotional foundation that eventually comes to characterize that child's later response to women and, ultimately, all others through the extended mother-complex and its association with the anima. Because of the neonate's inability to differentiate the actual experience of the mother from the archetypal mother-image, the good and bad characteristics of the experience of the mother may later be projected upon any person who provides some significant "hook" or similarity to the mother or the image of the mother (von Franz, 1980/1988; Jung, 1956/1967).

Normally, individuals learn gradually to differentiate between the actual mother and the archetypal image. In such cases, the mother emerges from the archetypal numen as a real person in her own right. If proper discrimination fails to develop, the man's relations with women will be fated to remain on an unconscious level. They will be dominated by unrealistically ideal or threatening images generated by the mother archetype. A woman under similar circumstances, would also develop a neurotic condition (Jung, 1959/1968a).

[I]f he allows his libido to get stuck in a childish milieu, and does not free it for higher purposes, he falls under the spell of unconscious compulsion. Wherever he may be, the unconscious will then recreate the infantile milieu by projecting his complexes all over again, and in defiance of his vital interests, the same dependence and lack of freedom which formerly characterized his relations with his parents. His destiny no longer lies in his own hands: his Τύχαι και Μοιραι (fortunes and fates) fall from the stars. The Stoics called this condition Heimarmene, compulsion by the stars, to which every "unredeemed" soul is subject. When the libido thus remains fixed in its most primitive form it keeps men on a correspondingly low level where they have no control over themselves and are at the mercy of their affects.

(Jung, 1956/1967, para. 644)

Although the archetypal image of the father appears somewhat later, his influence on the developing psyche determines specific kinds of relations to the outside world. These in turn provide "hooks" for projections relating to the specific developmental role of the father.

> The father represents the world of moral commandments and prohibitions. . . . The father is the representative of the spirit, whose function it is to oppose pure instinctuality. That is his archetypal role, which falls to him regardless of his personal qualities; hence he is often an object of neurotic fears for the son.
>
> (Ibid., para. 396)

Like the relation to the mother, the relation to the father has a strong influence upon the developing psyche. The archetypal predispositions are again found in a compensatory relation to the actual behavior of the father in order to provide a functional individual.

> In men, a positive father complex very often produces a certain credulity with regard to authority and a distinct willingness to bow down before all spiritual dogmas and values; while in women it induces the liveliest spiritual aspirations and interests. In dreams, it is always the father-figure from whom the decisive conviction, prohibitions, and wise counsels emanate. The invisibility of the source is frequently emphasized by the fact that it consists simply of an authoritative voice which passes final judgments. Mostly therefore it is the figure of a "wise old man" who symbolizes the spiritual factor.
>
> (Jung, 1959/1968a, para. 396)

Significantly, the idea of the father archetype has been recently called into question by Andrew Samuels (1993). Samuels holds that the father, as archetype, is not defined at any specifically biological stratum in the child's relation to the world (at least not after conception). The common Western image of father is easily replaced by a father, "of whatever sex" (p. 133 ff.). This is, of course, supported by the incredible variety of familial relations that obtain throughout the world. Whether, however, the father archetype possesses as full a claim on the organism as does the mother, his continuing appearance, clothed in the symbols of authority, rationality and spirit suggest its continuing viability.

In similar fashion, old patterns of friendship or enmity with parents, siblings and other family members may be projected on to others. More primitive idealizations rooted firmly in archetypal strata are also projected.

Jung also noted that the experience of identification was deeply sensual, rooted in the security of unconscious childhood.

> Sensuous feeling, or rather the feeling that is present in the sensuous state, is collective. It produces a relatedness or proneness to affect which always puts the individual in a state of *participation mystique*, a state of

partial identity with the sensed object. This identity expresses itself in a compulsive dependence on that object. . . .

(Jung, 1971, para. 146)

At the very root of group formation lie the tendencies in human beings towards projection and imitation. "Society is organized . . . less by law than by the propensity to imitation, implying equally suggestion, suggestibility and mental contagion" (1953/1966, para. 242).

Identification is an alienation of the subject from himself for the sake of the object, in which he is, so to speak, disguised. For example, identification with the father means, in practice, adopting all the father's ways of behaving, as though the son were the same as the father and not a separate individuality. Identification differs from *imitation* in that it is an *unconscious* imitation, whereas imitation is a conscious copying.

(Ibid., para. 738)

Identification always serves a purpose. The purpose, however, is often just out of the reach of conscious effort. Identity reflects a pattern of regression whereby the individual, frustrated in his efforts to attain some goal, unconsciously reverts to a more primitive pattern in order to obtain it. Cast in the light of his classic formulation of the regression of libido, group membership was seen to be identical with a regression to the symbiotic life of the neonate.

The sensuality of identity, identification and imitation is rooted in their common link to primal states: they are inherently regressive and are, therefore, self-reinforcing. In each there is a progressive intensification of the sense of union with the object and with it the reassertion of infantile patterns of omnipotence and security. Thus, imitation leads to identification. Identification promotes projection, and projections feed back into the system to provide a heightened sense of identity.

Identity is primarily an unconscious conformity with objects. It is not an equation, but an *a priori* likeness which was never the object of consciousness. Identity is responsible for the naive assumption that the psychology of one man is like that of another, and that the same motives occur everywhere, that what is agreeable to me must obviously be pleasurable for others, that what I find immoral must also be immoral for them, and so on. It is also responsible for the almost universal desire to correct in others what most needs correcting in one-self.

(Ibid., para. 742)

SUMMARY

Group membership is an important part of what it means to be human. From birth forward, even before birth, human beings are engaged in a continual dialogue between themselves and others. Imitation, projective identification and identity appear early and remain important to the existence of the individual throughout his or her life.

Group membership may be seen as the natural state of humankind for the following reasons:

1 The earliest experience of human existence is a unity with the mother. It is the benchmark against which all other unions are measured. It is experienced as empowered, safe and happy.
2 Projection is the earliest mode of understanding. It creates a sense of union by assimilating external objects to internal states or objects.
3 Any behavior that recreates that feeling of unity is, by definition, reinforcing or self-reinforcing.
4 *Participation mystique* and primitive identity are strengthened by the perception of sameness with others. These are regressive recreations of the sense of union originally experienced with the mother.
5 Imitation is an inherent capability of the human neonate. It is self-reinforcing in the neonate; because it recreates the physical sense of *participation mystique* in the adult, it is likewise self-reinforcing.
6 All groups are rooted in the sense of identity.

Chapter 11

Families, nations and thought

Although Jung never delineated a sociological analysis of groups, his psychology seems to support the division of groups into several broad categories. Because the collective unconscious is described as including specific strata related to ethnicity, there is in Jung's perception a biological root to national identity.

It cannot be denied that Jung wandered into dubious Lamarckian speculations with regard to the effect of the land itself on individual characteristics.[1] However, with some rationalization and re-evaluation of his observations, he can be understood to say that over periods of hundreds if not thousands of years, ethnicities select for specific traits through cultural practices and preferences. In so doing, they not only built up a strong biological propensity to prefer certain traits, but also made those traits the more egregious by actively selecting for them. In such contexts similarities abound and a sense of identity can easily be established.[2]

THE FAMILY

Jung observes that the family constellation provides the root archetypal pattern for all groups. He allows for cultural differences in expression of these patterns through the combined influence of the ethnic strata of the collective unconscious and cultural influences on family roles. The basic patterns are " ... husband, wife, father, mother, child. ... These ordinary everyday facts, which are eternally repeated, create the mightiest archetypes of all, whose ceaseless activity is everywhere apparent even in a rationalistic age like ours" (1960/1969, para. 336).

Families are heirs of child-rearing practices that reflect the cultural milieu. The cultural milieu is conjointly determined by ethnic traditions, class-specific practices and other factors. The peculiar adequacies and deficiencies of these traditions in regard to child-rearing are reflected in the compensations that mark personality development as a function of the "goodness of fit" between archetypal expectancies and the parental practices so determined. These traits are the mark of the class and the culture into which the child is born. They provide specific hooks for projection in the environment, commonalties which will serve to bind individuals into groups on the basis of class and ethnic perspective.

Families are part of the archetypal structure of the human organism. Jung makes no claim to the existence of a definitive structure for marriage, but emphasizes the specific elements which provide the necessary environment for the safeguarding and socialization of the infant human. In this he parallels the findings of many anthropologists to the effect that world-wide there exists great variability in the structure of marital relations (Fox, 1980/1983; Tiger and Fox, 1971/1989).

In a lengthy analysis of cross-cousin and sister-exchange marriages,[3] Jung suggests that these primitive forms may be the roots of the archetype expressed by the projection of anima/us. In all such situations the villages are divided into opposing segments, marriage classes or moieties, whose members may only marry members of specific classes. These classes are usually given names which designate natural opposites–antinomies " . . . east and west, high and low, day and night, male and female, water and land, left and right. It is not difficult to see from these that the two halves are felt to be antithetical and thus the expression of an endopsychic antithesis" (1954/1966, para. 434).

The crucial emphasis on family groupings has less to do with the specific form taken as it has upon the parental roles themselves. Someone must perform the maternal functions in a consistent manner. Someone else must fulfill the role of father, the voice of authority, and whether it is the biological father or the mother's brother makes little objective difference. However, to the extent that the persons assigned to the roles differ, to that extent will the personal characteristics of the individual differ from society to society.

Tiger and Fox note that in many societies it is, in fact, the brother–sister bond that provides the stability necessary for the safe growth of the family unit. In other societies related women live together, depending upon brothers and sons for some things, husbands for other needs and the other women in the group for yet other services. In general, they observe that the rules that define the mating bond – marriage – vary greatly from culture to culture. For these authors, the single most important factors in defining the nature of the family structure from culture to culture are essentially ecological and aim simply at the preservation of the mother–child unit.

> Far from representing the intrinsic morality of the mating bond, these rules suggest how precarious it really is. The great variety and depth of customs surrounding kinship and marriage are not expressions of an innate and ready tendency to form families: *they are devices to protect the mother–child unit from the potential fragility of the mating bond.*
>
> (Tiger and Fox, 1971/1989, p. 71)

From this perspective we might presume to say that the child-rearing practices in each culture provide a specific imprint upon the internalized maternal and paternal imagos. Second in importance to these, however, are the means by which the child is released from the protection of his or her parents and launched into the world of adulthood.

> The first bearer of the soul-image is always the mother; later it is borne by those women who arouse the man's feelings, whether in a positive or a negative sense. Because the mother is the first bearer of the soul-image separation from her is a delicate and important matter of the greatest educational significance. Accordingly among primitives we find a large number of rites designed to organize this separation. The mere fact of becoming adult, and of outward separation, is not enough; impressive initiations into the "men's house" and ceremonies of rebirth are still needed in order to make the separation from the mother (and hence from childhood) entirely effective.
>
> (Jung, 1953/1966, para. 314)

This passage from youth to adulthood is a transition which has of late received considerable attention in the United States. Nevertheless it still seems to be largely misunderstood.

For much of the last century the great Western mythic systems failed to provide significant initiatory experiences. Since the First World War, the universal draft has filled a significant part of the gap for Americans. The ordeal of basic training, including a separation into a world of men, humiliation, and the typically obscene banter of the drill sergeants, provided a significant parallel to the classical tribal ceremony. The accession to manhood, often including the first experience of sexual intercourse, became a landmark in the lives of those who experienced it. It is significant that it was the generation that came of age in the 1960s and 1970s that both resisted and brought an end to the draft, where the greatest sense of anomie appeared.

The "lost generation" needed to "find itself." The naive "love generation" was hopelessly idealistic. They believed what their mothers and fathers and Sunday school teachers had taught them, and failed to orient to the "real world." War, they said, was not healthy for children and other living things. They were the flower children.

> Just as the father acts as a protection against the dangers of the external world and thus serves the son as a model persona, so the mother protects him from the dangers that threaten from the darkness of his psyche. In the puberty rites, therefore, the initiate receives instructions about the things of "the other side," so that he is put in a position to dispense with his mother's protection.
>
> (Ibid., para. 315)

It is also striking how the national response to the war in Vietnam affected the returning military. Instead of receiving the hero's welcome, instead of having their manhood confirmed, those who had received the great initiation of war were ignored, cast aside, often vilified. The whole world was turned upside down, and a new disease was launched into national prominence: Post Traumatic Stress Syndrome.

There is strong reason to believe that the initiatory response is not only archetypally based, but that it represents one of several imprinting or pseudo-imprinting periods in the human life. Just as the archetypal imprint of the mother imago shapes the development of the entire psyche, it may be that a social imago must likewise be imprinted during or shortly after adolescence in order for the individual to become fully functional as a social being.

Robert Dilts (1990), following Leary (1989), suggests that there exist at least six discrete levels of imprint in the human organism. Each marks the opening of a new level of awareness and a new mode of consciousness. The earliest have to do with survival and identity bonds. Next come intellectual imprints, and then, at about adolescence, come social imprints that determine one's relation to the social world. These are followed by aesthetic and spiritual imprints.

Henderson suggests that one of the functions of the initiatory rite is a return to the state of mother–child identity, in order that the identity may be re-formed anew. It is in just such a re-formative regression that a re-imprinting, conceived of as a radical restructuring, could occur.

The ritual takes the novice back to the deepest level of original mother–child identity or ego-Self identity, thus forcing him to experience a symbolic death. In other words, his identity is temporarily dismembered or dissolved in the collective unconscious. From this state he is ceremonially rescued by the rite of new birth. This is the first act of true consolidation of the ego with the larger group, expressed as a totem, clan, or tribe, or all three combined.

(Henderson, 1964, p. 123)

According to Henderson, the archetype of initiation is activated at each passage from one stage of life to another: childhood to puberty, adolescence to adulthood, adulthood to middle age, middle age to old age. It may be most strongly activated at the time of passage to middle age. We may define these transitional points as special areas of sensitivity between the individual psyche and the collective environment. In each, the offerings and negligences of the surrounding society will mark the individual more deeply than at any other time.

NATIONALITIES AND ETHNIC GROUPS

National identities seem to develop from four separate strata of the Jungian psyche. At the deepest level are the layers of the collective unconscious which are common to specific national groups. On a level closer to consciousness are the imprints of parental influence and upbringing that indelibly stamp the child with those traits that identify him as a member of that culture. Closest to consciousness are the everyday formulae, the specific word patterns and meanings; myths, legends and traditions which comprise the collective consciousness and out of which a personal perspective on the world will grow. Finally, there is the individualized set of definitions used by each person to understand what is meant by his or her national identity.

It is not the will of individuals that moulds the destinies of nations, but suprapersonal factors, the spirit and the earth, which work in mysterious ways and in unfathomable darkness. It is useless to attack or praise nations since no one can alter them. Moreover, the "nation" (like the "state") is a personified concept that corresponds in reality only to a specific nuance of the individual psyche. The nation has no life of its own apart from the individual, and is therefore not an end in itself. It is nothing but an inborn character, and this may be a handicap or an advantage, and is at best only a means to an end. Thus in many ways it is an advantage to have been imprinted with the English national character in one's cradle. . . .

(Jung, 1964/1970, para. 921)

National identities, however, are relatively abstract. Certainly the needs of the nation are less salient than the needs of the family, tribe or clan. The nation as an abstract entity also ranks far below the local village or town. In fact, because it forms such a broad base of consensus, the issue of nationality may not come up until the individual is isolated or threatened specifically on the basis of nationality.

In a foreign country, nationality can form a strong base for establishing an identity. Like all groups, a group of co-nationals can provide a welcome respite to a stranger in a foreign country, and a comforting regression from the foreignness of the new country. The familiar language, the identity of background and other similarities breed the *participation mystique*. Under the spell of identification, the world can shrink to the point where a vast country seems a common neighborhood.

This explains the not uncommon phenomenon of two travelers meeting in a foreign land. Despite the fact that they live at opposite ends of the country, or if from the same state or province from different ends, they will swap names and addresses until they find some common link, as if they lived in the same small village all of their lives. In the midst of the foreign land, their common nationality becomes a strong bond and a great nation shrinks subjectively to the size of a village.

Jung noted that great nations may often be observed to express a certain average character. While the point comes close to being a simple stereotype, the idea that race, language, culture and ethnicity impact upon one's personality marks the idea as probable if not popular. If this were not so, the multitude of ethnic jokes, racial slurs, stereotypes and caricatures would be impossible to maintain.

Benjamin Whorf was a strong advocate of the idea that language affects thought. Lévi-Strauss views the mythic heritage of a people as their thinking tools. Marx tied culture in an absolute manner to the means of production and distribution. In like manner, George Herbert Mead saw that thought was related to action and the possibilities of manipulation. All of these ideas together strongly suggest the possibility of a national character (Lévi-Strauss, 1962/1966; Gouldner, 1970; Giddens, 1982; Aron, 1970; Miller, 1973/1980; Bandler and Grinder, 1975).

> Almost every great country has its collective attitude, which one might call its genius or *spiritus loci*. Sometimes you can catch it in a formula, sometimes it is more elusive, yet nonetheless it is indescribably present as a sort of atmosphere that permeates everything, the look of the people, their speech, behavior, clothing, smell, their interests, ideals, politics, philosophy, art, and even their religion. In a well-defined civilization with a solid historical foundation, such as for instance the French, you can easily discover the keynote of the French esprit: it is "La gloire," a most marked prestige psychology in its noblest as well as its most ridiculous forms. You find it in their speech, gestures, beliefs, in the style of everything, in politics and even in science.
>
> (Jung, 1964/1970, para. 972)

Jung characterized the Germans as captivated by abstract ideas and categories.

> In Germany it is the "idea" that is impersonated by everybody. There are no ordinary human beings, you are "Herr Professor" or "Herr Geheimrat. . . . Sometimes the German idea is right and sometimes it is wrong, but it never ceases to be an idea whether it belongs to the highest philosophy or is merely a foolish bias.
>
> (Ibid., para. 973)

The English were seen as upholding the ideal of the "gentleman" as an updated chivalry, and the Americans as embodying heroic ideals which led them to strive for excellence.

> America has a principle or idea or attitude, but it is surely not money. Often, when I was searching through the conscious and the unconscious mind of my American patients and pupils, I found something which I can only describe as a sort of Heroic Ideal. Your most idealistic effort is

concerned with bringing out the best in every man, and when you find a good man you naturally support him and push him on, until at last he is liable to collapse from sheer exertion, success, and triumph ... [I]n the schools ... every child is trained to be brave, courageous, efficient and a "good sport," a hero in short. There is no record which people will not kill themselves to break, even if it is the most appalling nonsense.

(Ibid., para. 976)

Such a spirit reflects, in addition to any archetypally conditioned characteristics from the ethnic strata of the collective unconscious, the compensatory constellation of specific archetypal qualities as a result of child-rearing and socialization processes specific to the group.

MYTH AND THE PERCEPTION OF REALITY

The specific practices of a people are usually rooted in an archetypal theme or myth that leaves its mark on the members of the culture. At its most basic, a myth is a coherent story, a narrative usually relating to the past, to the time of creation. Beyond that, the myth externally provides the proper patterns for living within the culture and ways of approaching specific kinds of problems that are encountered in everyday life (Eliade, 1990; von Franz, 1980/1988; Campbell, 1990; Lévi-Strauss, 1966).

According to Mircea Eliade, myths represent the eternally true narratives of beginnings and as such they constitute the paradigmatic patterns for all human activities. Myths, moreover, carry with them the power to transport the individual into the timeless realm of the primordial, there to participate in the original act of creation. "In traditional societies, one 'lives' the myth in the sense that one is seized by the sacred, exalting power of the events recollected or reenacted" (1990, p. 23).

Joseph Campbell has identified myths with the structure of life in a society. In each culture, myths provide the deepest and most immediately felt strata of meaning. A living myth bears the archetypal numen of self-evident meaning; for each member of its culture, the myth is the defining force and the controlling image.

[A] mythology is a control system, on the one hand framing its community to accord with an instituted order of nature and, on the other hand, by means of its symbolic pedagogic rites, conducting individuals through the ineluctable psychophysiological stages of transformation of a human life-time – birth, childhood, and adolescence, old age, and the release of death – in unbroken accord simultaneously with the requirements of this world and the rapture of participation in a manner of being beyond time.

(Campbell, 1986, p. 20)

Jung saw in these stories a projection of the structure of the human psyche. Myths, according to Jung, were not simply rules, or paradigms for action, neither were they the means to overcome contradictions. While all of these may reflect uses of myth, their fundamental purpose was to project meaning upon the world. This they did by projecting the structure of the psyche onto external reality making it thereby intelligible to the living psyche (1959/1968a). In the course of these projections, the world becomes populated by the personified contents of the collective unconscious. It is these archetypes, that, in the personae of the gods, provide the directives that define and give shape to each culture. The power of myth lies beneath the level of consciousness. From there it molds and shapes perceptions and understandings independent of the intellectual prowess of the subject. Rooted in archetypal structures, it carries an intuitive validity, it resonates with and defines the background assumptions of a culture, and formulates the core elements of the collective consciousness (Gouldner, 1970).

Bolen, Hillman and others have recognized that Western mythology tends to be dominated by specific patterns relating to sky gods. They tend to give shape to cultures in which the males are abstracting, unemotional men, cut off from their feelings and from each other while simultaneously disempowering the woman and devaluing the emotional and intuitive side of life.

> As the patriarchal world requires separation after separation of men, each cutting away cuts two ways: the boy who separates from his mother separates from her emotionally and cuts himself off from the inner part of himself that was close to her. The boy who goes to school and finds that he cannot show his innocence or ignorance, because it makes him an object of ridicule, adapts by imitating the acceptable attitude.... The boy who could cry when he was sad and learned not to, stopped his tears by walling himself off from his emotions. And there is a "men from the boys" cut-off time when something that is still tender in a young man is sacrificed so that he may join the ranks of men.
>
> (Bolen, 1989/1990, p. 284)

Long before women's liberation was fashionable, Jung called for a re-balancing of the Western psyche through the reintegration of the feminine part. He regularly pointed to the *de facto* incorporation of the Virgin Mary into the Catholic godhead as a watershed for Western civilization, bringing a feminine balance into what had been a male-dominated dynamic view of God (Matoon, 1981/1985; Jung 1959/1968b, 1969).

Kenneth Lambert (1977) points to the far-reaching effect of the dogma of the Assumption of the Virgin Mary. Both Jung and Lambert agree that the West is a very different place by virtue of this significant change in the collective consciousness of Western Christianity.

> Nevertheless, if we look both at the Roman Catholic Church and the world at large, 25 years later, we find changes that seem synchronous

with the symbolic shift. In the Church we find a radical rethinking about sex, marriage and bodily life. In the religious orders there is a crisis about the meaning and validity of poverty, chastity and obedience. Antagonism to the enforced celibacy of priests gathers force. A weakening of one-sided paternal authority has shown itself in the Mass where the Tridentine Rite in Latin, with its emphasis upon the mysterium and supremacy of God the Father, has given way to a rite expressing something more like a democratic family meal.

(Lambert, 1977, p. 171)

When myths change, all of life changes. Lambert continues on the secular side:

Outside the church, similar pressures for good or for bad express themselves, in Women's Liberation, in co-education, and in laws against sexual discrimination. Bodily existence, not only in terms of muscular experience and skills, but even more, today, in terms of an efflorescence of erotic and sexual experience, occupies a central interest. Egalitarian aims and a widespread sympathy with and understanding for criminals and deviants have become the trend, even as Mary used to plead the cause of sinners to mollify the severity of the Father God.

(Ibid., p. 171)

Out of the cult of the sky god comes the Hero as Warrior, Chief and Shaman; as controllers, dominators and power brokers. The Hero as Warrior, descends into the battle and obtains the treasure. In the material West it is a physical challenge and a financial reward; perhaps the Olympics and a career in commercial television. As the Chief he becomes a corporate raider or a military leader. His journey may be strewn with real broken bodies and real broken careers. Raw power and a real domain may be the reward that he seeks. As Shaman, the Western hero is the inventor–technologue who descends into the world of *physis* not like the alchemist to find himself but to find the rules of power that will *truly* turn lead to gold. He is, in company with the Chief and Warrior, the inventor of bombs and the polluter of rivers (Thompson, 1971).

Accordingly, we encounter the American Myth, characterized by the heroic ideal. Striving, enduring, suffering and obtaining are large parts of it, as are the ideals of freedom and independence. Davy Crockett, Daniel Boone, Wyatt Earp, Jesse James, Wild Bill Hickock, Buffalo Bill Cody: heroes, warriors, avatars of the sky god. Each is symbolic of a violent independence and disregard for human life. However they may have lived in real life, their memory evokes an uncrying, unshirking, unshakeable machismo. They were real men from the time when "men were men and women were women." These were men who reached out and took life where they found it – without regard, it might be said, even to its then current owner. The archetypal numen of the warrior god obscures the details of the individual life and like the seven immortals of China they live on as if gods.

Among the chiefs, our myths have sometimes enshrined a nobler breed. Take, for example, Washington and Lincoln. Washington, the demigod, skips coins across rivers that are almost too wide to swim. As a god of light, he is truthful to a fault – "Father, I cannot tell a lie." He is also highly born. And like the sky god Apollo, he uttered prophesy in his farewell speech and in dreams foretold the future of his country (Taylor, 1979).[4]

Lincoln fulfills the role of martyr and redeemer. He was a man of impeccable honesty (remember how many miles he walked to give someone the right change?), and lowly birth (as befits a messianic figure). Out of total obscurity he attained the highest office and provided a secular redemption for a divided country. Despite prophetic warnings not to go, he traveled to the site of his death. He led captivity captive, set the captives free, and gave up his own life at the hand of a traitor.[5] Just as Jesus of Nazareth drew to himself the messianic hopes of all peoples, the numen of Messiah clings to Lincoln among Americans.[6]

Within the mythos we find also scientist monks as entrepreneurs and as martyrs, as self giving and self aggrandizing. Thomas Edison, who embodies the American gifts of persistence, rebellion and invention, was also a self promoter and a brilliant salesman. He was a seventh son, educated primarily by his mother and his own curiosity. Possessed by a restless spirit, he embodied the Puritan ethic, sacrificing all for the sake of his calling. Remembering the Puritans' suspicion of too much sleep (Weber, 1958), we find Edison sleeping four hours a night. Remembering their exaltation of work, we find him virtually living at his Menlo Park laboratory. And finally, we see his hard-wired attitude summed up in his classic (if apocryphal) apothegm "Invention is one per cent inspiration and ninety-nine per cent perspiration."

George Washington Carver was born a slave. His mother was killed in a raid during which his father was stolen. He was raised from then on by the Carver family. His foster-father, significantly, bore the name Moses. After his emancipation he worked to put himself through high school and college. Unlike Edison, Carver was a devout Christian. Legend has it that at one point he prayed to God for wisdom, but being a humble man, he would only ask for wisdom regarding the peanut. Out of his efforts came a wellspring of new uses for the lowly legume, and his own well-deserved immortality.

In all of these examples, either the numen of a specific archetypal figure, the martyr, messiah, lawgiver or earth spirit, has enclothed an historical personage, or else (and perhaps simultaneously) they fulfill a role that seems to encode the promise of what America is expected to be. The "rags to riches" theme is common. It is related strongly to the secular religion of America that defines much of the American myth.

Robert N. Bellah, in *The Broken Covenant: American Civil Religion in Time of Trial*, reports that America was perceived simultaneously as a wilderness, a brand new land destined for God's elect, and as the Promised Land. The Revolution was understood as a conversion experience, and the signing of the Constitution as a sacramental covenant (Bellah, 1975). This identification of the new country with paradise developed further in the years after the founding of the Republic. Its echo is still heard in the idea that America's streets are "paved with gold," a clear reflection of the New Jerusalem. The new wilderness, the Land of Promise, the city whose streets are paved with gold, represented a land of opportunity. These very ideas, however, opened the possibility for the expression of the opposite pole of the Puritan work ethic as later expressed in the idea of distributive justice. If we remember that every archetype has two sides, and that both sides must have expression at some point, then it is not surprising that out of the Puritan ethic there should also arise the expectancy that the land owed one something.

Elizabeth Hirshman (1990) has discovered that the myth of secular immortality is a strong motivator amongst the wealthy. In her study of advertising images and the lifestyles of the American elite, she found a consistent appeal to a secularized concept of immortality: an immortality that might be gained either through great possessions, great wealth, great philanthropy or great talent. True to its Puritan roots, the image holds hard work, ability and originality as important proofs of "election."

Bellah sees just such a secular expression of the archetype of paradise in the classic New Testament contrast between the service of Mammon and the service of God. The search for secular immortality is a minor variant of the same theme. He notes:

> However sharply contradictory these motives might appear . . . a choice between God and Mammon, or God and the devil, they are at some deep level not unrelated. They can both be considered versions of the same mythic archetype: the quest for paradise; one for an earthly paradise in which impulses are gratified here and now, one for a heavenly paradise at some future time . . . there is little doubt that in the religious culture which is the chrysalis of American myth, the tension between two motives was conceived as one between worldly pleasures and the hereafter.
>
> (Bellah, 1975, p. 64)

The search for secular immortality does not end with wealth. Even a cursory look at the American concern for diet, health and longevity suggests that the gospel has finally concretized in the cultural canon of America in a secularized ideal of immortality. The archetype of paradise is still with us. Large groups, however, divide into dominant and repressed elements in clear analogy with the structure of the psyche. Accordingly a completely different mythic structure can be expected in the cultural unconscious.

Charles Silverman (1978/1980) reviews some of the crucial myths of the African-American culture. He points first to the Br'er Rabbit folk tales, as providing a significant mythical expression of the need to outsmart the oppressive white culture. The Uncle Remus stories, he notes, were not cute animal tales for children, but object lessons in the tools of logic and deceit necessary in the world of the oppressed minority. Unless Br'er Rabbit could consistently outsmart and outfox Br'er Bear, he would die.

The myth of the "Bad Nigger" also characterizes an essential portion of the mythic structure of the African-American community. The myth itself is rooted in the legendary figure of Stackolee.[7] Violence lies at its heart as the only means for the oppressed youth to assert his individuality.

> Manliness and virility are defined as random violence and joyless, indeed affectless sexuality. Stackolee is "a mean man, a purveyor of violence" who "does not hesitate to hurt, taunt, kill if someone offers him the slightest hint of challenge." ... Stackolee is "the archetypal bully blindly striking out, articulating or discharging his rage on any passing object or person." His violence seems to be an end in itself, for it solves nothing and is aimed at nothing; the badman is all style – more precisely, perhaps, all pose and bluster. Like so many young criminals, the badman is more concerned with demonstrating his "badness" than with achieving any goal; or accomplishing any purpose.
>
> (Silverman, 1978/1980, p. 199)

On a more positive note, recent evidence suggests that the images of Martin Luther King and Malcolm X have entered the canon of the African-American culture as strongly positive mythic images. Side by side with them are powerful images now being resurrected of black contributions to the American Dream.

Here we see that the racial problem in America, rather than lying simply in the negative projections of a dominant class, is hopelessly confounded with the problem of the self identity of the underclasses. The very roles available in the mythological corpus of the collective consciousness tend to reinforce the external projection.

Another important mythical system for the American black was in evangelical Christian religion. Although often indicted as the means whereby the slave-owner justified and emasculated his slaves, Christianity often provided a sense of hope and a possibility for success in the world despite the white man.

Fordham reminds us that according to Jung "when we think that we have discovered a new concept, myths will certainly have reflected it before" (1957, p. 118). This suggests the differentiation between monotheistic and polytheistic cultures mentioned by Frye (1982) and Henderson (1984). As is typical with the great mythical themes of a culture, each of these perspectives allows certain kinds of thought and proscribes others. Each gives its own distinct flavor to the manner in which life is experienced. In polytheistic cultures maternal imagery predominates. Life after death is shaped in terms of rebirth, reincarnation and the cycle of eternal birth and death. It is evolutionary and cyclical. In monotheistic cultures the paternal attitude predominates. It is linear and technical. Life after death comes through resurrection and recreation, the sovereign act of a sovereign creator. Myth molds thought.

Although Frye expressly rejected the theory of archetypes, he understood that myth and religion strongly impacted on the possibilities of language and thought. "Man," he said, "lives not directly or nakedly in nature like the animals, but within a mythological universe, a body of assumptions and beliefs developed from his existential concerns" (1982, p. xviii). Following Giambattista Vico, one of the foundational Renaissance thinkers for the modern scientific West, Frye saw that language historically followed three paths, each closely related to the religious/mythic structure embodied by the culture.

In the first, or metaphorical, phase of language, the unifying element of verbal expression is the "god," or personal nature-spirit. In the second phase the conception of a transcendent "God" moves into the center of the order of words. In the third phase the criterion of reality is the source of sense experience in the order of nature, where "God" is not to be found, and where "gods" are no longer believed in. Hence, in the third phase of language the word "God" becomes linguistically unfunctional, except when confined to special areas outside of its jurisdiction. Mythological space became separated from scientific space with the new astronomy of the seventeenth century, and mythological time from scientific time with nineteenth-century geology and biology.

(Frye, 1982, p. 15)

In cultures dominated by polytheistic conceptions, thought tends to be concrete,[8] language is oracular and declarative, words are power. Words are metaphors for things and they evoke their present reality. In those cultures dominated by a monotheistic conception of God, language becomes individualized and represents thought. Intellect separates from emotion, and subject from object. Language becomes metonymic. What was to the polytheist a sound fully and completely connected with its referent – a word of power – now becomes merely a sign. It no longer evokes the archetypal numen of meaning, it is only an abstract representation of a thought.

With abstraction, however, comes the possibility of idealized space and ordered realities. The scattered commands, oracular pronouncements and poetry of the metaphoric phase give way to the internally consistent, continuous prose of the metaphoric. In the final stage, language is descriptive. A representation is true only if its description corresponds to observed reality. Language is still characterized by continuous prose, but prose is now judged by its correspondence to external reality, not by its internal consistency. Because there is no conscious ordering of "third phase reality," no God or creator, Nietzsche was able to say that there is no such thing as a "law of nature," only necessities (Frye, 1982).

Myth and religion exist in a special relation to culture at large. As noted on page 88, culture, and the manner of thinking and means of communication, are closely related to the dominant myths that characterize a group. We find, however, that there exists also a feedback loop that, through the mechanism of compensation, allows social pressure to impact upon the social expressions of collective contents.

> Social, political, and religious conditions affect the collective unconscious in the sense that all those factors which are suppressed by the prevailing views or attitudes in the life of a society gradually accumulate in the collective unconscious and activate its contents. Certain individuals gifted with particularly strong intuition then become aware of the changes going on in it and translate these changes into communicable ideas. The new ideas spread rapidly because parallel changes have been taking place in the unconscious of other people.
>
> (Jung, 1960/1969, para. 594)

The collective unconscious exists as a dynamic field and responds to all of the vicissitudes of human existence. Charged as it is with the development and survival of the individual, it must always respond in such a manner as to balance out the unwarranted or excessive demands of the environment against the needs of the individual. In doing this, it brings different archetypal elements into central focus at different times. The relative salience of a symbol or symbol system in any culture is an index of its general applicability to the needs of that group. But the needs of the group change with external circumstances, and with them the relative salience of various symbolic elements of the group mythology also change. Frye notes:

> [T]he mythology of paganism seems to show a development. . . . It begins with local epiphanic gods and moves on to departmental gods with established functions, in proportion as societies grow from tribal to national entities. . . . With the rise of empires, whose rulers begin to think of themselves as rulers of the "world," we get a kind of mono- theism. . . . Imperial monotheism is usually an umbrella structure, and is normally tolerant of local cults, which it tends increasingly to regard as manifestations of a single god. This single god, who as a rule is a sky god, is in a peculiar sense the patron of the world ruler. . . .
>
> (Frye, 1982, p. 92)

Myth becomes not only the root of the possibility of certain kinds of thought, it can become their rationale, their legitimation. In this case the myth becomes part of the explanation of why the world is the way it is. This is, of course, the reciprocal function of the myth as the determiner of the way things can be. At this stage, the symbol has reached full bloom and, depending upon the stability of its contacts with the collective unconscious, it may or may not continue as a living determinant of the society through which it is manifested. When the mythic theme becomes so conscious that it becomes the legitimation of the current institutional patterns it takes on the role of universe maintenance.

Bellah notes:

> It is one of the oldest of sociological generalizations that any coherent and viable society rests on a common set of moral understandings about good and bad, right and wrong, in the realm of individual and social action. It is almost as widely held that these understandings must also in turn rest upon a common set of religious understandings that provide a picture of the universe in terms of which the moral understandings make sense. Such moral and religious understandings produce both a basic cultural legitimation for a society which is viewed as at least approximately in accord with them and a standard of judgment for the criticism of a society that is seen as deviating too from them.
>
> (Bellah, 1975, p. viii)

From the perspective of sociology, myth generally takes the form of legitimations for the current system of group function. But from the archetypal perspective they begin not so much as the rationale as the source of the behaviors themselves. This was illustrated in the Ta Chuan, the Great Treatise of the I Ching (Wilhelm, 1967/1971). In the Great Treatise, the hexagrams of the I Ching are explained as the inspiration for certain specific inventions and cultural innovations. While the actual attributions are without question mythical in the modern sense, they reflect the function of myth as the source of innovation and diversity.

When Pao Hsi ruled the world, after contemplating the heavens and the earth, he invented the eight trigrams of the I Ching. He did this in order to maintain an open line of communication with the gods. He then began a series of inventions which all relate back to the archetypal symbols embedded in the trigrams. For example, paragraph 5 relates: "He made knotted cords and used them for nets and baskets in hunting and fishing. He probably took this from the hexagram of the clinging" (ibid., p. 329). Wilhelm explains that a net consists of meshes and is used to catch things. The trigrams that make up the *clinging* have both of those meanings embedded in them. The symbol is visually a set of meshes, and the written character means to cling to or to be caught on something.

In the following passage, Shen Nung, the Divine Husbandman, invents the plow, again, after meditating upon the hexagrams:

When Pao Hsi's clan was gone, there sprang up the clan of the Divine Husbandman. He split a piece of wood for a plowshare and bent a piece of wood for the plow handle, and taught the whole world the advantage of laying open the earth with a plow. He probably took this from the hexagram of *increase.*

(Wilhelm, 1967, p. 330)

Wilhelm explains that the figure is composed of two trigrams associated with wood. One includes the idea of penetration and the other has the added meaning of earth.

The lesson of this admittedly obscure example is this: new forms of thought and action have their origins in the collective unconscious. Before an experience becomes part of the mythic corpus that defines a people, it must enter into consciousness. This was illustrated by the discovery of the trigrams and of the net and the plow through their combination into the hexagrams. Once a myth or other content of the collective unconscious has entered the cultural canon, as the trigrams did in Shen Nung's time, it can fertilize discovery and originality. This is true, even if it appears in as obscure a form as the I Ching, a symbol system with commentary. Insofar as the products of the mythic culture attract the structure of individual experience to themselves and reinforce the other mythic strains vital to the needs of the culture, they too may be incorporated into the collective consciousness. That they are incorporated into the conscious canon illustrates that the need for them, or a foreshadowing of them had already appeared in the unconscious.

We recall Jung's statement:

Social, political, and religious conditions affect the collective unconscious in the sense that all those factors which are suppressed by the prevailing views or attitudes in the life of a society gradually accumulate in the collective unconscious and activate its contents. Certain individuals gifted with particularly strong intuition then become aware of the changes going on in it and translate these changes into communicable ideas. The new ideas spread rapidly because parallel changes have been taking place in the unconscious of other people.

(Jung, 1960/1969, para. 594)

Cornford (1991) has, in a similar manner, unearthed a complex topological system in Greek religious thought that links each of the great schools of philosophy to a specific god, element and domain. Archetypally, his system parallels Jung's idea of the four personality types and their subsequent articulation into cultural patterns by Thompson (1971).

In these examples, we observe the archetype as the molder of thought and the stimulus for creativity on the personal and social level. On the level of the rationalized symbolic universe, however, they represent legitimations: "Bodies of theoretical tradition that integrate different provinces of meaning and encompass the institutional order in a symbolic totality" (Berger and Luckmann, 1967, p. 95).

SUMMARY

1 Groups have their roots in the structure of the family.
2 The family is more important than any specific form that it takes because it is the supplier of a consistent and safe developmental context for the child.
3 The personality and growth of the individual depends upon the specific care that the child receives from its family. Their response to the child's archetypally determined needs will determine the specific compensations that will shape his or her growth for the rest of his or her life.
4 The specific manner in which family constellations respond to the needs of the child are determined by the cultural milieu in which they themselves live.
5 There may be several imprinting phases with outcomes crucially dependent upon the nature of the cultural milieu at the time of their execution. One of these is the passage from adolescence into adulthood.
6 In America, the "initiation into manhood" was adequately handled for some time by the military draft.
7 Initiations entail a re-imprinting occasioned by the intentional breakdown of the conscious structure and its social reformulation in order to face the new reality.
8 National identities are often characterized as stereotypes; they are, however, rooted in the structure of the culture, religion and language of a people. In general, the collective consciousness of a group has a specific average character.
9 Myths shape reality. As the orderers of perception and the prescribers of action they have a determinative effect upon all members of the group.
10 The importance of a myth is determined by its relative salience within a culture.
11 Myths and culture live in a codetermining dialectic. Myth determines culture and culture defines the possibilities through which the mythic world is experienced.
12 The response of humans to their culture activates the collective unconscious through compensatory mechanisms; the unconscious reorganizes the archetypal elements that define the myth and either the myth is restructured, or a new myth appears.

13 The American mythic system is dominated by overly masculine sky-god images that have led to specific cultural characteristics.
14 The promulgation of the doctrine of the Assumption of the Virgin Mary signaled the emergence of a new concern for women's issues and the role of the feminine in the world.

Chapter 12

The structure of large groups

GENERAL CONSIDERATIONS

Sociologists in the "social facts" tradition generally see large groups and organizations as having the character of concrete entities apart from the people who make them up. As such they are perceived as facticities, coercive upon and external to the world of the individual. Apparently, Jung saw the same thing but framed his observations from a more cynical perspective (Durkheim, 1938/1964; Berger and Luckmann, 1967; Merton, 1967; Aron, 1970; Ritzer, 1980).

Jung saw large groups as social entities which had become autonomous by virtue of their hypostatization by the populace. They are, after all, only products of human consciousness but popular culture and social manipulators had turned them into "quasi-animate personalities."

> [S]ociety is nothing more than an abstract idea like the State. Both are hypostatized, that is, have become autonomous. The State in particular is turned into a quasi-animate personality from whom everything is expected. In reality it is only a camouflage for those individuals who know how to manipulate it.
>
> (Jung, 1964/1970, para. 504)

Accordingly, Jung saw that groups generally came into existence to meet a purpose or to fulfill a need.[1] In some cases groups are entered passively. In industrialized societies, large groups of workers were created by the development of the factory system. Large groups of students are produced by the various school systems. Insofar as they are passive groups, their influence relies upon the coercive or reinforcing effects of the milieu and upon the dual mechanisms of imitation/identification in their broadest mode of function. Even though there is no conscious surrender to group influence, the inherent susceptibility of humans to group influence naturally joins with the institutional reinforcement of uniformity to impel the individual into identification with the group.

In voluntary groups there exists the added dimension of personal projections, which have the effect of increasing the tendency to conformity through the mechanism of identification. As the individual has unconsciously assimilated some part of the group to his psychic structure, the shaping power of the voluntary group is all the more powerful.

The collective conscious tends to take on the character of the least common denominator, and its contents "purport to be generally accepted truths" and "reasonable generalities." Each group may project upon every other a definition or character that is more typical of the perceiving group than it is of the group perceived. One's perceptions of what a group may do for me when I am not a member may differ distinctly from my perceptions of the group as a member (Jung, 1960/1969).

Young people are often raised as idealists. They are taught, and firmly believe, that the criminal justice system performed its functions with the weighty solemnity suggested by the school books. As outsiders they project their expectations that judges are compassionate yet fair, weighing each decision with painful care; that prosecutors and attorneys seek truth and justice and are burdened with the deep moral, philosophical and humanitarian issues of each case brought to trial. Later, should they become more intimately involved with the system, they will suddenly discover people doing jobs, often in a perfunctory manner, and rarely with the pathos and angst they were taught to expect. Similarly, in the church, there is a tendency for many groups to project an aura of sanctity about the priests and ministers that is shattered the first time one hears a priest swear or sees a televangelist in his Mercedes.

Yet for every group that projects an ideal image upon these institutions, there is another that projects a negative image. Many groups have grown to perceive all policemen as dishonest, all lawyers as cheats and all judges corrupt. Similarly, there are groups that project their negative feelings upon the churches and all religious faith.

Each group has, amongst its common sense formulations and "reasonable generalities," what Schutz called shared typifications. These characterize the world both outside and inside the group. The typifications have a tendency first to define the group's perceptions in terms of specific emotional charges, and then to stabilize the average perception as a cultural definition, part of the perspective unique to the group. Berger and Luckmann refer to this process, especially as it occurs across generations and in the context of a linguistic system, as sedimentation (Schutz, 1967; Berger and Luckmann, 1967; Mannheim, 1936; Jung, 1960/1969).

The autonomy of such typifications arises from their reification as linguistic realities. The government is not only a sign that names a specific kind of institution, it carries with it some of the numen that each group projects upon it. As with all psychic phenomena, there exists a strong tendency to personify our projections. The government can become a "quasi-animate personality" by virtue of the life that I project into it (Jung, 1964/1970).

The objectivity of the institutional world "thickens" and "hardens," . . . The "there we go again" now becomes "This is how these things are done." A world so regarded attains a firmness in consciousness; it becomes real in an ever more massive way and it can no longer be changed so readily. For the children, especially in the early phases of their socialization into it, it becomes *the* world.

(Berger and Luckmann, 1967, p. 59)

The tendency to personalize and animate the objects that hold our projections is part of the primordial heritage of humanity. According to von Franz, the primitive or undifferentiated psyche (whether of the child or primitive) projects itself upon the external world. In so doing, it projects upon the world the very real and very lively centers of psychic action known as the archetypes.

The whole world was alive with demons and spirits, or, in other words, single components of the human psyche were for the most part unreflected and were seen out there in nature where the human being was confronted with them as parts of an objective "world."

(von Franz, 1980/1988, p. 36)

What we then did as children we continue to do as adults faced with an unknown quantity; we project the contents of the collective unconscious: *"wherever known reality stops, where we touch the unknown, there we project an archetypal image"* (von Franz, 1972/1986, p. 5).

In each kind of group there exists the tendency to emphasize one facet of the individual to the exclusion of all others. Whether in a work or educational situation, whether voluntary or essentially involuntary, the group tends to limit its interaction with the individual to a limited part of his or her entire range of functions.

The privileged position of the superior function is as detrimental to the individual as it is valuable to society. This detrimental effect has reached such a pitch that the mass organizations of our present day culture actually strive for the complete extinction of the individual, since their very existence depends upon a mechanized application of the privileged function of individual human beings. It is not man who counts, but his one differentiated function. Man no longer appears as man in our collective culture: he is merely represented by a function, what is more he identifies himself completely with his function and denies the relevance of the other inferior functions. Thus modern man is debased to a mere function, because it is this that represents a collective value and alone guarantees a possible livelihood.

(Jung, 1971, para. 109)

Here, Jung is offering a partial explanation for the division of labor in terms of his four psychological functions. The superior function determines whether a person will adapt to the world primarily in terms of thought, feeling, emotion or intuition. Each has its specific strengths and weaknesses. Thus, a "thinking type" would do well at an analytic profession, a "sensing type" might fare best as a laborer, craftsman or artist, while an "intuitive type" might serve as physician or poet. In general, however, Jung's argument is that modern mass society has eliminated the worth of the individual and has substituted for it a callous differentiation of humankind in terms of their labor value (Jung, 1971, 1960/1969).

An important secondary effect of this development is the pathological, one-sided identification of the individual with his or her working identity or persona. While mitigated to some extent by the modern culture of entertainment and the upsurge of interest in spirituality, there remains a strong tendency for individuals to identify with their occupational function. The question people most often ask seems to be "What do you do?", not "Who are you?"

> The persona is a complicated system of relations between the individual consciousness and society, fittingly enough a kind of mask, designed on the one hand to make a definite impression upon others, and, on the other, to conceal the true nature of the individual. . . . Society expects, and indeed must expect, every individual to play the part assigned to him as perfectly as possible, so that a man who is a parson must not only carry out his official functions objectively, but must at all times and in all places play the part of parson in a flawless manner. Society demands this as a kind of surety; each must stand at his post, here a cobbler, there a poet. No man is expected to be both. Nor is it advisable to be both. . . . Such a man would be "different" from other people, not quite reliable. In the academic world he would be a dilettante, in politics an "unpredictable" quantity, in religion a free thinker; in short, he would always be suspected of unreliability and incompetence, because society is convinced that only the cobbler who is not a poet can supply workmanlike shoes.
>
> (Jung, 1953/1966, para. 305)

Thus, society inevitably moves to limit the individual. This, however, was not viewed by Jung as a conscious imperative, but as part of the constant interplay between the pressure towards individuation and personal growth, and the call of the regressive tendencies of the unconscious past. While the group tends towards uniformity and anonymity, the urge to individuate requires personal distinction from the group as well as personal responsibility. Where the group tends to limit the individual to specific, narrowly defined functions, the urge to self realization emphasizes diversity in self discovery and self actualization.

> [S]uppression of individuality is nothing new, it is a relic of that archaic time when there was no individuality whatever. So it is not by any means

a recent suppression we are dealing with, but merely a new sense and awareness of the overwhelming power of the collective. . . . To the collective psyche every individual development is hateful that does not serve the ends of collectivity. Hence although the differentiation of the one function . . . is a development of an individual value, it is still so largely determined by views of the collective that, as we have seen, it becomes injurious to the individual himself.

(Jung, 1971, para. 123)

THE ARCHETYPAL DIMENSIONS OF LARGE GROUPS

Archetypal origins

Large groups inevitably develop and project an identity. The power to attract large numbers of individuals depends in all cases on the group's ability to constellate an archetypal image from the collective unconscious. Each group is centered around a specific formative factor, the archetypal image, as the hook for identification. These archetypally determined elements receive their individual stamp from the cultural milieu, the family constellation and other factors. As such they provide a meaning context which is familiar, and in which identification can prosper. Such a context tends to even out the differences between the members and emphasize the similarities. The one identifying element, the carrier of the projection, becomes the center of attention while other individual factors fade into the background.

Like the individual, a group is influenced by numerous typical factors, such as the family milieu, society, politics, outlook on life, religion. The bigger the group, the more the individuals composing it function as a collective entity, which is so powerful that it can reduce the individual consciousness to the point of extinction, and it does this the more easily if the individual lacks spiritual possessions of his own with an individual stamp. The group and what belongs to it cover up the lack of genuine individuality, just as parents act as substitutes for everything lacking in their children. In this respect the group exerts a seductive influence, for nothing is easier than a perseveration of infantile ways or a return to them.

(Jung, 1964/1970, para. 891)

In some cases, the group identity or structure corresponds to an archetypal element originally associated with a dying religious symbol system. This similarity provides hooks for the projection of the meanings originally associated with the religious symbol on to the newer group. Jung saw political ideologies as essentially displaced, secularized religions. Communism and capitalism were specific examples inspiring a religious style of devotion in the lives of their exponents.

In other circumstances, the group develops around a symbol newly arisen from the depths of the collective unconscious which represents a new way of perceiving the world. Such a symbol was the core of the Christian mythos as it developed around the life of Jesus of Nazareth. While many of the elements of the salvation story had previously appeared in diverse contexts, they had never before assembled in the context of a single life. When they did, Christ became the container of projections for individuals from many disparate religious groups, signaling that a truly new thing had been born into the world of consciousness (Jung, 1958/1969).

Archetypal themes

The centerpiece of Jung's theory is the idea of the archetype, the unconscious ordering factor and meaning bearer. One of the most common symbolic manifestations of the archetypal is revealed in the roles basic to a society. Even a child's rhyme seems to reflect certain basic themes:

Rich man, Poor man, Beggar man, Thief;
Doctor, Lawyer, Indian Chief.

More specific archetypal roles were discussed earlier (see Part II) in terms of archetypal sequences. Carol Pearson recounts six in her first work: the Innocent, the Orphan, the Martyr, the Wanderer, the Warrior and the Magician (1986/1989). In a similar vein, Mitroff reviews the work of Thompson (1971) and tentatively recommends four archetypes as presenting the "basic building blocks of society and all institutions." These are:

The Hunter or Warrior, the Shaman or Medicine Man, The Clown or Fool and the Chief... when they are institutionalized and developed further, as they have been in modern society, the Hunter becomes the Military; the Shaman, the Medical profession; the Fool, the Artist and Entertainment; and the Chief, the Manager and the Managerial Class.
(Mitroff, 1983, p. 395)

In a later work (1989), Mitroff presents a more comprehensive list of archetypes culled from the work of Paul Moxnes (1987). These include the Father, the Mother, the Son, the Daughter, the Slave or Servant, the Wiseman or Shaman, the Winner or Hero, and the Loser. More true to Jung, these are then split into antithetical components which give rise to a total of sixteen basic types. Table 12.1 is adapted from Mitroff with the addition of some typical messages that might be projected by the relevant role image.

Meditating on these possible "building blocks" one cannot help but recall Jung's observation that the archetypes are hopelessly intermingled. In the same manner, Mitroff points to his own observation of the fact that

Table 12.1 Archetypal figures from Mitroff and Moxnes

Archetype	Aspect	Fairy tales	Bible	Greek myths	Message
Father	Good Father	King	God	Zeus	I will guide/teach
	Bad Father	Troll/Beast	Devil	Hades	I will punish/enforce
Mother	Good Mother	Queen	Madonna/ St. Mary	Hera	I will care/nurture
	Bad Mother	Witch	Jezebel	Persephone	I will abandon
Son	Good Son	Crown Prince	Jesus	Apollo	I will obey
	Bad Son	Black Sheep	Antichrist/ Judas	Ares	I will disobey
Daughter	Good Daughter	Princess/ Virgin	Virgin Mary	Athene	I will follow/submit
	Bad Daughter	Whore/Witch	Mary Magdalene	Aphrodite	I won't
Slave/Servant	Good Slave	Courtier	Martha	Hermes	I will serve
	Bad Slave		Unjust Steward		I want mine/ serve me
Wiseman	Good Wiseman	Old Man	Jesus, Luke, Solomon	Asculapeus	I will teach/lead/heal/ empower
	Bad Wiseman		Balaam, Solomon		I will addict/lead astray/ deceive
Winner/Hero	Good Winner	Ash Lad	Abraham	Hercules, Perseus	I will save/give
	Bad Winner		Lot		Me first
Loser	Good Loser	Anonymous	Abraham	Prometheus	If at first you don't succeed . . .
	Bad Loser		Nabal		Life is not fair

One can "fix" some of the basic experiences around which the archetypes form, but one cannot fix the number or their shape. Indeed, one of the archetypes that always seems to form when he/she has captured the "complete set of archetypes" is an archetype having to do with precariousness, randomness, danger, and/or incompleteness. This archetype seems to function to alert one that the psyche may never fully succeed in fathoming itself in *fixed, static form*. Another closely accompanying kind of archetype that also seems to form is that of the trickster.

(Ibid., p. 392)

If we were to look for a base vocabulary of symbolic elements it would no doubt collapse several of the categories already noted. Because the archetypes are capable of almost infinite articulation and extension, the multiplication of possible root symbols is potentially endless.

They are genuine symbols precisely because they are ambiguous, full of half glimpsed meanings, and in the last resort inexhaustible. The ground principles, the αρχαι, of the unconscious are indescribable because of their wealth of reference, although in themselves recognizable. The discriminating intellect naturally keeps on trying to establish their singleness of meaning and thus misses the essential point; for what we can above all establish as the one thing consistent with their nature is their manifold meaning, their almost limitless wealth of reference, which makes any unilateral formulation impossible.

(Jung, 1959/1968a, para. 80)

For this reason, it may be best to limit oneself to the barest minimum of root types, understanding that within them and their interrelations all others pre-exist.

Jung specifically relates the archetypes of the Father, the Wise Old Man (the Magus or Shaman) and the Chief. He also finds the Mother and Daughter linked archetypally into one not only in the anima, but also in the myths of Demeter/Persephone. Likewise the Son and the Hero are eternally linked in the monomyth. Beyond these there lies only the archetype of wholeness, the self. And the self, whether as Mandala, Jewel, City, Child or Bride, returns us to the original categories. Yet, with regard specifically to the elements of culture, the possibility of a different list lingers (1956/ 1967, 1959/1968a).

William Irwin Thompson sees all social structures as rooted in four archetypal roles: the Chief, the Shaman, the Hunter and the Fool. In outlining his theory of four types, he was well aware of his affinities with Jung but also saw the consistent reappearance of the quaternio throughout history.

This model of four seems to be a persistent one; it recalls the rule of four in the Indian caste system, Plato, Vico, Blake, Marx, Yeats, Jung and McLuhan. So many people look out at reality and come up with a four-part structure that one cannot help but think that it expresses the nature of reality and/or the Kantian a priori pure categories of the understanding.

(Thompson, 1971, p. 78)

These archetypal roles match the four Jungian functions: Chief as thinker, Fool as feeler, Shaman as intuitive and Hunter as sensate. These four root types can be divided into the operational – the Chief and the Hunter – and the ideational – the Shaman and the Fool. They also appear as polar opposites, Chief v. Fool, and Shaman v. Hunter.

Thompson's insight, however, extends beyond the simple identification of these types to an analysis of the manner of their interaction on four different societal levels. All of society is based upon the conflict and coordination that occurs between the two perspectives – the ideational and the operational – as they are articulated in terms of the four basic roles.

In general, Thompson visualizes the process as two interacting vortices so arranged that the focus of the ideational vortex corresponds with the top of the operational vortex, and the top of the ideational vortex to the focus of the operational. It is a kind of ouroboric, metaphysical klein bottle. The specific strengths of the ideational members balance out the weaknesses of the operational members and *vice versa*: "Headman and Hunter realize the possibilities that Shaman and Clown do not, as Shaman and Clown realize the possibilities untouched by the others. Together the four form a stable group in which all the skills are balanced" (1971, p. 77).

At the level of tribal society where the division of labor has not proceeded to the point of setting up strong distinctions between roles, or strong oppositions between power bases, all are capable of working together. All must participate in the hunt, yet all retain their special roles and abilities. Charisma, knowledge and information are generally available.

With the arrival of the agrarian economy, elite specialists break up the unity of society into specialized realms of knowledge. From each of the fundamental roles there develops a specific realm of knowledge and specialization. Out of the tradition of the Chief comes the affairs of state. Out of the Shamanic tradition emerges religion. The military is derived from the role of the Hunter/Warrior and from the Fool emerges Art (see Figure 12.1).

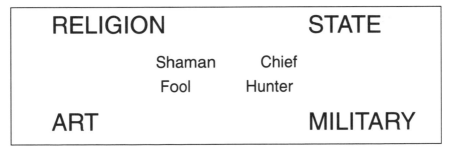

RELIGION   STATE

Shaman   Chief
Fool   Hunter

ART   MILITARY

Figure 12.1 The fundamental roles of society and their corresponding traditions

As the root categories are archetypal in nature, they also structure the divisions of knowledge as they appear in the agrarian economy. So, each field has its Chief, Shaman, Hunter and Fool who play out the same dynamic of opposites and complements as existed in the hunter/gatherer society. Thus, for the religious realm alone, the place of King is taken by the Bishop, the place of Shaman is given to the Theologian, the Mystic takes on the Fool's mantle and the Scribe becomes religion's Hunter/Warrior. Schematically, Table 12.2 displays the relations between the roles and the disciplines.

Table 12.2 The fundamental roles of society translated into four disciplines

	Operational roles		Ideational roles	
	Chief	Warrior	Shaman	Fool
State	King	General	High Priest	Apologist
Military	Commander	Foot Soldier	Strategist	Warrior–hero
Religion	Bishop	Scribe	Theologian	Mystic
Art	Publicist	Artisan	Celebrant	Satirist–critic

Thompson comments:

The duplication of the original four of the tribal community in every institution in urban society thus creates a field situation of simultaneous attraction and repulsion in which the Bishop administers the religion, the Scribe serves as the technician responsible for the important tool of writing, the Theologian relates the mythic tradition to the intellectual problems of society or the astronomical problems of the sacral calendar, and the mystic dwells in the religious consciousness all the others, presumably, are striving to achieve.

(Ibid., p. 81)

The operational poles within any given realm will generally compete with the ideational poles, each striving to expand their own hegemony throughout the entire discipline. Moreover, each individual fulfilling any of the roles so defined will likewise seek to expand his own authority and perspective throughout the entire system.

The Bishop thinks the Mystic is a foaming maniac; the Mystic thinks the Bishop is a callous money-grubber. The Scribe thinks the Theologian is a parasite upon his important work, and the Theologian thinks the Scribe is a mindless fool. In a stable institution the expansion of each will be checked by the mutual and complementary opposition of all.

(Ibid., pp. 81–2)

The system is maintained, however, by the mutual counterbalance of conflicting interest. Within the system there is a strong tendency for all individuals fulfilling the same archetypal role in any sphere of specialization to respond favorably to others fulfilling the same roles in other spheres. This has the net effect of counterbalancing the tendency of any one sphere to become absolutely dominant. Further, there is a marked tendency for each sphere to protect its own autonomy by defining claims to legitimate authority on its own terms. So, the state defines the rules of succession for the high priest in terms of routinized or traditional authority, not charisma.

Simultaneously, the religious sphere makes spiritual demands on the state in order to confirm its legitimacy in terms of charismatic authority.

> Let me make the anarchism as clear as possible by being as apodictic as possible: no political system can work because no political system can escape the structural contradictions inherent in the necessity of achieving values in a system which subverts the values themselves. No merely historical process can work for the individual or society, because no historical process can escape the structural contradictions of history.... Inverse entropy, the conservation of value in a world of chaos, comes from a religious transformation in which a disadvantage on one position of order becomes an advantage at a higher level of order.
>
> (Ibid., p. 86)

With the coming of the industrial society, the paradigm again recreates the four roles at a new logical level. On this level information unifies, abstracts and transforms. The state and its executive give rise to government; religion, through its theologians, creates education; the military's foot soldier becomes the precursor of industry; and out of art the critic/satirist gives rise to the media. In each new realm the archetypal dominants create a new level of differentiation. Here, however, all roles and all meanings are routinized. Education, government, the media and labor are industries which readily transfer individuals and information across boundaries unthinkable under previous paradigms. In the industrial, or post-industrial culture, the roles are retranslated from ideational/charismatic v. routine/operational to informational v. industrial, each with its distinctive culture.

> Industrial culture stresses sobriety, paternal wisdom, caution, thrift and the postponement of sensuous gratification in order to achieve long-term financial prosperity – all amounting to the familiar work ethic. Informational culture stresses joy, youthful spontaneity, energy, abandon, and the postponement of financial security in order to achieve immediate sensuous self-realization. Industrial culture is one of sexual repression, which finds its outlet in the power of mechanization. In the case of a wealthy industrialist, this power is sublimated into the acceptable forms of a man who dominates factories and industrial empires. In the case of a member of the industrial working class, the power is seen in his car, [or] motorcycle.... Informational culture is one of sexual expression in the complete body, which sublimates physical aggression into a form of erotic provocation of those who appear to be sexually repressed.
>
> (Ibid., p. 92)

With the final fruition of the third stage, the roles of Chief, Shaman, Warrior and Fool have become transformed into Manager, Scientist, Technician and Critic. Each role is recapitulated in each new level, as succeeding levels recapitulate the history of civilization in terms of global industry.

Lacking another, Thompson's perspective seems to be an accurate reflection of the archetypal structure of society and, as such, a crucial contribution to its understanding. What is especially attractive about Thompson's formulation is its self referential quality that reflects the holographic and fractal qualities of archetypal imagery (Zinkin, 1987; Part II of this text). Moreover, although we have not followed it thus far, at the fifth level, the system turns back upon itself and starts anew at the octave of its tribal beginning. This reflects once more an important property of the archetypes, especially as they are expressed in numbers. It is what von Franz (1974) characterized as the tendency for numbers to return to one. The alchemists also noted it in the doctrine of the *quinta essentia*, and Maria Prophetessa shadowed it in her curious maxim: " ... from the third comes the one as the fourth" (Jung, 1959/1968a, para. 430). That it appears here also provides strong evidence that Thompson has struck upon an important symbol system.

Archetypal styles

Each large group projects a specific archetypal image that characterizes not only its role, but the manner in which the role is carried out. Mitroff again points to corporate takeover styles varying in terms of whether they are seen as conquests, courtships, discoveries, duels or any of a number of archetypally defined approaches to an encounter with another group or person (1983).

Each group begins with a typological standard that relates to its specific means of interacting with the world. It may be introverted, redefining the world in accordance with its own dictates, as is done by some religious groups as well as certain highly secretive scientific enterprises. Bell Laboratories, before the break-up of American Telephone and Telegraph (AT&T), was a wholly owned research organization. It was typologically introverted with little concern for the outside world, except as that world appeared through the microscope of its researchers. The story is told that at the early Westinghouse labs, Bell's precursor organization, the only question asked of the scientists who were gathered there was "Are you having fun?"

On the other hand, an organization or group may be extroverted to varying degrees – always testing the waters with polls and samples much like a modern political campaign. Many modern corporations have taken on an extroverted style in their continuing quest for market dominance. Witness the "cheeseburger and cola wars" constantly being waged through the mass media. Here at the group level is the manifestation of Jung's extrovert, social entities totally committed to responding to the consumer – for the purpose of profit.

In smaller groups, likewise, the introvert/extrovert dichotomy appears. An Ouspensky study group is far more likely to be introverted than an evangelical Bible study group. Thus, a local group of Young Democrats will turn an extroverted face to the community, while an Alcoholics Anonymous group faces inward towards its members.

Sometimes the cultural idea is extroverted, and the chief value then lies with the object and man's relation to it: sometimes it is introverted, and the chief value lies with the subject and his relation to the idea. In the former case culture takes on a collective character, in the latter an individual one. It is therefore easy to understand how the influence of Christianity, whose principal is Christian love (and by counter-association, also its counterpart, the violation of individuality), a collective culture came about in which the individual is liable to be swallowed up because individual values are depreciated on principle.

(Jung, 1971, para. 110)

The style of an organization, or even of an era, has great impact upon the safety, sanity and satisfaction of its citizens or members. Ira Progoff has noted that styles of interaction characterize various time periods as a zeitgeist. One's career and livelihood could easily depend upon the goodness of fit between personal style and the spirit of the time or organization (1959).

He suggests that whereas the Middle Ages encouraged the introverted religious hermit to sit and meditate for years, today's zeitgeist requires a significantly more extroverted lifestyle. The personal revelation of the mystic is often held suspect while the new spirituality seems to encourage group awareness in men's groups, women's groups, support groups, etc. Witness the predilection for sound bites instead of meaningful discourse, and the relatively meaningless but mathematically correct sociology that now supplants scholarship in the tradition of Weber and Marx. This gives new meaning to the idea of someone born out of time.

A second level of archetypal analysis leads us back to the specific function favored by the group. Some groups (e.g. Mensa) are composed predominantly of thinking types. They are organized rationally, they communicate in terms of abstract signs. They may delight in chess games or discussion of theoretical physics. Their entire structure is dominated by the one function. The current rage in support groups emphasizes the "feeling side" of life. Other groups emphasize sensing or intuiting. Each of these may be expected to have the unconscious effect of attracting members possessed of the same dominant function and repelling those with a different dominant.

Jung understood that groups and cultures could prefer one function over another, and also saw that each culture adds a significant cant to the functions of consciousness operative within it.

This collective quality adheres not only to particular psychic elements or contents but to whole *functions*. Thus the thinking function as a whole can have a collective quality, when it possesses general validity and accords with the laws of logic. Similarly, the feeling function as a whole can be collective when it is identified with the general feeling and accords with the general expectations, the general moral consciousness, etc. In the same way sensation and intuition are collective when they are at the same time characteristic of a large group of men.

(Ibid., para. 692)

Western culture has come to consistently emphasize one function over the rest. Whatever the preferred function, Jung was scandalized by the tendency to reduce individuals to the value then preferred by the society or group.

The privileged position of the superior function is as detrimental to the individual as it is valuable to society. This detrimental effect has reached such a pitch that the mass organizations of our present day culture actually strive for the complete extinction of the individual, since their very existence depends upon a mechanized application of the privileged function of individual human beings. It is not man who counts, but his one differentiated function. Man no longer appears as man in our collective culture: he is merely represented by a function, what is more he identifies himself completely with his function and denies the relevance of the other inferior functions. Thus modern man is debased to a mere function, because it is this that represents a collective value and alone guarantees a possible livelihood.

(Ibid., para. 109)

This discussion of groups and functional styles immediately recalls Pitirim Sorokin's analysis of history and culture into ideational, sensate and idealistic supersystems. Sorokin appears to have differed from Jung in his decision to use three root types instead of four. (Whether this reflects Jung's mystical bias towards the number four or a problem with Sorokin's analysis cannot be addressed here.) The divisions are, however, not incompatible. Sorokin's ideational and sensate systems appear to correspond to Jung's sensing and intuiting functions; his idealistic culture seems to incorporate Jung's evaluative functions – thinking and feeling. The analysis is difficult because the perspectives are different. One is almost tempted to classify the ideational with introverted types and the sensate with the extroverts (Sorokin, 1985/1991).

Sorokin analyzed cultural history over a period of 2,500 years from the perspective of its organizing principles in art, truth systems, ethics and war. Of each he asked:

• What is the ultimate nature of reality? Is it spiritual, sensual/carnal or a balance of both?

- What is the nature of the needs to be satisfied? Are they abstract and transcendent, applicable to a different reality, or strictly for the here-and-now, dominated by physical considerations, or a balanced combination of the two?
- To what extent are different needs satisfied?
- What are the means of satisfaction?

In general, he differentiated the ideational/spiritual types who grounded their reality in a transcendent insensible realm from the sensate types who were grounded in the here-and-now of physical reality. Against these two he saw a third type, the idealistic, combining the best of the other two (Sorokin, 1985/1991; Maquet, 1951).

Each of these types also implied several transitional or mixed types. Ideational cultures might be ascetic–ideational, like monastic orders, or active–ideational evangelicals as in the early Christian Church. Sensate cultures may be active, seeking to change the world in which they live. "The great executives of history, the great conquerors, builders of empire are its incarnation" (Sorokin, 1985/1991, p. 28). They may also be passive, voluptuary and sybaritic, exploiters of the external reality in which they live. They might also be cynical in their sensuality, using ideational personae to obtain their own way. These are the hypocrites and vultures of the world. The idealistic cultures may be truly idealistic, integrating the ideational and sensate cultures into a balanced rhythm, or they may be pseudo-ideational types, dissatisfied with a portion which they did not choose but from which they cannot escape. Slaves, oppressed peoples, minorities and victims of calamity often fall into this category (ibid.).

From the Jungian perspective Sorokin seems to have been discussing the relative salience of the instinctual over the archetypal or spiritual poles in the course of Western civilization. Interestingly, Jung saw the functions of consciousness as capable of linear distribution in terms of their level of differentiation and capability of discrimination. This also represented a measure of the whole move of consciousness, from an instinctually based sensate system to an archetypally ordered and relatively spiritual system.

Jung noted that the non-evaluative functions were more archaic. Sensation "is given a priori, and unlike thinking and feeling is not subject to rational laws." Intuition is defined partially as unconscious perception. By comparison with the rational functions, they are more diffuse, less focused, less conscious. Feeling became the first evaluative response set. The capability of abstract thinking finally brought consciousness to a high level of development (1971, paras. 795–6).

Into this general background, the archetypal posture of the group is also projected. We have previously suggested that the archetypal vocabulary may be expressed in terms of three possible axes of organismic movement:

assimilative/accommodative, focusing/diffusing and approaching/avoiding.[2] These same poles apply to groups, especially to the styles of large groups. In order to see the potential effect of any group on the individual we must be prepared to characterize the group in terms of the following archetypal dimensions. Is it assimilative, dominating, aggressive, or accommodative, servile, passive? Does it possess a clear focus, or is it relatively diffuse in its direction, purpose and organizing principles? Does its general style involve movement towards a goal or goals, or movement away from some threat or threats?

These archetypal dimensions combine with the specific archetypal images and functional orientations to provide some very specific indices of an individual's or a group's archetypal character. Depending upon the immediate physical and psychological needs of the individual, he will be drawn to that group whose archetypal structure most nearly matches his own need structure. This will have been in part determined by the fulfillment or frustration of archetypal intent during key imprinting periods during the individual's life.

Sometimes the archetypal image of the group will be perceived only through the projection of the individual structure on to the group, and at other times, the group will actively project an image or symbol for public consumption. Corporate logos are often highly symbolic references to the specific archetypal image that the company embodies. At other times they are just nice picture-symbols out of context. Reynolds Aluminium presents a stylized St George slaying the dragon on its corporate logo. Whether the image is current or not, it apparently said something at one time about the way Reynolds saw itself and how it intended others to perceive it. Teleflora adopted the figure of Mercury/Hermes, presumably to illustrate its role of messenger, and with it the implied elements of speed and universal access. Colgate Palmolive is forever fighting allegations that its man-in-the-moon and star logo were inspired by Satan. The archetypal numen embodied in that image was so powerful that, despite corporate denials of any occult involvement, the company was forced to change the logo.

Underlying all such messages, however, are the deeper, less distinct messages of the collective unconscious: the domination of earth and instinctuality by the ego principle; the magical efficacy of the messenger god; the clarity and mystery of the night sky. All are powerful themes at the root of human experience.

More subtly the group task or organizational structure provides strong projective hooks. The Japanese corporation, providing "cradle to grave" care for its employees, and requiring absolute allegiance, projects a strong parental theme. Similarly, the Church, and more specifically, the Orthodox Churches project the mother imago on both conscious and unconscious levels. Other organizations clearly enact archetypal roles, and plainly evoke their images. The police, first aid or fire departments evoke projections of the hero archetype. The hospital, study group, or graduate seminar evoke the Healer, Magus and Shaman.

THE ARCHETYPAL STRUCTURE OF LARGE GROUPS

It is possible from Jung's writings to understand large groups as being possessed of a structure that parallels the structure of the individual psyche. From the perspective of systems theory such an arrangement would suggest that Jung's psychic elements represent relations between contents in accordance with the system's principle of systemic invariance. Piaget described such relations thus:

> As a first approximation, we may say that a structure is a system of transformations. Inasmuch as it is a system and not a mere collection of elements and their properties, these transformations involve laws: the structure is preserved or enriched by the interplay of its transformation laws. . . .

> (Piaget, 1970b, p. 5)

In her examination of the archetype in its relationship to Gestalt theory, Jacobi outlined the relationship of the systems elements, wholeness and self maintenance to the theory of archetypes.[3] The archetypes may be transposed and varied, subjected to transformations by various processes, but they always retain an invariant and recognizable structure. An archetype "may borrow its mode of manifestation from the most diverse spheres of reality and ideation and still retain its identity of meaning" (1974, pp. 54–5).

In Part II, we identified the elements of the psyche as archetypally ordered in their own right. As such, they must also partake of systems properties. As the archetypes, from a systems perspective, represent the rules of transformation which define the system and subsystems, we may expect the mark of their patterning to appear at every level of integration.[4]

One of the obvious implications of this is that groups should display several levels of function including a relatively conscious level corresponding to the ego, and a relatively unconscious function. We also expect that groups give expression to a collective unconscious, but this would tend to be more of a local activation of a universal structure and will be reflected in the division between the group executive and its unconscious.

The collective consciousness

It is clear that there exists a collective consciousness that acts as if it were a single entity. In large and small groups this would represent the formal definitions of the group, the public myths surrounding it and the general cultural milieu that it creates. Jung describes it as consisting of what "purport to be generally accepted truths ... [and] ... reasonable generalities" (1960/1969, para. 424). Despite its tendency to provide a unified front, the collective consciousness was seen by Jung to be a relatively low-level phenomenon. He hesitated to provide it with the dignity of a unitary element and repeatedly described it as a chaotic assemblage of commonly held ideas, the least common denominator.

Neumann seems to have provided a more useful perspective.

[W]ith the development and systematization of consciousness and the individual ego there arises a collective consciousness, a cultural canon characteristic for each culture and cultural epoch. There arises in other words, a configuration of archetypes, symbols, values and attitudes, upon which the unconscious archetypal contents are projected and which, fixated as myth and cult, becomes the dogmatic heritage of the group.

(Neumann, 1959/1974, pp. 86–7)

Just as the ego coalesces out of the early interactions between competing archetypal dominants, so every group coalesces about a certain set of commonly activated archetypal contents which tend to characterize its function, purpose and direction. These contents are represented in the official line of the group whether it is a religion, a corporation, a government or a culture. They give expression to what Neumann called the cultural canon.

In the group as in the individual, two psychic systems are at work, which can function smoothly only when they are attuned to each other. The one is the collective consciousness, the cultural canon, the system of the culture's supreme values toward which its education is oriented and which set their decisive stamp on the development of the individual consciousness. But side by side with this is the living substratum, the collective unconscious, in which new developments, transformations, revolutions and renewals are at all times foreshadowed and prepared and whose perpetual eruptions prevent the stagnation and death of a culture. But even if we see the group as an integral psychic field, the men in whom reside the compensatory unconscious forces necessary to the cultural canon and the culture of the particular time are also elements of this constellation.

(Ibid., p. 89)

Neumann is careful to note that individuals are the bearers of the life force that empowers the collective consciousness. Without individuals there can be no groups. In any formulation, the individual – who is the active conduit of unconscious energies – must be counted as part of the configuration.

There is a continuous interchange between the collective unconscious (which is alive in the unconscious of every individual in the group), the cultural canon (which represents the group's collective consciousness of those archetypal values which have become dogma), and the creative individuals in the group (in whom the new constellations of the collective unconscious achieve form and excursion).

(Ibid., p. 90)

The cultural canon, or collective consciousness, has the effect of channeling psychic energy into the specific pathways required by the institution or structure delimited by it. As such, the collective consciousness is a limiting structure. Positively, it tends to limit behavior to forms compatible with the manifest functions of the group.

[T]he cultural canon is not only a bond with the archetypal substratum of the unconscious. As "canon" it is also a means of limiting and fixating the intervention of the numinosum and excluding unpredictable creative forces. Thus the cultural canon is always a fortress of security; and since it is a systematic restriction to a dogmatic section of the numinosum, it carries with it the danger of one-sidedness and congealment. For the archetypal world is a dynamic world of change, and even the numinosum and the divine are mortal in the contingent form which can be apprehended by man.

(Ibid., p. 92)

The cultural canon consists of values, expectancies, definitions, prescriptions and proscriptions that define the conscious nature of the group. Correlatively, these same elements exclude the holders of conflicting values and definitions as either evil, subhuman or irrelevant.

Negatively, we see the collective stifling creativity and personal growth. With the coming of the collective comes also the diminution of individual responsibility.

The bigger the group, the more the individuals composing it function as a collective entity, which is so powerful that it can reduce the individual consciousness to the point of extinction, and it does this the more easily if the individual lacks spiritual possessions of his own with an individual stamp. The group and what belongs to it cover up the lack of genuine individuality, just as parents act as substitutes for everything lacking in their children. In this respect the group exerts a seductive influence, for nothing is easier than a perseveration of infantile ways or a return to them.

(Jung, 1964/1970, para. 891)

One of the marks of every psychic structure is the tendency to inertia, to resist change. Thus, the collective consciousness is profoundly conservative.

Every pattern of adaptation, outer and inner, is maintained in essentially the same unaltered form and anxiously defended against change until an equally strong or stronger impulse is able to displace it. Moreover, every such displacement or alteration is reacted to as a death-like threat to the ego.

(Whitmont, 1969, p. 246)

If we treat the cultural canon as the executive function of the group, we must assume that it will show the same conservative tendencies as the individual ego. This is the more so when we understand that identification with a group often entails a weakening of ego boundaries, hence the loss of individuality observed by Jung. Many will recall, from both positive and negative perspectives, the often quoted sentiment that identified one's country with one's honor, or one's country with one's mother – both were to be protected with the same vigor. Gang members are known for their violent reactions towards any show of disrespect for the "colors" or symbols of the group. Both examples represent a merging of personal identity with the group.

From the Jungian perspective, the collective consciousness is conservative, self perpetuating and grows increasingly inflexible over time. As guardian of the status quo, it limits individuality and any threat from below. As the relatively conscious agency of the group it actively represses the incompatible, inconsistent and unthinkable.

The group shadow

Just as the world of consciousness has its opposite in the psychic realm, there exists a dark underside to large groups. That which is not included in the collective consciousness by virtue of repression, forgetfulness or incomprehension may be said to belong to the group shadow.

[S]ince the unconscious, like the conscious, is both personal and collective, there also exists a *collective shadow* – the unrecognized, incompatible, and inferior side of a race, group, or nation. Because the shadow, whether personal or collective, contains all those aspects of the psyche which consciousness does not want to recognize, it is usually effectively repressed.

(Odjanyk, 1976, p. 70)

Jung described the shadow as a "sort of second personality, of a puerile and inferior character" (1959/1968a, para. 469). "The [shadow] . . . usually presents itself as the inferior or negative personality. It comprises that part of the collective unconscious which intrudes into the personal sphere, there forming the so-called personal unconscious" (1963/1970, pp. 107–8n).

On a collective level it is often expressed in the figure of the trickster.

The trickster is a collective shadow figure, a summation of all the inferior traits of character in individuals. And since the individual shadow is never absent as a component of personality, the collective figure can construct itself out of it continually. Not always of course, as a mythological figure, but, in consequence of the increasing repression and neglect of the original mythologems, as a corresponding projection on other social groups and nations.

(Jung, 1959/1968a, para. 484)

Key elements in the discussion of a collective shadow are the ideas that its contents may be actively repressed, or repressed through their incompatibility with the cultural canon. Both imply a dissociation between the conscious and unconscious aspects of the individual or group.

Neumann differentiates between repressed and suppressed contents. Suppression is: " . . . the deliberate elimination from consciousness of all those characteristics and tendencies in the personality which are out of harmony with the ethical value" (1959/1974, p. 34). He continues:

Suppression is a conscious achievement of the ego, and it is usually practised and cultivated in a systematic way. It is important to notice that in suppression a sacrifice is made which leads to suffering. This suffering is accepted, and for that reason the rejected contents and components of the personality still retain their connection with the ego.

(Neumann, 1959/1974, p. 34)

While suppressed contents retain contact with the executive, repressed contents are excluded from the conscious system altogether and, in the dark underground of the psyche or the social system, they grow with little or no relationship to the conscious values that exiled them. These forms of selective attention move readily from the personal to the social sphere where suppression gives the minority a voice while cynically ignoring any plea for justice; repression denies the problem and the cry altogether.

Jung saw that in individuals the dissociation between the shadow and the conscious mind always presented a danger to its subject.

Separation from his instinctual nature inevitably plunges civilized man into the conflict between conscious and unconscious, spirit and nature, knowledge and faith, a split that becomes pathological the moment his consciousness is no longer able to neglect or suppress his instinctual side.

(Jung, 1964/1970, para. 558)

The primary split that Jung observed was a dissociation between the rational and emotive functions in modern man. This grew out of the overvaluation of rationality brought about first by the Christianization of the West, then by the rationalization brought about by the industrial and scientific revolutions.

[J]ust as the intellect subjugated the psyche, so it subjugated Nature and begat on her an age of scientific technology that left less and less room for the natural and irrational man. Thus the foundations were laid for an inner opposition which today threatens the world with chaos. To make the reversal complete, all the powers of the underworld now hide behind reason and intellect. . . .

(Jung, 1959/1968a, para. 444)

On the level of national pathology, Jung diagnosed the denial of the shadow as one of the greatest dangers presented to modern man. Long before the emergence of National Socialism, he saw that the Germans,[5] in their forced conversion to Christianity, had repressed a violent, pagan aspect of their make-up which continued to exist as a significant part of their collective shadow.

Christianity split the Germanic barbarian into an upper and a lower half, and enabled him, by repressing the dark side, to domesticate the brighter half and fit it for civilization. But the lower, darker half still awaits redemption and a second spell of domestication. Until then it will remain associated with the vestiges of the prehistoric age, with the collective unconscious, which is subject to a peculiar and ever-increasing activation. As the Christian view of the world loses its authority, then menacingly will the "blond beast" be heard prowling about in its underground prison, ready at any minute to burst out with devastating consequences. When this happens in the individual it brings about a psychological revolution, but it can also take a social form.

(Jung, 1964/1970, para. 17)

Even though other countries may not have constellated so strong an image from their past, all groups stand in some danger of the eruption of the repressed forces of the unconscious.

In translating the idea of the shadow to the level of sociology, there are two possible means by which the dynamic pattern of the shadow expresses itself. In one we deal with a national shadow, as in the case of Nazi Germany. Here, a common and commonly repressed element of the collective unconscious, especially of the ethnic stratum of the collective unconscious, remains active. In times of national crisis this same element threatens to re-emerge as a mass psychosis. This is by far the most dangerous form.

The second form constellates the shadow as excluded groups. When we recognize that the executive has the property of focus, and that attention by its nature excludes information, we also see that necessary by-products of consciousness are the various levels of repression and suppression that result in the growth of the personal unconscious. At the group level this suggests that certain groups, institutional needs and problems may be relegated to a group, organizational or national unconscious as a side effect of the turning of attention somewhere else.

A large part of education ... teach[es] ... not what is, but what may be regarded as real; all human societies are at all times far more interested in instructing their members in the techniques of not looking, of overlooking and of looking the other way than in sharpening their observation, increasing their alertness and fostering their love of truth.

(Neumann, 1959/1974, p. 38)

This tendency is shown clearly in the example of functional sociology. Classical functionalism focused on the positive purpose served by a particular variable within the context of the phenomenon under study. Their classic question for the group or institution under study was: "How does this element contribute to the continuing existence of the larger whole; what is its function?" In so framing its view of the world, classical functionalism failed to examine those places where the institution harmed its members, or failed to acknowledge their real needs. Its critics viewed functionalism as extremely conservative. In its most exaggerated forms it ignored the underside of the dominant society and went so far as to ascribe positive functionality to injustice, discrimination and bigotry. Merton cited the critics who observed: "Functional theory is merely the orientation of the conservative social scientist who would defend the present order of things, just as it is, and who would attack the advisability of change, however moderate" (1957/1967, p. 37).

We observe the same principle in a dramatic fashion while applying Kuhn's (1969) theory of scientific revolutions to the study of science. As noted in the previous section, during periods of "normative science," all areas of a field of scientific study are determined by a specific perspective, the canon of that paradigm. Other approaches to science are ignored or actively disparaged. As a case in point, one might recall that when Freud originally announced his theory of sexual abuse, he was laughed out of the lecture hall. Similarly, Thompson (1971) recalls the absolute rejection afforded Immanuel Velikovsky and his theory of catastrophism when it was first presented in the 1950s. Whatever the merit of the theory, if it does not meet the requirements of the current canon or paradigm, it will be rejected.

Whenever the executive function operates in a state of alienation from the shadow, the focus is always too narrow to meet the needs of either a whole person or a whole society. Healthy societies require a certain level of communication between the conscious and unconscious functions. Western democracies, with all of their faults, have survived because they have been flexible enough to incorporate previously unconscious elements through modification of the collective canon.

A case in point is the historical growth of the United States government. The Constitution, when originally developed as a partial formulation of the collective canon for the emerging republic, was essentially conscious only of free, white males from a Jewish or Christian background. It may be argued that all the guarantees of freedom not only emerged from the Judeo-Christian canon, but were originally reserved for its adherents. The genius, however, of the Constitution was its appeal to archetypal levels of generality, and an inherent flexibility that allowed for the integration of new contents into the conscious canon. Thus, when those elements of society that had been relegated to the unconscious level of society developed enough energy, which were in this case represented by sympathetic voters and economic backing, they were included in the canon through a restructuring of its principles. This occurred with the emancipation of the slaves, the extension of voting rights to blacks, women's suffrage, and the Civil Rights movement of the 1960s. It is to be hoped that the process will continue.[6]

From this perspective, the American Constitution retains its viability through two mechanisms. First, it is a *true* symbol in the Jungian sense. This means that the Constitution is not subject to full interpretation or codification. As with all symbols, its meaning lies more in its numen than its rational analysis. This is a significant part of the reason why variant perspectives on the interpretation of the Constitution exist and flourish. It is a rich and living symbol. Second, *because* it is a living symbol it maintains an active avenue of communication between the unconscious elements of the society and the relatively conscious elements expressed as the collective consciousness of the dominant culture. This means that the defining symbol of the American experience will continue to function only insofar as it continues to provide an avenue of communication and a means of self transformation.

The separation between conscious and unconscious becomes pathological when the needs of the unconscious dynamism are no longer either susceptible of integration with the conscious system or suppressible, but threaten instead to overwhelm the ego. On the sociological level, this can occur as secondary groups and minorities grow in numbers or power to the point where their interests create a conflicting collective consciousness that is incompatible with dominant canon of values. The pathology becomes manifest when the old institutions prove to be so resistant to redefinition that violent means become the logical response.

Even if the resulting conflict seems to achieve resolution through a mass movement, Jung's perspective remains pessimistic. For Jung the only possible reformation of society comes through a change in the nature of the individual wrought through religious and moral awakening. Should mass movements effect a change, the same problems must resurface for they are bound up not in the nature of the social structure, but in the hearts of the people who create and compose the structure itself.

The accumulation of individuals who have got into this critical state starts off a mass movement purporting to be the champion of the suppressed. In accordance with the prevailing tendency of consciousness to seek the source of all ills in the outside world, the cry goes up for political and social changes which, it is supposed, would automatically solve the much deeper problem of split personality. Hence it is that whenever this demand is fulfilled, political and social conditions arise which bring the same ills back again in altered form. What then happens is a simple reversal: the underside comes to the top and the shadow takes the place of the light, and since the former is always anarchic and turbulent, the freedom of the "liberated" underdog must suffer Draconian curtailment.

(Jung, 1964/1970, para. 558)

Beyond being the repressed, unconscious and inexpressible, the shadow may also be the personification of what is evil, rejected or hated in one's self. There is also a tendency for the ignored to become the despised and for the alien to be identified with the enemy.

[N]ot only is the evil man experienced as alien but that the alien, in turn, is experienced as evil – is one of the basic facts of human psychology. It is a leitmotif which can be traced uninterruptedly from the psychology of primitives right down to the policy towards aliens of contemporary, so-called civilized states.

(Neumann, 1959/1974, p. 54)

Projection of the group shadow

From the neonatal stages onward, humankind retains the tendency to split off and ascribe to others – be they objects, individuals or groups – the deficiencies and disappointments that we experience in our own lives. Whatever is wrong, unpleasant or unknown in our own make-up is projected outward on to someone else.

Those upon whom our projections fall come in two kinds: those who provide significant "hooks" and those who provide a more or less blank screen.

Inside a nation, the aliens who provide the objects for this projection are the minorities; if these are of a different racial or ethnological projection or, better still, of a different colour, their suitability for this purpose is particularly obvious . . . the role of the alien which was played in former times by prisoners of war or shipwrecked mariners is now being played by the Chinese, the Negroes, and the Jews. The same principle governs the treatment of religious minorities in all religions; and the Fascist plays the same part in a Communist society as the Communist in a Fascist society.

(Neumann, 1990, p. 52)

Those who provide "hooks" for projection are often those who express the repressed portions of our own psyche. They live out our shadow, and are marked for it.

> The second class of people who play the part of victims in the scapegoat psychology are the "ethically inferior" – that is to say, those persons who fail to live up to the absolute values of the collective and who are also incapable of achieving ethical adaptation by developing a "facade personality." The ethically inferior (who include psychopaths and other pathological and atavistic persons, and in effect all those who belong to an earlier period in the evolution of mankind) are branded, punished and executed by the law and its officers. That at all events is what happens when it is not possible for this class of people to be made use of by the collective. In wartime, on the other hand, they are eagerly exploited.
>
> (Ibid., p. 53)

Whether positive or negative, the relatively unconscious elements of the group shadow may be projected outward upon other objects or groups. In general, positive projections attach to objects nearby while negative projections attach to those more distant. More often than not, that distance is an affective distance so that those closest to my group or perspective are more likely to receive positive projections; those farther from my position, opinion or appearance will more likely receive negative projections (Jung, 1960/1969; Odjanyk, 1976).

> Unconscious and repressed contents of the psyche readily lend them-selves to projection. Projection may be positive or negative and may be defined as the erroneous attribution of an individual's or a group's unconscious qualities to the environment or to another individual or group. Particularly, negative projections serve as defense mechanisms that help an individual or group avoid facing the incompatible and disturbing contents of the psyche. Such externalization of inner feeling-conflicts is one avenue by which the shadow is able to find an outward and socially acceptable expression. . . .
>
> (Odjanyk, 1976, p. 73)

Extreme projections of the positive shadow may be seen in some of the more militant proponents of environmentalism who project all evil on their fellow man and all good on Nature. Their counterparts in conservative circles who paint the ecological consciousness of the later twentieth century as satanic produce a similar kind of extreme projection. Similarly, classical Christianity projects all good on the Good God, and reserves all evil for the work of man. Jung and Odjanyk both point to the mutual projections by the Soviet Bloc and Western nations that maintained the Cold War. We may readily recall the Ayatollah Khomeini branding the United States as the Great Satan from whom all of the world's ills flowed.

There also appears to be a correlation between the level from which a projection emerges and the range of its application. The projection of personal faults seeks personal targets, small group projections are projected upon groups of similar size, and ethnic projections follow course.

Projections have what we might call different ranges, according to whether they stem from merely personal conditions or from deeper collective ones. Personal repressions and things of which we are unconscious manifest themselves in our immediate environment, in our circle of relatives and acquaintances. Collective contents such as religious, philosophical, political and social conflicts, select projection-carriers of a corresponding kind – Freemasons, Jesuits, Jews, Capitalists, Bolsheviks, Imperialists, etc.

(Jung, 1964/1970, para. 610)

In election years, the candidates all seek to be used as the bearers of projection for the positive hopes of the nation. During each election loaded words with strong archetypal/affective connections (e.g. peace, prosperity, jobs and responsibility) are dragged out in hope that individual projections will find a hook in the actions or message of the candidate. Tags like "the Ecology President" and "the Education President" are aimed specifically at the capture of projections.

Negative projections are often part of a whole constellation of effects that continue to trap minority groups into a cycle of self hatred and self destruction. The Protestant ethic of responsibility, dependability and diligence in work represents a major facet of the cultural consciousness in the majority white culture of North America. It produces, in turn, a shadow persona of lazy, shiftless and good for nothing. As the conscious ideal is white,[7] that is, the ideal of the cultural consciousness, the unconscious shadow is easily projected upon the black. In this case the recipient of the projection becomes less the enemy than the outcast. However, in the American South of the 1950s and 1960s and in apartheid South Africa, the black actually became the enemy.

Projections, whenever their recipient is unconscious of them, also evoke counter-projections. Thus, the black minority will respond unconsciously to the above projection by projecting his own shadow on the white majority – a conscious and ruthless oppressor, as well as an uptight, asexual weakling. However true or false either image may be, both, like the open ends of a Chinese finger puzzle, imprison the two parties in a world of unconscious tensions which can only be sorted out with the most extraordinary patience and effort on both sides.

The problem, however, is subject to further complications. Once a group is marked by the projections of a negative sort, those same projections can become part of its own shadow.

[C]ollective shadow projections have a cumulative effect. They activate and support various local and personal shadow projections, so that the recipient of the collective projection is confronted by negative feelings whichever way he turns. First, the culture as a whole defines him in shadow terms; then the locality in which he lives adds its own particular flavor; and finally, each individual with whom he comes into contact contributes his own personal shadow elements. The accumulated burden is so heavy that it is not surprising that members of shadow bearing groups are usually demoralized and depressed.

(Odjanyk, 1976, p. 83)

According to the Jungian position, the only way to short-circuit the vicious cycle of projections and re-projections embroiling racial and other large group relations is for each side to claim its own weakness and acknowledge its own part in the continuation of the error, independent of its original source.

A certain amount of consciousness and acceptance of the shadow ... checks the projection of the psyche's negative qualities upon others and the involuntary need for and creation of enemies, and it promotes a degree of modesty and humility and an increased sense of personal responsibility for the social and political problems of the world.

(Ibid., p. 77)

The group persona

Just as the normal individual projects an image that allows him to function in the world as a normal member of society, so groups can project images that may not be consistent with their actual goals or characteristics. It may be very important for a group or organization to be perceived as honest, reliable, or ecologically minded, especially if its failure to consciously project such an image will cost it money or prestige.

The group persona, like the individual persona, may be seen to represent the socially acceptable categories within which a society defines itself. Should the society be unable to provide a proper category, the function, whether good or bad, is relegated to the shadow.

Society actually requires that an individual have a category into which he can be fitted. Is he a doctor, lawyer, working man? Is he amiable, harsh, reliable? Society requires these easy classifications, and the individual in his turn seeks to create a mask to make such a classification possible.

(Progoff, 1953/1981, p. 84)

Likewise, Neumann observes:

The formation of the persona is, in fact as necessary as it is universal. The persona, the mask, what one passes for and what one appears to be, in contrast to one's real individual nature, corresponds to one's adaptation to the requirements of the age, of one's personal environment, and of the community. The persona is the cloak and the shell, the armour and the uniform, behind which and within which the individual conceals himself – from himself, often enough, as well as from the world. It is the self-control which hides what is uncontrolled and uncontrollable, the acceptable facade behind which the dark and strange, eccentric, secret and uncanny side of our nature remains invisible.

(Neumann, 1990, pp. 37–8)

To a large extent the nature of the personae available to the individual or group are a function of the structure of language and thought within a given society. They at once reflect and give tangible form to the shared typifications which bring men together within symbol systems (Schutz, 1967; Berger and Luckmann, 1967).

As this is true on the personal level, we can see quite readily how it appertains on the group level. For some groups the image is projected outward through advertising. For others it appears in the choice of a corporate logo or symbol.[8] For still others the group persona comes affixed to their role, and the expectations projected upon it. Doctors, nurses, the clergy, firemen and police step into the personae created by well-defined, archetypally ordered roles. Mitroff and Bennis (1989) document an entire industry devoted to just such "reality bending" in *The Unreality Industry*. There, they chronicle the development of an industry devoted to the projection and sale of false public images on every conceivable level.

A recent article in the *Journal of Marketing* suggests that for some purveyors of their trade, reality is a subjective variable that is constructed in the course of social interaction. As such, the idea of truth may be far less important as a variable in advertising than believability (Hunt, 1992). A case in point is derived from the Beech Nut fruit juice scandal during the late 1980s. In that case, the Beech Nut company was marketing an artificial apple-juice substitute, labeled as pure apple juice. Simultaneously, their ads proclaimed that the product was pure apple juice, and continued to proclaim a corporate concern for safety, purity and the welfare of children. Here, the public image of an otherwise reputable company was subverted to cover an illegal and potentially dangerous fraud.

Very often a group's public persona is very different from its reality. For some, Santeria provides just such a case of a projected persona that conflicts strongly with the actual practices of the group. In many cases the practitioners of Santeria are regular attendees at the local Roman Catholic church. Whenever possible, they send their children to parochial schools and appear externally to be devout Catholics. When questioned about their faith, however, we find that each of the saints, each member of the Trinity and the Holy Family, is identified with a Yoruban tribal deity. Their most essential worship involves shrines built in each home to the honor of the gods under their true names and may include elements of animal sacrifice.[9]

In this case, however, the projection of a standard Roman Catholic persona seems to be genuinely related to the survival of what would otherwise be a persecuted minority. Their projected identity shares survival characteristics with the Spanish Marrano Jews who took on a superficial conversion to Christianity in order to preserve themselves as a group (Ferm, 1945).

SUMMARY

The development of groups includes their transition from human products into external facticities. This process is understood in terms of the projection of shared definitions upon one group by another group.

- Groups are first perceived from without in terms of typifications provided by local cultural expectations regarding the nature of the group.
- These are usually uninformed projections based upon the peculiar identity of the perceiving group.
- Projections carry with them an archetypally derived sense of life and autonomy which is imposed upon their object.
- Such shared typifications have a tendency towards reification and concretization: they tend to become defined as real and, therefore, become real in their consequences.
- By their nature, groups tend to emphasize one facet of the individual. As a result they lead the individual to identify with his or her persona.

All groups possess an archetypally determined identity or meaning.

- All groups have an archetypal core of meaning which accounts for their selective ability to attract members.
- Because this core is archetypal in nature, and functions through the numinous attractive agency of the archetype, all groups may be said to be religious in nature.
- Secular groups arise when religious organizations become unable to hold the self-projections of their members.
- In such cases psychic energy splits from the main symbol system and adheres to secondary symbols from the secular context.

All archetypes are manifested by symbols which can appear as archetypal themes. The image projected by a group may differ from its governing image as a matter of style. This suggests that groups project personae as do humans.

- Archetypal themes on the level of social interaction are reflected for the most part in roles.

- One particularly elegant formulation is provided in terms of four root roles: the Warrior, the Shaman, the Chief and the Fool. These in turn may be articulated into four basic divisions of labor and four divisions of society.
- Groups are also characterized by archetypal styles. These reflect not only the actual archetypal image that forms the core of the group, but it also includes the intentional image that the group would like to project.
- Styles extend not only to groups but also to eras.
- The idea of a zeitgeist is a reference to an archetypal style preferred by a particular culture over a period of time.

As groups are made up of individuals, group structure reflects the psychic structure of humans. Each group has a conscious function corresponding to the ego. This is the collective consciousness or collective canon. It is formulated largely in terms of common sense and contractual definitions. The myths of a group, and its tradition contribute to the social canon.

The group shadow consists of those parts of the group or society that are either incompatible with the collective consciousness, or are inimical to it. Where a group's focus represents its conscious executive, its omissions, repressions and suppressions develop into a coherent whole which functions as a group shadow. In it are the minorities, the deviants, the forgotten and those upon whom the conscious executive has cast its shadow.

The shadow of the dominant group may be projected on any different, rejected or alien group. The shadow projected, however, is differentiated from the shadow group in that the projected shadow is a psychic condition projected upon the already excluded group. The projection of the shadow evokes a mutual re-projection of the subordinate group's own shadow. The process inevitably develops into near total mutual alienation. Shadow projection is to a large extent responsible for racial and ethnic conflict throughout the world.

Each group may be seen also to project some sort of persona or idealized image of itself into the world at large. The projected image may reflect reality, it may be cynical, or a necessary camouflage for an oppressed minority.

Chapter 13

Archetypal patterns in large groups

THE FRAGMENTATION OF RELIGIOUS SYMBOL SYSTEMS

Realizing that Jung's perspective on groups relied on the summation of individual action, one may nonetheless find specific patterns of large group action throughout the *Collected Works*. These patterns depend primarily upon the doctrine of the archetype that unites all humankind by means of deeply rooted similarities of disposition.[1] Archetypal activity could therefore be expected to affect all manner of men and women in similar situations so as to produce similar results. These similar responses had the general effect of binding them together into groups through the mechanism of projective identification. "Group observations have confirmed over and over again that the group subtly entices its members into mutual imitation and dependence, thereby holding out the promise of sparing them a painful confrontation with themselves" (1964/1970, para. 892).

While it is tempting to place inordinate value on social influences, Jung saw that social influences were more often than not the result of an interplay between archetypal mechanisms and environmental factors, cultural and otherwise. When human beings are cut off from natural modes of action and response (in a Marxist frame, one would describe it in terms of alienation from the means of production and the fruits of their labor), or when the natural modes of response are repressed by the values of an external culture, the unconscious naturally responds through the mechanism of compensation to bring the system into balance. During such times, the archetypes of the collective unconscious become activated in a compensatory manner and give rise to powerful symbols that seem to appear spontaneously in great masses of the people.

> Social, political, and religious conditions affect the collective unconscious in the sense that all those factors which are suppressed by the prevailing views or attitudes in the life of a society gradually accumulate in the collective unconscious and activate its contents. Certain individuals gifted with particularly strong intuition then become aware of the changes going

on in it and translate these changes into communicable ideas. The new ideas spread rapidly because parallel changes have been taking place in the unconscious of other people. There is a general readiness to accept the new ideas, although on the other hand they often meet with violent resistance. New ideas are not just the enemies of the old; they also appear as a rule in an extremely unacceptable form.

(Jung, 1960/1969, para. 594)

These ideas can unify the masses and become the center of powerful movements. In some cases the movements can be liberating; in others, as in Weimar Germany, they can be ultimately self-destructive (1958/1969, 1964/1970).

The classic pattern for the existence of large groups finds its roots in the spiritual life of the community.[2] When a content of the collective unconscious becomes constellated in a national group, or on any large scale, there is a tendency for specific symbols to arise and give voice to the content. Edward Edinger points to the projection of the self image as the essential archetypal component. Such projections are the source of stable but relatively unconscious societies.

When the collective psyche is in a stable state, the vast majority of individuals share a common living myth or deity. Each individual projects his inner God-image (the Self) to the religion of the community. The collective religion then serves as the container of the self for a multitude of individuals.

(Edinger, 1972, p. 65)

Times come, however, when social or natural forces inhibit the natural relations between the conscious and unconscious life of the individual. During such times of psychic tensions, new symbols and new meanings begin to arise out of the depths of the collective unconscious. These are compensatory responses. Their purpose is to mediate redress of the imbalance which originally called them out of the deep collective strata. They are often religious ideas, but they can also be political concepts, for, from Jung's perspective, many "isms" were either inherently religious or derived from originally religious patterns.

In such contexts the symbols are often messianic, promising a rebirth or the coming of a new age.

[H]onorific titles reproduce the essential qualities of the redeeming symbol. Its "divine" effect comes from the irresistible *dynamis* of the unconscious. The savior is always a figure endowed with magical power who makes the impossible possible. The symbol is the middle way along which the opposites flow together in a new movement, like a watercourse bringing fertility after a long drought.

(Jung, 1971, para. 443)

The symbolic element, whether overtly religious or political, unifies the people, brings promise of new levels of cooperation, empowerment, and ushers in a golden age. Thus, in the American system, while no one individual became the focus of the archetypal numen, the new Constitution became the holy writ of the Chosen People. To it accrued the archetypal projections that identify the saving individual. Bellah and others have shown repeatedly the strong and significant messianic flavor that accompanied the founding of the American nation (Bellah, 1975; Covey, 1961).

Moreover, Jung points to the fact that the arising symbol is often greeted as dangerous or threatening. It is often said to be bound up with destructive tendencies. Beyond the politics of power, the emergence of a new symbol provides added reason for the emergence of revolutionary movements.

> At all events the appearance of the redeeming symbol is closely connected with destruction and devastation. If the old were not ripe for death, nothing new would appear; and if the old were not injuriously blocking the way for the new, it could not and need not be rooted out.
>
> (Ibid., para. 446)

An essential distinction is made between living and dead symbols. A living symbol is empowered with archetypal energy. It captures the collective need of the moment and carries each individual in a tide of unconscious participation. The symbol is self-explanatory through the experience it evokes. When, however, the symbol no longer carries the numen of the archetypal core, and when the image fails to evoke the experience of faith as knowledge, then the symbol is subjected to intellectual examination. Its properties are defined, its meaning formulated and its life taken away. The symbol dies (Jung, 1959/1968a).

It will be remembered that one of the signal differences between conscious and unconscious contents is the inability of consciousness to abide by contradiction. Nothing in consciousness can be both good and bad, here and there, large and small. This coincidence of opposites is, however, a central quality of the collective unconscious. All of the archetypes are Janus-faced. They each contain within themselves a contradictory principle. They are both the best and the worst, the largest and the smallest. Each encompasses both a single response field and the whole of the psyche.

> It must be remembered, however, that this division is only true within the sphere of consciousness, where it is a necessary condition of thought. Logic says *tertium non datur*, meaning that we cannot envisage the opposites in their oneness. In other words, while the abolition of an obstinate antinomy can be no more than a postulate for us, this is by no means so for the unconscious, whose contents are without exception paradoxical or antinomial by nature, not excluding the category of being.
>
> (Jung, 1959/1968a, para. 419)

As an archetypal content is brought towards consciousness, some single facet of the symbol arises in consciousness. The ego, capable of only registering one aspect at a time, is forced by this restriction to act as if the whole content were represented in the part now conscious. As more of the symbol is revealed, the ego begins to swing between perspectives in the enantiodromic dance of opposites. Gradually, the dance gives rise to a third position that comprehends something of the depth of meaning hidden in the symbol and is represented by the unification of opposites. This is the symbolic function, the broadening of the interface between conscious and unconscious capabilities through symbolic means. It is comparable to the classical Hegelian dialectic and represents the means by which conceptual categories grow in number and sophistication.

Through this dialectic, the symbol forces the expansion of consciousness by concretizing some part of its own numinous content in a conscious formulation. In the end, the symbol is so crowded with the contents of consciousness that it is regarded consciously as fully understood and must be replaced by a new image (ibid.).

Activated unconscious contents always appear at first as projections on the outside world, but in the course of mental development they are gradually assimilated by consciousness and reshaped into conscious ideas that then forfeit their originally autonomous and personal character. As we know, some of the old gods have become, via astrology, nothing more than descriptive attributes (martial, jovial, saturnine, erotic, logical, lunatic, and so on).

(Jung, 1968a, para. 49)

Part of the outfall of this process is the development of new power centers based upon the same archetypal construction as the original symbol, but limited as to their ability to express or reveal the nature of its archetypal root. In some ways this is a recapitulation at the level of the symbol of the deintegration of the primal psyche. Just as the individual archetypes each reflect some major aspect of the primordial self, so the derived symbols[3] reflect some major pattern of the original symbol system.

The transfer of libido to other social institutions is accomplished by projection. Insofar as they display a major attribute of the original symbol system, they become fitting objects for the projection of the archetypal content.

[T]he projected suprapersonal value which has been withdrawn from the religious container will be reprojected onto some secular or political movement. But secular purposes are never an adequate container for religious meaning. When religious energy is applied to a secular object we have what can be described as idolization – which is spurious, unconscious religion.

(Edinger, 1972, p. 68)

One example that Jung gives is the archetypal claim of the church to total allegiance. The requirement of total obedience is a defining property of the archetype, and is expressed powerfully through living symbols. When, however, a major symbol system like the Western Church begins to die for large parts of the population (not necessarily for all), even the archetypal compulsion can split off and adhere to a discrete symbol system.

> As the authority of the Church fades, the State becomes the Church, since the totalitarian claim is bound to come out somewhere. First it was Socialism that entered into the Catholic heritage and again is experimenting with the crassest kind of *Gleichschaltung*[4] – not, indeed, with a view to buttressing up the kingdom of heaven but to producing an equally millenarian state of bliss (or its substitute) on earth. Russian Communism has therefore, quite logically, become the Totalitarian Church. . . . It is only consistent with the logic of history that after an age of clerical Gleichschaltung the turn should come for one practised by the secular State.
>
> (Jung, 1964/1970, para. 1,019)

LEGITIMATION AND THE RATIONALIZATION OF SYMBOLS

Large groups fall into several categories: there are national and ethnic groups, interest groups like corporations and large fraternal organizations, and religious denominations and sects. Within all of them there exists the possibility for bureaucratic structure. As we have seen each of these has an archetypal core that organizes its approach to the world and how the world perceives it. It is, moreover, constructed in terms of a psychic analog with the personal psyche, having an executive function, and relatively unconscious layers which, to a greater or lesser extent, are excluded from the executive.

In general, we may say that to the extent that the group's executive, the collective consciousness or cultural canon, exists close to the level of the collective unconscious, to that level will the executive function pass to collective symbols and the numen of traditional values. This is the common state of traditional societies. Weber (1968/1978) defined such groups as characterized by a charismatic[5] authority structure. To the extent that the executive is consciously constructed or develops around specific, conscious goals of its members, to that extent will the executive function require explicit codification and enforcement. This is typical of modern democracies and corporations. It was defined by Weber as having a legal/rational authority structure.

Max Weber identified three kinds of group structure which he called the three "pure types of legitimate domination." A group's authority structure, its executive, might be based upon legal/rational, traditional, or charismatic grounds.

In the case of legal authority, obedience is owed to the legally established impersonal order. It extends to the persons exercising the authority of office under it by virtue of the formal legality of their commands and only within the scope of authority of the office. In the case of traditional authority, obedience is owed to the *person* of the chief who occupies the traditionally sanctioned position of authority and who is (within its sphere) bound by tradition. But here the obligation of obedience is a matter of personal loyalty within the area of accustomed obligations. In the case of charismatic authority, it is the charismatically qualified leader as such who is obeyed by virtue of personal trust in his revelation, his heroism, or his exemplary qualities so far as they fall within the scope of the individual's belief in his charisma.

(Weber, 1968/1978, pp. 215–16)

These three types all devolve from the original charismatic form of authority in a process called by Weber the routinization of charisma. Weber noted that because charismatic authority is vested in the charismatic leader alone, there is, in general, no means for continuing the organization of followers. In order to ensure the continuation of the group and their livelihood, some means of transmission of authority must develop. Weber suggested that problems of succession might be solved by: a search for a new leader; designation by revelation or oracle; designation of a successor by the original leader; designation of a successor by the leader's staff; hereditary transfer; and ritual–magical transmission (ibid.).

These methods in turn seed the movement with patterns which will eventually result in relative devaluation of the original charism. In the examples noted above we find the following tendencies towards traditionalization or legalization: traditionalization of the charismatic person; rationalization of the legitimate means of consulting the oracle; transformation of charisma into an acquired or acquirable trait; transformation of charisma into a matter of due process; charisma as the right of birth independent of popular acknowledgment; and objectification of charisma as a transferable entity.

From the Jungian position we see first that charismatic authority rests neither in the leader nor in the people, but in the conformity of the leader to specific archetypal patterns in the collective unconscious, and specifically those constellated by the specific needs of the group in question (Jung, 1960/1969, para. 594). Jung uses the figure of Jesus of Nazareth as an example of the correspondence between archetypal projection and their object in the realm of charismatic leaders.

The whole pre-Christian and Gnostic theology of the near east wraps itself about him and turns him before our eyes into a dogmatic figure who has no more need of historicity. At a very early stage, therefore, the real Christ vanished behind the emotions and projections that swarmed about him from far and near; immediately and almost without a trace he was absorbed into the surrounding religious systems and moulded into their archetypal exponent. He became the collective figure whom the unconscious of his contemporaries expected to appear, and for this reason it is pointless to ask who he "really" was.

(Jung, 1958/1969, para. 228)

With Christ as an exemplar, it becomes clear that without the same levels of correspondence in the collective unconscious something less than world shaking is to be expected from the leader. In each of the solutions enumerated by Weber, some portion of the numen originally attached to the ruler is lost. The new leader ceases to be the full bearer of the projection as some part of the process or system attains symbolic value for the collective apart from the individual.

On a lesser scale a similar pattern of routinization of libido, or dispersion of projections, was observed in the development of the American system of government as practiced in seventeenth-century New England. In the early part of the seventeenth century, the vote was limited to landed members of the Church. These were communally recognized, confessing Christians, belonging to the local Puritan congregation. In a second stage, all landed citizens who could prove that their parents had been practicing members of the Church gained suffrage. Finally, in 1692, the vote was extended to all free and landed members of the community without reference to religion (Kirk, 1974).

Point for point this follows both schemes. If we recall Weber's observation that prosperity and diligence in one's calling were taken generally as proofs of election, and that the inscrutability of Divine Providence left all in doubt as to their eternal destination, we find a consistent logic applying itself as the archetypal authority moves from the individual believer to the family, to the community at large (1958).

The authority to vote was first vested in the charism extended to the individual believer as a member of the Body of Christ. All of the requirements for membership and theological definitions were derived from the scriptures by the Puritans. Presumably the charism was vested in a special guidance by the Holy Spirit through knowledge of the scriptures.

The logic of Puritanism, however, held that because one could not possibly know if one were among the elect, the argument could be made that being a Church member was no guarantee of salvation or of possession of the charism. When such membership, or possession of the specific charism that it implied, became untenable or difficult to prove, the projected authority was extended to those related to Church members. Again, we may presume that the influence of the family upon the child as well as the possible heritability of the trait (in accordance with scriptural principles) transferred the charism. So, some portion of the numen of salvation was transferred to those who belonged to the "right" families, as well as to those possessing character and land (ibid.). Finally, following the combined logic of the impossibility of choosing between the elect and the damned, and the popular conception of prosperity as a sign of election, the charism was transferred to those possessing property and good character.

In each stage there is a spread of libidinal energy from a relatively concentrated, symbolic focus to a more diffuse social object. There is, further, a movement of the recipient of the projection from a specific, albeit transcendent symbol – the true believer – to gradually more concrete and more general principles formulated along legal–rational lines.

MAX WEBER AND THE SPIRIT OF CAPITALISM: THE PATTERN OF SECULARIZATION

In the now classic study, *The Protestant Ethic and the Spirit of Capitalism* (1958), Max Weber traces the roots of that species of capitalistic endeavor characteristic of Western Protestantism to its root in the dogmatic structure of early Calvinist religion. His analysis can be understood on a point for point basis as an example of the concretization of the symbols that originally grew up around the figure of Christ and the Believer in the Christian Church.

Weber provisionally defines the spirit of capitalism in terms of the sense of religious and moral necessity that drives the businessman to pursue his calling. The calling itself may be any of a hundred means of sanctifying employment, but the ultimate gain is money. All this is seen to occur often in a context where there is no current religious exercise.

Among the denominations which began during the Reformation, the concept of calling as a secular duty sanctified by God arose in the several Churches. Within the Calvinist denominations salvation was held to be absolutely a matter of divine grace and predestination. God was, by definition, transcendent and unreachable, and He alone knew for sure who was saved and who was damned. There was no way for any member of the Church to know whether or not they were saved or damned, but as a pious life was one of the fruits of election, adherence to a biblically ordered life-style allowed a certain degree of confidence in one's election. One of the central means of expressing this election was by living out one's worldly occupation as a calling from God.

> The elected Christian is in the world only to increase this glory of God by fulfilling His commandments to the best of his ability. But God requires social achievement of the Christian because He wills that social life shall be organized according to his commandments, in accordance with that purpose. The social activity of the Christian in the world is

solely activity *in majorem gloriam dei*. This character is hence shared by labour in a calling which serves the mundane life of the community.

(Weber, 1958, p. 108)

There was, in the Calvinist perspective, no room for sin. Since good works were the proof of election, the elect were, by definition, not permitted the luxury of sin and repentance. Instead, the life was to become increasingly rationalized, demystified and ordered by the overwhelming need to prove one's election. Two consequences ensued. First, the Protestant was isolated from his peers as an individual seeking individual salvation. Second, life became subject to absolute rationalization and quantification.

Among the Puritans the waste of time became particularly sinful.

Waste of time is thus the first and in principle the deadliest of sins. The span of human life is infinitely short and precious to make sure of one's election. Loss of time through sociability, idle talk, luxury, even more sleep than is necessary for health, six to eight hours, is worthy of absolute moral condemnation. It does not yet hold ... that time is money, but the proposition is true in a certain spiritual sense. It is infinitely valuable because every hour lost is lost to labour for the glory of God. Thus inactive contemplation is also valueless, or even directly reprehensible if it is at the expense of one's daily work. For it is less pleasing to God than the active performance of His will in a calling.

(Ibid., p. 158)

According to Weber, the religious roots behind these ideas gradually died out, leaving behind them the ascetic mentality without religious conviction. In its wake were left the Western emphasis on the individual, the roots of the materialist science of the later Enlightenment, a strong bias towards uniformity and a rationalized world view.[6] In the context of religious asceticism

A specifically bourgeois economic ethic had grown up. With the con- sciousness of standing in the fullness of God's grace and being visibly blessed by Him, the bourgeois business man, as long as he remained within the bounds of formal correctness, as long as his moral conduct was spotless and the use to which he put his wealth was not objectionable, could follow his pecuniary interests as he would and feel that he was fulfilling a duty in doing so. The power of religious asceticism provided him in addition with sober, conscientious, and unusually industrious workmen, who clung to their work as to a life purpose willed by God.

(Ibid., p. 177)

Returning to the Jungian perspective, we find in the development of the capitalist spirit the disintegration of the symbol-complex defined by Calvinist Protestant Christianity.[7] As noted by Jung the rationalization of the symbol leads to its failure as a center for communal life and the resultant rise of a need to re-project the archetypal images originally held by religion. In the case of capitalism, the practical emphasis of Calvinist religion on asceticism and stewardship, linked to the strong sense of justification (now linked to the rational pursuit of one's calling), provide more than ample hooks for the projection of the numen of grace upon capitalist endeavor. Even removed from religion, capitalism has tended to be a religion in the West: "The outstanding current example of reprojection is the conflict between communism and capitalism. Communism in particular is clearly a secular religion which actively attempts to channel religious energies to secular and social ends" (Edinger, 1972, p. 68).

Following Weber's material we find specific stages in the development of the process.

1　A new symbol system arises out of the collective unconscious in response to some broadly experienced imbalance. It is formulated by certain visionaries who become the vehicles for specific versions of the message.
2　Early adherents are caught in the numen of the newly emergent symbol and enter fully into its meaning structure. The symbol system provides self-evident validity.
3　Later adherents are brought into the system by more rational modes of persuasion. As part of the process, an analytical set of explanations, practices and creeds develops about the symbol system which tend to replace a direct experience of the archetypal numen of the original symbol.
4　As group practice comes to depend less and less upon direct experience of the transcendent reality originally vested in the symbol, self projections once accruing to the symbol seek other objects. More often than not they attach to fragments of the original symbol system or its analogs in the community at large.
5　These secular symbols[8] now become the focus of libidinal energy originally reserved for the religious activity.

In the case of the Protestant ethic, certain ideas, among them the special character of each person as a unique individual, the concept of the equality of callings before God, and the insistence upon the rationalized or rule-based life, became especially charged elements in the collective consciousness that led to the growth of democracy in the succeeding centuries. Similarly, the transcendence of God, the demystification of the universe and the rationalization of life laid the foundations for the scientific revolution. Together these represent significant religious movements in the secularized West: the cult of the individual and the cult of scientism.

> [T]he Reformation . . . shattered the authority of the Church as a teacher.
> . . . The inevitable consequence was an increase in the importance of the

individual, which found expression in the modern ideals of humanity, social welfare, democracy, and equality. The decidedly individualistic trend of the latest developments is counterbalanced by a compensatory reversion to the collective man, whose authority at present is the sheer weight of the masses.

(Jung, 1964/1970, para. 326)

The early roots of rationalism and scientism were laid earlier in the Christian epoch even though their full fruition had to await the Reformation.

Increasingly it had to rationalize its doctrines in order to stem the flood of irrationality. This led, over the centuries, to that strange marriage of the originally irrational Christian message with human reason. . . . But to the degree that reason gradually gained the upper hand, the intellect asserted itself and demanded autonomy. And just as the intellect subjugated the psyche, so it subjugated Nature and begat on her an age of scientific technology that left less and less room for the natural and irrational man.

(1958/1969, para. 444)

The transfer of religious patterns into secular life was also observed by Jung in the tendency for human religions to develop representations of their deities that formed triads and trinities. He cites the ancient Egyptian trinities of Isis, Osiris and Horus, as well as father, son and Ka-mutef; the Indian trinity of Brahma, Vishnu and Shiva; and the Christian Trinity. All are marked by the archetypal pattern of the threefold godhead. These patterns were also seen to apply to governments which now function as the secular religions of the modern world.

If Communism, for instance, refers to Engels, Marx, Lenin, and so on as the "fathers" of the movement, it does not know that it is reviving an archetypal order of society that existed even in primitive times, thereby explaining the "religious" and "numinous" (i.e., fanatical) character of Communism.

(Ibid., para. 222)

One might suggest that even the American system of government is marked by the triadic index of divinity in its division between Legislative, Executive and Judicial branches. Jung's perception of the secular religions of the state was, however, profoundly pessimistic.

It is still too early to say what might be the consequences of a general recognition of the fatal parallelism between the State religion of the Marxists and the State religion of the Church. The absolutist claim of a *Civitas Dei* that is represented by man bears an unfortunate resemblance to the "Divinity" of the State, and the moral conclusion drawn by Ignatius Loyola from the authority of the Church ("the end sanctifies the means") anticipates the lie as a political instrument in an exceedingly dangerous way. Both demand unqualified submission to faith and thus curtail man's freedom, the one his freedom before God and the other his freedom before the State, thereby digging the grave for the individual.

(Jung, 1964/1970, para. 522)

GERMANY AND THE REGRESSION OF LIBIDO

By far the single most important group phenomenon treated by Jung in the *Collected Works* was the pagan revival and cataclysm in Nazi Germany. Jung saw the phenomenon as a revival of the latent potential of the more ancient pagan roots of the German psyche in the face of the crushing defeat and humiliation suffered during and after the First World War. As a whole, it is directly related to his theory of the regression of libido and the working out of the Hero's Journey as described in *Symbols of Transformation*.[9] It also represents a striking example of the appearance of what might be viewed as an individual pattern lived out at the level of national experience.

As we have noted, Jung saw that nations were composed of individuals, and that national behavior was explainable in terms of, first, the currents in the collective unconscious and, second, the sum of the responses of the individuals that comprise the nation. Jung notes:

> National Socialism was one of those psychological mass phenomena, one of those outbreaks of the collective unconscious about which I had been speaking for nearly twenty years. The driving forces of a psychological mass movement are essentially archetypal.

(Ibid., para. 474)

Of the collective unconscious, he notes:

> The psychology of the individual is reflected in the psychology of the nation. What the nation does is also done by each individual, and so long as the individual continues to do it, the nation will do likewise. Only a change in the attitude of the individual can initiate a change in the psychology of the nation. The great problems of humanity were never yet solved by general laws, but only through the regeneration of the attitudes of individuals.

(Jung, 1953/1966, p. 4)

The rise of the spirit of Wotan, as Jung characterized the Nazi movement, was founded on several elements (Jung, 1964/1970; Odjanyk, 1976; Baynes, 1941).

1 A dissociation in the German psyche that included a tendency to inferiority feelings.
2 A religious and educational system that emphasized submission to authority.
3 A powerful and just barely subconscious identity with the pre-Christian god, Wotan, representing both the highest potential of the German people and their greatest danger.
4 A striking blow at the national identity caused by their defeat in the First World War and the subsequent reparations.
5 Economic chaos brought on by the reparations imposed by the Treaty of Versailles.

Jung observed that different nationalities tended to reinforce certain traits. These traits could often be observed as part of the national character. They were explained as originating in the archetypal configurations which dominate the myths and, hence, the collective identity of the nation. Their power is expressed relative to the level at which these dominants affect the molding of the individual character through socialization.[10] Jung points out that the national character of Germany tended to be one-sidedly rational, almost completely denying feeling. This led to feelings of inferiority that were compensated for by an excessive insistence on precision and a desire to please. This level of alienation between psychic strata often leads to a complete denial of the shadow. As a result, the shadow is dissociated and projected outwards. This dissociation is also a symptom of neurosis, specifically hysteria.

> Ignorance of one's other side creates great inner insecurity. One does not really know who one is; one feels inferior somewhere and does not wish to know where the inferiority lies, with the result that a new inferiority is added to the original one. This sense of insecurity is the source of the hysteric's prestige psychology, of his need to make an impression, to flaunt his merits and insist on them, of his insatiable thirst for recognition, admiration, adulation, and longing to be loved.
>
> (Jung, 1964/1970, para. 425)

In the period preceding the World Wars, Germany had become a center of modern philosophy and theology. It was from Germany that Nietzsche proclaimed that "God is dead." It was likewise from Germany that Bultmann sought to demythologize Christianity. There too, Wellhausen laid the foundation work for the destruction of belief in scripture as either divine or inspired. According to Jung, Germany's Christian heritage was rooted in forced conversions during the Roman occupation. Its collective consciousness was still strongly flavored by pagan influences. Thus, it would not be a long step for many Germans to slough off a relatively superficial and all too rationalistic gospel for the wonders of the emotional tide of the cult of Wotan (ibid., Ferm, 1945).

As early as 1918 Jung had observed:

Christianity split the Germanic barbarian into an upper and a lower half, and enabled him, by repressing the dark side, to domesticate the brighter half and fit it for civilization. But the lower, darker half still awaits redemption and a second spell of domestication. Until then it will remain associated with the vestiges of the prehistoric age, with the collective unconscious, which is subject to a peculiar and ever-increasing activation. As the Christian view of the world loses its authority, the more menacingly will the "blond beast" be heard prowling about in its underground prison, ready at any minute to burst out with devastating consequences. When this happens in the individual it brings about a psychological revolution, but it can also take a social form.

(Ibid., para. 17)

The decline of Christianity was not, however, seen as a purely social influence. It was also a mark of the flow of the collective unconscious. The two inevitably move together. To understand this we recall that even where there is a cultural transmission of an archetypal theme, it is only adopted because of its resonance with a similar theme already present in the collective unconscious. Jung observes:

Social, political, and religious conditions affect the collective uncon-scious in the sense that all those factors which are suppressed by the pre-vailing views or attitudes in the life of a society gradually accumulate in the collective unconscious and activate its contents. Certain individuals gifted with particularly strong intuition then become aware of the changes going on in it and translate these changes into communicable ideas. The . . . new ideas spread rapidly because parallel changes have been taking place in the unconscious of other people. There is a general readiness to accept the new ideas, although on the other hand they often meet with violent resistance. New ideas are not just the enemies of the old; they also appear as a rule in an extremely unacceptable form.

(Jung, 1960/1969, para. 594)

With the end of the First World War, Germany was crushed and humili-ated. Already faced with an economy ravaged by the war, reparations imposed by the Treaty of Versailles drove it further into unemployment and hyper-inflation. The middle class faced the impossible tasks of making a living, somehow regaining face after a humiliating defeat, and just getting on with business. Throughout the nation, the impossibility of leading just such a normal life prepared the vast majority of Germans for a compensatory move in the collective unconscious.

As I have said, the uprush of mass instincts was symptomatic of a compensatory move of the unconscious. Such a move was possible because the conscious state of the people had become estranged from the natural laws of human existence. Thanks to industrialization, large portions of the population were uprooted and were herded together in large centres. This new form of existence – with its mass psychology and social dependence on the fluctuation of markets and wages – produced an individual who was unstable, insecure, and suggestible. He was aware that his life depended on boards of directors and captains of industry, and he supposed, rightly or wrongly, that they were chiefly motivated by financial interests. He knew that, no matter how conscientiously he worked, he could still fall a victim at any moment to economic changes which were utterly beyond his control. And there was nothing else for him to rely upon.

(Jung, 1964/1970, para. 453)

Again, this common response was neither simply social, nor at all mystical. It reflected the influence of external social factors upon the common biological heritage of the collective unconscious.

So far as a neurosis is really only a private affair, having its roots exclusively in personal causes, archetypes play no role at all. But if it is a question of general incompatibility or an otherwise injurious condition productive of neuroses in relatively large numbers of individuals, then we must assume the presence of constellated archetypes. Since neuroses are in most cases not just private concerns, but social phenomena, we must assume that archetypes are constellated in these cases too. The archetype corresponding to the situation is activated, and as a result those explosive and dangerous forces hidden in the archetype come into action, frequently with unpredictable consequences. There is no lunacy people under domination of an archetype will not fall prey to. If thirty years ago any had dared to predict that our psychological development was tending towards a revival of the medieval persecutions of the Jews, that Europe would again tremble before the Roman fasces and the tramp of legions, that people would once more give the Roman salute, as two thousand years ago, and that instead of the Christian cross, an archaic swastika would lure onwards millions of warriors ready for death – why, that man would have been hooted at as a mystical fool.

(Jung, 1959/1968a, para. 98)

It may be impossible to determine which, if any, of the above factors represented the one element that pushed the German psyche into psychosis. It is plain, however, from this point on, that the history of the National Socialist regime follows line by line the program of libidinal regression which in individuals no less than nations ends either in psychosis or rebirth.[11]

The regression of libido begins in a situation where the conscious individual is unable to differentiate a clear path. Either their symbol systems have grown weak, external frustrations have stopped their ability to go any further, or a tension between repressed and conscious elements has drained enough energy from consciousness that they can proceed no further. In such cases the individual may consciously enter a state of meditation, or be involuntarily drawn inward.

> When the libido leaves the bright upper world, whether from choice, or from inertia, or from fate, it sinks back into its own depths, into the source from which it originally flowed. . . . Whenever some great work is to be accomplished, before which a man recoils, doubtful of his strength, his libido streams back to the fountainhead – and this is the dangerous moment when the issue hangs between annihilation and new life. For if the libido gets stuck in the wonderland of this inner world, then for the upper world man is nothing but a shadow, he is already moribund or at least seriously ill. But if the libido manages to tear itself loose and force its way up again, something like a miracle happens: the journey to the underworld was a plunge into the fountain of youth, and the libido, apparently dead, wakes to renewed fruitfulness.
>
> (Jung, 1956/1967, para. 449)

In the case of the German people, the regression was prompted by the specific elements already noted. It was not voluntary, but it was apparently orchestrated by Adolph Hitler. The means of regression was the conscious use of the regressive tendencies of the mass media.

As Jung noted:

> A group experience takes place on a lower level of consciousness than the experience of an individual. This is due to the fact that, when many people gather together to share one common emotion, the total psyche emerging from the group is below the level of the individual psyche. If it is a very large group, the collective psyche will be more like the psyche of an animal, which is why the ethical attitude of large organizations is always doubtful. The psychology of a large crowd inevitably sinks to the level of mob psychology. If, therefore, I have a so-called collective experience as a member of a group, it takes place on a lower level of consciousness than if I had the experience by myself alone. That is why this group experience is very much more frequent than an individual experience of transformation. It is also much easier to achieve, because the presence of so many people together exerts great suggestive force. The individual in a crowd easily becomes the victim of his own suggestibility. It is only necessary for something to happen, for instance a proposal backed by the whole crowd, and we too are all for it, even if the proposal is immoral. In the crowd one feels no responsibility, but also no fear.
>
> (Jung, 1959/1968a, para. 225)

This was a mechanism not unknown to Hitler. Whereas Jung acknowledged that one of the greatest gifts of the Church to the Western world was the valuation of the individual, Hitler found the gift a barrier. While salvation was vested in individual action, Hitler sought to submerge the individual in the rule of the masses. Baynes quotes Hitler as follows:

> "To the Christian doctrine of the infinite significance of the individual human soul and of personal responsibility, I oppose with icy clarity the saving doctrine of the nothingness and insignificance of the individual human being, and of his continued existence in the visible immortality of the nation."
>
> (Baynes, 1941, pp. 42–3)

Further:

> "At a mass meeting, thought is eliminated. And because this is the state of mind I require, because it secures to me the best sounding-board for my speeches, I order everyone to attend the meetings, where they become part of the mass whether they like it or not, intellectuals and bourgeois as well as workers."
>
> (Ibid., p. 42)

Once the mechanism of regression was in place, imitation and the pull of the archetype would suffice to enthrall the German populace. Unlike a creative regression, in which the unconscious content is reintegrated with the restructured contents of consciousness, the Nazi episode represented a massive invasion of the pagan archetypes into German consciousness. They were not assimilated into pre-existent forms already conscious, but usurped them wholly. The usurpation was marked clearly by the book burnings, the persecution of the Jews, the re-institutionalization of the pagan religion and the appearance of oaths of allegiance and codes of belief, the *Gleichschaltungen* (Jung, 1964/1970).

> Regression carried to its logical conclusion means a linking back with the world of natural instincts, which in its formal or ideal aspect is a kind of *prima materia*. If this prima materia can be assimilated by the conscious mind it will bring about a reactivation and reorganization of its contents. But if the conscious mind proves incapable of assimilating the new contents pouring in from the unconscious, then a dangerous situation arises in which they keep their original, chaotic and archaic form and consequently disrupt the unity of consciousness. The resultant mental disturbance is therefore advisedly called schizophrenia, since it is a madness due to the splitting of the mind.
>
> (Jung, 1956/1967, para. 631)

A similar process, with a happier outcome, seems to have taken place in the first decade of American independence. The original Declaration of

Independence and, later, the Articles of Confederation, established an amorphous confederacy. This was a loose union of the original states sufficient to wage war against the British and to retain a minimal identity for the victorious states. When, however, the war was completed, the original formulation proved insufficient to meet the needs of the various interests involved. There was, first, the partial failure of a symbolic identity as the Articles of Confederation proved insufficient to provide a stable basis for a continuing government. This was followed by an intentional regression in terms of an in-turning. The Constitutional Conventions represented a conscious consideration of the real forces that would be necessary to form an ongoing government that would balance out the needs of the various groups represented. It also sought to integrate with those concerns a considered return to the principles upon which the original conscious union was based. Out of the pot came the Constitution: the symbolic formula which served to integrate the opposing forces then facing the nation. Its continued function as a symbol in the Jungian sense is underlined by the wealth of interpretations to which it gives rise. Only a true symbol could inspire so much disagreement.

SUMMARY

The fragmentation of symbol systems develops along the following lines:

1 A content of the collective unconscious arises as a numinous symbol into the conscious world of a group. This symbol receives near universal recognition and becomes the center of a religious symbol system.
2 As time goes on, more and more parts of the symbol become subject to rational interpretation and rationalized formulae. Because the abstracting quality of the conscious mind has the effect of blocking archetypal libido, a certain measure of the archetypal function of the symbol is frustrated.
3 The organismic energy naturally allotted to the blocked symbolic elements recedes into the unconscious where it seeks a different vehicle of manifestation.
4 In general, it will express itself either through a competing symbol, or through projection. It will attach to a secondary symbol that can carry much of the energy originally intended for the religious symbol.

We may summarize the mechanism of the regression of libido as follows:

• Every person, group or nation possesses some conscious focus, an executive function or interface with reality. In individuals it is called the ego complex. This is usually represented by the collective consciousness, the most general set of perspectives, traditions and practices common to a people or group.

- Underlying the conscious processes there exist unconscious processes corresponding to the collective unconscious and the group or national unconscious. For groups and nations, the unconscious is represented by minority interests, systemic contradictions which lie outside the consensus reality, actually censored or forgotten material and archetypally charged materials which would threaten the status quo. The collective unconscious is essentially the world of archetypes as it is for individuals.
- When the group executive becomes unable to function, through deadlock, frustration, external force or other inhibition, the current formulation of the executive may be dissolved, temporarily suspended, re-examined, or otherwise subjected to disassembly. This may come by violent revolution as well as by constitutional convention.
- In cases analogous to a healthy re-formulation of the ego, new elements from the collective and national unconscious are integrated into the executive. As a result the executive is restructured in order to accommodate the new contents. Originally, the new contents may appear as symbols (token examples), however, due to their truly symbolic nature; as time goes on, the symbolic measures are articulated in a rational manner consistent with the structure of the executive. In so doing they expand the options of the executive function by allowing the integration of other, previously repressed or unknowable contents.

The pattern of rationalization of symbols, paralleling Weber's routinization of charisma, takes the following steps:

1 A new symbol system arises out of the collective unconscious in response to some broadly experienced imbalance. It is formulated by certain visionaries who become the vehicles for specific versions of the message.
2 Early adherents are caught in the numen of the newly emergent symbol and enter fully into its meaning structure. The symbol system provides self-evident validity.
3 Later adherents are brought into the system by more rational modes of persuasion. As part of the process, an analytical set of explanations, practices and creeds develops about the symbol system which tend to replace a direct experience of the archetypal numen of the original symbol.
4 As group practice comes to depend less and less upon direct experience of the transcendent reality originally vested in the symbol, self projections once accruing to the symbol seek other objects. More often than not they attach to fragments of the original symbol system or its analogs in the community at large.
5 These secular symbols[12] now become the focus of libidinal energy originally reserved for the religious activity.

The tragedy of National Socialist Germany partook of both patterns with the added dimension that an underlying unconscious dominant, the spirit of Wotan, was lying ready to emerge. The specific elements that allowed the emergence of the dominant were:

- The effective destruction of the national identity.
- A growing rationalization and subsequent destruction of the Christian world view.
- A dissociated national identity.
- A tradition that emphasized obedience to authority.

Chapter 14

The problem of deviance

At heart, Jung saw that the germ of every kind of criminality dwells within each individual. Remembering that the archetypes possess a double nature, we see that every exalted virtue has its opposite pole in damnable crime or neurotic indulgence. The seeds are already present in man, their husbandry becomes another question (1971).

> If an archetype is not brought into reality consciously, there is no guarantee that it will be realized in its favourable form; on the contrary, there is all the more danger of a destructive regression. It seems as if the psyche were endowed with consciousness for the very purpose of preventing such destructive possibilities from happening.
>
> (Jung, 1964/1970, para. 475)

Beyond the innate propensity in all humans, Jung saw at least three possible sources for crime. First, he saw that criminality itself is often a fruit of repression. When otherwise acceptable urges are repressed, they eventually gain an extra charge of libido and can come to light in exaggerated form. What began as a minor deviation may later emerge as a major perversion or crime artificially inflated by the effort to subdue it. Neumann comments:

> It is a matter of common experience . . . that contents which are capable of becoming conscious but whose access to consciousness has been blocked become evil and destructive. We know from daily life that the inability or unwillingness to admit a fact or content or to "abreact" something as it is called, often makes a mountain – or rather an earthquake – out of a harmless molehill. The content which has been split off from consciousness becomes regressive and contaminated with other primitive, negative contents in the unconscious, with the result that, in an unstable personality, a minor irritation denied access to consciousness is not infrequently blown up into an excess of fury or a serious depression. In quite general terms, it can be stated that forces excluded from the conscious mind accumulate and build up a tension in the unconscious, and that this tension is quite definitely destructive.
>
> (Neumann, 1990, p. 49)

These are essentially neurotic crimes. Compulsive crimes like arson and kleptomania are typical of the form. In other cases the urge may occur once and, with expression, dissipate. Similarly, the repressed content returns empowered in an exaggerated and novel form. Thus, when in Weimar Germany, the Christian archetype descended below consciousness, the related image of Wotan was able to re-emerge in its place. The mechanism is exactly the same as that which appears in symptom substitution.

Second, and perhaps most important, Jung understood that the development of a healthy psyche was absolutely dependent upon the parents. If the parents were negligent, patterns of archetypal compensation could develop that would inevitably include elements of deviance and crime.

In his 1951 monograph, *Maternal Care and Mental Health*, John Bowlby pointed out that children who grew up in institutions without consistent loving were retarded physically, mentally and emotionally. Such children failed to develop a normal emotional life. Other children who were repeatedly separated from their mothers for significant time periods were found by Bowlby to lose the ability to respond to parents and other people on any deep emotional level. They were observed to become self-centered rather than other-oriented, and preoccupied with things instead of people. And, although capable of responding appropriately, the children had apparently become unable to care for anyone (Bowlby, 1951, cited by Stevens, 1982/ 1983, p. 96).

Since Bowlby, multiple ill-effects have been cataloged as following from the separation of the infant from its mother: developmental retardation, intellectual impairment, enuresis, delinquency and psychopathy. Hinde reports recent research that has correlated multiple hospitalizations or hospitalizations for more than a week before the age of five with decreased reading ability, delinquency and job instability. The problems were exacerbated if there were further hospitalizations between five and fifteen (1983, p. 216).

Eibl-Eibesfeldt reports that studies made in Bavaria in 1974 found that 34 per cent of prison inmates had been "love deprived and abused early in childhood." Another study found that only 5 per cent of the inmates of a German prison were raised with one stable reference person. Half of the inmates had had more than five reference figures before their fourteenth birthday (1990).

Third, Jung saw that group influence could provide a strong impetus for crime through two possible mechanisms. The first seems to be simply the fact that group membership in itself entails a lowering of the general moral level to the least common denominator. If the group possesses high standards, there may be no problem. However, in average or below average circumstances the group can provide the rationale for almost anything.

It is a notorious fact that the morality of society as a whole is in inverse ratio to its size; for the greater the aggregation of individuals, the more the individual factors are blotted out, and with them, morality, which rests entirely on the moral sense of the individual and the freedom necessary for this. Hence every man is, in a certain sense, unconsciously a worse man when he is in society than when acting alone; for he is carried by society and to that extent relieved of his individual responsibility. Any large company composed of wholly admirable people has the morality and the intelligence of an unwieldy, stupid, and violent animal. The bigger the organization, the more unavoidable is its immorality and blind stupidity.

(Jung, 1953/1966, para. 240)

Remembering that the main attraction of a group lies in its ability to compensate an archetypally determined psychic imbalance, it is possible for a group to exercise a strong compulsive power upon an individual. One need only recall the mass suicides and murders at Jonestown, Guyana, during the 1980s and the earlier Manson family murders, to bring home the archetypal power of group identity.

A second source of crime, closely related to simple group pressure, lies in acculturation to aberrant, alien or minority perspectives. Within the context of the group from which they sprung, the sentiments may be perfectly reasonable and rational. In the context of a group responding to a different symbolic authority system, the idea, sentiment or action may be illegal.

Inside a nation, the aliens who provide the objects for this projection are the minorities; if these are of a different racial or ethnological projection or, better still, of a different colour, their suitability for this purpose is particularly obvious . . . the role of the alien which was played in former times by prisoners of war or shipwrecked mariners is now being played by the Chinese, the Negroes, and the Jews. The same principle governs the treatment of religious minorities in all religions; and the Fascist plays the same part in a Communist society as the Communist in a Fascist society.

(Neumann, 1990, p. 52)

The aliens, however, divide into two types, those perceived as simply alien and upon whom the dominant society projects its shadow, as above, and those adjudged morally inferior.

The second class of people who play the part of victims in the scapegoat psychology are the "ethically inferior" – that is to say, those persons who fail to live up to the absolute values of the collective and who are also incapable of achieving ethical adaptation by developing a "facade personality". The ethically inferior (who include psychopaths and other pathological and atavistic persons, and in effect all those who belong to an earlier period in the evolution of mankind) are branded, punished and executed by the law and its officers. That at all events is what happens when it is not possible for this class of people to be made use of by the collective. In wartime, on the other hand, they are eagerly exploited.

(Ibid., p. 53)

The two kinds are, however, interchangeable. Both become the bearers of the dominant shadow, both are criminalized, both are excluded.

That these two classes of scapegoat victims are interchangeable – that not only is the evil man experienced as alien but that the alien, in turn, is experienced as evil – is one of the basic facts of human psychology. It is a leitmotif which can be traced uninterruptedly from the psychology of primitives right down to the policy towards aliens of contemporary, so-called civilised states.

(Ibid., p. 54)

Among the non-dominant groups are the simply alien whose activities are innocent if illegal. The peyote-smoking Native American Church in Oregon, for instance, fell into trouble with the State of Oregon when they continued to observe what they believed to be their right to free exercise of religion in violation of the State's anti-drug laws. Similarly, the coca-chewing natives of the High Andes practice a tradition of coca ingestion handed down from pre-Incan cultures. They have no concept that it might be harmful or dangerous. When the opportunity comes for the native Quechua or Aymara groups to turn coca into a cash crop, treaty obligations between the Spanish-speaking Peruvian government and the United States mean nothing.

Among those who actively bear the shadow of the dominant group, there stands the strong possibility that the projection of the shadow itself will propel them towards crime.

[C]ollective shadow projections have a cumulative effect. They activate and support various local and personal shadow projections, so that the recipient of the collective projection is confronted by negative feelings whichever way he turns. First, the culture as a whole defines him in shadow terms; then the locality in which he lives adds its own particular flavor; and finally, each individual with whom he comes into contact contributes his own personal shadow elements. The accumulated burden is so heavy that it is not surprising that members of shadow bearing groups are usually demoralized and depressed.

(Odjanyk, 1976, p. 83)

Howard Becker in the book *Outsiders* makes the point that deviance is a matter of the definition imposed by the observer. Similar to the Jungian position developed here, he saw that groups developed around common definitions.

[C]ulture arises essentially in response to a problem faced in common by a group of people, insofar as they are able to interact and communicate with one another effectively. People who engage in activities regarded as deviant typically have the problem that their view of what they do is not shared by other members of the society.

(Becker, 1966, p. 81)

Even when the culture is manifestly deviant from the surrounding groups, the individuals that comprise that group remain normal within its context. When, however, an individual is labeled as deviant, the label tends to stick. With the label comes an increased probability that further "deviant behavior" will occur (ibid.).

We may note further that the mythos that develops under such conditions can provide role models and archetypal patterns which perpetuate a "culture of deviance." Thus, under the pressure of segregation and repression there arose in the cultural unconscious of the African-American subculture the image of the "Bad Nigger," an archetypal role model capable of confronting the arbitrary violence and humiliation perpetrated by the dominant white culture. Technically this is a variant of the Hero or Warrior archetype. It is skewed, however, by the weight of negative projections coming from without into a less than admirable character.

Wherever the projections of the dominant culture define a group as deviant, if there is no redress after several generations, compensatory images from the collective unconscious appear as powerful symbols in the collective consciousness of the group. Unfortunately, such images have the result of further institutionalizing the conflict so that eventually the groups grow so far apart that they become incapable of cooperation.

Among the "ethically inferior" one finds criminals who instill criminal values in their children. Of these Anthony Stevens notes:

A child whose parents are criminals ... will develop a superego possessing some characteristics which society regards as "Bad" while his Shadow will incorporate unfulfilled capacities which society would deem "Good." ... However criminal the parents are in legal terms, provided that they have been loving and present through out the individual's childhood, they will succeed in actualizing much of the archetypal programme in the usual manner, thus rendering him capable of affection and loyalty to people whom he recognizes as his own kind.

(Stevens, 1982/1983, p. 216)

The Jungian perspective on deviance is, therefore, typically complex. True to his theory, even the archetype of the trickster is constellated in multiple causal paths.

Part V

Retrospect: analysis, conclusions

Chapter 15

Review

This book has sought to accomplish three things. First, to find out what Jung meant when he spoke about archetypes. Second, to discover if there were data from parallel fields that could help us to understand what the archetypes truly are. Finally, the theory of archetypes has been applied to the level of sociology.

THE NATURE OF THE ARCHETYPE

From a strictly Jungian perspective, we teased out the following basic characteristics of the archetype:

- An inherited predisposition to action and/or perception that has resulted from the "Crystallization of experience over time" (Samuels, 1985, p. 27; Jung 1953/1966, para. 151).
- It possesses a strong charge of libidinal energy and resultantly impels the organism to find corresponding data in the environment. It possesses a numinosity (Jung, 1971, para. 748).
- The archetype is never expressed except in terms of the accretions of life experience that it gathers to itself. It is then expressed in images, themes and motifs that reappear independent of cultural transmission or other non-heritable mechanisms (Jung, 1959/1968a, para. 155).
- The archetypal image is related to the instincts as it represents them to consciousness, evokes them as stimulus and represents their fulfillment as a goal or telos (Samuels, 1985, p. 29).
- The archetype is bipolar, Janus-faced. That is, it always presents two faces, upward and downward, inward and outward, good and bad, male and female, etc. (Jung, 1959/1968a, para. 413).
- Although individually distinct, the archetypes are contaminated with one another in their expression. This contamination is rooted in their common or singular source, the *unus mundus* of the collective unconscious (Jung, 1956/1967, para. 660).
- The archetype represents the organ of meaning as it mediates the

instinctual and spiritual poles of reality to the level of conscious experience through the symbolic function. It is simultaneously the voice of nature and the voice of spirit (Jung, 1971, para. 446).

Further examination of the characteristics of the archetypes found that Jung had expressly associated archetypal activity with instinctual activity and the flow of libido or life force. The numinous character of the archetypal image suggested the investment of life energy, as did its compulsive power. These suggested that archetypal patterns may be as fundamental to the structure of living systems of all kinds as they are to humans. The same idea was underlined by Fordham's (1957) suggestion that the deintegration of the primordial self into the archetypes represented the separation of an undifferentiated libido into separate functions starting with oral, anal and genital foci. The mutual contamination of the archetypes was now easily explainable in that they all spring from and express the same primordial life force.

As the investigation continued, it appeared more and more logical that what we deem to be archetypal has its root in some quality or qualities of living systems. In order to get a clearer picture of what this might mean, we examined the properties of living systems. From a Piagetian perspective these were designated wholeness, self maintenance and transformation. These are standard properties of complex systems. Piaget, however, gave special emphasis to self maintenance (1970b).

Self maintenance generally takes the form of homeostasis and is differentiated from inorganic models by three factors. First, organisms develop specific organs of self regulation that take over the systemic function. Second, the function of a living structure is tied to the effective function of the entire structure; structure and function are intimately tied together. Third, biological structures are dependent upon meaning. The idea of meaning at the level of organism, defined as assimilation to pre-existing structure, again pointed us towards an identity between the properties of life and the properties of the archetypes.

We were then led to examine the classical properties of life. These were defined as metabolism, irritability, adaptation, growth and reproduction. We immediately excluded metabolism (that living things are alive has little meaning) and reproduction (a special kind of adaptation) and for the same reason passed up growth. Concentrating on the two properties of adaptation and irritability, we identified the Piagetian processes of assimilation, accommodation and equilibration with adaptation, and the general principle of taxis with irritability. Having done this, we found that equilibration formed an excellent analog to the Bertalanffian idea of centration, and was naturally opposed to diffusion. So, from the two basic principles of living systems we developed three poles of activity: assimilative–accommodative, focused–diffuse and positive–negative taxes (Piaget and Inhelder, 1969; Bertalanffy, 1968).

Schematically, the developing information began to look very much like the spatial octahedron analyzed by Jung in *Aion*. It was immediately possible to associate up and down with assimilation and accommodation – assimilation retains its identity and absorbs the stimulus, while accommodation adapts to environmental stresses. Positive and negative taxes were likewise associated with forward and back. Centrated and non-centrated activity, however, presented a problem. They were not immediately understandable as analogs of right and left, and the meaning of the division seemed questionable on the level of protoplasm.

After some struggle, one of the important attributes of the goddess Hestia was discovered to be centering or focus. She was also the goddess of religious consciousness (Kirksey, 1980/1988). This led to the further association of unconscious versus conscious function, and left and right hemispheric activity with the basic directions left and right. Centration on the organismic level was the analog of consciousness on the psychic. Although the literal left and right had no meaning at the level of the simplest forms of life, they took on meaning later.

At this point, we had recreated the octahedron with each direction associated with a pattern of action displayed by living systems. These same patterns had also been associated with patterns of human action: up and down, assimilation and accommodation, dominance and submission; left and right, centrated and diffuse behavior, conscious–linear thought and unconscious non-linear thought; forward and back, attraction and repulsion, pleasure and pain, Eros and Thanatos.

These patterns were deemed to define the basic elements of archetypal action on all levels of interaction. Although at this level they do not explain the images generally associated with the archetypes, they do present a means of categorizing feeling patterns about images. We were, however, still left with the problem of the archetypal image.

In order to solve this problem, we turned to the idea of emergence and suggested that from the evidence provided by biology, artificial intelligence, ethology and developmental psychology, the archetype is no thing, but the emergent property of systems, selected or designed to emit specific behaviors in "expectation" of specific environmental consequences.

This conclusion was especially inspired by Hinde's (1983) analysis of the imprinting of the chick to its mother in terms of multiple, independent behavior components "designed" to identify and bond to the hen. While no one of the activities in themselves could have produced the imprint, and the imprint response could not be predicted from the aggregate of the behaviors in themselves, their concurrent expression produced the effect as an emergent property of the system.

Following up on this lead with Piaget's hierarchically structured schemata and the idea of subsumption architecture as it is now being explored in some artificial intelligence laboratories, it was determined that the archetype was an emergent property of subsystems interacting on the level of biology and physiology. Moreover, we saw that the emergent took the form of a functional expectancy, that is, a "readiness to perceive" aimed at the fulfillment of a specific psychic or physiological need. It was, we determined, more akin to a direction that received its meaning from the response it received than to any pre-formed image (Piaget and Inhelder, 1969; Freedman, 1991).

The archetypal image was now understood to have taken its form from the original "imprint," its first experiences with the "expected" object. The image itself, its affective tone and the direction it would subsequently impart to the growing organism would then be a function of the goodness of fit between the potential for fulfillment of the organismic "expectancy" and its actual fulfillment in the environment.

We were then led to reconsider the archetypal image, Jung's original formulation of the concept of the archetype. We now can see that part of Jung's confusion in usage stemmed from the fact that each archetype must be incarnated in an image of some sort, else it cannot appear. As an emergent property, its substance is irreducible to component elements and must often be confused with the image that it takes. If we had to define the archetype it would be in terms of the potential for image perception hidden in the interaction of the subsystems of the human organism. In fact, we should also acknowledge that Progoff's idea of a "dark image" rooted in the processes of life provides a clear indication of the nature of the archetype *an sich* (Jung, 1959/1968a; Hobson, 1961; Progoff, 1959).

After an exploration of the archetypal image as metaphor, and the root of metaphor, we returned to an examination of the spatial metaphor as somehow basic to the archetypal realm. Touching on the works of Yates, Casey and Hillman, we found that much archetypal activity can be interpreted in terms of a three-dimensional affective grid. We also found that every instinctual urge that emerges as an archetypal element will become a central element or lack focus, it will draw certain contents towards itself and repel others, it will appear to be desirable or repulsive, good or bad, worthy of approach or worth avoiding. Depending upon its relative salience or libidinal charge, it will either assimilate other patterns to itself, or accommodate to another pattern (Yates, 1966; Casey, 1974; Hillman, 1983/1988).

In summary, we have seen:

1 Archetypal responses are isomorphic with the basic response characteristics of living systems.
2 The idea of image is crucial to the idea of the archetype.
3 The archetype *an sich* may not exist until it emerges from systemic interactions as an image of the instant state of the system. In this, we vindicate Hillman's statement that the archetype is always phenomenal.
4 The abstract archetype exists only as a developmental pole, a set of possibilities of expression whose manifestation is only possible through the archetypal image.

5 The affective tone of an archetype may be described in terms of a three-dimensional scheme based upon salience (is it the center of activity, or does it function in the background, does it draw into focus or consciousness, or does it move from consciousness out of focus?); interactive style, its primary mode of interaction (does it draw to itself or assimilate other psychic contents, or does it accommodate to them?); and valence (is it "good" or "bad," does it attract or repel?).

THE ARCHETYPAL SEQUENCE

In Part II we spent some time looking over the structure of the Jungian psyche, its layers and elements and their relation one to another. A good deal of time was spent looking at various schemes of archetypal organization and activity.

Among the most subtle of these patterns was the capacity of the archetype to operate on many logical levels simultaneously. This is the key to the pattern of the descent of the libido. The same primal patterns that energize the single-celled amoeba are capable of energizing the adult human. The same part-objects that serve to link the newborn to its mother still operate in the ancient. Every level remains accessible to every other level and can reappear in the clothing of maturity at almost any time. This is the central reason that Hillman's definition of the archetypal works: any level of experience can be charged with archetypal energy and function as a symbol. This idea also links back to the idea of the holographic nature of the archetype as propounded by Zinkin and implied by Fordham.[1] Archetypal patterning often appears as self-consistent images and orderings at multiple levels of integration. The octahedron is one such image as is the Net of Indra and the Kabbalistic Tree of Life (Zinkin, 1987; Fordham, 1957; Campbell, 1972/1988).

Another level of self reference was seen when different archetypal roles could be assigned to a personality type, a specific task on the road to individuation at any stage, as well as a specific stage in personal growth.

The archetypes were then seen in the patterning of functional entities, whether as distinct elements of a psychic topology, or as the personalized inhabitants of an inner stage. That is, whether as the specific elements of the Jungian psyche: ego, shadow, collective unconscious, anima, persona, etc.; or as the personified relations of those elements – the king, the child, the great mother, the devouring mother, the treasure, the dragon, etc. The archetypes tend to take on patterns of action that are ultimately identifiable with the inner relations of the psyche, the external relations between individuals and the common experiences of all humankind.

The gods were seen to represent the culturally averaged manifestations of personality types as they were generally expressed within their ethnic locus. The gods, as dominant patterns, overpower and dominate the psychic landscape. They can, however, provide a metaphorical background against which specific patterns of behavior are emphasized and given a meaningful context. The gods are protean. Like all archetypal contents they have a tendency to overlap and merge one with another. Some quickly merge into more archaic forms, while others retain some level of individual identity throughout the process. In some cases the specific archetypal content may not be sufficiently differentiated to identify it clearly with one or another deity. For this reason, and the significant possibility of a dangerous psychic inflation, Hillman, Jung and others have emphasized the danger of over-identification with the gods. In any event, the progress of the archetypes through a life or situation provides specific clues for contextualizing current activities and predicting future directions (Hillman (ed.), 1980/1988; Miller, 1980/1988).

The most crucial pattern of archetypal activity, however, appears to be the pattern of the introversion of libido, the Hero's Journey. It expresses the basic theme of libidinal activity for the renewal and/or the destruction of an individual or a nation. In this return to the depths of the archetypal realm, self definitions are recreated to the good or ill of an individual or a society.

Throughout Jung's work, the pattern of regression appears as a recurring theme. It operates on every logical level and between levels as if the psyche were a vast system of interlocked convection currents sinking down from the surface and bringing up from the depths newly energized materials for the conscious world (1956/1967). Jung and others, before and since, have outlined the pattern clearly: there is a lowering of the level of conscious energy – the ego fails, the identity is lost, meaning fades, life grows stale. Under such conditions, unconscious contents may draw the individual down into their own depths, or unconscious contents may rise up to flood the conscious landscape. Willingly or unwillingly, as Odysseus or as Persephone, the ego is drawn down into a more archaic and less differentiated level. There it obtains contact with the patterns of childhood, the patterns of early life, or perhaps the primitives of life itself. In contact with these archetypal primitives, the ego must restructure itself, regain meaning and return to the world of light. In returning, it discovers whether it has found the treasure hard to attain, the princess, the elixir of life or the poison of poisons (Jung, 1956/1967; Campbell, 1949/1972).

On a personal level we see this happen in every major transition of life to a greater or lesser degree. On the larger scale of the whole life, it is the path of individuation. In the life of nations it can be a revivifying of national identity or the emergence of unspeakable monstrosities.

THE SOCIOLOGICAL PROSPECT

Before attempting to tease out sociological data from Jung's theory, it was necessary to establish some basis for doing so. Of all the social sciences, sociology seems the most racked by disagreement. Therefore, we turned to Kuhn's concept of the scientific paradigm to help organize some of the theoretical underbrush (1969).

Kuhn made the significant discovery that sciences did not develop along the steady incremental path that most of us had always assumed. He observed that they changed in revolutionary bursts that lead from one reigning perspective to another in a number of well-defined stages. He called these perspectives paradigms. Kuhn suggested that in periods of "normal science" the subject matter, approach to the subject matter and the interpretation of all results are controlled by the reigning paradigm. The paradigm was described most basically as the image of the subject matter.

Following Kuhn's position, George Ritzer (1980) applied the concept of the paradigm to the field of sociology. He determined that unlike mature sciences which are dominated by one paradigm, sociology was guided by three conflicting perspectives or paradigms. These were the Social Facts Paradigm, following in the tradition of Emile Durkheim; the Social Definitions Paradigm, following the tradition of Max Weber; and the Social Behavior Paradigm, in the tradition of radical behaviorist, B. F. Skinner. Each of these paradigms was presented as having a specific theoretical exemplar, an image of the subject matter and an outline derived from the metatheoretical considerations of one or another of its major exponents.

Having examined the various theoretical perspectives, we attempted to provide an outline of a sociology that might meet the needs of an integrated paradigm: one that truly bridged the gap between all three positions. Having derived that outline, it was decided that for the time being, a less detailed outline based upon the work of Berger and Luckmann would serve as a model for our exploration of the sociological implications of Jung's psychology. Accordingly, the following outline became the background for our researches into the possibility of an archetypal sociology (Berger and Luckmann, 1967).

I   Society as a product of human beings.

   A   What is the basis of intersubjectivity?
   B   What is the nature of the group?
   C   How do social structures arise out of individual experience?
   D   What is the relationship between the structure of the psyche and the structure of the group?

II   Society as objective reality.

   A   How are intersubjective typifications transformed into facticities?
   B   How do social facts gain their external and coercive properties?
   C   What mechanisms exist that foster the continued existence of social systems and social institutions?

1 What is the nature of authority?

2 What is the nature of legitimation and why is it necessary?

3 What is the nature and root of rationalization and why is it necessary?

D What mechanisms exist that account for the failure of groups and societies?

1 What is the source of contradiction, the seed of destruction?

2 How do we account for deviance?

III Man as a product of society.

A If society is a human product, how can man be a social product?

1 What is the nature of socialization?

2 How is the world of social relations perceived in the generations that have not helped to produce it?

3 What is the role of language in shaping behavior?

4 What is the role of religion in shaping behavior?

B What is the dialectic between man as producer and man as product of society?

1 What are the parameters of the human/social cybernetic loop?

2 To what level does man the product retain autonomy and the option to change the system?

THE ELEMENTS OF AN ARCHETYPAL SOCIOLOGY

Having now come to the heart of the matter, we began by analyzing the roots of intersubjectivity and the group. Both, according to Jung, were rooted in the archetypal structure of the human psyche. We saw that Jung perceived the human individual as a social creature, and found the roots of this nature in the archetypally conditioned bond between mother and child.

The archetypes, however, were not only responsible for binding individuals together, but they offered the possibility of communication based upon common perceptions of the world. So, the archetypes provided both a common perceptual capability, a common need hierarchy and an epigenetically determined propensity for sociality.

We also saw that, according to Jung, Levy-Bruhl, Durkheim and others, the group precedes individuality. Such archaic groups, whether on a desert island or in a Park Avenue penthouse, are characterized by a participation mystique. This was defined as a subsumption of the individual to the group experience so that he or she cannot differentiate between their own thoughts and the thoughts of the group. This particular state is identified by Jung as the affective equivalent of the mother/infant bond. It was seen to be a powerful impetus for the surrender of personal responsibility in favor of a group standard or decision (Jung, 1959/1968a; Durkheim, 1938/1964).

Groups were seen to be further rooted in three powerful behavioral elements: imitation, projection and identification. Jung believed that imitation was an important factor in group dynamics which led to a state of identification. Identification was a loss of self in the object. It was a recreation of the mother–infant unity and, so, a regressive state in which the participation mystique holds sway.

Projection is the unconscious tendency to attribute our own qualities, good or bad, to others. It is also the means by which we first become aware of archetypal activity: in our projections on to others. In the case of groups, paternal and maternal authority may be projected upon them, thus empowering or weakening their draw for the individual. Negative images may be projected upon them as in the case of minority groups or aliens, thus establishing the border of consensus and those who lie beyond the pale.

Groups, in general, have their archetypal basis in the family grouping. The family, however, is never hypostatized by Jung in any one form as perfect. In harmony with many anthropologists, Jung saw that the family is more important as the supplier of a consistent and safe developmental context for the child than as the exemplar for any archetypal family structure. The personality and psychic growth of the individual depends upon the specific kind of care and nurturance that the child receives from its family. Their response to the child's archetypally determined needs will determine the specific compensations that will shape his or her growth for the rest of his or her life.

Families do not live in isolation, but are always part of a cultural milieu. Therefore, the specific manner in which families respond to the needs of their children is at least partially determined by the local canon of values, or collective wisdom. According to Jung and his followers, this cultural variable provides a partial explanation for differences in national character. When the parent responds to the newborn child in accordance with culturally defined patterns of behavior, those cultural preferences provide a specific flavor to the archetypal image constellated in the newborn psyche. Thus, the psychic life of the child is determined in part through the interaction of the biological expectancy with the culturally determined parental practices (not to mention the parents' own idiosyncrasies).

One of the crucial points of interaction between the family and the society is the rite of initiation, the point of separation between childhood patterns and the newly emergent adult. This aspect of enculturation has proven so important that some authors have suggested that, like the early imprint of the maternal imago, there is a socio-sexual imprinting at puberty. Others have suggested that the human has several sensitive periods which serve a reorienting function strictly analogous to the original imprint during the early weeks of the infant's life. Jung saw initiation as a time of intentional regression of the individual in which libido was detached from the juvenile identity and created afresh with an adult identity.

National identities are rooted in the structure of the culture, religion and language of a people. In general, the collective consciousness of a group has a specific average character that molds the character of individuals throughout their lives. Although often relegated to the category of stereotypes, they represent a general tendency in the population.

One of the more significant means by which a population is ordered on an unconscious basis is through its myths. Myths represent the archetypal structure of consciousness and everyday life; they constitute a significant portion of the cultural canon, and the source of the patterns that structure everyday reality. Myths shape reality. As the orderers of perception and the prescribers of action they have a determinative effect upon all members of the group. Myths also reflect the movements of the collective unconscious by moving one or another theme or character into relative salience within the canon.

While myth is created by humans, it also reflects the psychoid collective unconscious in its universal and local manifestations. Each myth is a bricolage of symbols taken from the current canon to express the currents of the collective unconscious. Myths and culture live in a codetermining dialectic. Myth determines culture. Culture, however, is also defined by myth as the agent of the collective unconscious. The response of humans to specific elements of myth and tradition activates the collective unconscious through compensatory mechanisms. These can lead to a reformulation of the myth following the classic pattern of the regression of libido in which the unconscious reorganizes the archetypal elements that define the myth. Either the myth is restructured, or a new myth appears.

In the study of groups we examined the means whereby a group that is the product of human interaction becomes reified as an object outside of human influence. We also examined the archetypal structure of groups, beginning with the root archetypes from which they derive their meaning, their external manifestations and the roles they support. The development of groups includes their transition from human products into external facticities. This process is understood in terms of the projection of shared definitions upon one group by another.

When one group is encountered by another that is strange to it, it is first perceived in terms of the local expectations regarding the nature of this or that category of group. If the group is identified with the shadow of the perceiving groups, these typifications may be based upon archetypal projections of the shadow. Alternatively, they may be related to specific hooks for projection that are part of the group definition. They may also be accurate perceptions of the archetypal image about which the group coheres.

Projections carry with them an archetypally derived sense of life and autonomy which they necessarily impose upon their object. This is no less true in modern America where we personify the government, institutions and large groups as readily as non-industrial peoples project personality into trees, stars, shrubs or fetishes. With the projection of personality comes a sense of reality which is accorded it through the process of being named. The shared typifications by which a group is categorized carry with them an archetypally founded validity (intuitive validity) which is reinforced by the perceiving group (consensual validity). As a result, they have the tendency to be perceived as real in themselves and as having a real substance independent of the people who comprise them (reification). As a result, they become defined as real and become real in their consequences.

The archetypal dimensions of group existence focus about the archetypal core of group identity and the various means whereby it is expressed. All groups possess an archetypally determined identity or meaning. It is this core of meaning that accounts for their selective ability to attract members. Because this core is archetypal in nature, and functions through the numinous attractive agency of the archetype, all groups may be said to be religious in nature. This suggests that the meaning any individual seeks from group membership, except for the very pragmatic ends related to specific goals, is a contact with the numinous, directly apprehended meaning levels that are typical of the archetypes in their more powerful symbolic expressions.

For the most part, secular groups arise when religious organizations become unable to hold the self projections of its members and no longer provide an intuitive and self validating experience. In such cases, psychic energy splits from the main symbol system and gives rise to symbols appropriate to a secular context. This secularization has the effect of rationalizing the nature of election and of demystifying the world. As the archetypal energy, the meaning inherent in a religious symbol, dissipates over a broader and broader area, its ability to hold or command attention also dissipates. All archetypes are manifested by symbols and these can be understood as archetypal themes. The image projected by a group may differ from its governing image as a matter of style. This suggests that groups project personae as do humans.

On the level of social interaction, archetypal themes are reflected for the most part in roles. One particularly elegant formulation of archetypal roles and their relation to the structure of society is provided by Thompson (1971) in terms of four root roles: the Chief, the Warrior, the Fool and the Shaman. These may be articulated into four basic divisions of labor: the state, the military, art and religion. On subsequent levels these provide further differentiation of roles as the state gives rise to management and government, the military births industry, art brings along criticism and commentary, and religion fosters education.

Groups may also be characterized by archetypal styles. These reflect not only the actual archetypal image that forms the core of the group, but also include the intentional image that the group would like to project. Such styles may include specific orientations such as the Jungian functions and attitudes, or may reflect very specific roles for the group.

Whatever the role projected by a group as determinative of its archetypal style, it must be remembered that the archetype will be experienced in terms of the octahedral model discussed in Part I. Thus, every role will express itself in terms of a very specific affective tone that may be characterized in terms of the attentional (focused/unfocused), dispositional (accommodative/assimilative) and orientational (towards/away) poles. (Styles extend not only to groups but also to eras. The idea of a zeitgeist is a reference to an archetypal style preferred by a particular culture over a period of time.)

As groups are made up of individuals, group structure reflects the patterning of the human psyche. Each group has a conscious function corresponding to the ego. This is the collective consciousness or collective canon. It is formulated largely in terms of common sense and contractual definitions. The myths of a group and its tradition contribute to the social canon.

The group shadow consists of those parts of the group or society that are either incompatible with the collective consciousness or are inimical to it. Where a group's focus represents its conscious executive, its omissions, repressions and suppressions develop into a coherent whole which functions as a group shadow. This shadow has two separate identities in the social context. On the one hand, it represents the people who are excluded from the definition of the dominant culture's canon; on the other it represents the abstraction whose projection identifies aliens, strangers and others as worthy of exclusion.

Within the shadow – defined as a group – are the minorities, the deviants, the forgotten and others upon whom the conscious executive has cast its shadow. The shadow of the dominant group may be projected on any different, rejected or alien group. The projection of the shadow evokes a mutual re-projection of the subordinate group's own shadow. The process inevitably develops into a near total, mutual alienation. Shadow projection is, to a large extent, responsible for racial and ethnic conflict throughout the world (Neumann, 1990; Odjanyk, 1976).

Each group may also be seen to project some sort of persona or idealized image of itself into the world at large. The projected image may reflect reality, it may be cynical, or a necessary camouflage for an oppressed minority.

The fragmentation of symbol systems develops along the following lines. When the contents of the collective unconscious arise as a numinous symbol into the conscious world of a relatively homogeneous group, they will receive near universal recognition and become the center of a religious symbol system. As time goes on, more and more parts of the symbol become subject to rational interpretation and rationalized formulae. Because the abstracting quality of the conscious mind has the effect of blocking archetypal libido, a certain measure of the archetypal function of the symbol is frustrated.

As a direct result of this blockage, the organismic energy naturally allotted to the blocked symbolic elements recedes into the unconscious where it seeks a different vehicle of manifestation (once again the pattern of the regression of libido reappears). This new vehicle will express itself either through a competing symbol, or will, through projection, attach to a secondary symbol that can carry much of the energy originally intended for the religious symbol.

The basic form of the pattern of regressing libido as it applies to groups is as follows. Every person, group or nation possesses some conscious focus, an executive function or interface with reality. In individuals it is called the ego complex. This is usually represented by the collective consciousness, the most general set of perspectives, traditions and practices common to a people or group.

Underlying the conscious process there exist unconscious processes corresponding to the collective unconscious and the group or national unconscious. For groups and nations, the unconscious is represented by minority interests, systemic contradictions which lie outside of the consensus reality, actually censored or forgotten material and archetypally charged materials which would threaten the status quo. The collective unconscious is essentially the world of archetypes as it is for individuals. As groups are composed of individuals, the contents of their collective unconscious are reflected in the group patterns.

When the group executive becomes unable to function, through deadlock, frustration, external force or other inhibition, the current formulation of the executive may be dissolved, temporarily suspended, re-examined or otherwise subjected to disassembly. This may come by violent revolution as well as by constitutional convention.

In cases analogous to a healthy reformulation of the ego, new elements from the collective and group unconscious are integrated into the executive; as a result, the executive is restructured in order to accommodate the new contents. Originally, the new contents may appear as token examples. They hold forth an earnest of something better to come, but fall far short of that goal. However, due to their truly symbolic nature, these token measures are articulated in a manner that is both rational and consistent with the structure of the executive. In so doing, they gradually expand the options of the executive function by allowing the integration of other, previously repressed or unknowable contents.

The pattern of rationalization of symbols, already discussed as the fragmentation of symbols, was again discussed as paralleling Weber's routinization of charisma.

1   A new symbol system arises out of the collective unconscious in

response to some broadly experienced imbalance. It is formulated by certain visionaries who become the vehicles for specific versions of the message.

2 Early adherents are caught in the numen of the newly emergent symbol and enter fully into its meaning structure. The symbol system provides self-evident validity.

3 Later adherents are brought into the system by more rational modes of persuasion. As part of the process, an analytical set of explanations, practices and creeds develops about the symbol system. These rationalized rules and explanations tend to replace a direct experience of the archetypal numen of the original symbol with a code or canon of practices and beliefs which are incapable of carrying the libidinal charge born by the original symbol.

4 As group practice comes to depend less and less upon direct experience of the transcendent reality that was originally vested in the symbol, self projections once accruing to that symbol seek other objects. More often than not they attach to fragments of the original symbol system or its analogs in the community at large.

5 These secular symbols[2] now become the focus of libidinal energy originally reserved for the religious activity.

The tragedy of National Socialist Germany was a case where secularization combined with loss of identity (characteristic of the break-up of the ego in the regression paradigm), and the added dimension of possession by an unconscious dominant, the spirit of Wotan, led to insanity on a national scale. The specific elements that allowed the emergence of the dominant were as follows.

Germany had, at least since the Reformation, dissociated its national identity from its barbarian roots, overlaying them, like many Western nations, with a thin veneer of Christian civilization. In the process, Germany developed an over-dependence upon intellect at the expense of feeling. This led to a national sense of inferiority and a special vulnerability to irrational impulses from the collective unconscious.

Christianity had succeeded in holding back the Wotanic flood for some centuries. However, the growing rationalization of the Christian world view emerging from German seminaries during the hundred years that preceded the war helped to precipitate a crisis of faith for the German people. When these precursors combined with the economic depression that followed the First World War, their immediate effect was to constellate the pattern of the regression of libido. The German psyche receded from the light of consciousness and re-emerged with the spirit of Wotan, a spirit which, in the hands of a madman, eventually led the entire nation into psychosis.

Deviance was examined from the Jungian perspective and was found to emerge from several roots. These included, first, the innate propensity in all of humankind for both good and bad which is based upon the composition of human nature as a coincidence of opposites. Second, deviance was seen as arising from the effects of repression analogous to symptom magnification and symptom substitution. A third etiology was based upon group influence. Within this category there were two varieties. The first consisted essentially of peer pressure and group identity. The second was related to the possibility that one could have been socialized under aberrant or merely different conditions. The influence of shadow projections was seen as a powerful force in molding not only behavior, but the options available to the individual upon whom they fall.

Chapter 16

Retrospect: Jung and sociology

Having reviewed the basic content of the preceding pages, we must now ask whether the specific questions have been answered. Has Jung provided an adequate foundation for an archetypal sociology, or not?

SOCIETY AS A PRODUCT OF HUMAN BEINGS

The Jungian perspective provides an adequate vantage point for understanding the roots of intersubjectivity via several means. First, the collective unconscious provides a common access to the world for every human being. Because psychoid archetypes, at their most basic, are receptor-systems, we know that we are all perceiving essentially the same world. Continuing, we see that on the next higher levels of integration, the psychoid archetypes can be understood as the images of instinct in the psyche, or the instinct's image of itself. This is an indication that, in every corner of the earth, humankind is driven by the same basic needs, fears and failures. Not only do we perceive similarly, but we do so in the context of similar needs. On a further level we have the archetypes defined as the patterns of behavior common to all of humankind. From this we understand that people everywhere do the same general kinds of things. They are born, they marry, they have children, work and die (Jung, 1960/1969, 1959/1968a; Fordham, 1957).

These three levels alone suggest that the archetypal ordering of human existence provides for the possibility of intersubjectivity in terms of shared perception, needs and activities. The Jungian perspective holds more. Jung characterizes man as inherently social. He begins life in a symbiotic relation with another human, and spends much of his life seeking a return to that same state. Because that early symbiosis becomes the root of feelings of relatedness and belonging there is a strong tendency for people to be drawn into and overpowered by groups. Thus, intersubjectivity is founded, from the Jungian perspective, upon the psychoid base of the collective unconscious and upon the archetypally determined bond with the mother, which becomes the functional basis for all other interactions.

Each individual enters the world with specific developmental deficits or advantages that are the direct result of the adequacy of parental care during the early years. Through the mechanism of compensation, the self balances behavioral needs and predilections to offset developmental insufficiencies, thus providing the root of the individual personality. Groups develop out of the common needs that are created in the developmental sequence. The specific kinds of needs that develop within a specific milieu are determined in part by the structure of the collective consciousness, the givens of the culture. Insofar as these givens impact upon nurture and child rearing, they favor certain specific forms of compensation and need within each society. These societal definitions result in a receptivity to specific kinds of groups meeting specific kinds of needs from culture to culture.

Groups coalesce about just such archetypally determined need structures. They are maintained by two others: the continuing vitality of the organizing symbol and the ability of the group to either foster or frustrate individuality.

As each group builds up about a symbol, and depends upon that symbol for its meaning, the vitality of the symbol is a crucial element in the life of groups. If a symbol is alive it retains an active flow of libido between the conscious life and the collective unconscious. If this flow is maintained, its validity is perceived intuitively, it is self-validating. In the case of a religious group, this can be a crucial element. In secular groups, the symbolic element may be carried as an attitude among the other members.

Symbols are, by definition, the numinous expressions of the archetypes in consciousness. Through their manifold reference and multiple meanings they can never be fully known, and certainly are not human creations. When rationalization of the symbol system proceeds beyond a certain point, the conscious formulation begins to block the freedom of access between the symbol and the collective. At such times the symbol may simply die as a new symbol emerges to take its place, or it may be renewed through a regression to its roots in the collective unconscious. If the symbol can once again be restored, the group will continue.

Where the power of the collective unconscious is greatest, group relations will be characterized by the participation mystique in which the individual is unable to differentiate between his own thoughts and the thoughts of the group. This state is one of the powerful elements of group survival. It is fostered in part by imitation and conformity; these in turn give rise to identity. It is essentially identical to what Durkheim characterized as mechanical solidarity (1933/1964).

Just as individuals are shaped by the influence of social structure on parenting strategies, the social structure arises out of shared human experience. At root, the collective unconscious is the primary source of all social structures. The specifically human needs, as well as the locally determined needs, are reflected at their most basic form as archetypal elements of the collective conscious. Different myths, stories and traditions rise to differing degrees of importance within the group as the response of the system to imbalances in the conscious executive. Those that become most powerful will dominate the cultural canon and so become institutionalized.

Although there are archetypal elements that are constellated in response to specific environmental causes, there are other archetypes that arise spontaneously in the consciousness of many individuals simultaneously. They often mark a change in the level of the group consciousness. When this happens one might say that an idea's time has come. Insofar as it possesses both intuitive and consensual validity for those involved, it will probably be accepted into the cultural canon, where it will become subject to rationalization and institutionalization.

As it is passed on to the next generation, it tends to become less an element of personal experience and more a prescribed practice. No longer a true symbol, it becomes an emblem. Weber called this the routinization of charisma; Berger and Luckmann call it sedimentation. It is related to the idea that naming gives power (Weber, 1968/1978; Berger and Luckmann, 1967).

The structure of the group can be seen as reflecting the topology of the psyche in a broad sense. It possesses conscious and unconscious segments as well as persona and shadow analogs. At the level of the group, the expressed mythology, statements of purpose, legal charter or constitution, i.e., the cultural canon takes on the function of the ego or conscious executive. These constitute a central symbol system. Legitimation is tied to the level to which the executive remains open to the movements of the collective unconscious and is able to open to elements of the group shadow. Legitimation is a function of living symbols. Insofar as the symbol system retains its vitality, it will be perceived as legitimate and rational; traditional and charismatic legitimations will suffice to maintain order. Whenever a group loses the ability to reincorporate parts of the group shadow, or loses its dynamic relation to the collective unconscious, the executive symbol system dies, legitimation fails and the executive must resort to force (Neumann, 1990; Weber, 1968/1978).

The group shadow has two forms. First, it consists of all of the groups which do not match the definitions laid down by the cultural canon: aliens, inferiors, criminals, etc. Second, it consists of the negative projections by the dominant group upon the subordinate groups.

There are also group personae, masks projected by groups to gain some specific advantage among other groups. These take the form of misleading advertising, dummy laws and regulations, token memberships for minorities, etc.

SOCIETY AS OBJECTIVE REALITY

Social groups arise out of individual experience. When one group is encountered by another that is strange to it, the group is first perceived in terms of the local traditions or formulae, the common sense typifications of the collective consciousness. These typifications may be based upon archetypal projections upon the group by the community, especially if they are identified with the group shadow. In any case, they are related to the specific hooks for projection that are part of the group definition. They may or may not be accurate perceptions of the archetypal image about which the group coheres.

Projections carry with them an archetypally derived sense of life and autonomy which they necessarily impose upon their object. This is true in modern America where we readily personify the government, institutions and large groups as it is among non-industrial peoples who project personality into trees, stars, shrubs or fetishes. With the projection of personality comes a sense of reality, a reification which is also accorded a thing when it is named. The shared typifications by which a group is categorized carry with them an archetypally founded validity (intuitive validity) which is reinforced by the perceiving group (consensual validity). As a result, the perceived quality of the group or social structure, as well as the structure itself, has the tendency to be perceived as real in itself and as having a real substance independent of the people who comprise it (reification). As a result, they become defined as real and become real in their consequences. When these typifications are passed on to a new level of user, they will harden and become facts or rules about facts (Jung, 1959/1968a; von Franz, 1980/1988; Berger and Luckmann, 1967; Durkheim, 1933/1964).

Authority is first a response to an archetypal numen or practical situation. The authority figure is either intuitively and consensually worthy of authority, or he is capable of retaining it by main force. Insofar as the authority structure is secured by living symbols, it will be self-validating. Insofar as the system is dependent upon rationalizations and traditions, it will tend to require force. As noted already, there is an inverse relationship between the vitality of the symbol system embodied in the executive or collective consciousness of a group and the level to which force is necessary to validate the rule.

Beyond Weber's explanation that rationalization exists to ensure the continuity of the structure of a group or system after the charismatic leader is gone, rationalization is at once the cause and the result of the death of a symbol. When a living symbol is invested in a leader, his or her authority becomes a matter of fact. As the nature of the symbol is researched on deeper and deeper levels, it begins to dam up the flow of libido and the power of the symbol is depreciated. This leads to further rationalization, and a further limiting of the power of the symbol (Weber, 1968/1978; Jung, 1956/1967). Rationalization has another function in that it represents the attempt of the conscious element to wrest control of the structure of authority from the unconscious. It is often representative of a split within the individual or the group as to the need to control (Jung, 1960/1969).

Jung perceived that each archetype was capable of dual expression. It could produce the best and highest of results, or it could sink to the lowest depths. Each was characterized as a *complexio oppositorum*, a union of opposites. As such, a person of the highest morals can turn about and reveal just the opposite nature existing within himself.

Deviance was examined from the Jungian perspective and was found to emerge from several roots. These included, first, the innate propensity in all of humankind for both good and bad which is based upon the composition of human nature as a coincidence of opposites. They then included the effects of repression analogous to symptom magnification and symptom substitution. A third etiology was based upon group influence. Within this category there were two varieties. The first consisted essentially of peer pressure and group identity; the second was related to the possibility that one could have been socialized under aberrant or merely different conditions. The influence of shadow projections was seen as a powerful force in molding not only behavior, but the options available to the individual upon whom they fall (Odjanyk, 1976; Stevens, 1982/1983; Neumann, 1990; Jung, 1953/1966).

MAN AS A PRODUCT OF SOCIETY

Jung understood clearly the nature of the dialectic between man and society. Not only was society the creation of man, but it determined how he would be nurtured, socialized and initiated into the world. Yet, his response, as the only possible medium for the response of the collective unconscious, would join with others faced with situations similar to his and restructure the cultural canon in such a way that the problem would change the nature of the canon itself (1954/1966, 1964/1970).

Here, then, is the loop. Man creates culture through common consent to the intuitively validating cultural canon. The canon imposes practices of child rearing, socialization and initiation which impact upon the flow of libido in the psychic systems of each individual. Religion and language provide mythic and association systems that reinforce the more basic patterns, while myths and traditions reflect the more flexible patterns.

Insofar as the flow of libido is blocked or hindered through repression, suppression or inattention, the specific cultural contradictions and developmental deficits will call forth appropriate compensations from the collective unconscious. These compensations will take the form of the increased salience of certain mythic or traditional themes, or as an increase of the perceived importance of specific elements of the cultural canon. As these appear, compensatory movements in the collective unconscious will be experienced by others, who are perhaps not otherwise affected by the contradiction. If the response level of the collective unconscious is both strong enough and general enough, a reformulation of the collective canon may arise through any of a number of means, from legislation, through violent revolution, to total reformulation.

To the extent that man remains unconscious of his shadow, is content to be driven by the shared instinct or fails to set out on the path of individuation, he loses control over his own destiny. While the social structure determines much of what is possible for an individual to think or do, Jung felt that consciousness was possible and attainable for much of the human race.

Consciousness, however, required personal responsibility for personal choices. It required differentiating one's own thoughts from the thought of others, and the acknowledgment of one's own dragons in the shadows projected upon others. For as much hope as he held out for the person walking the path of individualization, Jung held out little or no hope for those who would not or could not awaken. For those satisfied with being cared for by the government, or protected from personal responsibility by the herd instinct, there would be no freedom. For those, however, who could become themselves, nothing was impossible.

The one area which has not really been covered in the above outline is language. Jung's works are full of etymological studies, and the relation between the cultural unconscious and linguistic patterns, as suggested by Henderson, was very tempting. However, like the archetypal significance of numbers, the archetypal study of linguistics is so complex that I have decided not to cover it here. This is a serious, but necessary flaw.

This is by no means a fully articulated sociology; it does however lay some of the groundwork upon which such an edifice may be built. At the very least, it provides a further link between the too long estranged worlds of sociology and psychology.

PARADIGMATIC CONSIDERATIONS

Looking again over the Jungian corpus, we find that Jung's statements on the nature of social life provide a means to understand each of the viewpoints outlined by Ritzer. In its breadth, we also find that the archetypal perspective provides a basis for an approach to sociology that integrates all three paradigms.

To begin with the Social Facts Paradigm, we have already shown how, through the mechanism of projection, the products of human activity become facticities, and further, how their association with archetypal content gives them an apparent life of their own. Although Jung saw this at the social level as a hypostatization of social constructs by the victims of manipulation, his ideas provide adequate formulations for the creation and maintenance of social facts that are external to and coercive upon the individual.

In the projection of the archetypal structure of the Jungian psyche on to groups, we have seen a means for understanding the roots of social division and inequality. We may also surmise that because of their archetypal root, there are no easy answers to such problems. As conflict, discrimination and separation appear to be rooted in the structure of human experience, we must look for and work towards a change of evolutionary nature in the individual psyche to effect a real difference. Jung suggested that these particular problems will remain with us until we individually become so conscious of our own shadows that we will no longer tolerate the exclusion of any human being.

In the process of differentiating conscious goals, each executive produces both latent and manifest functions and dysfunctions in accordance with Merton's (1967) formulation. The executive function of the group develops a formulation of the collective consciousness to express certain ideals and perform certain definitions. Conscious inclusions and exclusions form the manifest function of the decision; the unconscious results through repression, suppression, neglect and ignorance create the latent functions and dysfunctions of the group.

Conflict arises as a result of alienation of the groups controlling the collective conscious from those comprising the shadow and upon whom the collective shadow is projected. Marx (Marx and Engels, 1967a) understood and Mannheim (1936) echoed the idea that the upper class always determines the modes of consciousness in society. Jung would add that the mechanism whereby consciousness is determined is not so much the means of production as it is the instruments of consciousness, the collective canon. Conflict arises when the symbolic elements that unify existence cease to be sufficiently potent to justify the positions of each person to the satisfaction of all, or when those same symbols begin to die – failing to provide continuing patterns for the integration of the suppressed, repressed and forgotten elements of society.

Because the Jungian perspective is implicitly systems theoretical, it explains the cohesion of society through both archetypal and autopoetic mechanisms. As the manifestation of an integrated system, social systems and social structures show the systems property of self maintenance and systems organization. They are expressed as the emergent property of the interaction of the individuals, their collective consciousness and their interactions with the environment. The cohesion is further explained by the numen of the archetypal which draws the individuals into a systemic relation (Fidler, 1982).

From the social definitionist paradigm, the idea of meaning and its interpersonal communication become paramount. *Verstehen* easily makes the transition from sociology to depth psychology. The Jungian use, however, would not be limited to intentional actions alone, but through the unconscious it would integrate all faces of the human species (Weber, 1958/1968).

Meaning and the nature of continuing relations among people are elegantly explained by Jungian theory in terms of the archetype. As the organ and organizer of meaning that is common to all humans at the level of biology, the archetype provides a ready base for the existence of inter-subjective reality. The data of human experience is fully acceptable to the Jungian on the level of phenomenological observation. Further, the Schutzian world of shared typifications and recipe knowledge is easily identifiable with the collective consciousness (Berger and Luckmann, 1967; Schutz, 1967; Ritzer, 1980).

Even on the level of reinforcement theory we find the Jungian position providing new understandings as to the nature of reinforcement, generalization and other elements of learning theory. Although not explicitly covered in Part IV, Jung understood that any behavior not fully grounded in an instinctual system is doomed to disappear. He saw the archetypes as motivating forces, whose satisfaction was inherently reinforcing and whose frustration brought forth systemic compensations far beyond mere non-learning (1956/1967).

The generalization of learning takes on new meaning when we understand that metaphorical extension may be based upon the similarity of affective tone relating two circumstances, or the actual stimulus qualities of the circumstances themselves. In either case a continuing relation to an archetypal root is necessary to ensure the continued operation of the skill (Skinner, 1957).

On the broadest level Jung provides, through the collective unconscious, a means of integrating social theory rooted in the structure of the human psyche. With the groundwork of the archetypes, the possibility of inter-subjectivity receives a biological base closely related to the IRM. The continuing function of archetypal centers as organizers of meaning provides for the existence of symbolic centers about which meanings and groups can cohere. In part, because the symbols generated by the collective unconscious are associated with preconscious levels of existence, they are experienced as transcendent or numinous. Through their numen, the archetypes as represented in symbols become the center and source of mythic and cultural themes which guide the everyday life of individuals from culture to culture. Because the archetypes clothe themselves in the experiential vocabulary of the local culture, their expression through complex and symbol provides a mechanism to explain the differentiation of one culture or group from the next.

Chapter 17

Prospects: further research

Sociology and psychology have been estranged for far too long. There is here ample evidence for the possibility of the one benefiting from the other so that, out of the union of opposites, a new thing can be born.

We have already remarked upon the lack of socio-linguistic emphasis in this study. The question as to whether the archetypal substrate molds language or vice versa is crucial. Recent work by Paul Kugler (1983), demonstrating associative complexes surrounding the ideas of flower, virginity, sex and violence, provides significant leads for the further study of the archetype. Greenberg and Ruhlen's (1991) illustration of the spread of specific words surrounding the complex of mother, breast, suck and throat throughout both the Eurasiatic/Nostratic and Proto-Amerind language groups likewise deserves special attention from the Jungian population. Remembering von Franz's observation that the spread of symbols depends upon the readiness of the objective psyche, the peculiar patterns of linguistic drift reviewed by other scholars also becomes interesting.

An examination of language would also center upon the problem of whether language in itself can explain some of the effects that we identify as archetypal or if there does exist an archetypal reality that organizes human behavior. One of the most fruitful avenues of investigation would be the exploration of the base vocabulary used by scholars like Greenberg and Ruhlen (1991) for the multilateral comparison of languages. According to these authors there are categories of root concepts which are rarely if ever borrowed – words "that denote universal concepts such as personal pronouns, body parts and aspects of nature" (water and fire, for example). Here is fertile ground for further exploration.

Out of this study have come several other possibilities for continuing research. First among them is the nature of the archetype in its identity with living systems. Although our assertions are interesting and seem to be verified on the basis of past observations, a thorough critique and re-examination of the evidence needs to be made. One such study might entail a detailed hierarchical classification of human behaviors in order to determine if a hierarchical structure of schemata and emergents, as was suggested here, can be enumerated. Beginning with logical categories suggested by the early division of libido into oral, anal and genital venues, the research would then seek behavioral patterns clearly identifiable with the merger and overlap of the primitive divisions of libido.

Jung suggested just such a process in his analysis of the origins of art, already cited in Part II:

> [M]any complex functions, which today must be denied all trace of sexuality, were originally derived from the reproductive instinct.... Thus, we find the first stirrings of the artistic impulse in animals, but subservient to the reproductive instinct and limited to the breeding season. The original sexual character of these biological phenomena gradually disappears as they become organically fixed and achieve functional independence. Although there can be no doubt that music originally belonged to the reproductive sphere, it would be an unjustified and fantastic generalization to put music in the same category as sex.
>
> (Jung, 1956/1967, para. 194)

The prosecution of such a program would help to lay the groundwork for a clear understanding of the nature of associative systems. While it may also lead to absurd reductions and the tendency to lose any specificity in the archetype's manifold interrelations, its value would lie in the uncovering of specific forms of symbolic parallelisms between the different libidinal systems, and how they reunite at higher levels.

Several of the patterns of archetypal imagery that have appeared over the years are especially interesting. Thompson's fourfold division of society deserves serious consideration. It logically belongs in a discussion with Henderson's four cultural attitudes (1968, 1984), Jung's functions (1971), Stewart's fourfold affective scheme (1987) and Hillman's notion of topoi (1983/1988). These would also bear serious consideration in light of Cornford's unearthing of the topological roots of law and morality in the Greek tradition and the pattern of four that he uncovers there (1991).

Within this limited group we find not only the recurrence of the number four, but again, the strong odor of spatial relations, of place as related to concept, function, right and justice. All of this calls us to again examine Eliade's (1954/1971, 1976) concept of non-homogeneous space, and to look further at the archetypal dimensions suggested in Part I.

Another striking pattern that deserves serious attention is the self-referential patterning of archetypal energy. Thompson's roles (1971), Jung's regression of libido (1969), his analysis of the Trinitarian ages of man (1960/1969) and the alchemical wheel (1959/1968b), all represent self-referential loops which, upon realization of their ultimate goal, turn in upon themselves like the equations that plot chaotic attractors and fractal graphics. The consistent pattern of archetypal systems seems to be this strange loop[1] giving rise to self-consistent patterns at multiple levels of integration.

There is an important level of metaphorical understanding to be gleaned from a thorough understanding of chaotic systems, fractal mathematics and holography.

Ultimately, the holographic metaphor is irresistible. Fordham (1957) pointed to the fact that each archetype reflected the whole of the psyche and every other archetype as well. Joseph Campbell has reflected the basic pattern as the mythic net of Indra: "which is a net of gems, . . . at every crossing of one thread over another there is a gem reflecting all the other reflective gems. Everything arises in mutual relation to everything else" (1988, p. 229).

The octahedron as we have used it to understand the polarities of psychic experience is easily imagined into a fractal network of complexes (see Figure 17.1). A similar connection has already been made by Zinkin, Bohm, Peat, Wilbur and others. But, as we have seen in the few patterns already mentioned, self similarity, complexity and non-linear activity seem to be hallmarks of the activity of the collective unconscious (Zinkin, 1987; Bohm and Peat, 1987; Peat, 1991; Wilbur, 1985).

Figure 17.1 The fractal octahedron

Central to this study has been the pattern of the descent of the libido. The power of this single concept of Jung's is only now beginning to dawn upon me. Even when we talk of the self-referential and fractal properties of the other patterns, it appears that to a great extent we are talking about a pattern rooted in the descent of libido. This is a crucial avenue of study, it is the wheel that turns all the others and must become the center of further examination. From the biological to the sociological and spiritual levels of integration, it seems to be the key movement, against which all of the others are only variations on a theme.

I have not yet touched upon the reality of the archetype. This study has convinced me that because its existence is related to meaning and the nature of life, there may never be an adequate proof of either their existence or non-existence. Because they appear seemingly as emergents in complex phenomena, they will always be easily dismissed by those who seek more solid stuff. But, because they reappear consistently, and pattern perception and behavior at all levels of reality, they will always reappear as stumbling blocks to the empiricist. At this level they appear to be intimations of a different level of reality. Just as fractals and chaos theory intimate a different kind of ordering in the universe, so the archetype suggests a similar change on the level of pattern and meaning.

Andrew Samuels makes the interesting point that the archetypal is a perspective:

> The archetypal may be said to be found in the eye of the beholder and not in that which he beholds – an eye that interacts with images. The archetypal is a perspective defined in terms of its impact, depth, consequence and grip. The archetypal is in the emotional experience of perception and not in a pre-existing list of symbols.
>
> (Samuels, 1985, p. 53)

It is, however, unfortunate that this elegant formula does little to solve the riddle. Future research into the way complexes form, the spread of generalization in learning and other associative explorations will have to test the theory of archetypes on an empirical basis that is not possible here.

One of the implications of the theory of archetypes is that it is possible to target psychological and sociological interventions in such a way that they are congruent with belief and meaning structures in any individual or group. This is roughly equivalent to Jung's statement:

> [A] new adaptation or orientation of vital importance can only be achieved in accordance with the instincts. Lacking this, nothing durable results, only a convulsively willed, artificial product which proves in the long run to be incapable of life. No man can change himself into anything from sheer reason; he can only change into what he potentially is.
>
> (Jung, 1956/1967, para. 351)

All levels of human action are archetypally determined, from the instinctually driven Pavlovian conditional response to the heights of spiritual inspiration. Each partakes of the essential patterns of living systems. The identification of these primary patterns and their relation to any new behavior is always crucial to the acquisition of new behaviors or the shifting of others.

As we noted, from the Piagetian standpoint, learning consists in the assimilation of the new behavior to pre-existing schemata. From the Jungian perspective, we may translate this as learning consists in the assimilation of new behaviors to pre-existing complexes. For very young individuals learning is the assimilation of new behaviors to archetypal expectancies. The idea is rather like fitting round pegs in round holes. A round peg may fit in a star-shaped hole, but it will either be so small that it will fall out, or, if big enough, it will be damaged by the inner edges of the star. Neither case is satisfactory. The closer the fit, the longer the learning will last.

In some modern school systems the same basic logic has been applied. Here however, the libidinal drive takes the form of special interests which reveal the energized system (or centrated system) to which successful learning can be attached. Here, interest guides the learning process. All of the subjects come into the process of following a child's attempt to follow his interest. If a child is interested in building a house, he or she must read the instruction manual (reading), determine the necessary board feet of lumber (maths), and determine the angles for roofing, stairs, moldings, etc. (geometry). Education is related to the center of libido, the current driving interest. This is learning that lasts, because it taps into the center of libidinal activity.

In psychotherapy, a similar principle applies. Often the problem is addressed simply in terms of symptomatology, when in fact there are significant issues beyond the symptom that relate to archetypal drivers of the system that produces the symptom. Until this archetypal center is reached and an intervention applied, there can be no lasting results.

Ultimately, this relates to the principle of finding the center of the system (Bertalanffy's centration, again). Virginia Satir, Salvatore Minuchin and others teach that there is often one family member who is the controlling force in dysfunctional families. Once they have been dealt with, the family can often return to a normal level of interaction. Principally, we are talking about the same phenomenon, the archetypal core of the situation, embodied in a single individual's actions. Such centers are not always conscious. Therefore the psychologist must develop an archetypal science that will enable educators, therapists and social scientists to discover the center and direction of libidinal activity on any level of any system.

In the book, *Peace Child* (1974), Don Richards tells the story of a missionary who was frustrated by his inability to communicate with a relatively obscure non-industrial people. In that culture, significant value was placed upon the ability to use craft and deceit. One of the highest art forms that they acknowledged was the ability to deceive a friend. As a result, whenever he told them the Gospel story, Judas emerged as the hero. He was, after all, the most skilled of traitors. The missionary could find no means of overcoming this pattern until he discovered that another significant cultural element was embraced by the tradition of the peace child.

When the tribes warred with one another, there was often no possibility of peace. Since deceit and treachery were so highly valued, no overture of peace could be trusted. It was only when the headmen of the warring tribes were willing to give up their own children as hostages to the other camp in exchange for peace that a satisfactory conclusion could be made. Each chief had to place his most precious possession, his son, into the hands of a treacherous enemy in order to ensure the peace. Such peaces were frequently broken by the sacrifice of the children. Armed with this example, the missionaries used the obvious parallel with the Gospel and were able to effectively communicate their message.

The crucial issue here is that in every level of society there are mythical and cultural patterns that order human lives. If we begin with a broad understanding of the ideal types that occur within the culture, for that is exactly what the gods are, we are then provided with a significant tool for predicting, influencing or, at the very least, understanding behavior. What is suggested here is that the study of archetypes, as part of an integrated approach to the human sciences, can provide significant tools for communication and understanding. Someone who has become familiar with the expression of libidinal energies on several levels of experience develops a sensitivity to the underlying feeling tones by which they are differentiated one from another. With this tool, the tone associated with a set of behaviors leads straight to the root pattern.

It may, with some assurance, also be suggested that each society will be characterized not only by a specific set of archetypal patternings but by specific patterns that describe how each individual, group or society relates to another. At a very rudimentary level we have already seen how the gods of ancient Greece related one to another. This implies that, within Greek society, there was a strong possibility that individuals who constellate the pattern of one god will tend to associate with the other types in accordance with the pattern of that god. Thus, an Ares type might be strongly attracted by an Aphrodite type. He might likewise have real problems with father-figures, as Ares was the rejected son of Zeus. He might similarly be expected to compete with his brothers or intimates as Ares competed with Hephaistos for Aphrodite's affection. This also implies that the same kinds of behavior will follow the god's patterns as situations grow closer to the archetypal patterns related in the myths.

When a nation takes on the character of a god, we must also seek to determine the mythical patterns that it will act out. Jung's (1964/1970), Baynes's (1941) and Odjanyk's (1976) studies of the Nazi phenomenon reveal all too well how the gods are expressed at a national level. Diplomats can ill afford to be unaware of the behavior patterns that characterize the gods of the country with whom they have to deal, or the mythic patterns that shape the day to day reality of the people.

Nations enact archetypal roles as well. America as policeman to the world is an oft-reflected image. We need to understand how other nations characterize the Americans-as-police and themselves as either victims, criminals, prosecutors or bystanders. What specific roles do they act out in interaction with a policeman? How does their national role define the other countries with which they have to do? How is it expressed in their myths and symbols?

The question of the necessity of the archetype still remains with us. While we have associated it with the characteristics of living systems, and through living systems and Jung's definitions we have identified it as the source of meaning, we must still ask whether it is a necessary concept, or just one more intervening variable, one more power word or another unnecessarily complicated and complicating idea.

We have already said that the archetype *an sich* is no thing. It is an emergent property of living systems which, on each level of integration, gives expression to the basic attributes of life. It is only experienced subjectively and then in terms of a feeling tone that links images and actions in a meaningful manner. Whenever it is separated from feeling, the associations between the archetypal nodes become so unwieldy in their interconnectedness that all meaning is lost.

In the end, it is the continuing resonance of meaning, the constant reappearance of pattern and the recurrence of the familiar in every circumstance that recommends the archetype to our attention. That meaning and pattern exist suggests the existence of an underlying logos rooted in the structure of the universe itself. We know it intuitively. Our religions know it. We see it darkly in the recurring images of dream, myth and everyday existence. But just as we reach for it, it slips from our grasp, lost in some further complexity. Having traced a phenomenon evidenced in living systems at all levels, and as that phenomenon provides a consistent means of ordering and understanding the universe, we should hesitate to cast it off in favor of some less valuable reduction, lest in the process we diminish ourselves.

Notes

INTRODUCTION

1 Samuels (1989) refers to this reflexive nature of the psychological enterprise in *The Plural Psyche*.
2 Samuels (1985), p. 100.

1 THE NATURE OF THE ARCHETYPE

1 In this context, the anima/us represents not so much the internalized contra-sexual imprint, as a personification of the unconscious self.
2 I have been advised that the pejorative connotations of the word "contaminate" sometimes muddy the water in the context of archetypal expression. It is, how-ever, the term used in the English translations of Jung, von Franz and Neumann to express the intermingled nature of the archetypes, and their lack of any kind of conceptual "purity." I think that the term represents the Janus-faced nature of the attempt to define a pure type where none exists.
3 See pp. 17 and 59.
4 Fordham differentiates between the deintegrate, a natural subdivision of psychic function, and the products of disintegration or fragments. Deintegrates form an essential part of the developmental scheme of the psyche.
5 Libido, or libidinal activity, is the simple measure of energy afforded to any image or activity. Unlike Freud, Jung does not hang on it any specifically sex-ual connotation.
6 Psychoid was defined by Jung as a foundational biological state or condition below the level of the psyche that gives rise to psychic contents. Thus, the archetypes are the psychoid precursors of the archetypal images.
7 An autochthonic or autochthonous phenomenon appears independently, it is not obviously determined by the available causes and seems to spring indepen-dently from the earth.
8 The *Axis Mundi*, literally the world axis, is a universal theme identifying the meeting place of heaven and earth. It is closely related to the ideal of the world navel or *omphalos*.
9 The quaternio or quaternity refers to the recurring reflection of the four functions of consciousness in myth and image. The word refers generally to a pattern of four interrelated elements.
10 Lévi-Strauss compared the workings of the unconscious to the workings of the French bricoleur or handyman. This figure was known for his ingenious use of the odds and ends of past constructions in completely new contexts. In this

context "bricolage" refers to the reuse of previously acquired patterns in new circumstances.

11 Jung develops the idea of the self in terms of its expression on several different logical levels. First, it is the archetype of wholeness and the center of the psyche. Second, it is the existential whole, the entire psychic and somatic organism. Third, it represents in its teleological aspect the goal of the process of individuation.

12 Autopoiesis is the tendency of living systems to be self defining and self creating.

2 THE ARCHETYPAL DIMENSIONS

1 That is, a union of opposites.
2 IRM, Innate Release Mechanism, in ethology, that combination of eliciting stimulus and seemingly innate response system which has been used to explain specific kinds of apparently inborn or genetically determined response systems.

5 THE ARCHETYPAL SET

1 C. H. Waddington proposed that the development of an organism followed the contours of an epigenetic landscape or chreode in which the probable paths of development could be represented as deeper paths within a main developmental line (Lumsden and Wilson, 1981).
2 In Jungian usage, the self refers to the whole of the psyche. The SELF refers to the personalized aspect of the whole and the central archetype of order.
3 Like the term self, the psyche refers to the *whole* of the psychic apparatus, both conscious and unconscious.
4 Bricolage is applied by Lévi-Strauss to the manner in which the unconscious takes the data of conscious experience and uses it to construct new psychic edifices. See note 10, Chapter 1.
5 This discussion depends upon a full understanding of the concept of emergent properties found in the previous section.
6 J. J. Gibson theorized that perception and action depended upon properties of the world that were uniquely suited to the needs of an organism. These are real properties of physical objects, but they only take on meaning in terms of the observing, needing organism. One might say that the organism and the environment have been shaped together for their mutual affordances. In terms of this ecological psychology, the archetypes may be seen as providing the integration of perceptual possibilities that characterize affordances from the animal end (Gibson, 1977).
7 Eibl-Eibesfeldt (1990), Lumsden and Wilson (1981), Hinde (1983) and other authors have devoted long discussions to the effect of stimulus deprivation and early stimulus modification on sensory development in humans and other animals. With one voice they agree that the inborn component of perception is absolutely dependent upon environmental stimulation of a precisely determined kind for its proper development.
8 Scintillae are the archetypal sparks of consciousness at the core of every complex. Jung held the archetypes to be capable of expression as individual personalities (1960/1969).

6 THE ARCHETYPES AND THEIR IMAGES

1 The enantiodromia is the dance of opposites, the tendency for the ego to shift from one pole to its opposite in the comprehension of a new phenomenon.

2 The word self may represent any of three phases of the psychic system. First, it represents the individual as a whole. Second, it represents the central archetype, the archetype of order. Third, it represents the fullest realization of individual potential. All three overlap and intertwine, but are separated for the sake of clarity.

3 I call this manifestation of the self archetype the existential self.

4 Individuation is the Jungian process of psychic growth conceived as the realization of wholeness and fulfillment of the promised potential held out by the self as telos.

5 The nekyia is the technical term for the descent into the underworld.

6 The richness of these images and the ubiquity of the pattern is hinted at when we see the path applied as here to the introversion of libido, Samuels's (1989) application to the transference relations in therapy and our later application of the same pattern to social phenomena.

7 In the Inanna myth, the goddess travels to the underworld to redeem her brother. In the process she must surrender the seven tokens of her godhead and ultimately submit to death.

8 The citation of multiple versions for the interpretation of myth and fairy tales brings to mind Lévi-Strauss's similar practice as confirmation of the reliability of underlying unconscious processes to reveal themselves through the material (1962/1966).

9 Weltanschauung – a world view, perspective or attitude towards life.

10 A psychopomp is a leader of the souls of the dead in their journeys through the underworld.

11 The mural crown is a crown that looks like the wall of a fortified city.

12 The attributions of gods to signs are from Paul Christian's *The History and Practice of Magic*; the elementary attributions are from Israel Regardie's edition of Aleister Crowley's *777*. The need to consult different books arose from the sometimes erratic nature of Crowley's data with respect to the Greek gods.

7 THE SOCIOLOGICAL PROSPECT

1 We have purposefully not sought out the spiritual implications of the archetypal as it possesses an abundant and readily available literature.

2 In taking this tack, the author recognizes that there are problems both with Kuhn's idea of a paradigm and Ritzer's application of the view to sociology. Nevertheless, Ritzer's integrative approach will form the basis for defining our application of archetypal theory at the level of sociology.

8 THE PARADIGMS

1 Both Ritzer (1980) and Catlin (1938/1964) warn against the reification of the second kind of social fact as a distinctly non-Durkheimian proposition. They point to modern social factists as having generally fallen into the practice.

2 Buckley actually classes the modern functionalists with organic theories (1979, p. 13).

3 It is interesting to note that both Jung's and Piaget's conceptions of the origin

of consciousness similarly revolve about the separation of a stimulus-response chain and the resultant introduction of symbolic options. In their case, however, it seems to be more closely related to the separation between the IRM and the instinctual response, an unconditioned response paradigm. Conceptually, however, this is not a great distance.

4   Mead here anticipates an almost Piagetian relationship between abstraction and physical manipulation.

9   THE ROOTS OF INTERSUBJECTIVITY

1   Reification is the process whereby the world "loses its comprehensibility as a human enterprise and becomes fixated as a non-human, non-humanizable facticity. Typically the real relationship between man and his world is reversed in consciousness. Man, the producer of a world, is apprehended as its product" (Berger and Luckmann, 1967, p. 89).

2   See Part I.

3   Uroboric is a reference to the symbolic figure of the snake that swallows its own tail. It suggests a timeless and undifferentiated continuity, without beginning or end.

4   It is useful to recall at this point that the complex is the relatively dynamic field of personal experiences which gathers about an archetype. It is through the complex that the archetype at the core of the complex organizes behavior.

5   It should be noted that Lévi-Strauss's work, *The Savage Mind*, is aimed quite specifically at dispelling the notion that the mental habits of the non-industrialized peoples are unconscious or non-differentiated. While we believe that this is so to a much larger extent than Jung imagined, there is still such strong group identity in primitive circumstances that Jung's position remains valuable with only minor qualification.

6   It is difficult, if not impossible, in this day and age to give full credence to the demeaning and prejudiced observations that served as science a century ago. Nevertheless some of the social observations, especially those relating to the structure of society, still have a certain relevance.

7   William Irwin Thompson (1989/1990) makes the significant observation that the change observed by Jaynes was less a change from unconscious to conscious forms of action as it was a change to a more modern style of consciousness.

8   Libido and its strength may be understood as the level to which the life of an organism becomes centered on some activity. To the level that energy is diverted in the prosecution of some task we may say that the task is libidinally charged.

9   Throughout the application of Jung's observations to the realm of sociology, I will be using some very un-Jungian language, including the language of radical behaviorism. I believe that this is appropriate insofar as it provides a means of linking different logical levels and making the whole structure somewhat more understandable.

10 See the discussion of development in Part I.

11 One might argue that the perinatal union of infant and mother is an example of just such a physical unity.

11   FAMILIES, NATIONS AND THOUGHT

1   E.g., Jung's discursions on the physiognomy of the American people in paragraphs 93–9 of the same volume.

2 Lumsden and Wilson (1981) have estimated that a cultural trait takes about 1,000 years before it, or its closest biological precursors, becomes established in the gene pool by selection.

3 Jung's analysis preceded the publication of similar observations by anthropologist Lévi-Strauss by at least three years. This has led at least one author to accuse Lévi-Strauss of plagiarism. For a full discussion, see Eugene D'Aquili (1975) and Richard Gray (1991).

4 The vision is widely encountered in evangelical circles as is a prophetic interpretation of the Farewell Address. Charles Taylor records the vision as it appears in the 21 December 1950 issue of *Stars and Stripes* in his 1979 book, *World War III and the Destiny of America*.

5 Compare Ephesians 4:8: "when he ascended up on high, he led captivity captive, and gave gifts unto men."

6 Lincoln's rise from obscurity and his legendary homeliness further recall the messianic hymn in Isaiah 53.

7 The name is variously rendered as Stagolee, Stacker Lee, Staggerlee, etc. It is used here in accordance with Silverman.

8 We recall here Lévi-Strauss (1962/1966) and the primitive science of the concrete, and Jaynes's (1976) observation regarding the language in the *Iliad*.

12   THE STRUCTURE OF LARGE GROUPS

1 Here Jung is in complete accord with classical functionalism.

2 See Part I.

3 A more complete discussion of systems theory as applied to the Jungian psyche is provided in Part I.

4 While the archetype *an sich* is content-free, it is always expressed in terms of a content-filled image. This suggests that the abstract archetype represents a rule about the kinds of content that can be expressed by the feeling tone.

5 Throughout, following Jung's practice, I refer to the arising of Nazism as a German phenomenon. I am reminded by my associate, Florence Tomasulo, that Germany contains many diverse subcultures and the spread of National Socialism followed identifiable patterns in its spread through each. Moreover, we find its historic roots in Austria, a geopolitical unit quite distinct from Germany. For the sake of economy, however, our discussion will focus on the grosser unit.

6 This is by no means intended to say that the need for change has ceased to exist, or that the pace of change has not often lagged far behind the needs of the people. It is only a reflection of the fact that change has occurred and that there remains a mechanism within the system to make changes.

7 The ideal in this case may not be conscious. But imitation, contiguity and group pressure argue for the existence of a *de facto* white ideal.

8 See p. 291.

9 This data was gathered during an extensive personal interview with a Santera in Hudson County, New Jersey, during October 1989.

13   ARCHETYPAL PATTERNS IN LARGE GROUPS

1 It is important to reiterate that, although the Jungian system abounds with mystical events, the archetypal unity on the level of the collective unconscious was not conceived mystically but biologically in terms of the reflection of the instinct in consciousness. Further, there remains the common misconception

that the collective unconscious is operative as a world-soul. This could not be farther from the original conception. The collectivity here designated was only an expression of the common biological roots of human behavior, *not* a spiritual unity.

2 From the Jungian perspective, all groups find their root not only in a regressive mentality, but in religious feeling. Archetypal energy, the numinosum, tends to be expressed as religious energy. Primitive groups tend to retain the religious definitions that accompany everyday functions, but modern groups fail to acknowledge their essentially religious attachments to their groups.

3 A true symbol always represents an archetypal content that can never be made conscious. A derived symbol, as used here, is no less a symbol, but only focuses upon a different facet of the original. Like a hologram, each part of a symbol retains the image of the whole.

4 *Gleichschaltung* – conformation to a standard political or religious doctrine.

5 Charisma means literally a gift or anointing. In common English usage it has come to mean a magical appeal. The chrism, or (anglicized) the charism, is actually the oil or that which carries the gift. Here, however, it refers to the gift apart from any personal agency. In this context it is roughly equivalent to the idea of mana.

6 These specific elements are touched upon by Weber (1958) on pp. 105, 177 and 180.

7 That Weber discussed several brands of Christianity has not been lost sight of. We only reflect his emphasis on the Calvinistic pole.

8 The secondary symbol systems may be sects or new religions as well, but the emphasis here is on the secularization of religious material.

9 See p. 124.

10 See Chapter 9.

11 It was this possibility of a rebirth that seems to have led Jung to wait so long before condemning the Nazis, and the same hesitance which gave him the unwarranted reputation as a Nazi sympathizer. Jung consistently argued that the German people had been lured into psychosis by the ravings of a madman. It should also be noted that among the students of Jungian thought, Progoff (1953/1981) is the only one to have clearly identified the pattern of the regression of libido at the sociological level.

12 The secondary symbol systems may be sects or new religions as well, but the emphasis here is on the secularization of religious material.

15 REVIEW

1 While we recognize that Fordham did not use the term, the idea is present in his observation that every archetype reflects the whole (1957).

2 The secondary symbol systems may be sects or new religions as well, but the emphasis here is on the secularization of religious material.

17 PROSPECTS: FURTHER RESEARCH

1 Douglas Hoffstadter (1979) defines a strange loop as the phenomenon that occurs "whenever, by moving upwards (or downwards) through the levels of some hierarchical system, we unexpectedly find ourselves right back where we started" (p. 10).

References

Abrams, Denise, Reitman, Roger and Sylvester, Joan (1980). "The Paradigmatic Status of Sociology: Current Evaluations and Future Prospects." In George Ritzer, *Sociology: A Multiple Paradigm Science, Revised Edition* (pp. 266–87). Boston: Allyn and Bacon.

Aron, Raymond (1970). *Main Currents in Sociological Thought*, 3 vols (Richard Howard and Helen Weaver, trans.). New York: Doubleday.

Augros, Robert and Stanciu, George (1987). *The New Biology: Discovering the Wisdom in Nature*. Boston: Shambhala.

Bandler, Richard and Grinder, John (1975). *The Structure of Magic I*. Cupertino, CA.: Science and Behavior Books.

—— (1979). *Frogs into Princes*. Moab, UT: Real People Press.

Banville, Claude and Landry, Maurice (1989). "Can the Field of MIS be Disciplined: Social Aspects of Computing." *Communications of the ACM*, 32, 2: 48.

Baynes, H. G. (1941). *Germany Possessed*. New York: AMS Press.

Becker, Howard S. (1966). *Outsiders: Studies in the Sociology of Deviance*. New York: The Free Press.

Bellah, Robert N. (1975). *The Broken Covenant: American Civil Religion in Time of Trial*. New York: The Seabury Press.

Berger, Peter and Luckmann, Thomas (1967). *The Social Construction of Reality*. New York: Anchor Books.

Bertalanffy, Ludwig von (1968). *General Systems Theory*. New York: George Braziller.

Blair, Lawrence (1991). *Rhythms of Vision*. Rochester, VT: Destiny Books.

Blau, Peter (1964). *Exchange and Power in Social Life*. New York: John Wiley.

Bohm, David and Peat, F. David (1987). *Science Order and Creativity*. New York: Bantam.

Bolen, Jean Shinoda (1984/1985). *Goddesses in Every Woman*. New York: Harper and Row.

—— (1989/1990). *Gods in Every Man*. New York: Harper and Row.

Boulding, Kenneth E. (1966). *The Image: Knowledge in Life and Society*. Ann Arbor: University of Michigan Press.

Bowlby, John (1951). *Maternal Care and Mental Health*. New York: Columbia University Press. Cited by Stevens (1982/1983), p. 96.

—— (1958). "The Nature of the Child's Tie to his Mother." *International Journal of Psychoanalysis*, 39: 350–73.

Breger, Louis (1974). *From Instinct to Identity*. Englewood Cliffs, NJ: Prentice Hall.

Brooke, Roger (1991). *Jung and Phenomenology*. London: Routledge.

Broom, Leonard and Selznick, Philip (1963). *Sociology: A Text with Adapted Readings.* New York: Harper and Row.

Buckley, Walter (1979). *Sociology and Modern Systems Theory.* Englewood Cliffs, NJ: Prentice Hall.

Burell, Gibson and Morgan, Gareth (1979). *Sociological Paradigms and Organizational Analysis: Elements of the Sociology of Corporate Life.* London: Heinemann.

Campbell, Joseph (1949/1972). *The Hero with A Thousand Faces.* Princeton: Princeton University Press.

—— (1972/1988). *Myths to Live By.* New York: Bantam.

—— (1986). *The Inner Reaches Of Outer Space.* New York: Harper and Row.

—— (1988). *The Power of Myth.* New York: Doubleday.

—— (1990). "Myths from West to East." In Alexander Eliot, *The Universal Myths* (pp. 41–59). New York: Meridian.

Casey, E. (1974). "Towards an Archetypal Imagination." *Spring.*

Catlin, George E. G. (1938/1964). "Introduction to the Translation." In Emile Durkheim, *The Rules of the Sociological Method* (pp. ii–xxxvi). New York: The Free Press.

Chinoy, Ely and Hewit, John P. (1975). *The Sociological Perspective,* third edition. New York: Random House.

Christian, Paul (1963). *The History and Practice of Magic* (Ross Nichols, ed.). New York: Citadel.

Cirlot, J. E. (1962). *A Dictionary of Symbols.* New York: The Philosophical Library.

Compton, A. (1987). "Objects and Attitudes." *Journal of the American Psychoanalytic Association* 35, 3: 609–28.

Cornford, Francis MacDonald (1991). *From Religion to Philosophy: A Study in the Origins of Western Speculation.* Princeton: Princeton University Press.

Covey, Cyclone (1961). *The American Pilgrimage: The Roots of American History, Religion, and Culture.* New York : Collier Books.

Damasio, Antonio R. (1994). *Descartes' Error.* New York: G. P. Putnam.

D'Aquili, Eugene G. (1975). "The Influence of Jung on the Works of Lévi-Strauss." *The Journal of the History of Ideas,* XI: 41–6.

De Santillana, G. and von Dechend, H. (1969). *Hamlet's Mill.* Boston: Godine.

Dilts, Robert (1990). *Changing Belief Systems with NLP.* Cupertino, CA: Meta Publications.

Donovan, Denis M. (1989). "The Paraconscious." *The Journal of the American Academy of Psychoanalysis,* 17, 2: 223–51.

Durant, Will (1926). *The Story of Philosophy.* New York: Simon and Schuster.

Durkheim, Emile (1933/1964). *The Division of Labor in Society* (George Simpson, trans.). New York: The Free Press.

—— (1938/1964). *The Rules of the Sociological Method* (S. A. Solovay and J. H. Mueller, trans.). New York: The Free Press.

—— (1951/1966). *Suicide* (J. A. Spaulding and George Simpson, trans.). New York: The Free Press.

—— and Mauss, Marcel (1967). *Primitive Classification.* Chicago: University of Chicago Press.

Edinger, Edward F. (1972). *Ego and Archetype.* New York: Penguin.

Eibl-Eibesfeldt, Irenaeus (1990). *Human Ethology.* Alding DeGruyter.

Eliade, Mircea (1954/1971). *The Myth of the Eternal Return.* Princeton: Princeton University Press.

—— (1976). *Occultism, Witchcraft, and Cultural Fashions.* Chicago: The University of Chicago Press.

—— (1990). "Myths and Mythical Thought." In Alexander Eliot, *The Universal Myths* (pp. 14–40). New York: Meridian.

Ferm, Vergilius (1945). *An Encyclopedia of Religion*. New York: The Philosophical Library.

Fidler, Jay (1982). "The Holistic Paradigm and General Systems Theory." In *General Systems Theory and the Psychological Sciences*, Vol. 1 (Gray, Fidler and Battista, eds.). Seaside, California: General Systems Press.

Fishman, Daniel B., Rotgers, Frederick and Franks, Cyril (1988). *Paradigms in Behavior Therapy: Present and Promise*. New York: Springer Publishing.

Fordham, M. (1957). *New Developments in Analytical Psychology*. London: Routledge & Kegan Paul.

—— (1973/1980). *Analytical Psychology: A Modern Science*. London: Routledge & Kegan Paul.

—— (1981). "Neumann and Childhood.' *Journal of Analytical Psychology*, 26, 99–122.

Fox, Robin (1980/1983). *The Red Lamp of Incest*. Notre Dame, IN: Notre Dame University Press.

Fraiberg, Selma (1969). "Libidinal Object Constancy and Mental Representation." *Psychoanalytic Study of the Child*, 24: 9–47.

Frankfurt Institute for Social Research (1972). *Aspects of Sociology* (John Viertel, trans.). Boston: Beacon Press.

Freedman, David H. (1991). "Invasion of the Insect Robots." *Discover*, 12, 3, March.

Freud, Anna (1966). *The Ego and the Mechanisms of Defense*. New York: International Universities Press.

Freund, Julian (1969). *The Sociology of Max Weber*. New York: Pantheon.

Friedrichs, Robert (1970). *A Sociology of Sociology*. New York: The Free Press.

Frye, Northrop (1982). *The Great Code: The Bible and Literature*. New York: Harcourt Brace Jovanovich.

Fuller, R. Buckminster (1991). *Cosmography*. New York: Macmillan.

Furth, Hans G. (1969). *Piaget and Knowledge: Theoretical Foundations*. Englewood Cliffs, NJ: Prentice Hall.

Geigerich, W. (1975). "Ontogeny=Phylogeny? A Fundamental Critique of Neumann's Analytical Psychology." *Spring*, pp. 110–29.

Gerth, Hans and Mills, C. Wright (1946/1980). *From Max Weber: Essays in Sociology*. New York: Oxford University Press.

Giddens, Anthony (1982). *Capitalism and Modern Social Theory: An Analysis of the Writings of Marx, Durkheim and Weber*. New York: Cambridge University Press.

Ginsburg, Herbert and Opper, Sylvia (1969). *Piaget's Theory of Intellectual Development: An Introduction*. Englewood Cliffs, NJ: Prentice Hall.

Goldenberg, Naomi (1975). "Archetypal Psychology after Jung." *Spring*.

Goleman, Daniel (24 May 1988). "Personal Myths Bring Cohesion to the Chaos of Each Life." *The New York Times*, Sec. C, p. 1.

Gordon, Rosemary (1987). "Archetypes on the Couch." In *Archetypal Processes in Psychotherapy*. Wilmette, IL: Chiron Publications.

Gouldner, Alvin (1970). *The Coming Crisis of Western Sociology*. New York: Basic Books.

Graves, Robert (1955/1957). *The Greek Myths*. New York: George Braziller.

Gray, Richard (1991). "Jung and Lévi-Strauss Revisited: An Analysis of Common Themes." *The Mankind Quarterly*, XXXI, 3, Spring.

Greenberg, Joseph H. and Ruhlen, Merritt (1991). "Linguistic Origins of Native Americans." *Scientific American*, November, pp. 94–9.

Guggenbuhl-Craig, Adolf (1964). *Der Archetyp: The Archetype*. New York/Basle: Karger.

Halevi, Z. (1987). *Kabbalah and Psychology*. York Beach, ME: Samuel Weiser.

Hall, James A. (1977/1991). *Patterns of Dreaming*. Boston: Shambhala.

Hamlyn (pub.). (1959/1981). *The New Larousse Encyclopedia of Mythology*. New York: Hamlyn.

Hanna, Barbara (1981). *Encounters with the Soul: Active Imagination as Developed by C. G. Jung*. Los Angeles: Sigo Press.

Harding, Esther (1948/1973). *Psychic Energy: Its Source and Its Transformation*. Princeton: Princeton University Press.

Henderson, Jos. (1964). "The Archetype of Culture." In Adolph Guggenbuhl-Craig (ed.), *Der Archetyp: The Archetype* (pp. 3–14). Basel: S. Karger.

—— (1968). "Ancient Myths and Modern Man." In C. G. Jung (ed.), *Man and His Symbols* (pp. 95–156). New York: Doubleday.

—— (1984). *Cultural Attitudes in Psychological Perspective*. Toronto: Inner City Publishers.

Hillman, James (1972). *The Myth of Analysis*. Evanston, IL: Northwestern University Press.

—— (1975). *Loose Ends*. Dallas: Spring.

—— (1975/1977). *Revisioning Psychology*. New York: Harper Colophon.

—— (ed.). (1980/1988). *Facing the Gods*. Dallas: Spring.

—— (1980/1988a). "Dionysius in Jung's Writings." In James Hillman (ed.), *Facing the Gods*. Dallas: Spring.

—— (1980/1988b). "On the Necessity of Abnormal Psychology: Ananke and Athene." In James Hillman (ed.), *Facing the Gods*. Dallas: Spring.

—— (1983/1988). *Archetypal Psychology: A Brief Account*. Dallas: Spring.

Hinde, Robert (1983). *Biological Bases of Human Social Behavior*. New York: McGraw Hill.

Hirshman, Elizabeth (1990). "Secular Immortality and the American Ideology of Affluence." *Journal of Consumer Research*, 17, 1: 31.

Hobson, R. (1973). "The Archetypes of the Collective Unconscious." In Fordham (ed.), *Analytical Psychology: A Modern Science*. London: Routledge & Kegan Paul.

Hochman, Judy (1994). "Ahsen's Image Psychology." *Journal of Mental Imagery*, 18, 3–4: 1–118.

Hoffstadter, Douglas R. (1979). *Godel, Escher, Bach: An Eternal Golden Braid*. New York: Basic Books.

Hunt, Shelby D. (1992). "For Reason and Realism in Marketing." *Journal of Marketing*, 56, 2: 89.

Jacobi, Jolande (1974). *Complex, Archetype, Symbol in the Psychology of C. G. Jung*. Princeton: Princeton University Press.

Jaffe, Aniela (1984). *The Myth of Meaning in the Work of C. G. Jung* (R. F. C. Hull, trans.). Zurich: Daimon Verlag.

Jaynes, Julian (1976). *The Origin of Consciousness in the Breakdown of the Bicameral Mind*. Boston: Houghton Mifflin Co.

Jung, C. G. (1953/1966). *Two Essays on Analytical Psychology* (*CW7*). Princeton: Princeton University Press.

—— (1953/1968). *Psychology and Alchemy* (*CW12*). Princeton: Princeton University Press.

—— (1954/1966). *The Practice of Psychotherapy* (*CW16*) Princeton: Princeton University Press.

—— (1956/1967). *Symbols of Transformation* (*CW5*). Princeton: Princeton University Press.

—— (1958/1969). *Psychology and Religion* (*CW11*). Princeton: Princeton University Press.

—— (1959/1968a). *The Archetypes of the Collective Unconscious (CW9i)*. Princeton: Princeton University Press.

—— (1959/1968b). *Aion: Researches into the Phenomenology of the Self (CW9ii)*. Princeton: Princeton University Press.

—— (1960/1969). *The Structure and Dynamics of the Psyche (CW8)*. Princeton: Princeton University Press.

—— (1963/1970). *Mysterium Conjunctionis (CW14)*. Princeton: Princeton University Press.

—— (1964/1970). *Civilization in Transition (CW10)*. Princeton: Princeton University Press.

—— (1965). *Memories, Dreams, Reflections*. Princeton: Princeton University Press.

—— (1968a). *Alchemical Studies (CW13)*. Princeton: Princeton University Press.

—— (1968b). *Analytical Psychology: Its Theory and Practice*. New York: Vintage.

—— (ed.). (1968c). *Man and His Symbols*. New York: Doubleday.

—— (1969). *Psychology and Western Religion (CW11)*. Princeton: Princeton University Press.

—— (1971). *Psychological Types (CW6)*. Princeton: Princeton University Press.

—— and Kerenyi, C. (1949/1973). *Essays on a Science of Mythology*. Princeton: Princeton University Press.

Kirk, Russell (1974). *The Roots of American Order*. LaSalle, IL: Open Court.

Kirksey, Barbara (1980/1988). "Hestia: A Background of Psychological Focusing." In James Hillman (ed.), *The Gods Within*. Dallas: Spring.

Kugler, Paul (1983). *The Alchemy of Discourse: An Archetypal Approach*. Bucknell University Press.

Kuhn, Thomas (1969). *The Structure of Scientific Revolutions*. Chicago: University of Chicago Press.

Lambert, K. (1977). "Analytical Psychology and Historical Development in Western Consciousness." *Journal of Analytical Psychology*, 22, 1: 158–74.

Larsen, Stephen (1990). *The Mythic Imagination*. New York: Bantam.

Laski, Harold J. (1967). *Harold J. Laski on the Communist Manifesto: An Introduction Together with the Original Text and Prefaces by Karl Marx and Friedrich Engels*. New York: Mentor.

Laszlo, Irvin (1972). *Introduction to Systems Philosophy*. New York: Harper.

Laughlin, Charles D., McManus, John and D'Aquili, Eugene (1990). *Brain, Symbol and Experience: Toward a Neurophenomenology Of Human Consciousness*. Boston: New Science Library.

Leary, Timothy (1989). *Info-Psychology*. Las Vegas: Falcon Press.

Lester, David (1986). "Levels of Analysis in Systems Theories of Personality." *Psychology: A Quarterly Journal of Human Behavior*, 23, 2/3: 55–6.

—— (1987). "Systems Theories of Personality." *Psychology: A Quarterly Journal of Human Behavior*, 24, 3: 44–6.

Lévi-Strauss, Claude (1962/1966). *The Savage Mind*. Chicago: University of Chicago Press.

—— (1963). *Structural Anthropology*. New York: Harper Torchbooks.

Lumsden, Charles J. and Wilson, Edward O. (1981). *Genes, Mind, and Culture: The Coevolutionary Process*. Cambridge, MA: Harvard University Press.

Mahler, Margaret S., Pine, Fred and Bergman, Anni (1975). *The Psychological Birth of the Human Infant*. New York: Basic Books.

Mannheim, Karl (1936). *Ideology and Utopia* (Louis Wirth and Edward Shills, trans.). New York: Harvest Books.

Maquet, Jacques (1951). *The Sociology of Knowledge* (John F. Locke, trans.). New York: Beacon Press.

Marx, Karl and Engels, Friedrich (1967a). *The German Ideology* (R. Pascal, ed.). New York: International Publishers.

—— (1967b). *The Manifesto of the Communist Party*. In Harold J. Laski, *Harold J. Laski on the Communist Manifesto: An Introduction Together with the Original Text and Prefaces by Karl Marx and Friedrich Engels* (pp. 107–76). New York: Mentor.

Matoon, Mary Ann (1981/1985). *Jungian Psychology in Perspective*. New York: The Free Press.

Matthews, Boris (trans.) (1986). *The Herder Symbol Dictionary*. Wilmette, IL: Chiron Publications.

Maturana, Humberto and Varela, Francisco (1987). *The Tree of Knowledge: The Biological Roots of Human Understanding*. Boston: Shambhala.

Meltzoff, Andrew N. and Moore, M. Keith (1985). "Cognitive Foundations and Social Functions of Imitation and Intermodal Representation in Infancy." In Jacques Mehler and Robin Fox (eds), *Neonate Cognition: Beyond the Blooming Buzzing Confusion* (pp. 139–56). Hillsdale, NJ: Lawrence Erlbaum Associates.

Merton, Robert K. (1957/1967). *Social Theory and Social Structure*. New York: The Free Press.

Metzner, B., Burney, C. and Mahlberg, A. (1981). "Towards a Reformulation of the Typology of Functions." *The Journal of Analytical Psychology*, 26, 33–47.

Miller, David L. (1973/1980). *George Herbert Mead: Self, Language and the World*. Chicago: University of Chicago Press.

—— (1980/1988). "Red Riding Hood and Grand Mother Rhea: Images in a Psychology of Inflation." In James Hillman (ed.), *The Gods Within*. Dallas: Spring.

Mitroff, Ian I. (1983). "Archetypal Social Systems Analysis: On the Deeper Structure of Human Systems." *Academy of Management Review*, 8, 3: 387–97.

—— and Bennis, Warren (1989). *The Unreality Industry*. New York: Carol Publishing Group.

Moxnes, Paul (1987). "Deep Roles: An Archetypal Model of Organizational Roles." (Working paper, presented at the Third Conference on Organizational Symbolism in Corporate Culture, Milan, Italy, 26 June 1987.) Cited by Mitroff and Bennis, *The Unreality Industry*. New York: Carol Publishing Group.

Neumann, Erich (1954/1973). *The Origins and History of Consciousness*. Princeton: Princeton University Press.

—— (1955). *The Great Mother*. Princeton: Princeton University Press.

—— (1959/1974). *Art and the Creative Unconscious*. Princeton: Princeton University Press.

—— (1990). *Depth Psychology and a New Ethic* (E. Rolf, trans.). New York: Putnam.

Odjanyk, W. (1976). *Jung and Politics: The Political and Social Ideas of C. G. Jung*. New York: Harper and Row.

Pearson, Carol (1986/1989). *The Hero Within*. New York: Harper and Row.

Peat, F. David (1991). *The Philosopher's Stone*. New York: Bantam.

Perera, S. B. (1981). *Descent to the Goddess: A Way of Initiation for Women*. Toronto: Inner City Books.

Piaget, Jean (1970a). *Genetic Epistemology* (Eleanor Duckworth, trans.). New York: Columbia University Press.

—— (1970b). *Structuralism* (Chaninah Maschler, trans.). New York: Basic Books.

—— (1971). *Psychology and Epistemology* (Arnold Rosin, trans.). New York: Grossman Press.

—— and Inhelder, Barbel (1969). *The Psychology of the Child* (Helen Weaver, trans.). New York: Basic Books.

Plaut, A. (1975). "Object Constancy or Constant Object?" *Journal of Analytical Psychology*, 20, 2: 207–15.

Pribram, Karl H. (1984). "Emotion: A Neurobiological Approach." In Sherer, Klaus R. and Ekman, Paul (eds), *Approaches to Emotion*. Hillsdale, NJ: Erlbaum, p. 15.

Progoff, Ira (1953/1981). *Jung's Psychology and its Social Meaning*. New York: Dialog House Library.

—— (1959). *Depth Psychology and Modern Man*. New York: The Julian Press.

—— (1987). *Jung, Synchronicity and Human Destiny*. New York: The Julian Press.

Redfearn, J. W. T. (1973). "The Nature of Archetypal Activity: The Integration of Spiritual and Bodily Experience." *Journal of Analytical Psychology*, 18, 2: 127–45.

Regardie, Israel (ed.) (1973/1988). *777 and Other Qabalistic Writings of Aleister Crowley*. York Beach, ME: Samuel Weiser.

Reiser, Morton F. (1984). *Mind, Brain, Body: Toward a Convergence of Psychoanalysis and Neurobiology*. New York: Basic Books.

—— (1990). *Memory in Mind and Brain*. New York: Basic Books.

Richards, Don (1974). *Peace Child*. Ventura, CA: Regal.

Ritzer, George (1980). *Sociology: A Multiple Paradigm Science*. Boston: Allyn and Bacon.

Rucker, Rudy (1987). *Mind Tools*. Boston: Houghton Mifflin Co.

Samuels, Andrew. (1983). "The Theory of Archetypes in Jungian and Post-Jungian Analytical Psychology." *International Review of Psychoanalysis*, 10, p. 430.

—— (1985). *Jung and the Post-Jungians*. New York: Routledge & Kegan Paul.

—— (1989). *The Plural Psyche*. London: Routledge.

—— (1993). *The Political Psyche*. London: Routledge.

Schutz, Alfred (1967). *The Phenomenology of the Social World* (George Walsh and Frederick Lehnert, trans.). Evanston, IL: Northwestern University Press.

Shaw, Robert and Bransford, John (eds) (1977). *Perceiving, Acting and Knowing: Toward an Ecological Psychology*. Hillsdale, NJ: Erlbaum.

Sherer, Klaus R. and Ekman, Paul (eds) (1984). *Approaches to Emotion*. Hillsdale, NJ: Erlbaum.

Silverman, Charles E. (1978/1980). *Criminal Violence, Criminal Justice*. New York: Vintage Books.

Skinner, B. F. (1957). *Verbal Behavior*. Englewood Cliffs, NJ: Prentice Hall.

—— (1965). *Science and Human Behavior*. New York: Free Press.

—— (1969). *Contingencies of Reinforcement*. Englewood Cliffs, NJ: Appleton Century Crofts.

Sorokin, Pitrim (1985/1991). *Society, Culture and Social Change*. New York: Harper.

Spitz, Rene (1965). *The First Year of Life*. New York: International University Press.

Stein, L. (1967). "Introducing Not-Self." *Journal of Analytical Psychology*, 12, 2: 97–114.

Stein, Murray (1980/1988). "Hephaistos: A Pattern of Introversion." In James Hillman (ed.), *The Gods Within*. Dallas: Spring.

Stevens, Anthony (1982/1983). *Archetypes: A Natural History Of The Self*. New York: Quill.

—— (1986). "Thoughts on the Psychology of Religion and the Neurobiology of Archetypal Experience." *Zygon*, March 21, 1: 9–29.

Stewart, Louis (1987). "Affect and Archetypes in Analysis." In *Archetypal Processes in Psychotherapy*. Wilmette, IL: Chiron Publications.

Stewart. R. J. (1989). *The Elements of Creation Myth*. Shaftesbury, Dorset: Element Books.

Taylor, Charles R. (1979). *World War III and the Destiny of America*. Nashville: Sceptre.

The New English Bible (1961/1970). New York: Oxford University Press, Cambridge University Press.

Thompson, W. (1971). *At the Edge of History*. New York: Harper and Row.

—— (1989/1990). *The Imaginary Landscape: Making Worlds of Myth and Science*. New York: St. Martin's Press.

Tiger, Lionel and Fox, Robin (1971/1989). *The Imperial Animal*. New York: Henry Holt.

Timasheff, N. S. and Theodorson, G. A. (1976). *Sociological Theory: Its Nature and Growth*. New York: Random House.

Von Franz, Marie-Louise (1970). *The Interpretation of Fairytales*. Dallas: Spring.

—— (1972/1986). *Creation Myths*. Dallas: Spring.

—— (1974). *Number and Time*. Evanston, IL: Northwestern University Press.

—— (1978). *Time: Rhythm and Repose*. New York: Thames and Hudson.

—— (1980a). *On Divination and Synchronicity: The Psychology of Meaningful Chance*. Toronto: Inner City Books.

—— (1980b). *Redemption Motifs in Fairytales*. Toronto: Inner City Books.

—— (1980/1988). *Projection and Re-Collection*. LaSalle, IL: Open Court.

—— and Hillman, James (1971). *Lectures on Jung's Typology*. Dallas: Spring.

Wagner, Helmut (1970). *Alfred Schutz on Phenomenology and Social Relations*. Chicago: University of Chicago Press.

Wallich, Paul (1991). "Silicone Babies." *Scientific American*, December, 126.

Weber, Max (1958). *The Protestant Ethic and the Spirit of Capitalism* (Talcott Parsons, trans.). New York: Charles Scribner's Sons.

—— (1962/1980). *Basic Concepts in Sociology* (H. P. Secher, trans.). Secaucus, NJ: Citadel Press.

—— (1968/1978). *Economy and Society* (Guenther Roth and Claus Wittich, eds). Berkeley: University of California Press.

Whitmont, E. (1969). *The Symbolic Quest*. London: Barrie and Rockliff.

Wilbur, Ken (1985). *The Holographic Paradigm and Other Paradoxes*. Boston: Shambhala.

Wilhelm, Richard (1971). *I Ching or Book of Changes* (Cary F. Baynes, trans.). Princeton: Princeton University Press.

Williams, Mary (1963). "The Indivisibility of the Personal and Collective Unconscious." In Michael Fordham, *Analytical Psychology: A Modern Science*. London: Routledge & Kegan Paul.

Yates, Frances (1966). *The Art of Memory*. Chicago: University of Chicago Press.

Zinkin, Leonard (1987). "The Hologram as a Model For Analytical Psychology." *Journal of Analytical Psychology*, 32, 1–21.

Index

a priori 28, 51, 164
accommodation, assimilation 5, 23, 26ff, 30ff, 35ff, 41, 45ff, 53ff, 62, 64, 77, 258ff, 268, 284
Achilles 41
action theory 141
adaptation 23, 25, 25ff, 29, 39, 218, 258, 283
adolescence 172
Adorno, Theodor 151
affect image 52ff, 61f
affective tone 17, 19, 33, 54f, 58, 64, 260f, 268, 279
ages of man 281
aggregates 22, 25, 43
Agrippa, Cornelius 59
AI *see* artificial intelligence
alchemical wheel 281
alchemy, alchemist 13, 15, 96
algorithm 44
alienation 179, 268, 278
America, American 111, 183, 186, 189ff, 198, 222, 225, 232, 240, 246, 253f, 266, 275, 286
amoeba 39, 261
anima, animus 7, 11, 15, 72f, 80, 83ff, 88ff, 98ff, 109f, 168f, 177, 182, 206, 261
animal 18, 57
Aphrodite 107, 118f, 285
Apollo 107, 113f, 119
apperception 56
apprehension 36, 42, 56
arcana 60
archetypal constellation 115
archetypal dominants 115
archetypal field 12, 20, 52, 61, 71, 93, 113, 194, 232

archetypal image 5, 21, 24, 27, 47f, 51, 57, 63, 65, 69, 72, 88, 177, 210, 214, 257ff, 265ff, 275, 281
archetypal intent 57
archetypal mechanisms 7, 28
archetypal psychology 52, 105, 106
archetypal sequence 67
archetype *an sich* 2, 11, 20, 51, 63, 65, 260, 286
archetype, archetypal, 2, 4ff, 11ff, 27f, 31ff, 42, 46ff, 50ff, 67, 69, 71f, 75, 77f, 84, 88ff, 92ff, 101, 105f, 109, 111, 115f, 119ff, 125, 159, 164ff, 168, 176ff, 182, 184, 187, 190f, 196, 203f, 206f, 210f, 213ff, 228ff, 233f, 250, 257ff, 272ff
Ares 101, 119, 285
Artemis 101, 107, 109f, 118f
artificial intelligence (AI) 44, 64, 259
atemporal 34
Athena 107, 109f, 116, 118f
Augros, Robert and Stanciu, George 28–9
autochthonous 50
autonomy 146, 157, 200, 228, 264, 266, 275
autopoiesis 29, 41
axiom of Maria, 41
axis mundi 18, 36, 40
axis, axes 18, 30, 31, 36ff, 40ff, 59

"Bad Nigger" myth 192
barbarian 270
Bavaria 251
Baynes, H. G. 3, 286
Becker, Howard 253
behavioral science 3
behaviorism 26, 146, 149

Bellah, Robert N. 191, 195
Berger, Peter and Luckmann, Thomas 144, 263, 274f, 279
Bergson, Henri 24
Bertalanffy, Ludwig 22f, 27, 29, 37, 258, 284
biology, biological 3ff, 7, 13, 15, 17, 20, 25ff, 29, 32, 35, 39ff, 47, 51f, 54, 56f, 62ff, 90, 116, 258ff, 265, 279, 281, 283
bipolar, bipolarity 13, 31ff, 63, 76, 257
Bishop 208
Blair, Lawrence 1
Blau, Peter 149, 154
Bohm, David 282
Bolen, Jean Shinoda 109, 110, 111, 188
Boulding, Kenneth E. 57
boundaries 6, 25
Bowlby, John 63, 251
brain 4f, 15, 24, 34, 51
brain stem 24
bricolage, bricoleur 26, 72, 266
Brooke, Roger 4, 47, 52
Brooks, Rodney 44ff
Buckminster Fuller, R. 43

Calvinist, Calvinism 238
Camillo, Giulio 60
Campbell, Joseph 97, 187, 261, 282
canon, 167, 191f, 196, 216ff, 221f, 229, 234, 265ff, 270, 274, 276
Carver, George Washington 190
Casey, Edward 53, 59, 60, 65, 109, 260
castle 40
Catholic 188
causal interpretation 139
center 12, 16, 18, 22f, 34, 40, 42, 44, 53, 59ff, 116, 231, 261, 268, 279f, 284
centration/diffusion 22f, 27, 29f, 32, 34, 37, 40ff, 58, 61f, 64, 258f, 284
chaos, chaotic attractors 281ff
charisma 269, 274
chick, chicken 47, 48, 259
child 35, 40, 42, 45, 47f, 113, 165, 167, 172, 175, 181, 183, 254, 261, 264f, 273, 276, 284f
childish milieu 177
Christ 236
Christian, Christianity 118, 190, 204, 211, 213, 219, 220, 235ff, 238, 240, 242, 246, 249, 251, 270
Christian, Paul 235, 237, 240, 246
church 40, 188f, 200
Cirlot, J. E. 62

city 18, 37, 40, 42
coercion 263, 277
coevolution 14, 19
cognitypes 92f
collective canon, 268, 276, 278
collective consciousness 6, 133, 185, 188, 192, 196f, 215ff, 229, 239, 242, 247, 254, 266, 268, 273, 275, 278f
collective shadow 219, 226, 253, 278
collective unconscious 6f, 11, 13, 19, 21, 34f, 39, 50, 61, 63, 70f, 80, 82f, 85, 89, 91ff, 99, 101f, 109, 118, 164, 166ff, 169, 177, 181, 184f, 187f, 194ff, 197, 205f, 211, 214ff, 217, 220, 230ff, 235f, 239, 241, 243f, 247f, 257, 261, 266, 269ff, 272ff, 276, 279, 282
Columbus, Christopher 18
common sense 200, 268
communism 240
community 44, 161, 208, 270, 275
compensations 265, 276, 279
complex, complexes 5, 19, 20, 22f, 27, 28, 34, 35, 36, 41, 53, 58, 63, 70, 74, 80f, 83ff, 88ff, 104f, 153, 167, 169, 173, 177ff, 269, 279, 280, 282, 283, 284
complexio oppositorum 276
Compton, A. 35
compulsion 16, 23, 99, 169, 177, 179, 234, 251f, 258
compulsive crimes 251
condensation 51
conformity 168, 179, 273
conscious, consciousness 2, 4ff, 11ff, 16, 19, 21ff, 28f, 33ff, 41f, 51ff, 58, 61ff, 77, 96, 102, 154, 166, 172, 188, 200, 215, 218f, 222, 226, 232, 248, 257ff, 261f, 266, 268ff, 273ff, 277ff, 284
consensual validity 267, 274, 275
consensus 134, 265, 269
constellate, constellation 33, 35, 48, 51, 56f, 63, 84f, 87, 96, 105, 111, 113, 115ff, 120, 153, 166, 172, 181, 187, 197, 203, 216f, 220, 225, 231, 235, 244, 254, 265, 274, 285
Constitution 163, 191, 221f, 247f, 274
contaminated 11, 20, 63, 64, 257
content 19, 21, 26, 28, 33, 46, 47, 51, 55, 56, 61, 64, 83, 86, 91, 105, 125, 233, 247, 251, 262, 277
continuity 28, 41, 275
contradict, contradiction 31, 34, 76, 87,

152, 155ff, 188, 209, 232, 248, 264f,
    269, 276
co-ordinating, co-ordination 51
Cornford, Francis MacDonald 59, 109,
    196, 281
correspondence, correspondences 14,
    15, 17, 20, 35, 59, 64
creation 2, 17, 40, 276
creativity 217
crime, criminality 250, 252
crisis 127, 129, 270
criteria 18, 19
cross cultural 7
crystal, crystals 28, 40, 51, 55
cultural canon 167, 191, 196, 216ff, 234,
    266, 268, 274, 276
cultural milieu 265
cultural transmission 17, 50, 63, 257
culture 6, 11, 13f, 19, 28, 36, 78, 88ff,
    104, 106, 110, 133, 150ff, 161, 164,
    167, 170ff, 175, 182f, 185ff, 191ff,
    196f, 202f, 206, 209, 211ff, 216, 222,
    225f, 229f, 253f, 266, 268, 273, 276,
    279, 284, 285
culturgens 19
cybernetic 146, 157, 264

Damasio, Antonio R. 5
dark image 52, 53, 57, 62, 65, 260
de Santillana, G. and von Dechend, H.
    17, 18, 58, 59
death 3, 17, 34, 275
deintegrate, deintegration 12, 21, 22f,
    27, 33, 71, 81, 87
Demeter-Persephone 101, 103, 107,
    114, 117ff, 206
development, developmental 70, 74,
    126, 142, 164, 172, 173, 202, 216, 228,
    233, 238, 251, 259, 260, 265, 266, 272,
    276
deviance, deviant 157, 254, 264, 271
dialectic, dialectical 32, 83, 146, 157,
    197, 233, 264, 266, 276
diffusion 29, 30, 34, 40, 41, 62, 258
Dilts, Robert 184
Dionysius 101, 107, 113ff, 118, 120
discrimination (racial or sexual) 189,
    221, 278
discrimination of opposites 33, 91
diurnal cycles 15
Divine Husbandman 195
division of labor 134f, 137, 153, 171,
    201, 207

dominance 259, 261, 274
Donovan, Denis M. 41
dragon 55, 261
dreams 11, 18, 50, 53
Durkheim, Emile 6, 44, 132ff, 141, 148,
    150, 162, 171, 199, 263f, 273, 275
dynamic 5, 6, 21, 23, 33, 194, 274
dynatypes 93
dysfunctions 278

earth 37, 40, 42, 61
economy 81, 207
Edinger, Edward 12, 231, 233, 239
education 18, 221, 267, 284
ego 21, 22, 27, 28, 34, 40, 41, 69, 72, 75,
    81f, 85, 87ff, 91, 94ff, 99ff, 109, 122,
    167, 172, 173, 184, 214ff, 216, 218f,
    222, 229, 233, 247f, 248, 261f, 268ff,
    274f
ego development 81, 87, 167, 172
elan vital 24
Eliade, Mircea 36, 40, 42, 59, 60, 187, 281
emergent, emergent property 4, 22f, 25,
    43ff, 47f, 51, 54, 65, 69, 73f, 104, 142,
    149f, 239, 248, 259, 260, 278, 280,
    283, 286
emotion, emotions, emotional 13, 20,
    24, 33, 70, 84, 92, 102f, 106, 110, 115,
    136, 139, 170ff, 177, 188, 193, 200,
    202, 242, 245, 251, 283
energy 70, 91, 228, 237, 247, 257, 258,
    261, 262, 267, 269, 270, 281
Engels, Friedrich 240, 278
English 186
entelechy 24
environmental factors 2
epigenesis, epigenetic landscape 2, 19,
    154, 264
equilibration 23, 27, 28, 29, 30, 258
ergotrophic/trophotropic 34, 37
Eros and Thanatos 34, 259
ethnic groups 72, 181f, 185ff, 220, 225,
    229, 234, 261, 268
ethology, ethological 4, 35, 47, 65, 74,
    259
Euglena 39
Eurasiatic/Nostratic 280
exchange theory 148
excluded groups 155, 220
executive 209, 215, 218ff, 229, 234f,
    247f, 268f, 274f, 278
expect, expected, expectation 35, 46,
    48, 63, 65, 260, 265

extinction 147
extrovert 77, 211

facticity 263, 266, 277
fairy tale 11, 19, 88f, 101
family 71, 74, 92, 110, 135, 150, 162,
   164, 169, 174ff, 177f, 181f, 185, 189f,
   197, 203, 227, 236, 256, 265, 284
family constellation, 181, 197
fascinens 16
father 11, 15, 20, 46, 69, 75, 84f, 89f,
   91f, 169, 171, 177ff, 181ff, 189f, 204,
   206, 240, 285
feeling 16, 20, 58, 75ff, 132, 139, 146,
   162, 168, 170f, 174, 176, 178, 180,
   183, 188, 200, 202, 211ff, 226, 242,
   253, 259, 270, 272, 285f
feeling tone 5, 12, 19f, 28, 53, 58, 61f,
   90ff, 285f
Fidler, Jay 22
field 12, 16, 20, 41, 52, 61, 91, 93, 125,
   150
First World War 243, 270
Fishman, Daniel 43, 44
focus, foci 12, 16, 22, 29, 34, 40, 41, 59,
   61, 116, 248, 258, 259, 261, 267, 268,
   269, 270
Fool 82
Fordham, Michael 4, 12, 20ff, 27f, 35,
   46ff, 61, 74f, 81f, 87, 90, 164, 167,
   173, 192, 258, 261, 272, 282
fractal, fractals 281ff
fragmentation, 247, 268f
Fraiberg, Selma 35, 54
Frankfurt School *see* Adorno
Freedman, David H. 44f, 260
freedom 36, 273
Freud, Sigmund 34
Frobenius, Leo 94
Frye, Northrop 193
functionalism, functionalist 22, 131,
   134ff, 138, 153, 163
functions 6, 12, 21, 30, 34ff, 40ff, 63,
   69f, 76ff, 82, 85, 91, 95, 98, 119f, 155f,
   167, 171, 201ff, 206, 211ff, 213, 229,
   233f, 247f, 258, 267f, 278, 281
fundamental image 128, 131
Furth, Hans G. 4, 39

German, Germanic, Germans,
   Germany 3, 18, 104, 111, 118, 120,
   186, 220, 231, 241ff, 248, 251, 270
Giddens, Anthony 151, 186

Ginsburg, Herbert and Opper, Sylvia
   26, 45
gnosis 31
Gnostic 64
goal directedness 16
god, goddess 4, 12f, 32, 40, 58ff, 83f,
   86f, 89, 91f, 97, 100ff, 117ff, 171,
   188ff, 193ff, 214, 224, 228, 231, 237ff,
   241f, 285f
Goldenberg, Naomi 52
goodness of fit 38, 260
Gospel 285
government 200, 209, 216, 221, 236,
   240, 247, 266, 267, 275, 277
great mother 18, 261
Great Treatise 195
Greenberg, Joseph H. and Ruhlen,
   Merrit 280
group shadow 223, 229, 268, 274f
group, groups 6f, 11, 13f, 72, 89, 101,
   106, 111, 120f, 125, 128, 133, 135f,
   137f, 142f, 154ff, 161ff, 164f, 167ff,
   170ff, 174, 176ff, 179, 181, 185ff, 187,
   191, 197, 199ff, 204ff, 207, 210, 211f,
   214, 215ff, 218ff, 223ff, 226ff, 230ff,
   234, 247f, 251ff, 263ff, 283, 285

Halevi, Z. 40, 60
Hall, James A. 12, 20, 40
hand 47, 92, 142
healer 18
heaven 37, 40, 61
Hebrew 60
Hecate 114, 117f
heirs 181
helpful animal 18
Henderson, Joseph 3, 78, 184, 277, 281
Hephaistos 101, 107, 119, 285
Hera 107
Hermes 101, 107, 113, 116ff
hero 18, 94ff, 100, 187, 189, 204, 206,
   215, 254, 262, 285
hero's journey 94ff, 121, 173, 241, 262
Hestia, 107, 116, 259
hexagrams 195
hierarchical organization 22f, 71, 77,
   107, 137
hierarchy, hierarchies 23, 64, 69, 264,
   280
hierophany 59
Hillman, James 1, 5, 28, 52f, 55, 58f, 65,
   72, 77, 93, 105f, 109, 111, 114ff, 119,
   121, 188, 260ff, 281

Hinde, Robert 47, 259
Hirshman, Elizabeth 191
Hobson, R. 18, 260
Hochman, Judith 5
holistic 22, 26, 34, 151
holograph, holography, holographic
    metaphor 22, 210, 261, 282
Homans, George 148, 149
home 18, 37
homo sapiens 57
Husserl, Edmund 143
hypothalamus 34

ideal type 285
identification 48, 99, 105, 115, 118, 163,
    167f, 170, 172, 174ff, 177ff, 185, 199,
    202f, 218, 230, 262f, 265, 284
Iliad 102
image of the subject matter 128, 131,
    263
image, images 2, 5, 7, 16, 18, 21, 47f,
    50ff, 54ff, 58ff, 60ff, 63ff, 65, 69, 72,
    87f, 92, 128, 131, 177, 183, 192, 200,
    214, 226, 257ff, 263, 265ff, 272, 275,
    281, 283, 286
imaginal 34, 52, 58, 60, 109, 115
imago, imagos 63, 69, 72, 74, 84, 90,
    183f, 214, 265
imitation 176, 179, 180, 230, 246, 265,
    273
imprint, imprinting 20, 47f, 62, 90, 168f,
    175, 183ff, 197, 214, 259f, 265
individuality 175, 202, 264, 273
individuation 21f, 28, 31, 33, 70, 72, 76,
    80, 82, 85, 88ff, 94, 100, 102, 113f,
    121f, 163, 175, 202, 261, 262, 265, 277
inertia 46, 217
inferior function 41, 75f, 120, 201, 212
initiation 197, 265, 276
initiatory response 184
innate release mechanism (IRM) 35,
    62, 90, 164, 279
Innocent 98
instinct 2, 4, 12ff, 20, 24, 33f, 64, 272,
    277, 281
institutions 135ff, 144f, 149, 151, 153ff,
    157, 172, 195, 197, 200f, 204, 208,
    217, 220ff, 233, 254, 263, 267, 275
interactions 3, 5, 11, 22, 25, 27, 30, 43,
    45, 46, 49, 51, 56, 62, 216, 260, 272
interactive style 62, 65, 261
intersubjectivity 143ff, 153, 156, 161,
    174f, 263f, 272, 279

introvert 77, 211
intuition 24, 75, 78, 84, 152, 171, 194,
    196, 202, 212, 230, 243
intuitive validity 188, 267, 275
irritability 29, 258

Jacobi, Jolande 12, 90, 93, 215
Janus 13, 63f, 232, 257
Jaynes, Julian 101f, 171
Jesus of Nazareth 235
Joshua 97
Jungian sociology 3, 6

Kabbalah 40, 45, 261
Kerenyi, Carl 94, 113ff, 117ff
Kether 40
Kirksey, Barbara 259
Kore 92, 114, 117f
Kugler, Paul 280
Kuhn, Thomas 4, 8, 126ff, 130, 263

Lamarckian 181
Lambert, K. 188, 189
language 4, 18, 55, 85, 141f, 145, 150,
    157, 164, 175, 185f, 193, 197, 227,
    264, 266f, 276f, 280
Lazlo, Erwin 22
Leary, Timothy 34, 37, 184
legitimation 145, 156f, 194f, 196, 208,
    234ff, 264, 274
Lester, David 22
Lévi-Strauss, Claude 6, 21, 32, 37, 171f,
    186f
libido 5f, 12, 16, 20, 22, 28, 59, 63, 70f,
    74, 76ff, 88, 92, 94ff, 99, 101, 114,
    121, 163, 169f, 173, 177, 179, 233,
    236f, 241, 244f, 247f, 250, 257f, 260ff,
    265f, 269f, 273, 275f, 281, 283ff
limbic 5, 24
Lincoln, Abraham 190
linguistics 26, 277
living matter 15, 24, 51
living systems 4, 19, 23, 25, 28ff, 32ff,
    38f, 41, 46, 56ff, 64f, 70, 77, 109, 116,
    125, 258ff, 280, 284, 286
Logos 15, 17, 84, 107, 286
love generation, 183
Lumsden, Charles J. and Wilson,
    Edward O. 14, 19, 48, 49, 62

Magellan, Ferdinand 1
Mahler, Margaret S. 35
mandala 18, 40, 86, 92, 100, 206

manifest function 155, 278
Mannheim, Karl 152, 170, 200, 278
map 2, 3, 13, 24, 36, 60, 127
Maria Prophetessa 41
Martyr 99
Marx, Karl 109, 141, 150ff, 186, 278
Marxist 145, 151, 152, 171
mass instincts 243
maternal archetype 36, 48, 168
Maturana, Humberto and Varela,
    Francisco 5, 29
mature science 263
Maya 84
McAdams, Dan 107
Mead, George Herbert 4, 141f, 150,
    163, 186
meaning 4ff, 13, 16, 18, 21, 26f, 33, 36f,
    40ff, 45f, 50f, 54f, 57ff, 63, 65, 71, 76,
    78, 86ff, 89, 91ff, 98, 104, 106, 109f,
    121f, 125, 138ff, 143f, 150, 153, 170,
    185, 187ff, 193, 197, 203ff, 209, 215,
    222, 228, 231ff, 239, 248, 257ff, 262,
    266f, 273, 278f, 283, 286
mechanical solidarity 133f, 171, 173
Mediatrix 107
Merton, Robert 136, 278
Messiah 107
metaphor, metaphorical 35, 41, 54ff,
    57ff, 61, 65, 82, 105f, 109, 114f, 121,
    193, 260, 262, 279, 282
Metzner, B. 76, 120
Mexico 18
Miller, David L. 4, 105, 141, 165, 262
minority group 192, 219, 225, 228f, 248,
    252, 265, 268f
Minuchin, Salvatore 284
missionary 284
Mitroff, Ian 204f, 210, 227
mnemotechnicians 60
Moirae 59
moon 15, 60
morality 182, 251, 281
Moses and Khidr 97
mother 11, 15, 18, 20, 28, 35f, 46ff, 51,
    69, 84f, 88ff, 95ff, 107, 121, 154, 164,
    167ff, 175ff, 180ff, 188, 190, 206, 214,
    218, 251, 259, 261, 264f, 272, 280
motif 11, 14, 16ff, 40, 50, 63, 75, 86f, 89,
    96, 98f, 100, 157
mutual contamination 4, 17, 20ff, 61,
    63, 113, 257f
mystical 25, 244
myth, mythic, mythical 1, 6, 11f, 17ff,

36, 50, 52, 55, 58, 75, 85f, 88f, 94,
    96ff, 100f, 103ff, 109, 111, 113, 116ff,
    173, 183, 185f, 187ff, 192ff, 206, 208,
    215f, 219, 229, 231, 242, 254, 266,
    268, 273f, 276, 279, 285f

national pathology 220
National Socialism 120, 220, 241, 244,
    248, 270, 299
neonate, neonatal 35, 46ff, 164f, 167ff,
    174ff, 180, 223
net of Indra 261, 282
Neumann, Erich 3, 6, 74, 80, 82, 167,
    182, 216f, 219, 221, 223f, 226f, 250,
    252f, 274, 276,
Neurolinguistic Programming (NLP)
    176
neurotic crime 251
non-homogeneity 54, 59f, 281
normative science 128
norms 135f, 149f, 155
numen, numinous, numinosity 5f,
    16, 23, 33f, 38, 42, 52, 58, 61, 63,
    91, 103, 106, 118, 187, 190, 193, 200,
    214, 217, 222, 228, 232f, 234, 236f,
    239f, 247f, 257f, 267f, 270, 273, 275,
    278f

object relations 35, 168
objective psyche 13, 20, 86, 164, 280
observer variable 1
occult 60, 101, 107, 111, 214
octahedral, octahedron 31, 36, 37f, 40,
    42, 62ff, 109, 259, 261, 282
Odajnyk, Walter 3, 218, 226, 242, 253,
    268, 276, 286
Oedipus, oedipal 88, 97
omphalos 37
ontogenesis 15, 174
operant conditioning 146
organic solidarity 133f
organizations 228, 267
Orphan 99
Orpheus 17, 104
ouroboros, orobouric 2, 37ff, 169, 207
oxygen 43

paganism 194
Pao Hsi 195, 196
Paracelsus, Theophrastus 59
paradigm bridger 144
paradigm, paradigmatic 4, 8, 55, 125ff,
    130f, 135, 132ff, 138ff, 140, 144f,

146f, 150f, 156f, 187f, 209, 221, 263, 270, 277f
paradox 35, 39, 232
paramecia, paramecium 39, 57
parent, parents, parental ii, 63, 72, 90, 135, 162, 165f, 168ff, 172, 174, 177ff, 181ff, 185, 203, 214, 217, 236, 251, 254, 265, 273
participation mystique 6, 168, 170, 172, 174ff, 178, 180, 185, 264f, 273
pathology, pathological 58, 105f, 111, 202, 219, 222, 224, 252
pathologizing 106, 115
Pavlov, Ivan; Pavlovian 5, 142, 146, 165, 284
Peace Child 284
Pearson, Carol 98, 99, 100, 101
Peat, F. David 282
perceive, perception 2, 3, 5, 28, 34f, 41, 47, 56f, 63, 74, 78, 180, 197, 257, 260, 264, 266, 272, 283
Persephone 101, 107, 114f, 117f, 122, 206, 262
persona 7, 11, 69, 72, 80, 183, 202, 211, 213, 225ff, 261, 268, 274, 267f
personification 11, 70, 81f, 85, 105, 109, 169, 185, 188, 200, 223, 261, 266f, 275
phallus 88, 92
phenomenology 3, 279
Piaget, Jean 4f, 23, 25, 26f, 29, 39, 45, 56f, 64, 77, 165, 215, 258ff, 284
Piaget, Jean and Inhelder, Barbel 5, 27, 45, 258, 260
Pied Piper 18, 104
Plaut, Fred, 35
Plotinus 100
polar opposites 13, 33, 37, 76, 206
politics, political 126, 151, 156, 162f, 186, 194, 196, 202f, 209f, 223, 225f, 230ff, 241, 243
Poseidon 101, 103, 107, 117, 119
predisposition 2, 18ff, 47, 63, 102, 132, 178, 257
Pribram, Karl H. 34, 37
primordial image 5, 15, 21, 28, 50f, 55, 90, 96
Procrustes 111
Progoff, Ira 3, 22f, 52f, 61, 65, 80, 92ff, 161, 172, 211, 226, 260
projection 1f, 6, 15, 28, 35, 38f, 47, 72, 83ff, 92, 96, 102f, 156, 163, 169f, 174, 177ff, 182, 187, 192, 199ff, 203f, 210, 213f, 216, 219, 223ff, 231ff, 235ff,

239, 242, 247f, 252ff, 265ff, 271, 274ff
Prometheus 107
Protector 107
Proteus 114
protoplasmic image 52, 53, 61, 92ff
protozoans 39
provisional ego 27
psychoid 4, 7, 13, 17, 20, 54, 58, 62, 64, 69, 71f, 74, 164, 266, 272
puer, puer aeternus 11, 69, 85, 92
Puritans, Puritanism 190f, 236, 238

quaternio 18, 36, 40, 41, 42, 59, 75f, 109, 206

Radiolaria 39
rational action 140
rationalization 145, 157, 181, 197, 219, 234f, 238ff, 247ff, 264, 267ff, 273ff
Redfearn, J. W. T. 5, 53, 54, 61
reduction 2ff, 17, 143, 281, 286
reflection 12, 13, 47, 48, 50, 61
Reformation 237, 239f, 270
Regardie, Israel 40, 60
regression of libido 6, 95f, 114, 173f, 176, 179, 184f, 241, 244, 246f, 250, 262, 265f, 269f, 270, 273f, 281
reification 52, 267, 275
reinforcement 46, 155, 279
Reiser, Morton F. 41
releaser 35, 47
religion 17, 86f, 109, 135, 145, 150, 157, 162, 171, 186, 190ff, 197, 202f, 207ff, 216, 223, 231, 233, 236f, 239f, 252f, 264, 266f, 276, 286
Renaissance 60, 109, 193
repressed, repression 28, 62, 75, 82, 91, 111, 191, 209, 218ff, 223ff, 229f, 243, 245, 248, 250f, 254, 268f, 271, 276, 278
resonance 53, 58, 61, 286
Reynolds Aluminum 214
Richards, Don 284
Ritzer, George 4, 8, 125ff, 130ff, 138f, 141ff, 148, 154, 199, 263, 277, 279
robot, robotics 44ff
role, roles 6f, 19, 72, 80, 99, 101, 107, 113, 135ff, 145, 149, 153ff, 178, 181f, 190, 192, 195, 198, 204, 206ff, 214, 223, 227ff, 252, 254, 261, 264, 266ff, 281, 286
Roman Catholic Church 188, 227

routinization of charisma 6, 163, 156, 235f, 248, 269, 274

sacrifice 285
salience 22, 41, 62, 65, 72, 74, 194, 197, 213, 260f, 261, 266, 276
Samuels, Andrew 2f, 5, 22, 23, 63, 69, 82, 109, 178, 257, 283
Satir, Virginia 284
schema, schemata 27, 36, 42, 45f, 57, 70, 77, 259f, 284
Schutz, Alfred 143f, 163, 200, 227, 279
science 3, 15, 55, 127, 128, 263, 284
seasons 15
secular immortality 191, 246
secularization 191, 194, 203, 228, 233f, 237, 239f, 248, 267f, 270
sedimentation 200, 274
self 4, 11ff, 18, 21ff, 27f, 33f, 39ff, 46, 53, 58, 61, 69, 71f, 75, 81, 86ff, 92, 94, 96, 98f, 102, 113, 119, 135, 163, 173, 192, 202, 206, 209, 222f, 228, 231, 233, 239, 248, 258, 262, 265, 267, 270, 273
self maintenance 25, 41, 70, 215, 258, 278
self regulation 25, 26, 29, 72, 258
senex 11
sensual, sensuous, sensuality 13, 15, 107f, 162, 170f, 176, 178f, 209, 213
sephirah, sephiroth 60
sex, sexual, sexuality 33, 70f, 74, 83, 88, 95, 109, 116, 118, 168f, 173, 177f, 183, 189, 192, 209, 225, 265, 280f
shadow 6, 11, 32, 69, 72, 75, 77, 80, 82ff, 88f, 98, 218ff, 223ff, 229, 242, 252ff, 261, 266, 272, 274ff, 277ff
Shen Nung 195
Silverman, Charles E. 192
sinister 62
Skinner, B. F. 146, 147, 279
snake 2, 37
social behavior paradigm 146, 263
social class 152f, 156, 181ff, 192, 204, 209, 224, 243, 253, 278
social definitions paradigm 138, 144, 263
social facts 132ff, 137ff, 145, 148ff, 153, 155ff, 199, 263, 277
social facts paradigm 132, 135, 263, 277
social institutions see institutions
social structure 135ff, 141, 144ff, 149, 151, 155f, 206, 222, 263, 273, 275, 277f

social systems 135ff, 141, 145, 149, 157, 219, 263, 278
society 6, 58, 74, 80, 116, 122, 133ff, 136, 139, 142, 144ff, 156f, 161ff, 170f, 179, 182, 184, 187, 194ff, 201ff, 206ff, 212, 221ff, 226f, 229ff, 234, 240, 243, 251f, 254, 262, 263f, 265, 267f, 272f, 274f, 276f, 278, 281, 285
sociology, sociological 3f, 6ff, 123, 125ff, 130ff, 138ff, 141, 143f, 148, 150ff, 155, 159, 163, 171, 181, 195, 199, 211, 221, 257, 262f, 264, 272, 277f, 280
solidarity 134, 171, 273
Sorokin, Pitrim 212f
spiral, spirals 100
spirit 187, 237, 241, 258, 270
spiritual inspiration 284
spirituality 16, 33
Spitz, Rene 35
Stewart, Lewis 281
Stewart, R. J. 36, 37
stimulus 4, 26, 27, 29, 30, 31, 34, 35, 38, 41, 42, 46, 47, 48, 56, 61, 62, 63, 165, 257, 259, 279
structural elements 11, 72, 75
subjective, subjectivity 19, 56, 57
subsystems 22, 23, 28, 43, 45, 46, 87, 260
sun 15, 55, 60, 88
superior function 201, 212
superstructure 152
suppression 202, 219, 276, 278
symbiosis, symbiotic 35, 272
symbol, symbolic 4, 6f, 11ff, 18f, 32f, 37, 39f, 50ff, 57, 60, 64, 69, 71f, 86, 88f, 90ff, 95f, 101, 104, 109, 113, 115, 117, 121, 173, 178, 184, 187, 189, 194ff, 203ff, 210, 214, 216, 222, 227f, 230ff, 237ff, 241, 247f, 252, 254, 261, 266f, 268ff, 273ff, 279f, 281, 283
symbolic function 16, 63, 258
symbols, migration of, 13
symmetry 38, 39
symptom substitution 271, 276
synchronicity, synchronistic 24, 34
synergy 43
systems integration 22
systems organization 22f, 278
systems principles 22ff, 27
systems theory 3, 7, 23f, 125, 135, 215

tarot 60
taxis, taxes 29ff, 34, 258ff
Telos, teleological 22, 61, 63, 94, 257f
tertium non datur 33
thinking 78
Thompson, William Irwin 189, 196, 204, 206ff, 221, 267, 281
Tierra del Fuego 1
topoi 55, 281
topology, topological 69, 72, 196, 274, 281
traditions 18, 89, 127, 139, 170, 181, 185, 187, 197, 207ff, 229, 234, 249, 253, 266, 268f, 273ff, 281, 285
transformation 25, 26, 28, 46, 85, 95, 99, 258
transformation of libido 88, 99
transitional archetypes 11
treasure hard to attain 18, 262
tree 18, 60, 88
tree of life 18, 60
tree of paradise 88
trickster 11, 32, 218, 219
trophotropic *see* ergotrophic/ trophotropic
typifications 142ff, 145, 156, 200, 227f, 263, 266f, 275, 279

undifferentiated 40, 70f, 113, 165, 167, 169f, 173, 176, 201, 258
universal, universality 5, 15, 17, 18, 19, 27, 257
Unus Mundus 13, 63, 257
urbs 37

valence 62, 65, 261
values 5, 111, 135ff, 149ff, 172, 178, 203, 209, 216ff, 224, 230, 234, 254, 284f
vessel 40
Vico, Giambattista 193, 206

Vietnam 184
virgin 110
Virgin Mary 198
visual preference 48
von Franz, Marie Louise 5, 12, 13, 15, 18ff, 61, 71f, 76f, 84f, 88f, 93f, 103f, 116, 120, 166, 177, 187, 201, 210, 275, 280

walking 44, 45, 103, 277
Wanderer 99
Warrior 99, 107, 204
Washington, George 190
water 43, 44, 57, 94
Weber, Max 6, 138ff, 153, 163, 190, 211, 234ff, 237ff, 248, 263, 269, 274f, 278
Weltanschauung 111, 118, 127
West, Western (as cultural milieu) 101ff, 110, 171f, 178, 183, 188f, 193, 213, 219, 234, 237ff, 246, 270
West (as direction) 18, 94, 182
wheel 40, 281, 283
Whitmont, E. 167, 218
wholeness 39f, 72, 86, 167, 206, 258
Wholeness (as systems property) 22, 25, 27, 29, 215, 258
Whorf, Benjamin 186
Wilbur, Ken 282
Wilhelm, Richard 195, 196
womb 95
women's liberation 188
Wotan 111, 118, 120, 241f, 249, 251, 270

Yates, Francis 59, 60, 65, 109, 260

zeitgeist 229
Zeus 101, 103, 107, 113, 119, 285
Zinkin, Leonard 22, 261, 282
zodiac 60